NORB
630-670-6241

LEMONT AND ITS PEOPLE

1673 - 1910

Sonia Aamot Kallick

CHICAGO SPECTRUM PRESS
LOUISVILLE, KY 40207

CHICAGO SPECTRUM PRESS
4848 BROWNSBORO CENTER
LOUISVILLE, KY 40207
1-800-594-5190

Printed in the U.S.A.

10 9 8 7 6 5 4 3 2 1

ISBN: 1-886094-62-4

For All Lemont's Pioneers
Both Old And New

FOREWORD

Sonia Kallick loved Lemont. She devoted much of her life to learning and recording all she could about the history of our village and unselfishly sharing that invaluable knowledge with anyone and everyone who wanted to learn. This book distills two decades of her research into a work that was intended as a gift to the community, a demonstration of how much she cared for the rolling green hills, the church steeples, the limestone facades of downtown, and the wonderful citizens and characters that make Lemont so unique.

Sonia was born on March 11, 1933, in Chicago, Illinois. Her parents, Sven and Belle Aamot, were Norwegian immigrants who longed for a rural life and eventually purchased a farm and orchard in Downers Grove, where Sonia spent much of her childhood and formative years. She attended Downers Grove High School and went on to earn a Registered Nurse degree from the Cook County School of Nursing where she worked after graduation, and Bachelor of Science degree from the University of Illinois.

In 1956, she married Dr. Charles Kallick and moved to Lemont, where she settled down to be devoted wife and, in time, the mother of three children. She directed her considerable energies toward PTA, Girl and Cub Scouts, and parenting. But Sonia was ever curious about science, great literature, history, and especially about the village she had adopted as her own. When her children entered the Lemont public school system, she decided to become a teacher.

She taught grammar school at Old Central School in Lemont from 1967 through 1976, then she went back to college and earned a Masters Degree in Education at Lewis University in Lockport, Illinois, in 1977. Later, she began teaching at the Lemont Township High School, specializing in English Literature. She held this position until her retirement from teaching in 1995.

Sonia retired not because she was seeking rest and leisure, but because she now wanted to devote all her time to researching and writing about the colorful and fascinating history of Lemont.

In the early 1970s, Sonia began what became her third and perhaps most significant career, as a historian. This work ultimately led to a long list of achievements in historic preservation and education. A partial list of these achievements would be considered substantial for a devoted academician who spent an entire career in the field. How much more amazing, then, that they were achieved by a volunteer who held down a full-time job and raised three children. The following are a few of her most noteworthy achievements:

- Sonia helped lead the fight to create the Illinois and Michigan Canal National Historic Corridor, a designation signed into federal law by President Ronald Reagan in 1984. This park protects the waterway that created Lemont and helped make Chicago one of the world's leading cities.

- She was one of the founding members of the Lemont Area Historical Society, and worked hard to save the old stone church in which the Society's museum is now housed. As a volunteer on evenings and weekends, she helped create many of the museum's first displays, and spent endless hours promoting the Historical Society in our community.

- She directed the indexing of Lemont's "Centennial Book of History" in 1973, contributing extensively to the project and the Lemont Centennial celebration.

- She worked tirelessly to stop several attempts to demolish the Old Central School building, built in 1869. Old Central is perhaps Lemont's finest example of the limestone architecture that characterized our village. The school is now preserved as a local landmark, high atop the hill overlooking downtown.

- She advocated establishment of the Lemont Downtown Historic District, which has helped preserve many outstanding limestone structures and other historic buildings. This district has been a boon to Lemont's businesses and has helped create the atmosphere that makes Lemont a desirable place for newcomers to settle, keeping the town vibrant and alive.

- She played an integral part in the team of activists who commissioned the United States Bicentennial Mural in downtown Lemont. This noteworthy mural, painted by Caryl Yasko, depicts limestone quarry laborers cutting the stone that forms the foundations of Lemont.

- Last, but perhaps most importantly, she wrote her weekly newspaper column "Lemont and Its People" for more than twenty years, educating untold numbers of Lemont residents about the history of their home. Her hundreds of columns formed the basis for this book, on which she worked from 1994 until her untimely death in May of 1997.

In one of Sonia's many columns, she eloquently expressed her personal view of history, a view that informs every page of this work. "History is not about wars or politics," she wrote. "It's about ordinary people and why they did what they did. It's about the social and economic influences that make today and shape tomorrow."

Sonia was taken from us before she could see her history of the village set down in a bound volume for all time, but she was able to complete the material for the book. That she succeeded in her quest to document this everyday phenomenon, the making of history, is best demonstrated by the pages that follow. We hope and trust it will remain for a long time to come the definitive reference work describing Lemont's history.

We, her loved ones, now present this book to you, the citizens of Lemont, as an expression of the love she felt for you, and as our tribute to her life and many enduring accomplishments.

–*Charles, Steven, Karen, and Ingrid Kallick*

July 1997

TABLE OF CONTENTS

CHAPTER ONE

LEMONT

GEOGRAPHY, DISCOVERY, AND EXPLORATION

History is written in the landscape; our political, economic, social, and cultural record is the product of its surroundings. So it is that the story of Lemont is tied to its unique geography and geology, for Lemonters are privileged to live in one of the more unusual geological areas of Northern Illinois.

The Des Plaines Valley, which forms the northern boundary of the township, is the product of the forces that shaped the landscape over 10,000 years ago. This valley, about one mile wide and seventy feet deep, is surrounded by rocky bluffs and deep ravines. It was not formed by the erosive effects of the Des Plaines River but from glacial melt waters of the last ice age 10,000 to 12,000 years ago.

For a period lasting from 10,000 to 50,000 years ago, our area was covered by the Wisconsin glacier that extended as far south as the Illinois towns of Paris, Shelbyville, and Decatur and as far west as the Mississippi River. When the climate warmed, the glaciers melted, but not at a steady rate. At each advance or retreat, the glaciers acted like great scoops carrying soil, rocks, and debris along their path. This action created the topography we see today by depositing sand beaches called ridges, and rings of rock called moraines.

Three of the end moraines that circle Northern Illinois are called the Minooka, the Rockdale, and the Valpariso. The Valpariso moraine sweeps around the Chicagoland area and touches part of the northeastern section of our township. Known as Mount Forest Island, it is the site of the St. James of the Sag Church at 106th and Archer Avenue.

Des Plaines River. (Photo courtesy of Lemont Historical Society)

As the ice sheet made its final retreat, the melt waters collected in a glacial basin, a "super" Lake Michigan, called Lake Chicago by geologists. At the Sag, the intense pressure of the melt waters unable to flow through its ice-blocked outlets forced a break in the moraine. The water formed two outlets: one at the head of the Des Plaines Valley and the second at the present Sag. Both cuts joined at the west end of Mt. Forest Island to form our valley. During this geological event Mt. Forest was then isolated from the rest of the Valpariso moraine.

Where the waters met, they rushed southward to the Mississippi River and washed out most of the earlier clay and glacial fill deposits, exposing the dolomite limestone bedrock. Much later, this exposed bedrock would be used by pioneers as a natural resource that would become important in the development of our area, so important that it would be the main economic base of Lemont for over eighty years.

After the initial breakthrough, the flow of melt water ceased about 10,000 years ago, leaving the Des Plaines River to meander slowly through the valley. At a point east of our township, near Summit, where the Des Plaines River approached the Chicago River, a long marsh called Mud Lake was formed. East of that marsh there developed a low con-

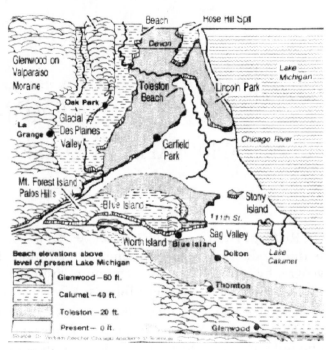

The three ancient beach levels of Lake Michigan. (Illustration courtesy of Chicago Academy of Natural Sciences)

tinental divide. Water east of the divide went into the Great Lakes system and eventually to the Atlantic. Water west of Mud Lake flowed into the Des Plaines, down the Illinois River to the Mississippi, and into the Gulf of Mexico.

This natural waterway system became another important resource of the area. On it a canoe could travel from the Northeastern section of our country to the Gulf with only one small portage through Summit's Mud Lake. F. Fryxell, an early local geologist, expressed the value of this system many years ago:

> Through this channel, carved thousands of years ago by a river now extinct, there passed a full and ceaseless stream of human activity. Providing, as it does, a natural route connecting the Great Lakes region with the Mississippi Valley. This valley is one of the greatest natural passes in our country. One more adapted for man's purposes could hardly be designed by man himself.[1]

So it developed that the Des Plaines River and this valley became a highway for human traffic. Therefore, the history of Lemont, like the history of our nation, is one of human movement and migration.

The first people to enter our area, after the meltwater formation of the valley, were the archaic Indians, who hunted and fished along the river and camped in the hidden and protected ravines. These Native Americans found the valley formations useful for survival because from the bluffs they could spot herds of bison and deer. Since game is hard to locate in wooded areas and even harder to find on the tall grass prairie, tribes or family clans that controlled the higher bluffs had an advantage.

These early Indians left few artifacts, but they did leave their mark with the development of an elaborate system of overland trails that linked all of the region into a network. As described by Bessie Pierce:

> On the hunt, in trade, and in war, they had beaten these paths, later to become the course of men destined to establish permanent homes in the region. These trails followed the natural features of the land, traversing ridges and high ground, touching lakes and rivers, and dipping into depressions for shortcuts.[2]

The trails that traversed Lemont Township followed natural formations. Our main trail was along the south side of the Des Plaines River from Lake Michigan through the Mud Lake portage past future Lemont to the Illinois River Valley. This trail had the advantage of cover and good hunting. It could be traveled on foot or by water. Traffic along the way became so common that many traditional campsites developed, which were used by the Indians, fur traders, and early explorers. Camps were located on the "hogback" at Sag, on the three islands that once fronted Lemont,[3] and on land near the three local seep springs; these seep springs were on the east Main Street bluffs, near the parking lot at Lockport Street and West Main, and on Bluff Road. Another favorite campsite was on Isle La Cache at 135th Street and the river in Will County.

Elevated ridge trails were used in the spring when the water was high, or in the winter when snow blocked the valley. They were also used during tribal conflicts, so a traveler could see across the prairie. Present day Archer Avenue follows an ancient high ridge trail. Driving today along this road from the Sag to Lockport one can see how the street follows a high point on the landscape, one that would remain dry and would offer a view of the horizon.

Two other important ancient trails crossed our township. One began in Lemont at State Street and New Avenue at the Des Plaines River and went due south through Homer, Marley, and New Lenox to join the important Sauk Trail. The other trail was a branch of the Portage Trail that cut east off Archer Avenue along present 131st Street to the Lake Calumet region. Every driver who gets frustrated by the odd angle of the intersection at 131st and Archer should remember it was an old Indian pathway not designed for the modern automobile.

Many other trails crossed in the Sag. The Buffalo Trail went north to the Downers Grove-Darien area. A minor section of the Portage Trail went southeast toward Chicago and, finally, there was a route to Hinsdale that crossed the Chicago and Joliet trail, a trail that is now part of I-55 and Route 53. There is no question that the Native Americans left a legacy on our landscape and the way we move around that landscape.

Since these pathways were known to fur traders and explorers, it was only natural that they would be a part of the first patterns of western exploration and that they were the routes that the pioneer settlers would follow into our township. By the time the later settlers arrived, most of our local Indians were gone and thus our knowledge of them and the ancient tribes before them is limited. Our first pioneer generations were too busy building and plowing the earth to pay attention to fragile artifacts left that might give us a picture of the Indian before the arrival of Western man. Sadly, this is still true today. As we build in the township and village we lose information hidden in the ground around us. For example, archaeological studies of the Brown property on New Avenue reveal that there are ten recorded prehistory habitation sites within a mile of that area. The bluffs there contain large deposits of chert, hard limestone nodules, which were necessary for making arrowheads and tools. There can be no doubt that some archaic Lemont tool-maker tribes inhabited this section of our township.[4]

Not all archeological sites are lost. Some remain in the valley, on Argonne property, on some upland farms, and in the Cook County Forest Preserves, waiting to be explored.

We do not know the exact time that Native Americans first came to our township, but evidence suggests it was sometime around 5,000 to 6,000 years ago. However, we do know the date when they left our land. It was in the fall of 1835, when by treaty they moved West.

What recorded information we have begins in the 1600s with the French fur traders and missionaries who were impressed with the land and its people.[5] The French arrived here when our country was only a group of towns and villages along the Eastern coast. They had plans to extend the French Empire down the Mississippi and isolate the English Colonies. With the advantage of easy travel into the interior of our country by way of the St. Lawrence Waterway and the Great Lakes, it was only natural that the French should be in our area first.

They found the whole south Lake Michigan area to Central Illinois inhabited by natives classified as the Northeastern Woodland Indian. Based on language structure these groups belonged to one general tribe called the Algonkians, who functioned separately in clans based on special relationships. However, Helen Tanner has shown that Indian groupings were dynamic and not static; the villages were mixed, and there was a good deal of intermarriage between individual groups. Also, many of the clans took in refugees. Thus, all the Great Lakes Indians spoke several languages and dialects.[6]

The Woodland Indians knew little of the archaic natives who had occupied the land before them. The simple hunters and fishermen who met the first French explorers referred to their predecessors only as the ancient ones.[7] In our region there was a succession of three different branches of the Algonkian family: the Illini, the Miami, and the Pottawat-

The Illiniwek greet Fr. Marquette and Joliet. Note Fr. Marquette holds a calumet, or peace pipe. The rock formation in the background is Starved Rock. (Illustration courtesy of Illinois State Historical Society)

The Des Plaines River. (Photo courtesy of Lemont Historical Society)

omi. This succession of tribes occurred because Indians were nomadic and the boundaries of their hunting areas shifted, depending upon game migration patterns and intertribal conflicts. Yet, in spite of these pressures, tribes seldom moved too far from their original lands, and operated a balanced system without crowding each other's hunting grounds.

This life continued without major disruption until Western man arrived. To feed the fashion tastes of Europe, the fur traders entered this naturally balanced economic and ecological system the Indians had developed over the centuries. Suddenly, there was a demand for beaver, fox, muskrat, and other New World furs. As a result, the Indians of the eastern coastal areas, who had the first Western contacts, began to over-trap game and to extend their control over certain significant game lands for their own tribe. As they needed more hunting areas intertribal fighting and conflict developed, which was encouraged by the French and English for their own gain.

Tribes from the northeast began moving west and south toward the Lake Michigan area. This caused tension between tribes already here and the newcomers. Since there was land enough in the early days, often the established tribes would simply move westward. Therefore, we have the succession of tribes reported by the early explorers and missionaries.

The Illini were the first inhabitants discovered by the French. Joliet and Marquette, who saw Lemont Township as early as 1673, found them to be a cooperative and peaceful nation. Robert Howard reports they were the descendants of the ancient tribes that had long ago developed the Middle Mississippi civilization of great pyramid cities like Cahokia Mound, but by the 1600s had been forced by constant warfare to return to a simpler culture.[8]

The Illini group included such branches as the Kaskaskia, Cakokia, Michegamea, Peoria, and Tamara. The story is that their name came about when the French explorers asked the Indians by what name they called themselves. They replied "Illiniwek," an

Algonkian word meaning "man." It probably conveyed the idea that the tribe considered itself superior to other men, including the French. The French took the name, dropped the last two syllables and added a French ending, hence the name Illinois.[9] The territory the French called Illinois covered not only our present state, but large parts of Wisconsin, Iowa, and Missouri.

Marquette and Joliet met the Illini Indians when they explored the region looking for the Mississippi River and its course through the new land. They explored Wisconsin to the Mississippi and on their return trip the Indians suggested the Illinois River and the Des Plaines Valley as a short cut back to Green Bay. This is how our valley became recorded in history. It was during this trip that Joliet conceived the idea that a small canal could be built through the portage at Mud Lake making future travel much easier. It took over 175 years for his vision to be completed, with the building of the Illinois and Michigan Canal. We see that landmark on our Lemont landscape every time we go downtown.

Marquette also wrote about the beauty of the whole Des Plaines and Illinois River Valley system. He stated in his journal:

> We have seen nothing like this river that we enter, as the fertility of the soil, its prairies and woods; its cattle (bison), elk, deer, wildcats, bustards, swans, ducks, parroquets, and even beaver. There are many small lakes and rivers. That on which we sail is wide, deep, and still . . . In the spring and during part of the summer there is only one portage of half a league.[10]

And so our land was discovered by Western man, a fact that would, in the end, drive away those very natives who greeted them in friendship. But for a period of over 100 years the land would remain undisturbed as Nelson Algren's poetic prose describes:

> To the east were the moving waters as far as the eyes could follow. To the west a sea of grass as far as wind might reach.[11]

ENDNOTES

[1]F.M. Fryxell, *The Physiography of the Region of Chicago* (Chicago: University of Chicago, 1927), p. 21.

[2]Bessie Pierce, *A History of Chicago* (New York: Knopf, 1940), vol. 2, p. 5.

[3]This was before the construction of the Sanitary Ship Canal (1893-1900).

[4]Theodore Karamanski, *Brown Property Evaluation* (Chicago: Loyola University, 1986), p. 17.

[5]Robert Sutton, *The Prairie State* (Grand Rapids: Eerdmans, 1970), p. 3.

[6]Peter Gorner, "Back on the Map," *Chicago Tribune*, January 22, 1987, "Tempo Section," pp.1-3.

[7]Sutton, *The Prairie State*, p. 3.

[8]Robert Howard, *Illinois: A History of the Prairie State* (Grand Rapids: Eerdmans, 1972), p. 12.

[9]*Ibid*, p. 20.

[10]Pierce, *A History of Chicago* (New York: Knopf, 1940), vol. 1, p. 7.

[11]Nelson Algren, *Chicago: City on the Make* (New York: McGraw-Hill, 1983), p. 10.

CHAPTER TWO

NATIVE PEOPLE OF OUR AREA

The Illini were eager to welcome the French explorers and fur traders for their weapons and for protection from the Iroquois Confederation, which consisted of the five nations of the Mohawks, Oneidas, Onondagas, Cayugas, and Senecas. The Iroquois were excellent fighters and had pressured the Illini southward. When the French explorer LaSalle built Fort Saint Louis in 1682, at Starved Rock, many Illini gathered there for safety, living in villages with mat covered dwellings containing six to 12 families. The tribe was agriculture based, raising crops of maize, beans, squash, and pumpkins. Twice a year, in the spring and winter, small bands migrated to hunt game. They processed the meat caught and brought it back to the main camp. Father Marquette reported his observations on the Illini in his journal:

> They are mild and tractable in their disposition, as we experienced in the reception they gave us. They have many wives, of whom they are extremely jealous; they watch them carefully, and cut off their nose or ears when they do not behave well; I saw several who bore the marks of infidelity. They are well formed, and very adroit in using the bow and arrow; they use guns also, which they buy of our Indian allies who trade with the French; they use them especially to terrify their enemies by the noise and smoke. The others lying too far west, have never seen them, and do not know their use. . . Their only clothes are skins: their women always dress modestly and decently. The men do not take any pains to cover themselves. Through what superstition I know not, some Illinois while yet young, assume female dress, and keep it all their life. There is a mystery about it, for they never marry, and glory in debasing themselves to do all that is done by women; yet they go to war, though not allowed to use a bow and arrow, only a club. They are permitted to sing but not to dance; they attend councils and nothing can be decided without their advice; finally, by profession of an extraordinary life, they pass for manitous, or persons of consequence.[1]

With the arrival of the fur traders, the Indians gave up many traditional skills of living off the land. Traders introduced metal and weapons that soon replaced the bow and arrow. With trade goods there was no need to spend time chipping away a stubborn piece of chert when a gun or a metal arrow tip was much more effective. Metal cooking pots replaced handmade pottery. Glass beads from the factories of France and Bohemia replaced

Starved Rock. (Photo courtesy of Lemont Historical Society)

the carefully cut and dyed porcupine quills used for decorations. Woolen and cotton cloth replaced deerskins. Metal axes and knives replaced stones. Within a generation, the tools of the Illini were brought from the stone age to "modern" times. The traders also brought two other things that began the destruction of the Native American way of life: white man's diseases and alcohol.

Although the English won, French rule over our area ended slowly after the French and Indian War. Pontiac, the great Ottawa chief, sided with the French and when he was murdered at Cahokia in 1769, by a Kaskaskia Indian, the Lake Tribes, all allies of Pontiac, vowed to seek vengeance. Members of the Lake Tribes included the Ottawa, Chippewa, and Potawatomi. Braves from these tribes fought and reduced the remaining Illini to a handful. It was this struggle that began the legend of Starved Rock. According to local lore, a band of Illini fled to the top of the rock, where, deprived of food and water, they died of thirst and famine.[2]

Although this story is widely believed, it has never been authenticated. Beaten and scattered, the few remaining Illini Indians joined other wandering tribes and were moved to Oklahoma in the early 1800s. By that time there were only 150 members remaining of the once great tribe.[3]

It was now the time of the Potawatomi and the Miami to live and hunt on our land. The Potawatomi became the principal tribe controlling what was to be Lemont from the early 1700s to 1833. The Potawatomi, as the Illini before them, formed an alliance with the French fur traders. This gave them control of most of the trade in the Chicago region, which they protected by controlling traffic on the Des Plaines River and through the Chicago Portage. Travel between our area and the southern end of Lake Michigan was common for the nomadic tribes. The Potawatomi had originated much farther east and north and pushed by the Iroquois Confederacy, they came by way of the eastern shore of Lake Michigan from the region around St. Joseph, Michigan. Two famous Indian trails, the Illini and the Sauk, had branches in our township that led to St. Joseph.

Our local Potawatomi had two divisions, the Woodland-Mission Pottawatomi and the Prairie Potawatomi. However, as was reported by early explorers, the band often included members of other related groups.[4]

The name Potawatomi means "people of the place of the fire." The name in Potawatomi is "nI'nabe'k." According to their legends, they were chosen people of their god — The Great Spirit — to be the keepers of the sacred fire. Fire was sacred, to them because it protects from the cold, cooks and preserves meat, and offers protection from dark nights and wild animals. The Potawatomi believed that they were the special tribe that had first received fire and had given it to all other tribes.

The tribe was regarded by outsiders as a good friend but a bad enemy. Their friendliness was noted by Allouez in 1666, and Dablon in 1670 and 1718.[5]

The yearly pattern of the Amerindian of our area, before extensive Western contact, was based on the seasons, a pattern that was repeated for centuries. In the springtime the tribe members would return during the "moon of the melting snow" from their various winter grounds, to begin tapping maple trees for sugar and syrup. In our area the major village was located on Mt. Forest Island in the Sag. That site was not only a village, but also a signal and chipping station.[6]

Early Illini Indian dress. The painting depicts a group with La Crosse style equipment. (Illustration courtesy of Illinois State Historical Society)

The winter villages and minor encampments that we know about in Lemont were east of the Will-Cook County line, in Romeoville, and across the Des Plaines River along Bluff Road. There must have been others because we know that before Western contact, there were at least 21 major villages in the Chicago area, a fact recorded by archaeologists.[7]

All Potawatomi villages were located on waterways such as the Chicago River, the Des Plaines, the Calumet, and the DuPage. They also camped along washes and runs, such as Big Run and Long Run, and lakes, such as Lake Michigan and the Chain of Lakes. Winter encampments were made up of small family groups, so in the spring when the whole tribe gathered together again, it was traditional to hold a medicine feast to "bury the dead." All those who died the previous year were remembered, and their relatives gave away goods belonging to the deceased as remembrance presents to friends. This act often reduced the family to poverty, but it was done to show the Great Spirit that they were humble and wanted his pity on their sorrow.

The caches, storage areas for corn, cornmeal, and dried meat prepared the previous fall, were then opened and the lodges repaired for the summer. Women began planting corn, beans, squash, pumpkins, and melons. This farming was always the woman's responsibility. The ground was broken with pointed sticks and the seeds planted. This means that corn and the other unique American plants were developed by the Native American women who crossbred plants and saved seeds that were hardy, exchanging them with other tribes. The Native American woman contributed more to our landscape and life than we realize. Many plants they developed over centuries are the basis of our American agricultural and economic system.[8]

While the women planted, men went on short hunting trips and exchanged stories about events during the winter season. To outsiders this division of labor was often misjudged. It was said that the men were "lazy." This was a misunderstanding based on a lack of knowledge about how much work was required for hunting game to keep the tribe supplied. When the crops were in there was a feast featuring the Crane Dance. Single women, dressed in their best, danced for the young braves who then selected the woman they wished to have for a wife. The brave would tell his mother, who would call on the mother of the young woman.[9]

Several rites have been reported as part of the engagement agreement. One was that the brave would go to the wigwam while all were asleep, or pretending to be asleep, and bring a lighted stick. He would awaken the maiden. If she blew out the flame, the ceremony was ended and he would appear at the lodge the next morning, now a member of the family. Others report that if a woman accepted a blanket offered by a young man and wrapped it around her then an agreement was reached. If the girl did not blow out the light, or accept a blanket, the brave would have to court her.[10]

In the evening he would sit outside the lodge, playing a courting tune on the Indian flute until he was invited in to make another nightly visit. Usually, the young couple lived together for a year before final marriage arrangements were made. There was no formal ceremony but there would be an exchange of gifts and goods to seal the contract. Braves could have two or three wives. The "sororate," marrying the sister of a dead wife, was also common. It appeared to the early missionaries and traders that there were many more women than men in the tribes. This may account for the tradition of multiple wives.[11]

A woman, if unhappy, could return to her parent's lodge at any time, no matter what she had done or how many children she brought with her.

In the cycle of the seasons, summer was the best time. However, it was not the restful idyllic world we like to imagine. Subsistence living requires constant work so that food supplies are preserved. Berries had to be picked and dried or packed in oil. Meat and fish had to be smoked and packed away, while clothing, pottery, mats, and weapons had to be made during the warm days of summer. It is surprising that even today, an inventory of our valley in the *I & M Heritage Corridor* by Michael McNerney reveals no less than 30 edible small mammals, if you are willing to include mice and voles.[12]

The Indians also had large mammals such as deer, bear, fox, wolf and dog as part of their diet. Add to that at least two types of frogs, nine types of edible turtles, 22 types of birds, and 34 species of fish and you have some idea of the protein available.[13] As for food-bearing plants, we know of 23 different types of leaves, fruits, and nuts that still grow in the area. This harvest, besides their domesticated foods, made most seasons for the Potawatomi plentiful.[14]

Fall was occupied with the final harvesting of crops. When winter began, those strong enough to travel broke camp for winter quarters. Winter was spent following game and preserving what was not eaten. As the fur trader began to affect the economic life of the Indian, winter encampments became very important, for it was the winter pelts of the fur-bearing animals that commanded the best prices. Often fur traders, many of whom married into the tribes, would travel with the winter groups to make sure they got the best pelts. Meanwhile, the old and ill remained in the permanent camp near the caches of food.

Corn was the mainstay of the Indian diet. Any other meat, fish, vegetable, or fruit available would often be added to the corn, according to individual taste. This was cooked as a kind of stew. Marquette, in his journal, described the Illini dish he called *Sagamity* as an Indian corn meal boiled in water and seasoned with fat. Special occasions required a feast. An example of such a menu was recorded as follows:

> Two White fish boiled in water. Tongue and breast of deer,
> Wood hens. Hind feet of bear. Tail of a beaver Broth made
> from several meats. Dog meat, corn, beans, squash and pump-
> kin. Beverage: Sassafras or maple syrup beaten in water.[15]

All food preparation was the domain of the woman. Recognition of the female influence in developing the Indian grains, along with economically important tobacco, is shown in this Indian legend from our Midwestern tribes:

> A beautiful woman was seen to descend from the clouds and
> alight upon the earth by two braves who had killed a deer and
> were sitting by the fire roasting it to eat. They were aston-
> ished seeing her, and decided she must be hungry, They went
> to her taking a piece of the roasted venison with them. They
> gave it to her and she ate it. She told them to return to the
> spot where she was sitting, at the end of one year, a cycle of
> our seasons. At that time they would find a reward for their
> kindness. She then ascended to the clouds and disappeared.
> The two returned to their village and explained what had hap-
> pened; but, of course, the others laughed. When the year was
> up they returned with a group of villagers. At the spot they
> found corn growing where her right hand had rested, beans
> growing where her left hand had rested; and, above all, to-
> bacco where she had been sitting.[16]

Tobacco was important even if it was not a food. Tobacco and the calumet pipe were part of the native mystery and awe of life. Father Marquette recorded:

> It now only remains to speak of the calumet, which there is
> nothing among them more mysterious or more esteemed. Men
> do not pay to the crowns and scepters of kings the honor they

pay to it; it seems to be the god of peace and war, the arbiter of life and death. Carry it about you and show it, and you can march fearlessly amid enemies, who even in the heat of battle lay down their arms when it is shown . . . There is a calumet for peace, and one for war, distinguished only by the color of the feathers with which they are adorned . . . They use them for settling disputes, strengthening alliances, and speaking to strangers. It is made of red polished stone, like marble, so pierced that one end serves to hold the tobacco while the other is fastened on the stem, which is a stick two feet long, as thick as a common cane, and pierced in the middle . . . They esteem it in particular because they regard it as the calumet of the sun; and, in fact, they present it to him to smoke when they wish to obtain calm, or rain, or fair weather. They scruple to bathe at the beginning of the summer, or eat new fruits, till they have danced to it.[17]

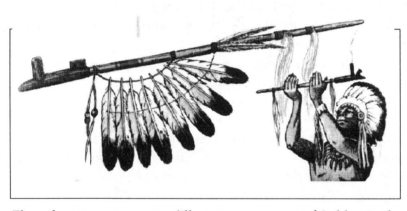

The calumet or peace pipe. (Illustration courtesy of Golden Books Publishing)

Ceremonies centering around tobacco and the calumet pipe were very important to the well-being of the tribe. Robert and Pat Ritzenthaler describe it as the, "unifying cord, the thread of communication between the human element and the spiritual powers."[18] Indians believed that the spirits, *manidog*, liked tobacco and the only way they could get it was from the Indian, by smoke or by dry offerings.

Because so many acts of life required the guidance of the spirits, tobacco was scattered to insure safe travel, used for protection from places considered dangerous, spread on graves as an offering, given to bind an agreement, used as an invitation to a feast, and considered a wonderful gift. Tobacco smoke was used by medicine men to drive away bad spirits in a patient. The smoke was often blown in the ear of someone suffering from an earache. Tobacco was the important ingredient in the spiritual obligations of the individual, his clan, and his tribe. Adults, male and female, smoked tobacco in pipes. Children were not allowed this privilege. The Woodland Indian mixed his tobacco with a material called *Kinnikinnick*, a term that means "what is mixed."[19] This was made of the inner bark of willows and dogwood, or sumac leaves, and added to the smoking mixture. Most Indians preferred the diluted combination.[20]

Besides the essential food crops, Indians grew and gathered plants for their medicinal qualities. Our early pioneers learned to depend on such Indian treatments as milkweed juice for warts and the root of the blueflag iris for a sore mouth. A mixture of raspberry and blackberry juice plus the leaves of hoarhound and spearmint was boiled together for croup, asthma, or any breathing problems. White oak bark was soaked in water for burns. It is interesting to consider that this combination would produce tannic acid, a common treatment for burns until the development of our modern techniques.

Other remedies included mayapple for stomach complaints, dried wild grapes for boils, black willow bark for skin disorders, sassafras for sluggishness, chestnut leaves for coughs, wild cherry tea for hiccoughs, mullien for bee stings, prickly ash for mosquito bites and infections, elm bark tea for sore throats, and wild ginger tea for colds.[21]

Most medicines were collected and prepared by the women although occasionally the medicine man, working as a specialist on a difficult case, would prepare his own formulas. Infectious disease posed little problem for the Indians before contact with Western man. The tribes were small isolated groups that had infrequent interaction outside their own clans. Colds and viruses would spread through a tribe only after festivals and gatherings that included other tribes. The greatest medical risks were accidents, acute surgical problems such as appendicitis, and compound broken bones. This type of injury usually caused death. Diseases brought by Western contact included tuberculosis, measles, cholera, smallpox, and typhus. Because the Amerindian peoples had never experienced these infections, they had no resistance and entire tribes were destroyed by epidemics.

When these new diseases began in the villages, the clans would break camp fearing some powerful magic was responsible for the illness. The tragic part of this behavior was that those who fled would seek refuge in other tribes and by that behavior spread the infection. This transfer of Western European diseases did have one ironic twist. There is some evidence that the Indians may have given Western man a disease in return. Some medical historians claim that Columbus's men came back to the Old World with a disease that was to be the shameful scourge of the "civilized" world — syphilis.[22]

Along with food, the Indian woman also had the main responsibility for providing shelter for the family. As the harvest season ended and just before winter set in, the women would ask permission to go to the swamps and marshes to gather rushes to be made into mats. The Des Plaines Valley has many sites to find cattails, the favorite plant of this area used for these mats.

The chief woman had to give her permission for this annual trip, at a special feast. After the feast, the women would then travel to the wetlands and set up temporary camp. On the morning of the first day, the chief woman would conduct prayers facing east toward the sunrise, for this was the path of life, east to west as the sun moved, from the beginning of life to the western afterworld. She would also offer prayers to the water, to her clan ancestors, the sky, the earth, and to the spirit of each direction. Almost all Potawatomi rituals involve the number four, four seasons, four directions, four elements — water, earth, sky, and the spirit world.[23]

After this ritual she would enter the swamp and cut the first reeds. The cattails were selected before they developed seeds. The main stem was removed and the leaves carefully trimmed and bundled, and stored in the shade. The next day the ends were sealed in scalding water, dried and returned for storage in a cool, dry, dark spot. When enough rushes were collected, the women returned to the village to begin making mats. Many cattail leaves were required since all the wigwams were covered with these mats and mats were also used to sit and sleep on.[24]

To weave the mats, the cattail leaves were laid flat and opened as wide as possible. With a simple under and over weaving, the mats were completed. The ends of the mats were folded back into the woven portion so they would not ravel. Sometimes cat tail stems were used for mats, then the stems were sewn together on a cord. This type of mat was good for insulation during the winter. The best mats, those used inside the wigwam, were often made of rushes and fiber from the basswood tree. These mats were woven on a frame. The warps were the rushes and the weft twisted basswood fibers plaited or twined across.[25]

To build the wigwam frame, lodge poles from slender saplings were also cut and prepared by the women. Young saplings were trimmed and all bark removed and these were set in a circle or oblong shape about one to two feet apart. One end of each pole was driven into the ground and the other ends lashed together in a domed wigwam shape. The mats were draped over the frame, starting at the bottom so they would overlap. Then they were pinned with large thorns or lashed with deerhide. It took many mats to make a wind and water-tight wigwam. In some areas bark and skins were also used to cover the homes.[26]

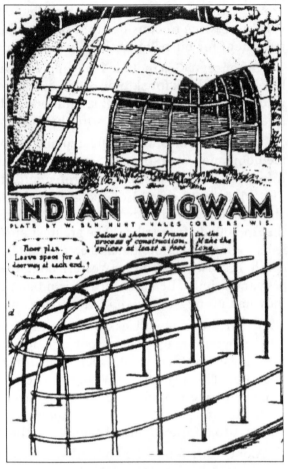

The Wigwam, by W. Ben Hunt

Clearly this type of shelter was not the home of a completely nomadic tribe. When camp broke for the seasonal cycles the mats were removed but the framework remained. Upon return in the spring the shelter could be quickly repaired and covered. A simple wigwam could be also built during an emergency. If conditions demanded immediate shelter, Indians would bend and lash four or five live saplings together throwing mats and covering over the makeshift home. The housing they developed suited our local environment and examples of wigwams can still be seen in use today as summer fishing camps on reservations in Wisconsin.[27]

The fireplace was located in the middle of the home in a depressed spot lined with stones to keep ashes in place and to retain heat. Cooking was done indoors only in inclement weather.

On the top of the wigwam there was an opening to allow smoke to escape. It could be closed in wet or cold weather. Doorways were covered with animal skins. Around the inside were bunks made of small branches lashed together for seating or sleeping. Clothing and goods were stored in deerskin wrappings and woven bags placed under the bunks.

The homes were warm, dry, and uncluttered, although probably small for our modern way of living. However, the Indian spent very little time indoors; only cold and rain would send the family inside.[28]

Clothing worn by the Potawatomi, before contact with the Western world, was made of animal skins. In fact, skins were used for many other items including shields, boats, lashings, decorations, drums, containers, robes, blankets, shelter, and many different household objects. Skins of most animals could be used, but bison and deer were preferred because of their size. Larger skins did not need piecing. Skin work was of three types: rawhide, deerskin, and buckskin.

> Rawhide was untanned skin, cream-colored, tough, light-weight, waterproof, hard but flexible, and unbreakable. When fresh it could be molded, but when dry it was like plastic.[29]

Rawhide was made by staking out the fresh skin and chipping off the flesh and tissue with a buffalo or deer leg bone. The hide was then dried in the sun and scraped. A tool made out of an antler was used to scrape and thin the skin. The skin was then turned over and the hair removed. From this rawhide Woodland Indians made items such as snowshoes, drums, and boxes. It was also an essential material for bindings.

Deerskin and buckskin differ only that buckskin was smoked to make it softer and more pliable. Deerskin was difficult to prepare. The fresh skin was treated in several different ways depending on the tribal custom. Usually the hide was placed in a kettle of water along with wood ashes. The hide remained in the water for two or three days; it then was taken out and all the flesh and hair scraped off. The hide was tanned by smearing it with a paste of the brains and liver of the animal and working this mixture into the skin with a piece of deer rib. It was then washed, stretched, and dried. Finally, the skin was lashed to a frame and beamed, or worked with a stick or bone, until it was soft.[30]

Patterns were cut out of the prepared skin with a stone knife, and the seams were sewed together by puncturing holes with a bone and lacing the deerskin with sinew. The lower hems were fringed for decoration. Men and boys of the Potawatomi tribes wore only a breech cloth and moccasins most of the year. These were decorated with designs common to the Woodland Potawatomi. Although each design was unique, all designs done by a tribe followed a certain traditional style so that anyone could tell the tribe or clan by its dress and decorations.

In late fall and winter, or for special occasions, the men wore buckskin shirts and leggings. In the coldest weather, both men and women wrapped themselves in blankets of buffalo and animal skins. Potawatomi braves wore roach head decorations, not a full feathered headdress, as it would be foolish to travel through the woods with a feathered bonnet. The roach was made of a strip of animal skin with intact hair. This could be deerskin or porcupine guard hair. It often had one or two hawk or eagle feathers attached. Young Potawatomi braves shaved their heads leaving only a scalp lock in the center. The roach was attached to this strip of hair.

The Woodland Roach head dress,
by W. Ben Hunt

Favorite male decorations were necklaces made from bear claws. The claws would sometimes be alternated with beads made from the wingbones of birds and various seeds. Later, glass beads and silver medals from Europe and the Colonies became part of the neckwear.

The sash was a clothing item unique to the Eastern Woodland tribes. It was made from vegetable fiber mixed with buffalo, fox, dog, or other animal hair. At first these sashes were not woven on a frame but plaited, that is, they were done by what we call finger weaving or macrame. Loom weaving was a later development. Sashes were worn around the waist, tied around the arms or legs, wrapped around the head like a turban, or hung over one or both shoulders in a bandolier fashion.[31]

Fine examples of sashes were highly valued and often traded. Voyagers traveling and collecting furs in the area often wore these sashes as part of their working costume. Footwear was, of course, the moccasin. The Woodland moccasin was made from a single piece of leather with an added decorated cuff.[32]

Besides prepared skins, furs of animals were used to make hats for men and were decorated with beads and ribbon work. This fashion developed after contact with Europeans and often looked like the popular European tri-cornered hats of the 1700s. Furs of small mammals were also popular for medicine bags and clan bundles, which had a special place in the spiritual world of the Indian.

Clothing for the women and children was based on long-sleeved, loose fitting buckskin dresses, belted at the waist and lined from the waist to the knees. The old style dress was a two-piece costume, a jumper style dress worn under a skin caplet draped on the shoulders. Leggings were tied on at the knees and were both decorative and practical. They protected the ankles from insect bites and irritating plants and added color and design to the costume. The long fringed dress reaching to the ankles that we picture as native clothing was a late design influenced by contact with the clothing of the pioneers.[33]

The dresses were decorated with porcupine quills dyed in juice obtained from local plants such as the pokeberry, yellow dock, and goldenseal, along with cedar bark, and walnuts from trees. Quill work was a true Woodland native art. The porcupine has smooth, shiny quills up to five inches long; if placed in water they become pliable and can be bent and twisted. These quills were worked in many different ways — they could be wrapped and sewn to the buckskin, they could be twisted and folded as they were sewn to the skin, or they could be woven.[34]

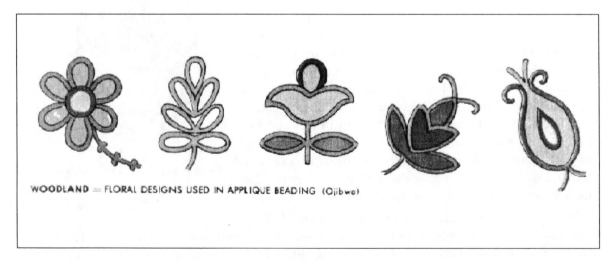

WOODLAND — FLORAL DESIGNS USED IN APPLIQUE BEADING (Ojibwa)

Woodland designs.(Illustration courtesy of Golden Books Publishing)

When these woven quill bands were pushed tightly together, they looked like small cylinder shaped beads. The fur traders saw this and realized that glass beads would be an excellent substitute for the tedious quill work. Beads were introduced on the Eastern seaboard around 1675, so the glass factories of France and Bohemia found a new market in what could be called the "third world" of the 1700s — our own Midwest. It is intriguing to think that 150 years later some descendants of those same European glass workers would be living here and working our quarries and farms.

The Indian women adapted the glass bead to an art form based on their own traditional designs. Their skill with these beads was remarkable and many sophisticated Europeans, recognizing the value of these handmade items, began collecting beadwork brought back by the traders in the late 1700s. Bead work, like quill work, was done several different ways. It was netted, spot-stitched, or lazy-stitched; woven bead work was done with cross warp weaving only after the introduction from Europe of the heddle. Most Potawatomi work was spot-stitching wherein the beads were threaded then laid in place and sewn down. This method was favored because Woodland Indian designs were often asymmetrical floral patterns that required more creative freedom than could be achieved with woven or netted work.[35]

Later Woodland designs were influenced by contact with European embroidery because those designs appear in work about the same time that glass beads became available. The first beads used were large and called pony beads; smaller seed beads were introduced shortly afterwards.[36]

Fashion then, as now, was not static. We think of Indian dress as some Hollywood outfit frozen in time, but this was not true. Indian women and men wanted clothing that was unique. The fur traders brought materials never seen before and those materials quickly became a part of the Native American dress. Trader cloth, a dark blue wool flannel, became popular with the Potawatomi by the end of the 1700s for three reasons: first, the skins and pelts had become too valuable for use as clothing; secondly, woven material was much easier to sew than skins; and, finally, it became fashionable.

The search for fashion ideas was no different on the frontier than it is now in our highly sophisticated world. The Indian women copied clothing ideas they saw on the Europeans and adapted those ideas in their own way. Patterns and designs also came from other tribes. For example, certain floral bead designs slowly traveled from east to west as one tribe after another learned the patterns. The quality of style and design work a woman did on her family clothing was a reflection of her ability and was considered a serious pursuit.

A last addition to the native costume of the Potawatomi of this area was ribbon applique. Ribbons of silk or satin from the traders were cut into designs and sewn onto leather or other cloth. With the introduction of the metal needle and cotton thread, it was possible to do more intricate work and some ribbon applique involved multi-level cutwork with many colors. These beautiful trimmings were used mostly on robes and shirts.[37]

In spite of the changes in dress over the years and in spite of the fact that much of the change was adaption from Western clothing, the Native American considered his costume an important part of his identity. It was as important to him as the three-piece suit is to the business man, or the rock tee-shirt and jeans to the teenager. Evidence for this fact comes to us in two ways: those Indians who intermarried and entered the world of the French or English traders gave up their Indian dress; those who held to their identity refused to give up the dress even when there could be social or financial gain. In early Chicago, Billy Caldwell, also known as Sauganash, was a mixed blood son of a British army officer and a Potawatomi woman. He received a Catholic school education in Detroit, and later offered to pay the school tuition of any Potawatomi child who would wear European clothing. No one accepted his offer.[38]

Descent in the Potawatomi tribes was patrilineal, men were required to marry outside their clan, and certain formal relationships controlled family life. Respect was due between brothers and sisters, children and parents, and children-in-law and parents-in-law.[39]

The Potawatomi had a complicated pattern of family and spiritual obligations. Besides his duties to the whole tribe, the Indian was also part of a smaller clan or totem group. Each group believed it was descended from a sacred animal. These totems formed smaller villages or encampments and were an extended family of sisters, brothers, and cousins from two or three families. Totem groups carried the name of the sacred animal that was their ancestor, such as the bear, deer, rabbit, hawk, or beaver. These animal ancestors conveyed power and special gifts to the totem which were based on the qualities of the animal. For example, a group could gain courage from the bear, or intelligence from the fox, or swiftness from the deer.

All animals, plants, and inanimate objects held a special nature or spirit. This spirit was called *manitou*, or *manido*. The idea is not easy to trans-

Potawatomi Chief Me-No-Quet. Little of his dress shows European influence. Note the trader medal. (Illustration courtesy of Illinois State Historical Society)

late to our modern concept of the world but was very real to people living close to nature. There were gods of the sun, the lakes, and the four directions. There was an afterlife, better than the one here. When an Indian died, his spirit rose to the sky and followed the Milky Way to a good land in the Western sky, which was ruled over by *Tcibiabos*, brother of the Potawatomi hero *Wisaka*. There also existed a greater spirit, owner of all these worldly *manitous,* called the Great Spirit. However, "he was inert and did not intervene in man's affairs."[40]

The totem spirit was worshiped in special ceremonies using sacred clan bundles. They contained objects the Indians believed would give them special power and were handed down from generation to generation. The bundles were often of deer or beaver skin filled with such fetish items as shells, wampum, medals from French or English traders, feathers of a different shape or color, or natural objects that were unique in some way. It makes sense that if every object has a spirit, then any object that was unusual would have more power. So any strangely shaped stone, twig, or natural formation was collected for the bundle.

Potawatomi Chief Wa-Baun-See. Note his European style dress, especially the military influence. He also wears a trader medal. (Illustration courtesy of Illinois State Historical Society)

The bundles could not be dishonored by any improper ethical conduct by any member of the totem, or the whole tribe would suffer. Each bundle had a legend or a history connected with it; this bound the totem to its past and its departed members and this history of the clan took on a special religious meaning. Legends would vary. Sometimes the bundle came into being as the result of some ancestor's dream, sometimes the bundle contained gifts from the clan's originators, and sometimes it was given to the clan by the hero, *Wisaka*.

Those Indians entrusted with the care of the clan bundle belonged to the medicine society, a priest group that held power to cure illness and prolong life. They were responsible for guarding and retelling the sacred stories and myths of the clan. When the stories were related in special ceremonies, each object of the clan bundle would serve to remind the medicine man and his audience, visually, of the story that went with the object. Since the Potawatomi did not have a written language, all information about their ethics, history, religion, philosophy, and science had to be transmitted orally and the clan bundle with its objects helped to do this.

The medicine men, or *shamans*, were of two types. A *chasgied* used herbs and talking with spirits. He also was often practiced in ventriloquism and sleight of hand tricks. His medicine was powerful but benign.[41] The other medicine man was called a *wabeno*; he was considered more powerful but could be malevolent. He usually offered protection from disease or evil. Potawatomis believed that wabenos could control weather, handle hot coals, and could transform themselves into animals.[42]

Sometimes shamans in a tribe would try to acquire power and followers. This type of struggle, when it occurred, created "considerable suspicion and paranoia among the tribe members."[43]

The world of the Potawatomi was a world filled with good and bad forces. One of the most feared evil forces was *Kegangize*, or The Great Horned Water Panther. It was natural to people who lived near water to have suffered any number of tragic mishaps, so they were careful when near water for the panther could attack any time and drag his victim to a watery death.[44]

Clearly the Indian was not a carefree savage. He had many very important spiritual responsibilities to his family, to his clan, and his tribe. He was required to meet these obligations or the whole group could suffer. Yet, the practice of his religion was an individual responsibility and there were few organized group religious activities. He was personally obligated to recognize and appease the spirit world around him.[45]

Moreover, he had to think of the group before himself. If he had corn or meat, he had to share with those in need and share his blankets and shelter with those who were cold. He had to conduct himself so that he did not dishonor his clan bundle, for any misconduct seen or unseen by others was known to the bundle. If a Potawatomi failed to do these things, he could be banished from the clan, from his loved ones, and from the protection of the clan bundle.

The Potawatomi religious and cultural world view was successful and comprehensive until Western contact. Intermarriage with French and English fur traders disrupted the clan structures because Western men could see no reasons why they were required to follow taboos that involved elaborate systems they failed to understand. The fur trader often had "powerful magic" items that the Indians had never seen before, which would displace the power of the local shaman. Moreover, the missionaries introduced a new, personal, monotheistic view of God and man's relationship with that God. All these factors weakened old traditions.

Childhood for the Potawatomi was very pleasant. Children were indulged, and seldom punished or reprimanded.[46] They had an extended family. Father and uncles were called father. Mother and aunts were called mother. This pattern developed because a man would often marry sisters in a family, so a special kinship existed in the family unit. Even when a brave was not married to the sisters of one family this aunt-mother, uncle-father relationship was established.

The infant was taken everywhere on a cradle board, measuring two feet long and ten inches wide, with a foot brace on one end and a hickory hoop around the head for protection. Sphagnum moss was placed in a shallow bark tray under the infant, which acted as a diaper and a cushion, so the disposable diaper is not a new invention.[47]

To keep warm during the winter, the babies' feet were wrapped in rabbit skin or cattail moss. Infants on the cradle board also wore a pair of tiny moccasins with holes in the soles. These were a charm to protect the baby from death, for if death came to lure the child away, the child could say: "But I can't come with you. See, my moccasins have holes in them."[48]

The baby's body was completely bound with only the head showing. Arms were freed when the child could grasp and focus its eyes. Attached to the hickory hoop around the head were colorful playthings. The Indian women did, by instinct, the very same thing that child psychologists tell us to do today — surround the infant with stimulating and colorful objects to develop an awareness of the sensory world. The objects dangling from the cradle board hoop had more use, however, than just playthings; they were also charms. These articles could be feathers, shells, pinecones, wampum, or any unusual natural items. Always included was a pouch containing the child's dried umbilical cord; it was believed that the Indian child gained wisdom by keeping this cord. If the child did not guard his cord it was thought that he would spend his life "searching for something" and would become foolish without it.[49]

The baby stayed on the cradle board for about a year, but he or she was removed every day for three or more hours for bathing and exercise. Weaning was done around two years of age and the children weaned to fish broth and soft vegetables. The Indians did practice birth control by mechanical and herbal means, especially during seasons with a small harvest, so a child could usually nurse until two or older.

To name a child, the parents called in a paid Namer. The Namer had a special relationship with the child, something like a godparent today. The designation the Namer selected could be based on a dream or some natural event. Sometimes it came from the weather or an animal that appeared at an auspicious time. The infant's special name was seldom used, however. Later, when the child was around six or seven years old, he or she was given another name based also on a dream or an event. This became its common name.

Usually, most hunting and tribal customs were taught to a boy by an uncle or male relative along with the father. Indians recognized the emotional difficulties that can arise when a father tries to teach his son any skill. The same pattern followed for girls; they learned food preparation and domestic chores from their mothers along with aunts and other female relatives.

However, this idyllic childhood was not without its limits. Customs regarding food were elaborate. Even very young children were required to fast on occasions for a day or more. This was done for spiritual and religious reasons and also to teach the child patience and restraint, because a child had to be trained for times of famine. The Potawatomi had a code that required you not to look at food while others ate and never to talk of food when there was hunger.

Young children often were controlled by fear. They were told tales of an owl that would carry away children who did not go right to sleep. Some clans had a "frightener" who dressed in ragged clothes and wore an owl mask. He was sent out when it got late to chase children back to their homes. Some clans placed "ugly and frightening forms" near areas too dangerous for children.[50]

Young boys were also trained to withstand pain and it was considered a sign of weakness to express pain of any kind. So, boys were encouraged to bathe in icy waters during the winter to strengthen their endurance.[51]

Puberty brought on adulthood: for the girls it began with menarche and for the boys it began with the vision quest. With the first menses the girl was isolated in a special hut built for this monthly event. There she was instructed by the women on her duties and obligations as a woman of the tribe. The female cycle was considered powerful magic and capable of harming warriors and hunters, so all women were isolated in the hut during their menses when the tribe was encamped and not on the move.[52]

The vision quest was required of all young males. In the Potawatomi world of good and bad forces the male needed a special protection that was personal. This was his own *manitou* and to find it adolescent Potawatomi had to undertake a special ceremony. He painted his face black with charcoal and withdrew from the tribe to fast. There he remained isolated from the tribe without food and unprotected except for his own weapons and skills. This was done until he had a dream or experience that revealed his personal *manitou*. Once the vision came, the *spirit/manitou* would protect him throughout his lifetime. The *manitou* could be an animal, a star, the moon, the west wind — anything in the whole of nature, since all things had power. The boy would remain protected by his special *manitou* as long as he worshiped it, made sacrifices to it, and held special feasts in its honor. From this vision he would make his own medicine bundle for protection from the bad forces of the world.

Old age was venerated. Few made it to the golden years since life was hard, so elders, who could recall the past and use that experience to advise the young, were called on for all important tribal decisions. When the older members of the tribe could no longer travel the yearly hunting cycles they stayed in the main camp near food and under the protection of a few braves who remained with them.

When death came, the deceased were dressed in their finest clothing and buried with their prized possessions for the trip to the land beyond the Milky Way. The burial site was important since the Potawatomi were semi-nomadic and followed a set pattern of travel. This meant that they would pass near family burial sites some time during the year. One of the many unhappy problems that came with removal of the Potawatomi from our area to the western lands was their inability to visit the grave sites of their ancestors.

A measure we in Western society use to decide the cultural development of a civilization is based on the quality of its arts and artifacts. Since the Potawatomi were small nomadic bands they left no major monuments — they did not build temples nor did they build elaborate tumuli mounds as some Indian civilizations before them. Nevertheless, they did develop attractive and useful objects that showed a sensitivity to beauty, form, and design. The problem is that most of their objects were organic, made of natural materials and fibers from fields and woods. These decay rapidly if not protected from the elements.

Besides clothing design and quill and bead work, the Potawatomi used clay, stone, bone, wood, and plant fibers to make equipment needed for everyday life. Algonquin pottery was fashioned from local clay, which was mixed with sand or gravel as a tempering material. The pots were made by the simple coil method, rolled into snakelike shapes and built up, then formed around gourds or baskets. The gourds or baskets were left in the clay to be burned away as the pottery was fired. Firing was done by baking the pot in hot coals. Most of the Potawatomi pots had round or pointed bottoms as they were designed to hang over a fire and not rest on the ground. When used for storage they were placed on their side. The top of the vessel was usually squared off and decorated with an incised geometric design.[53]

The contrast between the rounded or tapered bottom and the square rim was pleasing to the eye, and the squared rim made stirring and serving easy. Because the Potawatomi did travel frequently, the pottery was subject to breakage and, therefore, it was not developed to the fine artistic level of the non-nomadic tribes such as the Indians of the Southwest.

Stone was one of the more important raw materials for the Indians. It was easy to find stones that had shapes that could be adapted for use. Grinders, pounders, hammer-stones, and anvils can be found anywhere in our area. It is in the chipping and forming of specialized tools that we see the level of development of a tribe. Arrowheads here were made of chert, a gray-blue material found as nodules in limestone formations. These nodules had to be broken out of the rock layers along our bluffs. Two types of chipping techniques were used. First, percussion chipping was done on the nodule with a hammer stone. This method broke off smaller flakes of the chert. Then came pressure chipping to finish the arrowhead. A tool of bone or antler was used and pressed against the chert as it rested on another stone. This pressure against the stone broke off small chips from the opposite surface to form the arrow tip.[54]

To make the arrow shaft, the Indians would dry a bundle of shoots near a fire for a few weeks. Then they were sanded and straightened by using grease and heat. The arrow was then fletched with tail feathers to control flight. Arrows used for fish, birds, and small game had small bird points, sometimes made of bone. Those for warfare and hunting big game had large sharp arrowheads attached to the tip with sinew.[55]

The stone objects that we find around Lemont are all that is left to remind us of the time of the Indian. If you have an arrowhead, or other worked artifact, take it out and look at the craftsmanship that went into its making. You are holding the work from some distant Native American's life. You are touching our past.

Horn and bone were other raw materials that were available to the Native American. They were fashioned into knife handles, needles, hooks, and blades. Bones were also good decorations, because the composition of bone lends itself to carving and polishing. From the woods the Indians had an abundant supply of bark, plant fibers, and wood, from which bowls, cups, spoons, and ladles were carved by the men. Each person had his or her own spoon and bowl, which was carried to feasts, where food was transferred from a large cooking pot to the personal bowls.[56]

Long grasses were woven into coil baskets made like coiled pottery. Thin strips of grasses were wrapped into a bundle that was coiled around in a continuous spiral. As new material was added to the coil, lashing stitches were used to bind it together and sew it to the next loop of the coil.

The women also used plant fibers to weave into bags and other articles of clothing. Woodland finger weaving was done on a small frame. The fibers, basswood inner bark, buffalo wool, milkweed, and other plants, were woven spirally around the warp. The result of this simple process was beautiful and colorful.

Decorations done by the Indians on their household objects were not only for beauty but also for the magic that the symbols contained. The curve and the circle, repeated themes in Potawatomi design, were the symbols for life and for the cycles of the seasons. Animal designs represented the various totem clans. Plants and flowers reflected the *manitous* of nature. Any design with four points was dedicated to the four winds or the four elements: sky, earth, water, and the spirit world. Often the decorations would contain items that stood for the personal *manitou* of the owner. So Indian craftsman-artists approached their designs considering both its beauty and its spiritual meaning, certainly a sign of a highly civilized people.

ENDNOTES

[1]Robert Sutton, *The Prairie State: The Colonial Years to 1860* (Grand Rapids: Eerdmans, 1970), p. 59.

[2]Robert Sutton, *The Heartland* (Lake Forest, IL: Deerpath Publishing, 1982), p. 36.

[3]Jacqueline Peterson, "The Founding Fathers," *Ethnic Chicago*, ed. Melvin Holli, (Grand Rapids: Eerdmans, 1987), p. 302.

[4]James Clifton, "Chicago Was Theirs," *Chicago History*, (Chicago: Chicago Historical Society, Spring 1970), p. 7.

[5]Peterson, "The Founding Fathers, p. 302

[6]Chipping stations were areas with a large amount of chert, the hard dolomite needed for making arrowheads.

[7]Jacqueline Peterson, "The Absorption of French-Indian Chicago, 1816-1837," *Ethnic Chicago*, ed. Melvin Holli, 4th ed., (Grand Rapids: Eerdmans, 1995,) p. 19.

[8]For a discussion of the role of primitive woman in developing agriculture and domestic life see Lewis Mumford, *The City In History* (New York: Harcourt Brace & World, 1961), pp. 12-28.

[9]Donald Jackson, *Blackhawk* (Urbana: Illinois Books, 1969), pp. 90-91.

[10]Robert and Pat Ritzenthaler, *The Woodland Indians of the Western Great Lakes* (Garden City, NY: Natural History Press, 1983), p. 39.

[11]*Ibid,* p.38.

[12]Michael McNerney and Virgil Noble, *An Inventory and Evaluation of Known Archaeological Resources in the Illinois and Michigan Heritage Corridor* (Carbondale: American Resources Group, 1987), vol.1, pp. 18-20.

[13]*Ibid*

[14]Robert Sutton, *The Prairie State*, pp. 57-58.

[15]*Indians of Early Chicago* (Chicago: Field Museum, Booklet, 1970).

[16]Jackson, *Blackhawk,* p. 93.

[17]Robert Sutton, *The Prairie State*, pp. 59-60.

[18]*Ibid*., p. 92.

[19]Ritzenthaler, *The Woodland Indians,* p. 68.

[20]The Ritzenthalers discuss the question of why Indians used *kinnikinnick* when tobacco was a plentiful crop. They thought that since the Indians used the plant without processing or aging, as is done now, that it was too strong or rank in the undiluted state. Adding the *kinnikinnick* made a mellow smoke.

[21]Frances Densmore, *How Indians Use Wild plants For Food, Medicine & Crafts* (New York: Dover Books, 1974), pp. 286-294. This book is based on material from the Northern Woodland Chippewa tribes so some of the plants she lists were not available here. However, medicines were traded between tribes along with other foods and materials.

[22]Gerald Mandell, R. Gordon Douglas, and John Bennett, *Principles and Practice of Infectious Diseases* (New York: Churchill Livingstone, 1979), vol. 2, p. 1821.

[23]Clifton, "Chicago Was Theirs," p. 7.

[24]Oliver LaFarge, *A Pictorial History of the American Indian* (New York: Bonanza, 1974), p. 60.

[25]Andrew Whiteford, *North American Indian Arts*, ed. Herbert Zim, (New York: Golden Press, 1973), p. 60.

[26]Ritzenthaler, *The Woodland Indians,* p. 57.

[27]La Farge, *History of the American Indian,* p. 61. The Ritzenthalers also report viewing Woodland wigwam housing being used by a band of Kickapoos located in northern Mexico in 1952. See *The Woodland Indians,* p. 58.

[28]Ritzenthaler, *The Woodland Indians,* p. 59.

[29]Whiteford, *North American Indian Arts,* p. 78.

[30]*Ibid.,* p. 77.

[31]*Ibid,* p. 63.

[32]*Ibid,* p. 81.

[33]Ritzenthaler, *The Woodland Indians,* p. 55.

[34]Whiteford, *North American Indian Arts,* p. 87.

[35]*Ibid.,* p. 91.

[36]*Ibid.,* p. 92.

[37]Ritzenthaler, *The Woodland Indians,* p. 74.

[38]Jacqueline Peterson, "Wild Chicago," *The Ethnic Frontier,* ed. Melvin Holli, (Grand Rapids: Eerdmans, 1977), p. 57.

[39]Ritzenthaler, *The Woodland Indians,* p. 46.

[40]David Edmund, *The Potawatomi: Keepers of the Fire* (Norman, OK: University of Oklahoma, 1987), p. 61.

[41]Ritzenthaler, *The Woodland Indians,* pp. 95-108.

[42]Edmunds, *The Potawatomi,* p. 20.

[43]*Ibid.,* p. 21.

[44]*Ibid.,* p. 20.

[45]Ritzenthaler, *The Woodland Indians,* p. 85.

[46]*Ibid,* p. 33. The authors comment on the lack of tension in child rearing tactics by traditional Indian families even today. They believe that this attitude accounts for what is "popularly and tritely, but not wholly inaccurately called the 'stoic' in the Indian."

[47]Edmunds, *The Potawatomi,* p. 18.

[48]Ritzenthaler, *The Woodland Indians,* p. 29.

[49]*Ibid,* p. 30.

[50]*Ibid.,* p. 34.

[51]Edmunds, *The Potawatomi,* p. 19.

[52]*Ibid.,* p. 19.

[53]Whiteford, *North American Indian Arts,* p. 20.

[54]*Ibid.,* p. 112.

[55]Roland Eisenbeis, "Bows and Arrows: Part Two, *Nature Bulletin, Cook County Forest Preserve* (Chicago: Cook County District, 1976)

[56]Ritzenthaler, *The Woodland Indians,* p. 62.

CHAPTER THREE

THE INDIAN AND
THE CONTACT PERIOD

By the 1600s, even as the Indians lived out their cycle of the seasons, Western Europe began to impose its power politics on our wilderness. For almost 100 years, three countries struggled to control the land that was to become Illinois and Lemont. The French, English, and Spanish not only fought each other in Europe, but brought those wars to our continent to try to gain land and trading power.

The French came first with the establishment of military posts and missions shortly after Joliet and Marquette viewed the Illinois Valley and Lemont Township in 1673. LaSalle followed, traveling the Illinois River and building Fort Crevecoeur at Lake Peoria in 1679. LaSalle along with Tonti, his companion, had a dream of a French Empire along the whole Mississippi Valley. From Crevecoeur, LaSalle extended his exploration to the Gulf of Mexico and claimed the region for the King of France, calling it Louisiana. He then returned to the Upper Illinois Valley, where he built Fort Saint Louis at Starved Rock. The Indians and fur trade were an essential element in his plan for an empire which, however, failed.

LaSalle was recalled to France and returned with an assignment to establish a settlement at the mouth of the Mississippi. There he was murdered by his followers. Meanwhile, Tonti and the Illini Indians at Fort Saint Louis, who were in constant warfare from the Iroquois, moved back to Crevecoeur. But, the French government, with its complicated court politics, canceled Tonti's fur trade contract and he went south to Mobile, where he died.

Tonti and LaSalle may not have built an empire, but they did open the Illinois country to small French settlements in the south and along the Mississippi. These towns dealt mostly in fur trade and agriculture. The trade was largely carried on along the Mississippi, but some came through the Upper Illinois Valley to Canada. It is estimated that almost three thousand inhabitants lived in these Illinois-French villages until the end of the French and Indian War.[1] It was easy for the fur traders to collect and move goods because they could work within an already highly developed economic system — for hundreds of years native tribes had created their own extensive trade routes for exchanging products.

There is a local tradition that the French also established a fort or stockade in our area near Mt. Forest Island. A.T. Andreas' *History of Cook County: 1885* contains an article by Albert Hager, quoting Dr. Boyer of Chicago reporting on this fort:

> I have many times visited, when on hunting excursions the
> remains of an old fort located . . . at the crossing of the old
> Sag Trail, which crossed the Ausagaunashkee swamp
> [Sagaunaskee slough], and was the only crossing east of the
> DesPlaines River prior to the building of the Archer [Sag]
> bridge in 1836. The remains of the fort, situated north of the

Sag and near the crossing, were on elevated timber land, commanding a view of the surrounding country . . . I first saw it in 1833 and since have visited it often. I feel sure it was not built during the Sac War, from its appearance . . . It seems probable that it was the work of French fur traders or explorers as there were trees a century old growing in its environs . . . It evidently was the work of an enlightened people, skilled in the science of warfare.[2]

In an addition there is a short statement from Alexander Reid, an old pioneer of Lemont Township, who wrote that:

Thirty-seven years ago [1846] when plowing a piece of land on the south side of the Sag at a depth of 10-12 inches, [I] found about a bushel-basket full of arrow flints and . . . about 60 to 75 stone axes, of all sizes about 3 or 4 rods from the margin of the Sag.[3]

The site mentioned in both reports is located about three miles southwest of the village of Willow Springs near the edge of Lemont Township.[4]

After the French and Indian War (1755-1763), France was defeated in America and Europe, and was forced to sign the Treaty of Paris (1763) that ceded all of her land east of the Mississippi. However, French forts and villages remained in the Illinois territory with the support of our local Indians. The Indians regarded the French as their friends and were convinced that the British would push them off their land and rob them of their hunting grounds.

It took until 1765 for the English to establish some control over the trade and the Indians of the Illinois wilderness. Some independent English and Scotch traders did quite well, but generally, the Indians resisted trade with the English. The British had little time to establish military power in the region before the American Revolution began and troops were removed from the frontier to fight in the East.

When the Revolution ended in 1783, all the area north of the Ohio and east of the Mississippi that had been under English rule became part of the United States and was named "the Northwest Territory." It was now up to the our new country to try to establish control over the wilderness frontier. Americans, eager for land, began moving into Indian country, a movement that would shape the next period of our nation's history. The natural result of this expansion was a series of conflicts, raids, and wars between the Indians and the pioneers. Settlers demanded protection and the army was called in to police the situation.

After several small victories, the Indians of the Midwest suffered a major defeat at the Battle of Fallen Timbers, in 1794, in Ohio.[5] As a result, the Treaty of Grenville was signed in 1795, ending the wars and demanding that the Indians deal only with Americans in the future. Several areas were set aside for the construction of forts and trading factories; one of these was at the present site of Chicago.[6]

This location was chosen because it was at the head of the Chicago-Portage route and because there already was a small community of fur traders and Indians at the site. One of the first non-native settlers was Jean Baptiste Du Sable, a French speaking black man, who arrived in 1784 built a cabin and trading post, and married a Potawatomi woman.[7]

The site at Lake Michigan was designated to protect the western frontier from the English still remaining in the area. It also was to serve as a factory[8] in the Indian fur trade and as a police force between the Indians and the settlers. Congress, however, was slow in appropriating funds and it was not until 1804 that the United States government sent a party to build Fort Dearborn. The original company was small, having one captain, one

John Kinzie home in early Chicago. (Illustration courtesy of Illinois Historical Society)

second lieutenant, one ensign, four sergeants, three corporals, four musicians, one surgeon's mate, and 44 privates.[9]

Outside the fort, John Kinzie set up a trading station. The local Indians traveled the Des Plaines River carrying pelts and other trade goods to the station at the fort. Furs and other products from more distant areas were brought in to the post by traders. Most of the fur traders worked for the American Fur Company, signing contracts for two to five years. They were paid wages that ranged from 250 livres to 750 livres and then received their outfits, consisting of two cotton shirts, a Mackinaw blanket, and trade goods for the Indians. They left the headquarters of their employer at Chicago or other outposts[10] in the fall to spend the months until spring at their wintering grounds. Their food, when with the natives, consisted principally of fish, wild game, salt pork, corn, and tallow.[11] These traders returned to the posts in the spring and the furs they collected were sent to Mackinac and from there to New York.

So, at the start of the 19th Century the small settlement at the mouth of the Chicago River had only a few permanent settlers, some Indians, some mixed French and Indian families, some fur traders, and the troops stationed at the fort. It was an isolated post. At the time the westernmost state was Ohio and it contained no more than about 200,000 people. The only other non-native settlements west of Ohio were small groups of pioneers around forts or trading posts at Detroit, Saint Joseph, Fort Wayne, and Mackinac. All other land was in control of the Indians.

Because of the traders and the Kinzie family who dealt with the different Indian clans, we know the names of some natives and we have some idea of them as human beings.[12] Traders formed close and loyal friendships with the leaders of the tribes. Some also married into totem clans and their children often served as interpreters between the native and non-native populations. Of the early Indian leaders, two are of special local interest: Black Partridge and Kepotah (Keepataw). Information on both men is sketchy, since most of what we know comes from the Kinzie family records.[13]

Black Partridge's Indian name was Muck-ke-tay-pe-nay. He was considered spokesman for his local band in the early 1800s. His main village was located on the Au Sable Creek in section 32 of Au Sable township in Grundy County.[14] From that point his tribe controlled the lower end of the Des Plaines-Illinois waterway route. His dealings with the early pioneers were always honorable and he influenced his tribe to work with the settlers.[15]

To honor him and as part of treaty recognition of the Indian nations, he was given a peace medal by the Jefferson administration. This medal was part of a series of peace medals adopted by the United States government with an image of Jefferson, "the Great White Father," on the obverse side. Medals were an important part of the trader-Indian relationship on the frontier. They became a magical symbol of tribal power and power with Western man. The medals became part of tribal legends handed down to following generations.

The French and English started the custom by handing out medals to the leaders of tribes that had trading agreements with them. These medals became so significant that when new trade deals were struck, all former issues had to be recalled to be replaced by symbols of the new governmental alliance. Black Partridge wore his medal with pride, and since it bound him to maintaining peace, he spent a good deal of time arbitrating squabbles between the American authorities and the Indians.

His tribe ranged from the Au Sable area along the Illinois River south and to the Chicago area north, following the yearly pattern of the semi-nomadic Potawatomi. Black Partridge's band sometimes met with another tribe led by Kepotah. Kepotah's (Keepataw) clan originated in Saint Joseph, Michigan, around a trading post and settlement there. Their band wandered as far west as our area following the Sauk and Illini trails. It was not unusual for tribes to travel over 200 miles while looking for food and game. It is estimated that under the best of hunting and food gathering conditions it took at least one square mile to support ten people and it took considerably more territory to hunt for the fur traders. Land area that was sufficient for the demands of small tribes had to increase once the trader became part of the economic system.

An example of the ecological devastation the trade created can be understood in the amount of goods supplied by the Indians of the Illinois Valley during the winter season of 1816. That year traders shipped the hides of 10,000 deer, 300 bears, 10,000 racoons, 400 otters, and beaver, cat, fox, and mink for a total value of 23,700 dollars. Ten thousand pounds of maple sugar were also shipped.[16]

Recorded for 1819 was 286,000 pounds of deer tallow, 300 pounds of feathers, and 1,000 pounds of beeswax, so the Indian trade did not just involve fur-bearing animals.[17]

In the early years of Fort Dearborn, Kepotah, Black Partridge and other Indians traded not only with Kinzie and the American government, but also continued to maintain their old ties with the English. Indians made yearly trips to Malden, Canada, where they received presents from the British for their friendship. Native Americans did not see conflict in this arrangement, as they did not understand the political dealings of the major powers; they were used to tribal customs based on interpersonal relationships. This continued contact with the English led to disaster for Fort Dearborn and a heroic role for Black Partridge and Kepotah during the "Second War for Independence," or the War of 1812.

When the War of 1812 began, most local Indians favored the English, since they felt that the British had treated them fairly in the fur trade and because the English were not interested in acquiring land. Trouble began after the Battle of Tippecanoe in 1811. Many young braves became angry and eager to stop the flow of pioneer settlers into the region. They found leadership under the idealistic Indian, Tecumseh, who had served as a brigadier general in the British Army. He had a vision of a confederation of all tribes that would drive out Western man from Indian lands.

Tecumseh preached two main themes among the local Indians. First, temperance — whiskey should be abolished; and secondly, socialism — all private property should be abolished. The second idea was not unique to Native Americans, who were trained to share from early childhood. Temperance, however, was a difficult choice for people newly introduced to liquor. The French had introduced brandy, the English rum, and the Americans corn whiskey, all in an attempt to control and manipulate Indian behavior.

War was offically declared in June of 1812 and tension soon developed between the Indians and the Americans at Fort Dearborn. When the English captured Fort Michillimackinac, the American government decided that Fort Dearborn could not be defended and the occupants should retreat from the frontier to Fort Wayne, in the Indiana Territory.

On August 12, 1812, a council was held with the local Indians, including Black Partridge and Kepotah, to tell them that the Dearborn garrison was moving out. They were informed that the factory goods would be distributed among the bands. In return they were asked to give the company safe conduct to Fort Wayne. The next day all goods, except the ammunition and liquor, were disbursed. On the 14th, Captain Wells and an escort of Miami Indians arrived from Fort Wayne to accompany the garrison. Another council was held with Indians around the fort and this time open anger and hostility was expressed against whites, mainly Americans. Black Partridge tried to counsel the commander by warning him of the danger, but Captain Heald decided to abandon the fort.

Later that evening, in the most telling move of all, Black Partridge returned to the fort and gave Captain Heald the trading medal that he wore. He explained that he had worn the medal as a token of mutual friendship, but his young men were resolved to bathe their hands with the blood of the whites. He could not restrain them, and would not wear a token of peace, while compelled to act as an enemy.[18]

On the 15th the garrison marched out, led by Miami Indians from Fort Wayne. Captain Wells, an old Indian scout, blackened his face with powder, a traditional sign of trouble. Meanwhile, Mr. Kinzie was notified by a friendly Indian that he should not send his family with the garrison. Instead, it was suggested that the family be placed in a boat and taken to Saint Joseph, in Michigan Territory. The boat contained Mrs. Kinzie, four children, a nurse, a clerk, two servants, and boatmen. This boat was kept out of sight during the battle. After the massacre the boat was guided by natives with enough power and prestige to protect the family from harm. One of those was Kepotah.

Both Kepotah and Black Partridge were present at the massacre as it was their duty to be there as tribal leaders, although they did not agree with the action of the braves. Decisions on tribal matters, including wars and raiding parties, were done by vote, and if most of the braves wanted to take an action, no one could stop them. To maintain position in the tribe, Kepotah and Black Partridge had to be there. However, it was reported that neither one took part in the killing and worked to save those they could. Kepotah kept guard over the Kinzie family and Black Partridge rescued Mrs. Helm, a step-daughter of Mrs. Kinzie, from the middle of the battle and dragged her to safety in the lake.[19]

The actual attack occurred a mile from the fort. Twenty-six soldiers, 12 militia men, Captain Wells, two women, and 12 children died, their bodies left to the wind and sand. Their bones were not collected and buried until four years later when Kinzie returned to reopen the Indian trade.[20] Immediately after the massacre, Kepotah took those Kinzie family members he saved to Saint Joseph, finally escorting them to Detroit. There he insisted that the English, who had by then captured Detroit, take care of the family. He visited them frequently and was visiting when General McArthur retook Detroit for the American forces. When General Harrison arrived, Kepotah and the general simultaneously were guests in the Kinzie house. It was reported that they enjoyed each other's company.[21]

The war between the United States and England ended on December 24, 1814, and the U.S. promptly began negotiations with the tribes of our area who had supported the British. Our government looked upon the Indians as nations and therefore felt that they must sign a peace treaty with the United States, in the same manner as the English did. In July of 1815, many of the Northern tribes gathered on the right bank of the Mississippi, a few miles from Missouri, and there signed treaties of peace.

A separate treaty for the Potawatomies declared "that the parties are desirous of re-establishing peace and friendship between themselves, and being placed in every respect on the same footing upon which they stood before the war with Great Britain," and further declared, "that every act of hostility shall be mutually forgiven and that there shall be perpetual peace between all citizens of the United States and individuals of the Pottawatomie tribes, and that they have to agree to surrender all prisoners they have in their hands."[22]

The last item was included because Potawawtomi tribes frequently captured settlers and other Indians for ransom. Black Partridge, happy to live in peace, was one of the signers of this pact.

On July 4, 1816, the Fort at Chicago was rebuilt and the quiet life of the frontier outpost in our area returned.

ENDNOTES

[1]Robert Sutton, *The Heartland* (Lake Forest, IL: Deerpath, 1982), p. 23.

[2]A.T. Andreas, *History of Cook County Illinois: 1885* (Evansville: Unigraphics, 1976), p. 56.

[3]*Ibid.*, p. 60.

[4]*Ibid.*, p. 824.

[5]The name came about because a tornado had destroyed the trees before the battle. General "Mad" Anthony Wayne commanded the troops.

[6]Sutton, *The Heartland,* p.38.

[7]Bessie Pierce, *A History of Chicago* (New York: Knopf, 1940), vol. 1, p. 12.

[8]The word "factory" comes from the Latin "agent." The factory on the frontier was a trading post.

[9]Pierce, *A History of Chicago,* vol. 1, p. 16.

[10]Stations were located at Mackinac, Chicago, Peoria, and other outposts along the river and lake systems.

[11]Andreas, *History of Cook County,* p. 92.

[12]See Juliette Kinzie's book, *Wau-Bun,* first published in 1856. Recent reprint, (Portage, WI: The National Society of the Colonial Dames of America in the State of Wisconsin, 1989). Her work is autobiographical and tends to flatter the family.

[13]Kinzie, *Wau-Bun,* pp. 140-199.

[14]Virginia Brown, ed., *Grundy County Landmarks* (Morris, IL: Grundy County Historical Society, 1981), p. 49.

[15]Zeb Eastman, *Chicago Magazine: 1857* (Chicago: Chicago Historical Bookworks, 1978), p. 108.

[16]Robert Howard, *Illinois: A History of the Prairie State* (Grand Rapids: Eerdmans, 1972), p. 94. The sugar represents over 58,000 gallons of maple: it takes 40-50 gallons of sap to make one gallon of syrup, and one gallon of syrup makes about seven pounds of sugar.

[17]*Ibid.,* p. 94.

[18]Eastman, *Chicago Magazine,* p. 110, and Kinzie, *Wau-Bun,* p. 171.

[19]Kinzie, *Wau-Bun,* pp. 176-177. The Chicago Historical Society has on display a statue depicting this event.

[20]Eastman, *Chicago Magazine,* p. 116.

[21]*Ibid.,* p. 106.

[22]*Ibid.,* p. 198.

U.S. HISTORY

1810: *United States Population 7,239,881.*

1811: *William Harrison Defeats Indians under Tecumseh at Tippecanoe — Earthquake on New Madrid Fault in Southern Illinois and Surrounding States.*

1812: *Louisiana Becomes a State — U.S. Declares War on England.*

1813: *Americans Capture Toronto — Detroit is Occupied by the Americans — Peoria [Ft. Clark] Built on the Site of Black Partridge's Destroyed Village.*

1814: *English Burn Washington D.C. — Treaty of Ghent Ends War of 1812 — Francis Scott Key Writes "Star Spangled Banner."*

1815: *Battle of New Orleans.*

1816: *Indiana Becomes a State — Fort Dearborn is Rebuilt After Its Destruction in 1812.*

1817: *James Monroe is President — Mississippi Becomes a State — Erie Canal is Started between Buffalo and Albany, Finished in 1825.*

1818: *Illinois Becomes a State — Andrew Jackson Suppresses Seminole Uprising in Florida.*

1819: *Alabama Becomes a State — Florida is Purchased from Spain.*

LEMONT HISTORY

1812: *Fort Dearborn Massacre — Black Partridge and Kepotah Help Some Settlers.*

1813: *Indians and British Fur Trading in the Area — No Permanent Non-Native Settlers in the Lemont Area.*

1816: *Major Stephen Long Surveys the Proposed Illinois and Michigan Canal Area — New Fort Dearborn Built.*

1818: *Illinois Becomes the 21st State — Our Area and Ten Northern Counties Included in the New State Boundaries in Anticipation of the I & M Canal.*

1819: *Fur Trade with Indians Continues But is on the Decline — Fur Station in Lemont in Area of Present State and Main Streets.*

CHAPTER FOUR

EARLY CHICAGOLAND AND THE REMOVAL OF THE INDIANS

With the rebuilding of Fort Dearborn in 1816, more traders and settlers came to the area. The economy was based, however, on either supplying the needs of the garrison or on the fur trade. It was an economy that was unable to sustain a large population. Nevertheless, the frontier outpost was not ignored by the government. The war with England, in 1812, had renewed the idea of a canal connecting Lake Michigan and the Illinois River. This plan was not only for commerce, but also viewed as a defense system for the more western lands. The *Niles Register* of August, 1814, praised the idea:

> By the Illinois River it is probable that Buffalo, in New York, may be united with New Orleans, by inland navigation, through Lakes Erie, Huron, and Michigan, and down the Mississippi. What a route! How stupendous the idea! How dwindles the importance of the canals of Europe compared with this water communication! If it should ever take place [and it is said the opening can be easily made] the territory will become the seat of an immense commerce and market for the commodities of all regions.[1]

With this idea in mind, another treaty was concluded with the Indians in the fall of 1816. Black Partridge, whose second village had been ordered destroyed by Governor Edwards because of the war, and other Potawatomi Indians signed a compact that ceded away a tract of land under the name of the Indian Boundary. This land was bounded as follows:

> Beginning on the left bank of the Fox River; thence running so as to cross the Sandy (Au Sable) Creek, ten miles above its mouth; thence in a direct line to a point ten miles of the west end of the portage between Chicago Creek, which empties into Lake Michigan, and the River Des Plaines, a fork of the Illinois; thence in a direct line to a point on Lake Michigan, ten miles northward of the mouth of Chicago Creek; thence along the lake to a point ten miles southward of the mouth of the said Chicago Creek; thence in a direct line to a point on the Kankakee and the Illinois River to the mouth of the Fox, and thence to the beginning.[2]

Reading this legal description, which is difficult even for us, makes one wonder how much Black Partridge and the other leaders understood these formal treaties.

By purchasing this section, the United States government could control the vital Chicago Portage and the Des Plaines-Illinois waterway for the day that the I & M canal project could be built. The Potawatomis received for this strip of land — containing our present twenty miles of the whole section on either side of the waterway system from Chicago to Ottawa, a "considerable amount of goods." They were also given a promise of one thousand dollars worth of goods at cost price, for that year, and twelve succeeding years, to be delivered to them on some point of the Illinois River, not lower down than Peoria.

Since there were few settlers in the region, the impact of the sale was not immedietly apparent. Indians did not understand the concept of buying land and thought that they could remain forever hunting and following their yearly cycle simply avoiding those few whites who did settle, trade, and farm. There was no way that Black Partridge, Kepotah, and the others could know of the stream of pioneers who would come in the years to follow. At the most, the settlement at Chicago had one hundred non-natives. It was a village of fur traders, their employees, "clerks, *voyagers*, and *engage's* of French, British, American, Indian and mixed extraction."[3]

However, within a few years conditions changed. As early as 1821, there was pressure from the settlers to have Indians moved. Fear of the Indian discouraged newcomers and hindered development. Meanwhile, the fur trade declined as the Chicagoland region became over-hunted. As a result, the Native American was less economically important to the settlement at Chicago. With frontier expansion and settlers demanding farm land, the Indian agency pushed Natives for more concessions. Kepotah and the others then found themselves forced to sign the Treaty of Chicago. This paper deeded the Indian lands around the southern end of Lake Michigan to the U.S. government. Kepotah signed as one of the St. Joseph chiefs.[4]

This section, along with other lands to the west, was the final holding of the Potawatomis in our part of Illinois. Kepotah's summer and winter hunting grounds in the Des Plaines Valley were already gone, sold with the Indian Boundary purchase. Now his spring and fall village lands were taken. For the grant of the lovely area along southern Lake Michigan the tribe was paid 5,000 dollars each year for twenty years, and 1,000 dollars a year for the support of a blacksmith and a teacher, two skills the tribe considered essential for adaption to the modern age.[5]

It is easy to question now why we had to force the Native American from his lands in this manner, but there really was no way that the early settlers and the Indian could live together because their social and cultural values were so different. The early settlers, except for the French fur traders, seldom took time to understand the Indian and lived in constant fear of harm. The country would not open up until new settlers were reassured that the Indians would be moved.

The western pioneer came with a drive to control and manage nature, to till the soil, cut down trees, and to make the land pay. Peterson calls it a "concept of linear progress with the future only obtainable by cheating the present, by conserving time, currency, and emotion-walking the straight line."[6] To the Potawatomi the earth was here to enjoy. It was a mother to all and not meant to be manipulated, owned, or controlled. To do such a thing would anger the *Manitous* of the world and bring sickness and death to the tribe. The Indians felt free to roam settlers' lands and to take what food or cattle they might need, just as deer and game were there for all to take.

Though many missionaries and social agencies tried to develop some interest in farming and "western ways" among the Potawatomis, most of it met with failure.[7] First, crop raising, even on the small scale that the tribes did, was women's work and therefore not a proper way for a man to live. Secondly, remaining in one area was confining mentally and socially to a semi-nomadic tribe. Moreover, there were other ethical conflicts. The early pioneer wanted to acquire material things to show his status in society, while Native Americans were suspicious of individuals who collected too many material possessions. For example, when a Potawatomi died, many of his belongings were given away by his widow to friends. Often Indians held feasts and distributed many of their possessions as "love gifts" for those who attended.

Pioneers looked to tomorrow and the great cities that would arise from their efforts. The Potawatomi seldom lived beyond today; life would come as it came. The pioneer admired action and aggressiveness. The Potawatomi admired patience and stoicism, and his children were trained to be patient, to wait. The Indian also had little concern for time, which was not measured in hours and minutes, but in days and seasons.

The two groups were so different that cultural clashes were bound to happen. Tension developed as early as 1827, when the settlement at Chicago had only 14 taxpayers and 35 voters. At that time, in spite of the treaties, the Indians remained in the area because of their fur trade dependence. Relations became especially tense when the tribes came to the fort in large groups for their yearly payments. Bessie Pierce reports an incident in 1827:

> In the evening following the annual payment . . . a dance held in the soldiers' barracks was interrupted by a storm and a bolt of lightning set fire to these quarters and destroyed them, together with the storehouse and a portion of the guardhouse. The combined efforts of the inhabitants were required to check the course of the flames, during which Big Foot's band of Pottawatomies, who had remained after the payment, refused to lend assistance.[8]

A week after this strange act, the fort learned about the outbreak of the Winnebago War in the Wisconsin territory. The settlement then became concerned that Big Foot might be planning to attack Chicago and took measures for its defense. This event never happened, but it added to the paranoia of the pioneers. In 1832, another "Indian Scare" began when the Sauk and Fox tribes returned to Illinois from Iowa, starting the Black Hawk War.

Most of the fighting occurred west of the Chicagoland area, but many outlying settlers sought shelter at Fort Dearborn. The pioneers crowded into the fort, or their own defense stockades, and remained until the first two companies of the U.S. regular army arrived from Fort Niagara.[9] When they arrived, those already in the fort were forced to find shelter elsewhere so the troops could be housed. This was a blessing, because the troops under General Scott brought Asiatic cholera with them and the fort became a hospital. Two hundred men became ill and 58 died. One regiment in that war was led by Colonel Jacob Fry, who later became a Commissioner of the I & M Canal.[10]

As for the Black Hawk War, it ended at the Battle of Bad Axe, near the Mississippi River in Wisconsin, "in a heavy slaughter that almost extinguished the Sauk tribe; the warriors, old people, woman, and children were driven into the water and then ambushed as they tried to reach the west bank. Black Hawk escaped but was soon captured." [11]

This war did accomplish two things. First, many of the troops from the East were introduced to the beauty of Northern Illinois land that was available for settlement. Secondly, the war forced the government to press for the final removal of the Indians from

Illinois so it could be opened for development. The treaty for removal was signed in 1833. Robert Howard writes about the event:

> Summoned to a council in the autumn . . . the tribes, long dependent upon the white man, were unable to resist. Some five thousand set up their camps for five miles around the village. The chiefs insisted they did not want to sell, but the white man provided whiskey and food in quantity. The town was in an around the clock uproar . . . John D. Canton described it as a carnival of lost souls [12]

Another observer of the scene recorded:

> It is a grievous thing that government is not strong enough to put a stop to the shameful and scandalous sale of whiskey to these poor miserable wretches. But here lie the casks of it for sale under the very eyes of the commissioners, met together for purposes that demanded sobriety should be maintained. Were it only that no one should be able to lay at the door an accusation of unfair dealing, and of having taken advantage of the hapless Indian in a bargain, whereby the people of the United States were to be so greatly a gainer and such was the state of things day by day.[13]

Even as the payments were made to the Indians there were salesmen hawking all kinds of wares to part the Indian from what money was gained from the sale. Years later, Nelson Algren would look on it all as "The Great Hustle," part of his view of Chicago as a "City on the Make":

> Yankee and Voyageur, the Irish and the Dutch, Indian traders and Indian agents, halfbreed and quarterbreed and no breed at all, in the final counting they were all of a single breed. They all had hustler's blood . . . They hustled the land, they hustled the Indian, they hustled by night and they hustled by day. They hustled guns and furs and peltries, grog and the blood-red whiskey dye; they hustled with dice or a deck or a derringer. And decided the Indians were wasting every good hustler's time. Slept till noon and scolded the Indians for being lazy. Paid the Pottawatomies off in cash in the cool of the Indian evening: and had the cash back to the dime by break of the Indian dawn. [14]

Shortly after signing, bands of Indians began leaving and by 1835 the last remaining groups headed West. There was sadness in leaving the familiar land and, yet, conditions had changed so much with the advancing frontier that most of the Indians looked forward to a new life in a wilderness not hemmed in by farm fences and civilized society.

So passed one of the many groups that would come to live in our region over the progression of history. The Native American is unique because he represents 97 percent of man's known habitation in our valley, prairies, and woods. We, of recorded history, can claim only three percent of human time in Lemont.

To finish the story of the Indians of Lemont, we need a last postscript on the life of the Prairie Band of the Potawatomi, Lemont's and Chicagoland's Indians. Most local histories have the Potawatomi disappearing never to be mentioned again, but they did not disappear. Some escaped to Canada, some moved to the more remote areas of Michigan and Wisconsin, and some, who intermarried, stayed on.[15]

However, most of the Prairie Band moved. As a group they were adaptable, having moved, over a period of less than 150 years, from Lake Huron to Northern and Central Illinois. During that period they had changed from a totally nomadic life to a semi-agricultural society, and, during those years, they drove out most of the other tribes of the region, gaining control of the fur trade.

With the coming of pioneers and development, power over their own lives was lost and the Prairie Band leaders felt the move westward would be another chance for the Indian way of life, as they knew it, to survive. They had no idea how rapidly the frontier would advance on them again. Reports of the new lands were not hopeful. In 1835, a scouting party visited the Iowa region given to them and came back with the information that "there was scarcely timber enough for wigwams, there were no sugar trees . . . and warlike tribes lived to the north." Yet the leaders felt they had no choice but to leave.[16]

While living here, the Prairie Potawatomi had developed the yearly pattern of small seasonal migration for summer planting and winter hunting dependent on goods supplied by the fur traders. They had adapted so completely to this life that by the time they were faced with mass migration all older subsistence skills had been forgotten, and it became necessary for the tribe to hire American scouts to guide and feed the band as it moved west. Many contractors took advantage of the tribal groups by serving bad food, charging exorbitant prices, and, worst of all, guiding them to the wrong area — the Platte River country of Missouri rather than to the Western Iowa lands that they had been given.[17] So within a year the Prairie Band had to move again.

Because it took time to develop a new pattern of hunting and planting in a different area, the tribe spent its first few years in Iowa depending upon government handouts. There were many — traders, settlers, missionaries, and storekeepers — who preferred this dependency. With money from the government, the tribe was an economic factor in the Iowa frontier, and as long as they remained near the government agencies they could be civilized, contained, and educated to Western ways.

Tribal elders soon recognized that they were repeating the pattern of assimilation and dependence that had weakened their customs and survival skills before, so they began to move westward and to adapt to the plains. "In Western Iowa they were free from any real efforts to 'civilize' them."[18] Missionaries and teachers sent to the tribe were rejected as a danger to the development of a lifestyle for survival. Because of this self-imposed isolation, the Prairie Band regained their old skills and established new hunting grounds out of the lands used by the powerful Dakotas. As a result, between 1838 and 1854, the Potawatomi were frequently at war with the Dakotas and the Pawnee. In fact, the Dakotas, numbering around 28,000, were in constant fear of the Potawatomi, numbering only 2,000.[19]

The army garrison at Council Bluffs did not interfere in the struggle as they considered the Potawatomi a good buffer against the Dakotas. But no matter what success the tribe had, they could not stop the frontier as it moved west. Within ten years the wilderness of Iowa was carved into farms and the Potawatomi were again under pressure to change their life patterns to become small farmers or to move on. The tribe struggled with the problem until one of its leaders, Waubansee, had a vision, an important sign to the Potawatomi. It came to Waubansee to give up trying to deal with the local Indian agents and go directly to Washington to talk to President Polk. So, in 1845, Waubansee and his sub-chiefs traveled to the nation's capital and met with the President. There they arranged for a place in Kansas in trade for the Iowa lands. Reservations were becoming difficult to obtain and this choice on the Kaw River was much smaller than the Iowa site. It also would one day be surrounded by the area of Topeka, Kansas.

Conditional with this move was the fact that the Prairie Band would have to share the reservation with the Mission Band of Potawatomi, an assimilated and mission-educated tribe. This was a situation that neither group liked. The Prairie Band considered the Mission Band untrue to their heritage, while the Mission Band, naturally, considered the Chicago Indians heathen savages.

In the years that followed, the new land was soon coveted by real estate and railroad speculators. Eager to please government authorities, the Mission Band Indians submitted to a division of their lands. The Prairie Band held out for a reservation and finally achieved a very small portion of the original holding.[20]

It was too small to support the whole population, so the young were forced out and adapted to Western culture. Nevertheless, the descendants of this tribe remain loyal to the area to this day, although many live in other parts of the United States, and tribe members return to the small reservation for reunions and ceremonies. James Clifton tells of a visit to the reservation and of a drum ceremony that he viewed, an updated version of an ancient ritual created by their once neighbors in Iowa, the Dakota Santee. The ceremony was done to insure that the Prairie Band would endure. Clifton was moved to say:

> I watched inside the drum circle the children of Black Partridge who had rescued Captain Helm's wife; of the English half-breed Billy Caldwell; of Waubansee; of the French-half breed La Clair, who had interpreted for the garrison's [Ft. Dearborn] surrender following the massacre . . . and of all the young braves and war chiefs who had bested Captain Helm and his troops on the beach south of the Chicago River. The distant grandfathers of these same Pottawatomi had traded in respected friendship with John Kinzie . . . Although Chicagoans may have forgotten the Prairie People who they knew as warriors and as "Chicago's Own Indians." . . . The Prairie Band in Kansas has never forgotten Chicago nor their victory over Fort Dearborn. Even today somewhere on the edge of Little Soldier Creek on the Kansas reservation is buried safely in an old copper kettle, now too dangerous to handle, a sacred Pottawatomi war bundle . . . The very war bundle that a Chicako Pottawatomi shaman appealed to for spiritual power and victory in the dark night of August 11, 1812 . . .[21]

So, after over 160 years since they left, the remnants of the local Indians still survive in spite of overwhelming changes in their culture and environment. There on the Kansas Plains near the little town of Mayetta, the last descendants of the Prairie Band struggle to adapt to a modern world without losing their unique heritage of customs and traditions. The population of the tribe is over 4,000 with about 500 living on the 11 square mile reservation. In a real sense they are repeating a struggle that every immigrant to this country has to follow, how to adapt to a new world without losing those important values and traditions of the old ways.

ENDNOTES

[1]Zeb Eastman, *Chicago Magazine: 1857* (Chicago: Chicago Historical Bookworks, 1978), p. 383.

[2]*Ibid.*, p. 198

[3]Jacqueline Peterson, "Wild Chicago," *The Ethnic Frontier,* ed. Melvin Holli and Peter d'A. Jones (Grand Rapids: Eerdmans, 1977), p. 35.

[4]Bessie Pierce, *A History of Chicago* (New York: Knopf, 1940), vol. 1., p. 29.

[5]*Ibid.*, p.29.

[6]Jacqueline Peterson, "Absorption of French-Indian Chicago 1816-1837," *The Ethnic Frontier*, ed. Melvin Holli and Peter d'A. Jones, 4th edition, (Grand Rapids: Eerdmans, 1995), p. 49.

[7]Robert Berkhofer, Jr., *The White Man's Indian* (New York: Vintage Books, 1979), p. 150. Berkhofer discusses how the federal system supported missionaries in their attempts to develop what was thought of as Christian Civilization. This reformation of the Native American was to create a "model husband and wife, who farmed private property, attended church faithfully, could read and write and keep accounts, and participate in the government as American citizens."

[8]Pierce, *A History of Chicago,* vol. 1, p. 35.

[9]John Lamb, *A Corridor in Time* (Romeoville: Lewis University, 1987), p. 16.

[10]Fry Landing on the I & M Canal downtown is named for him.

[11]Robert Howard, *Illinois: A History of the Prairie State* (Grand Rapids: Eerdmans, 1972), p.152.

[12]*Ibid.*, p. 153.

[13]Robert Sutton, *The Prairie State: Colonial Years to 1860,* (Grand Rapids: Eerdmans, 1970), p. 232.

[14]Nelson Algren, *Chicago: City on the Make* (New York: McGraw-Hill, 1983), p. 12.

[15]These other Bands include the Citizens Band in Oklahoma, the Forest Band in Wisconsin, the Hannahville Band in northern Michigan, the Pokagon and Huron Bands in southern Michigan and northern Indiana, and the Stoney Point and Kettle Bands in Canada. The Potawatomi now have a home page on the internet and are developing an orthography for the language so it can be taught.

[16]Ellen Whitney, "Indian History and the Indians of Illinois," *Journal of the Illinois State Historical Society* (Springfield: Illinois State Historical Society, May, 1976), p. 145.

[17]James Clifton, "Chicago Was Theirs," *Chicago History* (Chicago: Chicago Historical Society, Spring, 1970), p.12.

[18]*Ibid*., p. 12.
[19]*Ibid*., p. 13.
[20]*Ibid*., p. 15.
[21]*Ibid*., p. 9.

U.S. HISTORY

1820: *Missouri Compromise — Maine Enters as Free State and Missouri as Slave State — U.S. Law Fixes Land Prices at Minimum of $1.25 an Acre.*

1821: *Monroe's Second Term — Population of U.S. at 9.6 Million.*

1822: *Government Trading Post at Chicago Closed.*

1823: *Monroe Doctrine — First Steamboat Up the Mississippi.*

1824: *John Q. Adams is President — Marquis De Lafayette Visits U.S. by Invitation of Congress.*

1825: *Erie Canal Completed.*

1826: *U.S. is 50 Years Old — John Adams and Thomas Jefferson Both Die on July 4, 1826.*

1827: *Audubon Publishes* Birds of North America.

1828: *Andrew Jackson is President — Noah Webster Publishes* The American Dictionary *— First U.S. Railroad in Baltimore — Soldiers Return to Fort Dearborn.*

1829: *Jackson Attacks the Bank System — More Canals in the East: Delaware & Chesapeake, Delaware & Hudson, Oswego, Farmington, and the Cumberland & Oxford.*

LEMONT HISTORY

1821: *Potawatomi, Ottawa, and Chippewa Give Up Lands in Michigan and the Right-of-Way to Ft. Wayne.*

1823: *Military Forces at Ft. Dearborn Withdraw — Chicago a Small Village of French-Canadians, Indians, and a Few Settlers from the East.*

1825: *First School Law in Illinois.*

1826: *Mark Beaubien Opens the Saugnash Tavern in Chicago.*

CHAPTER FIVE

THE I & M CANAL
AND EARLY DEVELOPMENT

When Illinois was offered statehood in 1818, it was because of the increase in population in the southern part of the territory along the Mississippi and Ohio Rivers. Since water was the main means of transportation, city and village settlements along the waterways were a normal growth pattern. This relationship of water transportation to economic development led to the canal building craze that swept the United States and Europe in the early part of the 1800s. Communities not located on natural waterways saw the need to create their own. With great fanfare, New York began the Erie Canal and our Representatives in Congress, not to be outdone, already were considering the power of a canal linking Lake Michigan and the Illinois River. Therefore, when the borders of our new state were established, Illinois Representives in Congress worked to move the northern boundary 41 miles northward to 42°30" N., so Illinois could have full control of the Chicago River, the lake shore harbor, and the portage.

The result of this maneuver was to remove construction of the proposed I & M Canal from a national project located in a territory to a project that would need mainly local state support. The national government, with its debt from the War of 1812, was reluctant to aid in any canal construction, so the burden fell upon the new state. This delayed the project since so little of Illinois' population lived in our area and, therefore, there was no real financial support for the canal. All capital had to come from Eastern bankers or Europe.

Finally, in 1822, the federal government did grant the state the right to ninety feet of land on both sides of the proposed canal. With this small beginning a canal commission, the first of many, was created in 1823 and the commission hired Justus Post and Rene Paul to survey the Indian Boundary area. Post and Paul selected five possible routes through the valley, but money continued to be a problem and the commission was dissolved to be replaced by a private stock company that also failed. In 1827, the state convinced Congress to grant public lands they held in Illinois for sale to finance the canal. So half of the Indian Boundary lands, alternating sections five miles on either side of the proposed canal, were given to a new commission. This amounted to a total of 290,915 acres, 113,000 of which was prairie land. Congress added some conditions: the work must be started in five years, it must be finished in 20 years, and tolls should be forever free to the United States government.

In our area the canal land sections were 12, 14, 20 (downtown Lemont), 22, 24, 26, 28, 30, 32, 34, and 36. In 1830, the Canal Commission platted two towns, Chicago and Ottawa, and offered lots for sale. The response was disappointing. The Commission raised only 18,000 dollars. However, the publicity and the prospect of a major construction project on the frontier attracted the attention of land speculators, contractors, workers, farmers, and shopkeepers from the East, and some began settling in the area.

The canal was delayed again, for a short while, because some capitalists, looking at newer transportation ideas, proposed that a railroad instead of a canal be built in the corridor.[1] In 1833, Illinois Congressman Duncan fought for the canal and for federal support by listing his objections to the idea of a railroad. His points were the basic arguments that turned popular support back to the original canal idea:

> [Such] transportation [railroad] would fall into the hands of a few monopolists. The cost risk, and delay of transhipment would be great; and many if not most of the articles raised in the country could not be transported on a railroad . . . If a canal should be made, such as I have spoken of, every man who did not desire to put his material into a steamboat [the newest form of water transportation at that time], could use his own craft, his own means, and his own time; could go to market and return with little or no expense; while the citizens of other states could pass from Lake Michigan to New Orleans without the expense of transhipment . . . or delay. Experience has shown that railroads grow worse with use, require repairing from the moment they are made, and last about 15 years [steel rails had yet to be developed]; while canals improve every day, and last forever.[2]

The canal project won out but the federal government was still unwilling to give more aid to the Commission. It fell on the state to take over the burden of internal improvements and when the state legislature met in Vandalia in 1836, a bill was introduced to sell 10,000,000 dollars worth of bonds to underwrite the canal and other state projects. These infrastructure improvements were driven by the wild land speculation that swept the new state. Governor Thomas Ford, who served from 1842 to 1846, disapproved of encumbering the young government with such a financial burden. In his history of that era he commented "speculation was the order of the day and every possible means was hastily and greedily adopted to give an artificial value to property."[3]

Abraham Lincoln, then a Whig floor leader, worked hard for the passage of that bill, so hard that in later years one legislator seemed to recall Lincoln as a member of the Committee on Internal Improvements. He was not. He worked for the bill because he believed in the future growth of Illinois, which he felt could be achieved faster by developing new transportation corridors. Without his efforts during his years in the Illinois legislature the I & M Canal might never have been built and Lemont might not exist. There are some historians who insist that Lincoln traded votes on the Internal Improvement Bill for votes to have the state capital moved to Springfield.[4] Others, including Senator Paul Simon, who studied the voting records during that session, dispute this idea.[5] They contend that Lincoln was acting only out of the belief that the state could back its indebtedness. It is interesting that Stephen A. Douglas worked along with Lincoln to deliver this bill. Future years would find them divided on many issues, but for canal and transportation development in Illinois, both men were in accord.

So, in 1836, with enough backing to begin the I & M Canal, another commission was appointed composed of Gurdon S. Hubbard, William F. Thornton, William Archer, and

Jacob B. Fry. On July 4, 1836, ground was broken at Bridgeport, in Chicago, to begin the work. William Gooding was appointed the canal engineer. In fact, "Gooding was a key figure in the history of the canal and was affiliated in some way with it until his death in 1878."[6]

The first plan chosen for the canal was what was called the "deep cut," or a system of direct supply of water from Lake Michigan through the Chicago River to the canal. The cut was to be 60 feet wide at the surface, 36 feet wide at the base, and six feet deep. This design raised the original estimate to 8,654,000 dollars, a huge sum when considering that 33 years before, the United States government had paid only 12,000,000 dollars for the entire Louisiana Purchase.

To help carry supplies for construction, Archer Road was laid out from Chicago to Lockport, crossing diagonally through what would someday be Lemont Township. The road cost 40,000 dollars to build, supported by money raised from land sales. A.T. Andreas reports that there was some question about the cost and development of this road "since Colonel Archer had extensive property in Lockport which the road seemed designed to benefit."[7]

Archer Road, following the old Indian trail, was important in the early growth of Lemont. The first farm settlers of the township developed lands close to the road, knowing that good wagon and stage transportation was crucial for getting their produce to market. For them, and for others, the completion of the waterway was still a long way off.

Frontier settlers came for many reasons including opportunities for a new life. Historians studying the westward movement describe three main types who opened the new lands. That same pattern was followed here in Lemont.[8] The first arrivals were young, daring, and, generally, unmarried men. They built makeshift cabins, raised some corn (which was usually converted to whiskey), pumpkins, vegetables, and a few animals. They

An example of an early frontier shelter in Lemont, circa 1840s. The photo dates from the 1890s, when the cabin continued to serve as a shelter for hunters and those running trap lines. (Photo courtesy of Lemont Historical Society)

A permanent Lemont pioneer cabin, circa 1880s, which was probably built in the 1850s. Note the modern additions of windows and a wood stove chimney. (Photo courtesy of Lemont Historical Society)

took water from streams and springs and lived mainly by hunting and trapping. Free from the restrictions of civilization, they were not very different from the Indians who lived around them. "When they heard the sound of a neighbor's gun, it was time for them to move on."[9]

We know very few of their names since they were a transient group. They settled in one place only for a short while and lived with a rifle and axe. These frontier men seldom claimed or paid for the lands they lived on, but often sold their small improvements to those that followed.

The second group that came were the true pioneers. Coming with families, they built log houses with rooms, sunk wells, and cleared the timber land. They grew grain, vegetables, and planted fruit trees. They had animals for meat and milk. At first their farming was simply for subsistence, but later they would produce enough to sell as cash crops. These pioneers often were land hungry and purchased as much as they could in anticipation of the new settlers to come. They were also a restless group, often moving westward after five or ten years. It is remarkable how many of our early settlers, or their children, went to California during the "gold rush" years of 1849 to 1851, looking for adventure, such as Jeremiah Luther and his three sons, who went overland in 1850. Jeremiah died on the journey, as did his youngest son, and only Job and Seth Luther returned. Mancel Talcott went to the gold fields in 1850 and returned two years later with enough money to buy quarry lands with Horace Singer. S.W. Norton made the trip by sea and returned with 4,000 dollars. Three of the Sullivan brothers, John, Tim and Eugene, also joined in the adventure. We know the names of this second wave as they are memorialized in place names around the township, such as Bell and Derby Roads, Singer Hill, Brown Drive, Walker Road, Archer Avenue, Norton Drive, Pruxne Street, Talcott Street, and Smith Road.

The local settlers were able to break the thick prairie sod for farming because of the invention of a Homer Township farmer, John Lane. In 1833, Lane attached a steel saw blade to the wooden moldboard of his plow, making cutting the sod much easier. Before his development, breaking the sod required gang plowing with four to eight yoke of oxen.[10] There is a stone mounment to Lane, on 7th Street and Gougar Road, in Homer Township. The irony here is that Lane may have been the inventor, but the plow that became known throughout the Midwest was designed by John Deere at Grand Detour, Illinois.[11]

The third type of pioneer included more specialized farmers and professional men like doctors, lawyers, editors, preachers, mechanics, politicians, land speculators, semi-skilled workers, and educators. This was the group who wanted roots. They planned a lifetime in our area and intended that their children would remain here. When they arrived, they set out to develop those institutions that represented civilization such as churches, schools, stores, roads, aid societies, and local government.[12]

These settlers came because the economy of the East offered little opportunity for economic security. Land-poor citizens heard stories about land available in our area from soldiers returning from the Black Hawk War. During the 1830s New England farmers also heard a popular ballad that advertised our state enthusiastically:

> Come leave the field of childhood
> Worn out by long employ.
> And travel West and settle
> In the state of Illinois.
> Your family is growing up
> Your boys you must employ
> Come till the rich prairies
> In the state of Illinois.

Taking that advice, many came looking for the promised rich lands, so many that by 1840, only ten years after the first land holding settlers arrived, every available section of DuPage Township had been sold. The same would have been true for our township except that the I & M Commission reserved some of the sections for later sale.

Those who came in the 1830s to farm came at the right time because food and grains were needed for the expanding population. Since transportation routes were still primitive, the early settlers of the Chicago area were forced to depend upon food shipments overland from Indiana or by water through the Great Lakes. The cost of shipping was added to the price of the goods, and such staple items as flour and meat became very expensive. In 1835 the *Chicago Democrat* reported, "Flour is selling here at $12 a barrel and indeed it is almost impossible to obtain provisions of the meat kind at any price." Three weeks later the same flour was selling for 20 dollars a barrel.[13] Therefore, locally grown products were in demand to feed the urban population and the canal workers as construction began on the I & M Canal.

Most of our first farmers came from New England, and in a country so newly formed into a nation, they tended to identify themselves with their home county, region, or state. Nationalism was still a new idea that began with the War of 1812, but for most pioneers "back home" was a local regional area. "Anyone from a state east of the Ohio River was called a Yankee and all others Hoosiers. For state identification Ohio pioneers were called Buckeyes, Kentuckians were Corncrackers, and Michigan newcomers called Wolverines."[14] Illinois natives gained the name Suckers. The origin of the name is unclear, but it has been suggested that it derived from small crawfish holes on the prairie that held fresh water. These holes were a source of water for travelers. A person spying such a depression would announce it by shouting "a sucker!"

Few pioneers from the Southern states came in the first wave of settlers because migration patterns are often linear, based on the shortest transportation route available. This pattern is largely true even today. Most newcomers to Lemont come from the Southern or Southwestern suburbs or Chicago's South Side because they follow roads and transportation corridors that are familiar when looking for a place to live. Aside from easy transportation and work location, one other reason people move to a place is that they already know someone living there. This truth also influenced migration patterns in the 1830s. It was easier to move to a settlement where friends and family already lived.

The usual way a farm homestead was selected was for the father, or some adult member of the family, to take the first trip West to view potential sites. The trip from the East could be made by wagon or by water over the Great Lakes. Arriving in the Chicago area, the settler would contact a land agent or explore available lands himself. This was done by following developed trails and roads. Because Lemont was crossed by the new Archer Road and several Indian trails, many of our first farms were located along or near these routes. Some homesteaders, looking for communities, were sold undeveloped lots in platted towns that promised a future settlement with streets, city squares, water, and all the comforts of towns back East. Shady real estate dealers existed then, as now, and such communities as Sag Station, Des Plaines, Athens, Hastings, Emmetsburg, Keepataw, and Amsterdam all existed on maps of the area. Often, these towns disappeared or never were developed. The same pattern was true for most of the open lands in our area; the real estate boom of the early 1830s created paper towns throughout Northern Illinois. In Downers Grove Township, across the valley, the towns of Lace, Marion, Byrneville, Cass, Center Cass, Orchard, and Barbers Corners either never were built or never grew and are now forgotten.

The first farmer settlers, after considering how close the land was to a road or trail, looked for a place that had woods, water, and open land. They needed the wood for shelter and fuel and water for their own use and for livestock. An ideal site would have a fast running stream that was spring fed, for then it could be used for waterpower equipment to grind grain or saw wood. If a stream or run were not available, the property needed a small wetland, pond, or slough, evidence that a shallow well would produce water. Easterners wanted open land for pasture only because they believed, at first, that prairie land that could not support trees could not support crops.[15]

Once the land was selected, a crude shelter was built unless there were improvements already made that could be bought from some rifleman-pioneer who was ready to move on. Such shelters were usually one-room log cabins with a loft above for sleeping. The logs were fastened with wooden pegs and the space between the logs was filled with clay and sticks. There were two approaches to these log cabins; one was in the French style with the logs set vertically in a trench and anchored with cross beams; the other was in the Scandinavian style with the logs laid horizontally and notched at the ends. Few had any windows, as glass was hard to bring out to the frontier. All had some form of fireplace for heating and cooking.

Next, the farmer planted a small crop. The home and crops established the settlers' rights before titles to the lands could be cleared and the land put up for sale. Sometimes early squatters remained on a section of land many years before they purchased it.

After establishing the homestead, a family member would return East to bring the rest of the family to their new home on the frontier. Returning farmers often brought such vivid descriptions of the rich soil and great opportunities in northern Illinois that extended families of brothers, sisters, cousins, and in-laws would come back with them to the new West. Such was the case with Jeremiah Luther, who came from New York to our township in 1833 and settled on sections 34, 37, and 11 of the canal land adjoining Archer Road at its northwest corner. When he returned to get his family, he was joined by his brother-in-law from Vermont, William Derby, and two other families, those of Orange Chauncey and Joshua Smith.[16] Together they divided the section and established a small farming community.[17] Forbes Miner also came to the area in 1833.[18] Miner was a member of a family that had been in the area as early as 1828. A Reverend Miner worked as a missionary in Kanakakee until his death from a fever in 1829. He had a son, Henry D. Miner, who was only eight at the time and was sent back to relatives in the East only to return with them in 1833.

It was a difficult struggle until the first crops were harvested. There was little hard money available and almost all transactions were on a barter basis. William Derby came to Lemont with a team of horses, a wagon and harness, a few household goods, and 40 dollars cash. He had to sell his team to get enough money to pay for his land as it came to market early.[19] The Miner and Luther families cut local timber in the winter to get money to pay for their land. The boys of these families also worked in Wisconsin lumber camps when the harvest years were bad. At one of these camps in 1843, Henry and Tom Miner and three of the Luther brothers met Louis Labute. Labute had been a fisherman on Rock Island off Door County, Wisconsin. He told them that money could be made net fishing and sold them his rig. From that time on there was a Lemont colony of fishermen on Rock Island and Washington Island; they would fish in the spring and summer and return to Lemont in the fall.[20]

Because of the movement westward, the New England states lost vast populations to Illinois in the 1830s and 40s. It was the beginning of a physical expansion of this country that would sweep West and not end until the 1890s when little government land was left to homestead.

ENDNOTES

[1]John Lamb, *A Corridor in Time* (Romeoville: Lewis University, 1987), p. 12.

[2]Lewis Spitznagel, *Canal or Railroad* (Lockport, IL: Illinois Canal Society, 1984), pp. 8-9.

[3]Thomas Ford, *A History of Illinois: 1818-1847* (Springfield, IL: Illinois State Historical Society), p. 124.

[4]Theodore Pease, *The Story of Illinois* (Chicago: University of Illinois, 1975), p. 125. See also Ford, *A History of Illinois*. Ford refers to the group that worked with Lincoln as the "Long Nine." Ford was a Democrat. All of the "Long Nine" were Whigs, except one.

[5]Robert Howard, *Illinois: A History of the Prairie State* (Grand Rapids: Eerdmans, 1972), p.199.

[6]Lamb, *A Corridor in Time*, p. 12.

[7]A.T. Andreas, *History of Cook County, Illinois: 1885* (Evansville: Unigraphics, 1976), p. 150.

[8]Allan Nevins and Henry Commager, *A Pocket History of the United States* (New York: Washington Square Press, 1956), p. 179.

[9]*Ibid.*

[10]W.J. Beecher, "The Lost Prairie," *Chicago History* (Chicago: Chicago Historical Society, Spring-Summer, 1973), p. 168.

[11]*Ibid.* Beecher suggests that both men came on the idea at the same time. In any case it was Deere's marketing that made him the fortune. By 1840 he had made 40 plows. Deere changed the moldboard to wrought iron, and by 1847 the company had moved to Moline and was producing 10,000 plows a year.

[12]Nevins, *A Pocket History of the United States*, p. 186.

[13]Bessie Pierce, *A History of Chicago* (New York: Knopf, 1940), vol. 1., p. 50.

[14]George Woodruff, *A History of Will County* (Evansville: Unigraphics, 1973), p. 253.

[15]Katherine Richardson, "An Analysis of Land Parcel and Landscape Change in LaSalle County," *Settling the Upper Illinois Valley*, ed. Michael Conzen and Melissa Morales (Chicago: University of Chicago, 1989), p. 113.

[16]Andreas, *History of Cook County*, p. 847.

[17]*Ibid.*, p. 852.

[18]*Ibid.*, p. 847. Life in early Lemont may have been hard on the family. One of the early divorce petitions registered in Cook County is that of Forbes Miner vs. Cornelia S. Miner, reported in the *Chicago Daily American*, February 5, 1841.

[19]*Ibid.*, p. 852.

[20]Conon Eaton, *Rock Island* (Sturgeon Bay, WI: Bay Print, 1979), p. 13.

U.S. HISTORY

1830: *Abe Lincoln Comes to Illinois.*

1831: *Slave Revolt by Nat Turner, 55 Die — Chloroform Invented — German Immigration to America: 15,000 — U.S. Population: 12.8 Million — First Cook County Elections.*

1832: *Jackson is Reelected — New England Anti-Slavery Society Formed — Chicago Has 300 People.*

1833: *Whig Party Begins — Jackson Moves against All Banks — Chicago Incorporates As a Village.*

1834: *Lincoln Becomes an Assemblyman in the Illinois Legislature — McCormick Patents His Reaper — Last Bear Killed in the City of Chicago — First Murder in Chicago.*

1835: *Texas Secedes from Mexico — Halley's Comet — Chicago Population: 2000 — Liberty Bell Cracks Tolling for Chief Justice Marshall.*

1836: *The Battle for the Alamo — Texas Wins Independence — Chicago Population: 4179 — Chicago Becomes a City.*

1837: *Martin Van Buren is President — Michigan Becomes a State — Electric Telegraph Invented — Lovejoy Killed in Alton for Pro-Abolitionist Stand.*

1838: *The American Navy Has 15 Ships.*

1839: *First Baseball Field, Cooperstown.*

LEMONT HISTORY

1830: *Chicago Platted with I&M Canal in Mind — Year of the Deep Snow, Four Feet Deep for Two Months.*

1831: *Large Indian Encampment on Big Run in Homer Township — Joliet Founded.*

1832: *Blackhawk War, Local Settlers John Barber, Seth Wescott, and John Miller Go to Ft. Dearborn for Safety — Cholera Breaks Out among Soldiers Sent to Fight Blackhawk.*

1833: *Indians Give Up All Lands around the Area and Prepare to Move West — Lemont Settlers Are Jeremiah Luther, Forbes Miner, and Nathan Lee.*

1834: *Settlers This Year Include: William Derby, Orange Chauncey, Joshua Smith, H. Martin, Tom and Winfred Claffy, John Russel, Sealy Spaulding, and Adam Boyce.*

1835: *Pioneers Are Royce and Israel Blodgett and Tom Williams — Indians Leave the Area.*

1836: *I&M Canal Work Begins — Canal Workers Settle in Camps Along the Site of the Proposed Construction.*

1837: *N.J. Brown Has Contract for the I&M Canal in Athens Precinct [Lemont] — Two Towns That Never Develop are Platted in Our Area: Amsterdam [Section 22], and Harmonsville [Section 14] — Des Plaines [Section 11] is Developed and Contains Many Canal Workers and Their Families — Augustus Doolin Holds I&M Contract on Section 13.*

1838: *Cholera and Typhoid All Summer, Many Canal Workers Die — Irish West of Town Hold First Strike in Northern Illinois, They Destroy All Goods and Buildings of Contractor James Brooks — Sag Bridge is Developed As a Village — Joshua Bell Has a Hotel in the Sag and Farms Section 25.*

1839: *Keepataw Subdivision is Platted [Section 20] in July — Athens is Platted [Section 20] in August — Emmetsburg is Platted [Section 30] in October — Derby School on Archer Road Starts Classes As Does Village School at the State and Main Street Area.*

CHAPTER SIX

EARLY LAND DEVELOPMENT AND SPECULATORS

It is hard to say who were the very first riflemen-pioneers to reside in our area, since recorded purchase of land did not begin until 1835 and most of the history we know deals only with the written record. The nature of our earliest frontiersman was such that they neither signed nor registered any legal documents and so passed on unrecorded.

We do know that by 1830 a Nathan Lee settled in section 30 west of the present town of Lemont, along the Des Plaines River; and in 1831, a Vermonter, Robert Strang, came to the region and established a cabin on the east bank of the DuPage River. The land they found was pristine and lovely. George Woodruff wrote about our Des Plaines Valley as it appeared to the newcomers from the East:

> When the white people first began to settle here they found
> the prairie teaming [sic] with wild flowers and their beauty
> and fragrance surpassing all [that] they have ever dreamed of
> loveliness. Some of the more romantic of them say it seemed
> as if the whole earth had been converted into green grass,
> blue sky, blooming flowers, and glorious sunshine.[1]

It was a land far different from the dark, wet, and gloomy forests of New England.

Other early settlers identified include Mr. Kinney in the Sag, 1831; and John Barber, Seth Westcott, and John Miller in south DuPage, in 1832. There were also those already in Lemont Township, including Jeremiah Luther and Forbes Miner in 1833, along with William Derby, Orange Chauncey, Joshua Smith, Hylon Martin, Tom Claffy, and Winfred Claffy in 1834. That same year saw John Russel, Seely Spaulding, and Adam Boyce locate in the south DuPage region.

Most of Lemont's early farmers stayed in the eastern part of the township, except sections 12, 30, and 20. The latter sections fronted the proposed I & M Canal and were along the Des Plaines River; therefore they were considered choice lands for speculators.

The eastern part of the township was popular for three reasons. First, most of the sections offered for sale initially by the Canal Commission were in that part of Lemont Township. Secondly, the western sections are hilly and have a hard clay topsoil that is difficult to work. Finally, the main transportation route, Archer Road, ran diagonally through the eastern half, offering better access to markets.

In January of 1835, the first government land sales were held for our township. The main purchases were in section 12, Mt. Forest; section 30, west of present Lemont from 127th Street north to the river; and sections 34, 36, and 26 near 131st and Derby. Sections 34, 36, and 26 were purchased for the first farming complex.

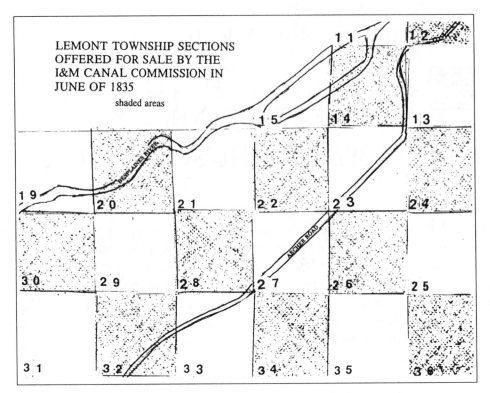

(Illustration courtesy of Lemont Historical Society)

The following are registered as having bought land at the initial sale in the first months of 1835:

> January: Section 12 — Wm. Bemen, Crandall Bemen,
> Harrison Fay, John Kinzie & H. Pearson, Ben Lisenby.
> February: Section 30 — John and Dan Brewer.
> April: Section 30 — John Miller.
> May: Section 34 — Jeremiah Luther, Wm. Derby.

By the second sale of public lands, in June, speculation fever based on final plans for the canal swept the population. When word spread that the east half of Mather's addition in Chicago, originally purchased for 5,000 dollars, sold for 80,000 dollars, people began buying any land they could, most of it sight unseen and mortgaged with every bit of real property they owned. The craze was so wild that some land owners made over 100 percent returns on a few months' investments.[2]

The experience of 1835 was impossible to comprehend. Speculators drove prices so high that within five days in June, 186 lots were sold for 1,041,344 dollars.[3] To outsiders, "it seemed if some prevalent mania [had] infected the whole people."[4] The land rage was such that:

> Auctioneers reigned as the high priests of speculation, the
> walls of their rooms [were] covered with maps and town plats
> . . . representations in the form of lithograph maps [of planned
> or proposed towns] were hung upon the walls of public build-
> ings, in the bar rooms of hotels, and in every place likely to
> attract attention.[5]

At this point the paper towns of the Lemont area mentioned before were created, bought, and sold. They included Emmetsburg, in section 30, platted by Hunter, Johnson and Davidson.[6] There also was Des Plaines, in section 14, platted and owned by the Canal Commission. This town had a population of canal workers and suppliers numbering over 1,000 at one time. There was Hastings in section 22; Harmonsville, Amsterdam, and Sag Bridge in section 13 and 14; and Athens in 20, platted by Hiram Hugunin, a Democratic party man with federal connections.

Keepataw (or Keepotaw) by Hunter and Pearson, also in section 20, was surveyed in 1836 and was laid out along section lines following the true north-south pattern. Its street plan was of five one-acre blocks containing ten lots to the block. The plat fronted on the Des Plaines River. The owners had a river town in mind in spite of the knowledge that the I & M would run through the site. Some street names of the Keepataw paper town included Pearson, Erie, Huron, Michigan, Superior, and Ohio, names we still find on the near north side of Chicago. The only name that remains was Steffens which was changed to Stephens, after Stephen Truesdell's addition to Athens. The later subdivisions of Athens, Truesdells, and Lemont were laid out in alignment with the I & M Canal. This arrangement explains the buildings and streets in the downtown that appear at odd angles.

The June land mania of 1835 had section transactions with rapid turnover. By that month the following had bought or sold lands in our township: Section 14: Armstead Ruynon, John Will, L. Smith, Phillip Lathan, John Kinzie, H. Pearson, Henry Gaines, Laurence Carroll, and Patrick Carroll. Section 20: John Kinzie, H. Pearson, William Eagan, Nathan Lee, George Sturtevant. Section 22: Sam Foster, Hale Mason, Amanda Minor, Holder Sisson. Section 24: John Kinzie, H. Pearson, John Champlain, David Clark, Walter Newberry, Sarah Spaulding. Section 26: John Kinzie, H. Pearson, John Champlain, Amanda Minor, Walter Newberry. Section 28: I. Blip, Sam Spring, George Sturtevant. Section 30: John Cody, Ed Keunter, Nelson Lee, Nathan Lee. Section 32: John Brewer, Martin Ford, David Parrish, Lyman Klezen, Van Klezen. Section 36: P. Blip, Addison Green, Lawrence Grove, Ed Martin, Joseph Meeker.[7]

Towns along the proposed canal were planned approximately every ten miles because horses and mules were unable to pull barges without rest or change for longer distances. Our first settled community was named Athens, and was part of the canal system plan, while Romeoville was called Rome. This was because the country was experiencing a classical revival due to the traditional old world educational system based on ancient classical authors, and a deep public sympathy for the Greeks who were then fighting for their own independence from the Turks.

Many lots were sold in the paper town of Athens, but few ever built on the location that was on the north and south sides of the proposed canal, east of the old Pure Aluminum plant site at Talcott and Holmes Streets. Almost all these land transactions were carried out by large land brokers.

One of the major land auction firms in Chicagoland was Garrett, Brown and Brother, located on the corner of LaSalle and South Water in Chicago. The company was so successful that they sold 1,800,000 dollars of real and personal property in the first ten months of 1835.[8] Two of the company's partners were Nathaniel J. and Daniel Brown, men who became important pioneers and developers of our Lemont area. The company had a unique way of advertising their sales. Nathaniel (known as N.J.) Brown told how they hired a "town crier" called Colonel George, a black man who was dressed in full military uniform and mounted on a white horse. He rode around Chicago crying out the goods, wares, and lands to be sold that day and at every corner the crowds flocked around him to hear what was available.[9]

Real estate speculation was seen as the fast track to wealth in our area in the 1830s. There was nothing else to sell for capital, as Illinois' Governor Ford remembered:

> Every vessel coming west was loaded with money and means, bound for Chicago, the great fairyland of fortunes . . . enough did come to satisfy the insatiable greediness of the Chicago sharpers and speculators they frequently consigned their wares to eastern markets. Thus a vessel would be freighted with land and town lots for New York and Boston markets for less than the cost of a barrel of flour. In fact, lands and town lots were the staple of the country, and were the only articles of export.[10]

Lemont's Nathaniel Brown, and his brothers Lemuel, Daniel, William, and Benjamin, typify the young settlers who came to our frontier and built their fortunes on land speculation. It must be said, however, that we have knowledge of their lives because their biographies were recorded. This does not make them more important to the development of Lemont than all the others who built our community. It just happens that their stories were written because they became economically successful and established a social standing in the community.

When historians at the end of the 19th Century began to look back at the record of Lemont and the Chicago area, they contacted those pioneers who had made a name for themselves. Publishers like A.T. Andreas compiled one of the earliest books, *The History of Cook County — 1885*, by sending out salesmen to interview prominent people. He had a two-fold purpose in his plan. One was to try to record the 70 year history of this area before those who had pioneered passed away. The second was to sell copies of his books to those whose biographies appeared in its pages. So the result is that we do have a history of the early days, but a history that reflects those people who had economic or political power in the community and their view of events. Therein is the failure of so many local histories; they often exclude the stories of ordinary people. If we only had more letters or journals from the canal and quarry men, or the records from farmers, storekeepers, and homeowners, we could get a comprehensive view of life in the early days. But few are available, and therefore we must depend on the sources we do have to get a picture of Lemont and some of its settlers, like Nathaniel J. Brown.[11]

N. J. Brown was born in Vermont in 1812. His father was a canal contractor who moved his family of 12 children from Vermont to New York to Ann Arbor, following the frontier.[12] Because they were constantly on the move, Nathaniel never received more than a grade school education. In Ann Arbor, at the age of 14, he began working for his older brother Anson, who ran a stage line from Detroit to the mouth of the St. Joseph River. Anson had established many important connections in that area. He subdivided an early part of Ann Arbor and he served as a postmaster under the Jackson administration. Working as an agent for his brother, N.J. rode through the Michigan wilderness and became aware of the great timber resources avail able. So he saved his money, and, by the time he was 22, purchased land in Kent County and began to cut timber. He borrowed capital and bought machinery to build his own saw mill near the present site of Grand Rapids.[13]

Nathaniel realized that lumber would command a higher price in Chicago where the town's growth was so rapid that the timber supply from Wisconsin and Michigan could not keep pace. The open prairie lands settled by the new pioneers lacked wood for building and burning. Pine, then as now, was the preferred wood. The wood was even-grained, typically 50 feet in height and straight, because it dropped its lower limbs. The large trees had trunks that could range up to six feet in diameter, which meant heartwood that was clear and without knots. The best part was that pine was soft, easy to work, and grained to take paint. The lack of roads required that wood be transported by river and streams. Pine, as opposed to some hardwoods, was easy to float.[14]

Working day and night, N.J. and a few lumbermen cut trees through the fall and winter of 1834. They worked so hard that by the spring of 1835 they had cut and trimmed six schooner loads of wood. With the aid of an old Maine lumberman, high water, and good luck, the youthful Nathaniel floated the rafts of timber down the shallow Grand River to Grand Haven. There Brown arranged for a schooner from Detroit, the *White Pigeon*, to take the cargo to Chicago.

After a winter of hard work, risk, and borrowed capital, he sailed with great expectations for the new city. The ship arrived on April 4, 1835, but instead of open arms and a great sale, Nathaniel found himself in a political situation as old as the great city of Chicago.[15] He had no clout. In spite of the fact the lumber was needed, the young upstart found himself locked out by the lumbermen from Wisconsin who controlled the market.

Brown, being a stubborn Yankee, insisted that he had a right to sell his cargo and ended up being arrested by the local dealers. He finally solved the problem by paying six dollars for a permit to the County Commissioners. His business judgement was correct; he had little difficulty in selling his lumber, getting the impressive sum of 28 dollars per thousand feet — an excellent profit.[16] He took the payments in silver coin, having the natural Yankee suspicion of any paper or script money. He packed the silver in axe boxes — 1,000 dollars a box — and deposited it at the warehouse of Newberry and Dole.[17]

From that sum he had drafts drawn for payments on his debts and to continue the lumbering business. He also entered a partnership with Augustus Garrett, forming a land and forwarding company called Garrett and Brown, later to become Garrett, Brown, and Brother with the addition of N.J.'s brother Daniel. At first, Nathaniel spent much of his time in Michigan purchasing land in that state and leaving the sales activity to Garrett in Chicago. He made an agreement that all of his profits should be invested in Chicago lots and canal lands when they went on public sale in June of 1835. The sales went so well that when N.J. returned to Chicago he found that the partnership had acquired large blocks of Chicago lots, plus over 3,000 acres of land in the surrounding area.[18]

Suddenly N.J. was a partner in what was to be the one of the most famous auction houses in the West. Garrett, Brown, and Brother dealt not only in lands but in goods of every kind that were often traded for lands or town lots. The business expanded to Milwaukee, Sheboygan, Manitowoc, Joliet, Lockport, Lemont, Kankakee, Peru, and other places in the Midwest. Land speculation was so wild that while it lasted, the company held over 9,000 acres of land in and around Chicago.[19]

Young Nathaniel left little to chance. For example, when the Wisconsin legislature first met in Belmont in 1836, he sent a friend to the meeting to find out where the new state capital was to be located. The site had to be registered at the Milwaukee land office, so his spy, Jerry Ford of Jefferson, Michigan, arranged for the three fastest horses he could find and stationed them between Belmont and Milwaukee. Brown then traveled to Milwaukee to be ready to file the necessary papers. Ford arrived 18 hours before any official word was received and Brown managed to buy up 5,000 acres of Madison land for $1.25 an acre. He also found that a Buffalo resident held 1,400 acres of land in that area, so he sent a special messenger to New York to purchase it. Part of the University of Wisconsin is now located on that property.[20]

At the height of his power and wealth, N. J. was asked by General William Thornton, President of the Board of Canal Commissioners, to complete two sections of the newly proposed I & M Canal running through Lemont. Nathaniel agreed to begin the work and it was a lucky chance for him, because by 1837 real estate speculations died as the national economy began to falter. The firm of Garrett and Brown was dissolved. Nathaniel's life now entered a phase that would tie him to the history of Lemont — the building of the I & M Canal.

ENDNOTES

[1]George Woodruff, *A History of Will County* (Evansville: Unigraphics, 1973), p. 535.

[2]Bessie Pierce, *A History of Chicago* (New York: Knopf, 1940), vol. 1, p. 58.

[3]*Ibid.*, p. 65.

[4]Finis Farr, *Chicago* (New Rochelle: Arlington Press, 1973), p. 42.

[5] Pierce, *A History of Chicago*, p. 65.

[6]The name Emmetsburg has a number of possible sources. Robert Emmet was an Irish Nationalist who led the uprising of 1803. He was captured and hanged by the English. There is also an Emmitsburgh, Maryland, where Father Plunkett, one of the first Catholic priests who served the area, studied. He could have been the source for the name of the land registration. Oral tradition confuses Emmetsburg with Haytown. Haytown was located west of the intersection of today's State and Main Streets. It, too, was largely inhabited by canal workers. Many believe that the name Haytown came from huts with thatched hay roofing, but this is unlikely. It probably came from the fact that the workers also raised and cut hay for extra cash.

[7]Note the names of Chicago pioneers who speculated on Lemont lands. Kinzie, Pearson, and Newberry all made a good deal of money on land transactions. John Kinzie was the son of the early trader, Kinzie.

[8]Pierce, *A History of Chicago*, p. 65.

[9]Howard Conrad, "Nathaniel Brown," *The National Magazine* (1887), p. 7; and Farr, *Chicago,* p. 40.

[10]Thomas Ford, *A History of Illinois: From its Commencement As A State in 1818 to 1847* (Chicago: University of Illinois Press, 1995), p. 123.

[11] Andreas lists the following biographies from Lemont in 1885: William Bell, John G. Bodenschatz, Rev. Joseph Bollman, N. J. Brown, W.S. Brown, Isaac Cleveland, Milton Cleveland, William Derby, Augustus Doolin, John Doolin, Rev. J.E. Hogan, Christopher Johnson, James Lister, Job S. Luther, I. McCauley, Hylon Martin, Fred Miner, Rev. Leopold Moczygemba, Dewitt Clinton Norton, Alex Reid, Joseph Rood M.D., Horace Singer, Daniel Skelly, Mancell Talcott, John Tedens, James Tripp, Rev. W. Uffenbeck, Lorenz Valentien, Mathew Warner, and Joel Wells.

[12] Theodore Karamanski, *Brown Property Evaluation* (Chicago: Loyola University, 1986), p. 2.

[13] *Ibid.*, p. 3.

[14] William Cronon, *Nature's Metropolis: Chicago and the Great West* (New York: W.W. Norton & Company, 1991), pp. 152-153.

[15] Conrad, p. 4.

[16] *Ibid.*, p. 5.

[17] *Ibid.*, p. 5.

[18] *Ibid.*, p. 6.

[19] *Ibid.*, p. 7.

[20] *Ibid.*, p. 8.

CHAPTER SEVEN

THE BUILDING
OF THE I & M CANAL
The Start: 1836-1838

In 1836, the promise of the construction of the canal became the center of future hopes for the development of our area. So it was that on July 4, the I & M Canal began with a big celebration in the small city of Chicago. The citizens assembled in the public square at the signal of three cannons from Fort Dearborn. Colonel Archer and Canal Commissioner T.W. Smith turned the first shovel full of earth at Bridgeport to symbolize the beginning of construction.[1] In an interview in his later years, N.J. Brown recalled the event with its wild frontier flavor:

> The celebration of the event had been extensively prepared for, and widely advertised. People came from all parts of the county, in all sorts of conveyances — in boats, in wagons, on horseback and on foot — to witness the demonstration at Bridgeport, with Gurdon Hubbard as master of ceremonies . . . That the crowd was enthusiastic to the point of hilarity was attested to by the fact that they . . . converted a spring, located near where the ceremony of "breaking ground" for the canal was to take place, into a veritable fountain of the kind of liquor which cheers and inebriates . . . Whiskey and lemons [were] mixed in the spring, and the beverage was free to all comers.[2]

N.J. remembered, that as a result, the local citizens and troops continued the party well into the night. His own company, Garrett and Brown, contributed to the celebration:

> [There was] a mammoth stock of goods of all kinds stored, and among other things were a stock of liquor and a stock of Connecticut eight-day clocks. Every time the procession passed . . . they stopped to sample the liquors, and when this had been done the soldiers would form a line and give an exhibition of their marksmanship, the target being one of the eight-day clocks set out on the street for that purpose. Each time they fired a volley a clock was demolished, and a new one was set out to await their return. It is not probable that Chicago has had since that time a celebration so unique in its character.[3]

In spite of the hope attached to this major construction project, the economic pressures of the late 1830s deepened and much of Chicagoland's business came to a halt. Many early land speculators, a number of whom had purchased Lemont properties, returned to the East, but N.J. and his brothers believed in the future of the area and remained. It was at this time that Brown was asked to take up the contracts of C.B. Dodson at sections 51 and 52 in Lemont, because Dodson was unable to complete his part of the project. Brown, who was looking for capital, joined with L.C. Hugunin to finish these two sections. The work they did was from the east end of Talcott Street to what is now the Will-Cook County line.

Many problems faced both the contractors and laborers in building the canal. The project was a massive undertaking extending 96 miles through all types of terrain. There was a shortage of both labor and supplies. This shortage, naturally, led to inflated costs for the contractors, many of whom underestimated their costs and went bankrupt. Moreover, the canal, like any government project, was constantly struggling against red tape and inadequate funding.

The plan for the canal, after opening the divide between Lake Michigan and the Des Plaines River, was for it to follow the natural descent of 141 feet to the Illinois River. The drop was to be controlled with 15 locks along the route. The steepest drop, 40 feet in four miles, is between Lockport and Joliet and it was to have four locks to control traffic.[4]

The project was divided into three sections: the summit level from Bridgeport to Lockport, the middle section from Lockport to Seneca, and the western section from Seneca to LaSalle-Peru.

The summit level, our section, was planned so the cut through the divide would be lower than Lake Michigan, called the deep cut. It was part of the plan that this cut would reverse the flow of the Chicago River and produce enough current in the canal so that towns along the route could have water power for industry. However, the state, already in financial difficulty, could not fund the deep cut and, as a compromise, a lock was planned where the Chicago River and the canal join, with a steam-driven pump installed to lift water from the river into the canal.[5] This proved inadequate, so a feeder canal was built from the Little Calumet River at Blue Island to attempt to add more water to the system.[6]

Overseeing canal construction was difficult. First there was a labor shortage; then transportation difficulties inflated the cost of goods. As a result our early local farmers who could supply the canal population did quite well. A journal kept by N.J. Brown lists a food contract for 300 hogs for his men, and that same year A.T. Andreas reports 6,000 hogs slaughtered and pickled for canal laborers.[7] A comparison of prices in 1836 and 1843, when economic problems stopped most work on the canal, will give an idea of the financial strain of start-up costs that many small contractors faced at the beginning of the project. In 1836, laborers were paid 40 dollars a month, while in 1843 it was 16 dollars a month. In 1836, a horse, necessary for transportation and construction, cost 100 dollars; by 1843 the price was 60 dollars. In 1836, flour by the barrel was 11 dollars, and by 1843 it sold for $3.50.[8]

Nevertheless, the I & M Canal payroll from 1837 to 1841 of over 75,000 dollars a month was "the saving factor in the economic situation of the time, supplying the area with money and capital until the development of an agricultural surplus."[9] At the beginning of the project, to lower labor costs since so few people lived in the area, contractors advertised for workers in the East and in Canada.[10] The Canadian connection was via

Lock on the Illinois and Michigan Canal. (Illustration courtesy of Illinois and Michigan Heritage Corridor Commission)

the lake system and many Canadians came here. However, because of the local labor shortage, some of those who arrived soon left canal work for the better wages and working conditions offered by area farmers and shopkeepers.

Nathaniel Brown realized the difficulty in obtaining laborers and sent a personal agent to Montreal and Quebec. There his agent interviewed and contracted 500 men for Brown's canal section, most of them Irish or French from the poorer working classes. All histories of the I & M Canal mention the contributions of the Irish and Germans, but the contribution of the French is often overlooked.

The presence of both French and Irish laborers, many of whom were Catholic, required spiritual support. Brown's biography in *The National Magazine* of 1887 describes the need for priests and gives an interesting sidelight to the origin of Lemont's Saint Patrick's Parish. According to various sources there are two conflicting dates and two different priests credited with founding the church.[11] The latest research has Saint Patrick's formed in April of 1839 by Father Plunkett, known as the "Irish priest." Other records have the parish organized in 1840 by Father DuPontavice and Father St. Polla of the Diocese of Vincennes, known as the "French priests." N. J. Brown reported that both priests, Father DuPontavice and Father Plunkett, were working in the area simultaneously and that either "one or the other made his home with [me] for more than two years."[12] Those years would be the periods from 1838 to 1840, so it appears that Saint Patrick's did have two founders.

Brown's reasons for having the priests stay with him was to help him promote temperance and morality among his workers to keep down conflicts. He discovered that when his laborers came to Lemont, he had to deal with dislikes and hatreds imported from Ireland and Canada. The Irish laborers were divided into two elements, the Corkonians and the Fardowns and they were antagonistic to each other, while the French from Canada were the sworn enemies of both these clans. Brown reported that, "The management and control of these men was no easy task. They were a turbulent, riotous lot, much given to drinking [and] . . . their quarrels were apt to be serious in their results."[13]

Almost everyone contracting on the canal recognized the problems with liquor, but felt it necessary to sell spirits and to dispense whiskey free three times during the working day. It was believed that whiskey offered medicinal protection against waterborne diseases and helped the men get through the 14 to 15 hour workdays. Nathaniel Brown, however, was a temperance man. He wanted sobriety from his workers, both for discipline and better workmanship. Perhaps he had learned from the failed experience of the previous contractor. Anyway, he called on Father DuPontavice and Father Plunkett to organize a Father Matthew Temperance Society among the workers. It was the first of its kind organized in Northern Illinois and about 300 of his men "put on the badge of the order." As a reward N.J. gave each man who took the pledge a dollar more in wages each month that they stayed off liquor.[14]

Brown's biographer reported that the result of this local temperance society was that during the five years of Brown's canal project, "not a saloon was to be found on the section of which he had control, nor could any intoxicating liquors be obtained there. There were no drunken carousals nor riotous assemblies, and the men in his employ were recognized as the most orderly and well behaved set of men on the line of the canal."[15]

This approach worked for Brown, as he was one of the first contractors to finish his section in spite of the fact he started late and that much of his section was through stone outcroppings. As the work on the canal progressed, the need for labor increased and contractors began to appeal for workers overseas. Handbills circulated throughout Europe offering 26 dollars a month plus food and lodging for unskilled workers on the canal. The Irish and the Germans were the largest groups to respond. It was said that all you needed to build a canal were a pick, a shovel, a wheelbarrow, and an Irishman. The Irish came in such large numbers that a popular ballad of the day made fun of these workers:

> Young Barney O'Toole was a broth of a boy,
> Who crossed the sea with Pat Malloy.
> They landed one night — it was raining withal,
> and the next day they got work on the raging canawl.

The Irish came because of overcrowding, political unrest and, later, from 1846 to 1848, because of famine. Political problems developed in Ireland when a young Irishman, Daniel O'Connell, fostered agitation against the Protestant English authorities. The landowners responded by encouraging immigration to reduce the Catholic population. In 1840, Ireland had 8,000,000 people, compared to a population of around 5,500,000 today.[16] Landowners often paid passage for the emigres, who were mostly under-educated and unskilled.

Father DuPontavice commented on the sad state of these men who came to work the canal in a letter to the Diocese of Vincennes:

> Many Irish immigrants twenty and thirty years old have never
> made their first communion. They scarcely know there is a
> God; they are ashamed to attend Catechism and when they
> do come they do not understand the instruction.[17]

The immigrant Irish canal laborers settled on the work site or in five communities in the township: Sag Bridge, section 12; Des Plaines, section 14, owned by the Canal Commission; Corktown east of the Des Plaines settlement; Haytown west of State and Main; and Emmetsburg in section 30.

The other wave of early immigrants, the Germans, also came because of political unrest. The 1830s and 1840s in Europe were a time of upheaval, and in Germany, liberal students were censured for the murder of a conservative writer. A series of repressive measures including the dismissal of teachers, press censorship, and arrests sent many young Germans to the United States, and eventually to Illinois to work on the I & M

Canal. They, too, were housed in tent and shack towns along the project. The Germans had a language barrier and tended to keep to their own group. However, many German immigrants had the advantage of an education and eventually worked themselves into positions of supervision once they learned English, much to the anger of the Irish and French who were here earlier.

Conditions were severe and life hard for the canal workers. Because they were considered inferior by local inhabitants, canalers were isolated from the general social life of the community. Religious differences also became a source of misunderstandings and hatred. Pioneer life for the New England Yankee contractors and farmers centered on the Protestant church, and they found the ceremonies and rituals of the Catholic Church strange.

Tent housing at the work site was dormitory style with 20 to 24 men to a tent.[18] No bedding was supplied so it was necessary for the workers to find their own bedding. Personal hygiene was difficult to maintain and workers had to contend with lice and fleas most of the time, which exposed them to typhus. Their living conditions also helped spread tuberculosis and other diseases of overcrowding. The canal was built with hand tools and black powder, much of it through marshy bottom land, so that men stood in water a good deal of the time and were subject to such endemic waterborne diseases as dysentery, typhoid, and cholera.

Eighteen thirty-eight, the year after Brown began his contract, was a bad year for the project. The problems of that year represent the struggles both worker and contractor had to endure to build the canal that brought so much to Lemont and Northern Illinois.

ENDNOTES

[1]A.T. Andreas, *History of Cook County* (Evansville: Unigraphics, 1976), p. 150.

[2]Howard Conrad, "Western Real Estate Speculation Fifty Years Ago: Chicago's Famous Auction House," *The National Magazine* (1887), p. 13.

[3]*Ibid.*, p. 14.

[4]John Lamb, *A Corridor in Time* (Romeoville, IL: Lewis University, 1987), p. 12.

[5]*Ibid.*, p. 13.

[6]*Ibid.*, pp. 13-14.

[7]Andreas, *History of Cook County,* p. 328.

[8]James Putman, *The Illinois and Michigan Canal* (Chicago: University of Chicago Press, 1918), p. 61.

[9]Bessie Pierce, *A History of Chicago* (New York: Knopf, 1940), vol.1., p. 71.

[10]*Ibid.*, p. 38.

[11]See Barbara Buschman ed., *Lemont Centennial Book 1873-1973* (Des Plaines, IL: King/Mann Yearbook Center, 1973), p. 108.

[12]Conrad, "Western Real Estate Speculation Fifty Years Ago," p. 13.

[13]*Ibid*.

[14]See, Pierce, *A History of Chicago,* vol. 1., pp. 256-261. Pierce has a discussion of the temperance movement in Chicago during the 1833-43 period. By 1843, there were four temperance societies active in the area with a membership of almost 2,000.

[15]Conrad, "Western Real Estate Speculation Fifty Years Ago," pp. 13-14.

[16]1995 population figures including Northern Ireland. *The World Almanac Book of Facts* (Mawah, N.J.: Funk & Wagnalls, 1996), pp. 775, 830.

[17]Charles Rosenburg, *The Cholera Years* (Chicago: University of Chicago Press, 1962), p. 123.

[18]Elmer Ott, "The I & M Waterway," *Lions Magazine*, Jan. 1966, p. 5.

CHAPTER EIGHT

THE I & M CANAL
AND LOCAL POLITICS

The Early Years: 1838-1840

In the spring of 1838, laborers on sections 54 and 55, near present-day Romeoville,[1] became so upset with working conditions that they destroyed their tent town, job store, other homes, and the home of their contractor, James Brooks. Local settlers and other contractors organized a *posse comitatus*, a civilian militia police force, to put down the riot and many workers were hurt. This, naturally, increased tension between the canal workers and the local population.

To add to the problems of the project, there was a drought from July to November and work was suspended for periods because of a disease called canal cholera. It was not a true cholera but was some form of a deadly gastrointestinal disease that could not be controlled. Judge Blodgett of DuPage Township, who worked in the Lemont area as a rod man in his youth, described the illness as similiar to yellow fever and believed that it came from the malarious exhalations of the upturned soil and hard work in the hot sun, combined with meals of poor salt pork and bread. The victims would become feverish and then be seized with black vomit, a sign of gastric hemorrhage. Death came within eight hours after the vomiting.[2] Often the dead remained where they fell for days because of fear of the epidemic. Over 500 men died that summer of the illness and it took heroic efforts by priests and circuit preachers to get the dead buried.[3]

The daily routine on the canal began at 6:30 in the morning. For most workers a pail of whiskey was passed at 10:00 a.m.[4] Each man was given a jigger (one and a half ounces), or a gill (four ounces), from a tin cup. At noon there was an hour for lunch, usually salted pork, and at 3:00 p.m. another ration of whiskey. Work ended anywhere from 6:00 to 8:00 p.m., depending upon the contractor. By the time the men returned for the evening meal there was little time for anything but sleep.

If it rained, work was halted and the men were not paid. Those workers not lodged in company dorms had to pay board, work or not.

Lonely men in a strange country often drank too much, got into fights, and sometimes met violent deaths. Accidents were common among the unskilled laborers and there was, of course, no such thing as health insurance or disability compensation. Unscrupulous foremen or contractors would sometimes start disagreements that led to fights so disrupting that no one was paid, and from 1837 to 1842 many contractors, short on hard money, paid their workers in script, much of which was never redeemable, especially as the state grew closer to bankruptcy. However, in spite of all the problems, by the end of 1838, all sections of the canal were under contract except the section from Dresden to Marseilles.

Contractors of record for the line through our area, starting in the Sag and running to Lockport/Romeoville, were:

39-40: Irvin, Kettering[5] & Co.

41-42: Dodd, Morehouse & Co.

River Section: John Bracken.

45: Seth Kershaw, Alton & Pestana, Balentine & Douglass.

46: Coburn & Granger and Smith, Granger & Co.

47-48: Wm. Avery.

49: A. McGroves, L.C. Hugunin, J.& S. Clifford.

50: Groves, Hugunin & Rodgers.[6]

51-52: C.B. Dodson (taken over by Hugunin & N.J. Brown).

53: Gavin & Johnson, E.M. Daggett, J.& D. Roberts.

54-55: James Brooks.[7]

56-57: Stewarts, Sanger & Wallace.

58-59: John Boyer and Pruyne[8], Negus & Rodgers.

The social conflict and dislike for the canal workers, especially the Irish, by the local population is recorded in Woodruff's book, *The History of Will County*. He reports a newspaper article by a Lockport reporter who complains of the Irish in this negative and stereotypical way:

> They have frequent fights. Representatives from different parts of Ireland gather into separate settlements and raise old songs and war cries that have so often torn "the Harp of Erin" to tatters, they have reenacted there freshing dramas of "Donneybrook Fair"[9] and the "Kilkenny Cats" in which every spring of the shillalah was rampant and restless. Funerals and wakes follow on the heels of each other, the wakes being productive of more wakes.[10]

A good part of the dislike was political as well as religious, for the canal men were largely Democrats and their presence created very large Democratic majorities in national and local elections. It was said that "the first thought of the Irishman when he arrives in this country is the right of franchise."[11] That was true, for the Irish came to this country with an understanding of urban politics. They were familiar with the English political system and had a knowledge of organization. Funchion points out that "from the 1790s to the 1820s they [the Irish] had watched the landlords form tenants into effective voting blocs, and in the 1820s they had participated in O'Connell's successful drive to weld the Irish masses into . . . a political force to win Catholic emancipation. The Irish clearly came to the United States well schooled in politics and electioneering tactics."[12]

It was reported that during the Presidential election of 1840, some canalers voted not less than 20 times apiece, and it was estimated that along the I & M Canal there were probably 5,000 illegal votes for Van Buren.[13] This did not bother N.J. Brown who, until the Civil War, considered himself a Jacksonian Democrat. He found the pioneer political experiences along the canal as peculiarly interesting. Lemont, Athens Precinct, was known as the banner Democratic precinct of Cook County and was always a stop for politicians. Brown loved to tell about the day in 1838 when a young man rode up to his door and said:

> I am Stephen A. Douglas, and I am a candidate for Congress
> in this district. I want to get my dinner and have my horse
> fed, and then I want to make a speech to your men.[14]

Brown had never seen Douglas before and he was not impressed. Douglas was short, wore a linsey-woolsey suit, his trousers were tucked in his boots, he had on a slouch hat, and rode a lean, hungry horse. N.J. felt that Douglas, this short rumpled man, would not make a favorable physical impression on his tough workers and he told him so. His advice was direct and honest:

> Mr. Douglas, my men are all Jacksonian men, and if you will
> just quietly go along to Naperville, where you said you were
> going, and not let my men see you, they won't know what a
> diminutive little cuss you are, and I will guarantee that you
> will get every one of their votes.[15]

Douglas took his advice and when election day came every man in our section of Athens Precinct cast his vote for Stephen Douglas.

Wm. B. Ogden, the first mayor of Chicago, made his maiden speech for state senator of Illinois from N.J. Brown's company store on the canal, and there he was undermined by an Irish lawyer, Patrick Ballingall, who jumped up during his speech and said: "Boys, don't vote for Ogden. He's a rich man and a land-grabber who don't sympathize with the working man . . . I'm the man to vote for because you can depend on me to do what is right by you."[16] Ballingall carried the precinct. Odgen, in a bitter letter, revealed his feelings and the feelings of many pioneer settlers. "It is well known that a large portion, perhaps a majority, of the voters in this district are unnaturalized foreigners. It is also known that this foreign influence is perverted to the election of men unfit for office, and that the foreign populations in Cook and Will Counties have asserted the right, as they hold the power, to elect officers for the sole reason that they are Irish."[17]

Naturally, the presence of a large group of workers on the canal encouraged politicians to campaign for their votes. Lemont had visits from almost all of the local office seekers of the day. If they made any promises to improve conditions for the men those promises certainly were not kept. However, the campaigns were a source of amusement and interest to the laborers. Some old political games that Chicagoland loves so much had their beginnings during these days of the canal construction.

When Daniel Lynch, a canal contractor and tavern keeper at Bridgeport, ran for sheriff of Cook County, he established his main headquarters at McKays Tavern above present Lemont, out of reach of N.J. Brown's liquor free zone. There he rolled a barrel of whiskey into the street, knocked out the head, called together as big a crowd as he could collect and, of course, he gathered a large crowd. He passed around tin cups of whiskey while he made his speech:

> Now me byes', it's Daniel O'Connelly of Ireland [calling up
> the spirit of the hero of their hearts from their days in Ire-
> land]; but pretty soon it'll be Daniel O'Lynch of America, yez'll
> be hearing of. Come up me boys and have a sup. [18]

With a short speech and plenty of whiskey, Daniel Lynch had no trouble carrying the precinct. Others found new ways to get the canal vote from the Lemont workers. Ebenezer Peck, who later went on to become an important lawyer in Illinois government, began his career running for the State Legislature. He came to Lemont and made the usual flowery speech typical of the time, but unlike so many other candidates he did not leave. Instead, he stayed for a couple of days, meeting and talking with the men on an individual basis. He also added a gimmick that has become familiar to us today. He brought his own "advance men or claque." Brown described the campaign this way:

> Starting out early the next morning on horseback, he took a big Irishman on behind him, and together they spent the day interviewing voters. As they traveled about from place to place, the Irishman made good use of his lungs, by doffing his hat and cheering lustily for Peck, whenever anybody was in hearing distance of them . . . of course Mr. Peck made a favorable impression on the voters of Athens precinct, and he was elected to the office he sought.[19]

The power of the canal workers as a voting bloc became important and fed the beginning of a backlash, the early start of the movement of Know-Nothingism, a nativist party that wanted restrictions on voting and citizenship requirements.[20] In July of 1840, the Chicago newspaper the *Daily Democrat* published a petition addressed to the Congress asking them to deprive all foreigners not already enfranchised of the right of suffrage in the United States. It was signed by 250 residents of Cook County, most living in Chicago. The petition was ignored by the Congress, for the newcomers to this country already had enough power to be heard. What the petition did do was to haunt most of its signers. For years afterwards, anyone running for office who had signed that petition was roundly defeated by German, Irish, and Scandinavian voters.[21]

The historian Samuel Morison claimed that the only people who really took much interest in immigrants, such as canal workers, were the "contractors who used their labor, the politicians who wanted their votes, and the priests who preferred ghetto-like isolation for their flocks."[22] This may have been true for some who exploited the newcomers, but it must be said that there were local people who felt compassion and concern for the plight of the immigrant workers. There were efforts to collect money to help those who were sick or injured. A 5,000 dollar assistance payment for the poor on the canal was raised in 1838, and in 1839, as money for the canal was withheld by the state, Mayor Raymond of Chicago donated all of his salary for the relief of canal workers.[23]

In spite of bad times, most workers remained, holding the belief that the canal would eventually be completed. Many settled in the area and became a part of the Lemont community. This included its politics, for the love of politics, especially for the Irish, never faded. Those canal men that stayed here and their families that followed made remarkable political contributions to our community. Lemont's Irish probably make up no more than fifteen percent of our population, yet since 1873, over 57 percent of our mayors have been of Irish descent, a remarkable record. The breakdown for our other nationalities serving as mayors, based on surnames is: English/Scot—15 percent; Polish—10 percent; Swedish—eight percent; German—10 percent.

Even with the economic problems of 1838-39, Brown and several local contractors were able to keep working and meeting the payroll through 1839 and 1840, mostly by using their own resources in the belief that they would eventually be repaid with interest. Brown did his part by drive and determination. His own workers could see that he was personally involved in the project. An example of how directly he conducted and controlled his affairs was when he spent one day on horseback in order to get pay for his men. He began by riding from Lemont to Lockport where he made his estimate of the payroll at the office of the Canal Commissioners. He then rode from Lockport to Chicago where he drew the money due him and his men and returned to Lemont, traveling 73 miles on horseback to meet the payroll that evening.[24]

N.J.'s work on the canal contract did not help his own financial condition because the state, which had been borrowing funds from the East and England, found itself caught in a world financial crisis. It was overextended with too many internal improvement projects and threatened to default. Abraham Lincoln, then in the State Legislature, struggled to keep funds for the I & M Canal. He helped to pass a tax of 25 cents per 100 dollars of assessed valuation on all real property in Illinois. By the next session attempts to repeal the Internal Improvement Bill were even stronger. The state was in debt 17,000,000 dollars and many of its grandiose projects uncompleted. However, Lincoln and his friends fought to salvage the great dream of the Illinois and Michigan Canal. They supported and pushed a bond issue of 1,500,000 dollars to obtain enough money to continue work on the canal while the commission looked for other sources of revenue. Lemont owes its existence at least in part to Lincoln, who realized that an unfinished canal would be of no value. It was necessary to spend or obtain more money to make the project pay off.

Brown's frustration with the financial arrangements reached a crisis point in June of 1843. He must have had some disagreement with General Jacob Fry as he forwarded the following letter to Governor Ford:

> Dear Sir,
>
> Being a contractor on the Ill. & Mich. canal, on the rock cut, and having been invited by General Fry to settle with him on the part of the State and surrender my contract up to him, I find there will be a small balance due me if I should take this course. This amount Genl. Fry proposes to pay in State Script, without interest from this date.
>
> This is not my construction of the law, but that it shall have an annual interest upon its fact until paid at the rate of Six per cent and this will be a poor compensation, for the money we had invested in getting our buildings, machinery & tools for the completion of the work. Will you have the goodness to give me your views on this subject and also instruct General Fry what course to pursue with contractors. Please direct your communications to me at this place.
>
> I will now say on the part of myself and my contractors on the Summit Division of this canal, we should be most happy to have the honor of meeting with you at Lockport, or any other point on that line that may best suit your convience.
>
> Your Obedient Servant,
>
> N.J. Brown[25]

Although generally opposed to encumbering the new state with more debt, Governor Ford did finally see the need to support some system to help the contractors. However, many lost money on the project, including Brown, yet he persisted.

ENDNOTES

[1] The area was also called Martin's Landing.

[2] Sonia Kallick, *Lemont Ancedotes* (Lemont, IL: Lemont Area Historical Society, 1975).

[3] See Rev. Norman Werling, *The First Catholic Church in Joliet, Illinois*, Surname Index by Nancy Thornton (Baltimore: Gateway Press, 1987), pp. 39-42.

[4] This was not done at Brown's section.

[5] John Kettering not only contracted part of the canal, but was a partner in one of the first quarries, Illinois Stone & Lime. By 1860, he accumulated 580 acres in section 34. The home he built is now called Willow Lane Farm. See, Jonathan Keyes, "Agriculture Hinterland: A Profile of the Lemont Township Community in 1860," *Looking For Lemont*, ed. Michael Conzen and Carl A. Zimring (Chicago: University of Chicago, 1995), pp. 25-26.

[6] There is a letter dated 1847 in the Canal Archives containing a request from Lemuel Brown (N.J. Brown's brother) to allow him to finish sections 50-51 as a supervisor. The present supervisor was about to leave. He offers to take charge for $1.75 a day, as "the work was near his residence." Part of this work would have been under N.J.'s contract.

[7] The contractor whose men rioted in 1838.

[8] Note that the original plat of Athens in Lemont has a Pruyne Street. Peter Pruyne served as a state senator from 1836 to 1838.

[9] The Doonybrook was once a suburb of Dublin. There King John, in 1204, granted the citizens a charter to hold an annual fair to raise money for upkeep of the city walls. For the following 651 years the fair was held in August on the banks of the Dodder River. It soon gained fame for the drinking and brawling that went along with its commercial activity and the word has become part of our language. It ended in 1855, so some of our canal workers may have experienced the real Doonybrook Fair.

[10] George Woodruff, *A History of Will County* (Evansville: Unigraphics, 1973), pp. 428-429.

[11] *Ibid.*, p. 431.

[12] Michael Funchion, "Irish Chicago" *Ethnic Chicago*, ed. Melvin Holli and Peter d'A. Jones (Grand Rapids: Eerdmans, 1977), p. 29. Daniel O' Connell, called "the Liberator," (1775-1847) was an Irish leader who formed the New Catholic Association in Ireland. It worked to defeat candidates sponsored by the large landowners.

[13] Woodruff, *A History of Will County*, p. 431.

[14] Howard Conrad, "Western Real Estate Speculation Fifty Years Ago," *The National Magazine* (Chicago, 1887), p. 15.

[15] *Ibid.* It is interesting how in this interview that N.J. Brown did not feel it was wrong for him to imply that he controlled the votes of his workers. If this was true he had tremendous political power.

[16] *Ibid.*, pp. 15-16.

[17] Bessie Pierce, *A History of Chicago* (New York: Knopf, 1940), vol. 1., p. 377.

[18] Conrad, "Western Real Estate Speculation Fifty Years Ago," p. 16.

[19] *Ibid.*

[20] A.T. Andreas, *A History of Cook County Illinois: 1885* (Evansville: Unigraphics, 1976), p. 386.

[21] *Ibid.*

[22]Samuel Morison, *The Oxford History of the American People* (New York: The New American Library, 1972), vol. 2., p. 229.

[23]Pierce, *A History of Chicago,* vol. 1., p. 264.

[24]Conrad, "Western Real Estate Speculation Fifty Years Ago," p. 16.

[25]Brown family papers, Lemont Area Historical Society.

CHAPTER NINE

THE I & M CANAL COMPLETED

Lemont Becomes a Township: 1840-1850

Faced with monetary problems in the early 1840s, the I & M Commission tried many ways to finance canal work. One idea was to move the branch bank of Illinois to Lockport and to issue paper notes in a variety of denominations. This succeeded for only a short time because the notes became useless except to buy land from the state holdings.[1]

Meanwhile, Brown and other contractors, lacking any capital source, tried to refloat loans. They employed General Thornton to go East and to Europe to negotiate the sale of 1,000,000 dollars of canal bonds subscribed at par. Thornton's efforts raised 95,000 dollars from Illinois, 270,000 dollars from New York, and 721,000 dollars from French and English sources. When Thornton returned, the funds acquired were divided at the going rate, so Brown and the other contractors had a financial loss.[2] Nathaniel Brown made up some of this loss by retailing goods in the area as Garrett, Brown & Brother had done before the land speculation boom. He had a small general store and, in 1844, was ordering clothing and household supplies from New York for resale.[3]

Another scheme to save money was to have all building supplies bought by a central source so that companies selling cement, shovels, powder, pry bars, and other needed materials could not outbid each other, thus driving up prices for contractors. This idea of unit buying worked. The building where the canal supplies were stored is now part of the restored Gaylord Building in Lockport and was designed by Jacob Fry.

Tough times in the early 1840s did not stop all work on the canal. In spite of the difficulties some contractors continued to struggle from payroll to payroll with the hope that financial problems would be resolved. So as the project continued, Lemont attracted more workers, farmers, and merchants. The official population of Lemont in 1840 was 2,107. This was divided between the Athens/Keepataw listing of 1,662 and the Des Plaines listing of 445. The population was probably higher than reported because Emmetsburg, and Haytown are not listed, nor the small settlement at the corner of the Des Plaines River that was known as Corktown,[4] nor is the community at Sag Bridge. Still it was a sizeable population for that time since Chicago had only 4,470 people.

Because of its size, Lemont became an official postal station in 1840 and was listed as Keepataw from the plat of that name registered in 1836 in the south section 20 of the township. The first postmaster was John Roosevelt, Jr. That year also saw our Irish canal workers stage a St. Patrick's Day parade in town, a well-attended affair. Lemont can take credit for one of the first St. Patrick's Day parades in the Chicagoland area.[5]

The canal construction and growth that continued here, while the nation suffered an economic depression, brought N.J. Brown's brother, Lemuel, to the community. Lemuel had worked for N.J. in his younger years and then went into the trading and land business in Michigan. He served as the first county recorder of Shiauassa County in Michigan and its first postmaster. He had, like his brother, done quite well and by age 23 owned land, was married, and had 3,000 dollars. However, the bubble burst by the end of the 1830s when President Jackson instituted the sub-treasury and specie was demanded in payment for lands. This, combined with a stabilization of the population in Michigan, offered little land for speculation.

Never one to remain and let the frontier pass him by, Lemuel sold his farm, tavern, and all interests and moved to Keepataw/Athens, where the new growth offered opportunities. Lemuel, like N.J., had political connections and was appointed village postmaster by 1841.[6] He also served as justice of the peace for twelve years. Lemuel is important to our history, not only because he worked in the Brown family enterprises but because he was the man who named Lemont.

While the post office designation for the area was Keepataw, the planned I & M Canal stop was called Athens, a confusing state of affairs. However, Keepataw was our official name until the reorganization of Cook County. In 1846 the county began to organize with an effort to standardize township boundaries and town names. Township boundaries then were not clear; for example, part of Palos and our township were joined, while many areas in Illinois had towns with the same names. This made delivery of mail and governmental control difficult. Lemuel was asked to be one of the officials delegated to visit every township in Cook County to set in motion the structure needed to meet the new state law demanding such organization.[7]

Lemuel accepted the appointment for our township. Perhaps he is to blame, rather than geography, for the fact that our township is missing sections. Anyway, the meeting to pick names was heated. Two new names were needed, one for the community and one for the township. As for town names, Athens could not be retained because an older town near Springfield had the same name. Keepataw was not favored because the population felt Indian names made a town on the new frontier sound too uncivilized. It was also rejected because the platted area, Keepataw, was largely commercial, a bit seedy, and had fallen into receivership.

It was then decided that the main town and the township should have the same name, as that would make mailing and taxing easier. For some unknown reason the name Palmyra was selected and used for about a month between April and May of 1850. The name was familiar to some Easterners from the New York town of the same name located on the New York canal system. It certainly was a historically appropriate name. Palmyra was an ancient Syrian city that was the trade center between the East and West; caravans traveled through that city and fortunes were made in transportation and trade. No doubt, the people of our area saw themselves as the center of transportation with the I & M Canal and the railroad to come. Palmyra could have been rejected for several reasons. First, the reference may have been unclear to many Lemonters because most were frontier children who had little opportunity for formal education and would not have understood the allusion. Secondly, the name did carry an association from Palmyra, New York, which was connected with the then feared Mormons and their prophet, Joseph Smith, for it was there he had his vision that led to the founding of the Church of the Latter-Day Saints.[8] Finally, it is believed by some that the name Palmyra was a code word used on the underground railway to smuggle slaves to Canada, for the ancient city enjoyed the status of a *civitas libera,* or free city, under Emperor Hadrian.

There is a local tradition that the Brown family and other Methodists and Baptists in Lemont and Downers Grove Township were an important link on the freedom railway. Oral anecdotes relate that the underground limestone bunkers on the Brown farm, which once held black powder for building the canal, were used to hide escaping slaves. Perhaps there was political opposition to hiding runaway slaves, or at least to advertising the fact.

In any case, there was a demand for a new name. The committee reached a point where they were eager for any reasonable suggestion. Lemuel Brown offered La Mont, assumed by the public to be French for "the mountain," a reference to our hills.[9] It was accepted as a name for both the town and the township but was modified to Lemont. It is part of our folklore that it became Lemont by taking the first part of Lemuel's name and adding it to "-ont." Where Lemuel got the idea for the name Lamont or Lemont is not recorded. There is, however, a Lemont and a Lemont Furnace in Pennsylvania, and a Lemont in France.

The man who named Lemont was restless and was on the move west by 1853, this time to try his hand at land speculation in Iowa. He settled in Clinton County, Iowa. There he served as sheriff and justice of the peace while farming. There is a small rural town, called LaMont, in Iowa, but no one knows if it was named by Lemuel. From Iowa he went to Kansas and raised cattle for 10 years. By 1883, he was too tired to follow the frontier any longer. It was time to retire and of all the places he had seen and of all the new lands he had explored, he chose to spend his last years in Lemont. He died in 1894 and was buried in the Brown family cemetery overlooking the town he named.

When Lemuel joined Nathaniel, the town and the new canal held promise but there were hard days. Lemuel was lucky to have the political connections to get positions as justice of the peace and as postmaster, for work on the canal was so slow that the future of the village and the canal looked bleak. It took another agreement by the state to give all the land assets to a board of trustees who then sold the lands and borrowed enough money, again, to push the project forward. This time with a depressed economy, depressed prices, and an excess of labor, it was finally possible to complete the I & M Canal. In the spring of 1848 it was ready for commerce.

Construction of the I & M Canal changed our area. The first change was during the actual construction which brought workers, many of whom stayed. It also brought a payroll into the area that encouraged those services needed to support a work force. The money attracted stores, blacksmiths, saloons, boarding houses, mechanics, carpenters, cobblers, hotel keepers, anything needed by people with money to spend. The sale of public lands at cheap prices to raise money for the canal offered opportunities to those who wished to farm for a living. Canal construction created a full-blown community in twelve years, a remarkably swift time.

The second effect was from the economy of the canal itself. Lemont became a shipping point for goods and people along the canal area. Farmers brought in goods and purchased needed supplies, thereby making the town the center of their social, religious, and economic activity. Many townspeople made their living largely by offering services to the agriculture community.

Compromises had to be made to complete construction at a reasonable cost, including abandoning the deep cut plan for a shallow cut with water being supplied from the Calumet, Fox, and Kankakee Rivers. When the completed canal was opened, the first boat to travel it was the *General Fry*, named for the Canal Commissioner. The *General Fry* passed through our section on April 10, 1848. It went from Lockport to Chicago towed by a propeller craft, the *A. Rossiter*. The use of a propeller craft could suggest that the horses and mule barns were not in full operation at the time.

The first trip the entire length of the canal was done by the barge the *General Thornton*. It arrived in Chicago from LaSalle on April 23, carrying sugar. Canal records set April 19, 1848, as the official opening date of the canal.[10]

There were problems even that first year. Putnam, in his book, reported:

> For several months after the opening . . . its efficiency was adversely affected by an insufficient supply of water on the Summit level. The Calumet feeder had not been finished yet and water had to be pumped into the canal from the Chicago River at Bridgeport.[11]

Other difficulties included the fact that the upper area of the Summit level was built through very porous soil so that water leaked out of the banks. That problem did not happen in Lemont for the part of our canal that was not cut through stone was carved through our notorious clay, which holds water. Another problem was a serious oversight because no one had planned on enough boats to meet the sudden demand for freight and passenger traffic. At the opening of the canal there were only 16 boats in commission for service.[12]

However, by the end of the first season most of the difficulties were worked out and tolls amounted to 878,090 dollars while the expenses were 48,197 dollars. When the canal first opened, passenger service was its main source of revenue until the railroads began to compete for passengers.[13] Among the more famous passengers on the boats were Abraham Lincoln, his wife Mary, and their five year-old son Robert,[14] who traveled through Lemont on October 8, 1848.[15]

It is one of those patterns of history that technology often surpasses man's ability to understand change. The I & M Canal was built at the end of the great canal building period of this country. It was a time when men had visions of connecting all of America's waterways into a highway system that would be efficient, noiseless, and would offer waterpower as a source of energy to communities. Yet, even as the canal was in its planning stages, the idea of rail transportation was being developed and the first train in the Chicago area had its maiden run from Chicago to the Des Plaines River in the fall of the same year the canal opened.[16]

Still, the completion of the I & M Canal was an economic boost to all of northern Illinois. It offered both passenger and freight transportation at a low cost. The rate for freight boats was three and a half cents per mile, and for passengers, six cents a mile. Added was a passenger charge of four mills per mile for anyone over eight years old.[17]

One of the best known passenger barges was called *Queen of the Prairie*. It had a 50-foot cabin and was nine feet wide and seven feet high.[18] It held as many as 50 people traveling at six miles per hour. The trip from Chicago to LaSalle usually took 22 hours. That may seem slow but it was an improvement over any other means of transportation available in those days. The packet boats also allowed passengers to carry household goods up to 60 pounds free, something that the stagecoaches could not do.

Except for the crowded sleeping sections, with curtains separating men and women, travel was pleasant. Travelers could sit on the deck on nice days and watch the prairies and small towns drift slowly by. The pace was such that passengers could get off and walk along with the barge for stretches. Boats were pulled by horses or mules, until the arrival of steam powered tugboats in the 1860s. Work horses or mules were attached to a 150-foot line lashed to the midsection of the barge. These animals were led by a muleboy who walked along the towpath to keep them moving.[19] The crew was usually composed of a captain and a poleman whose job was to keep the boat from sticking or hitting the sides of the canal. Barns for changing animals were located from ten to 15 miles apart. Lemont had a barn on the east side of Stephen Street along the north side of the canal. The animal change was combined with a station and rest stop. For some barge men it was the home port, and often a small section of boarding houses and saloons that catered to bargemen only grew up around the animal barns. Such was the case in Lemont. Many bargemen had a rough reputation, not unlike sailors in seaport towns, and towns like Lemont and Sag Bridge tried to isolate their activities to one section of town. In Lemont that section became well known as early as the 1860s, when it acquired the name of Smokey Row. Here in 1865, Pete Boyle murdered Con Brown, a notorious bounty jumper who had enlisted in and deserted from the Union Army over 20 times.[20] Smokey Row was destined to acquire an even greater fame.

Freight boats on the canal were pulled by mules in teams of four. They traveled at a slower speed, usually around three miles an hour.[21] The freight business remained an important part of the economy of the corridor even after passenger traffic decreased. Chronic problems of the canal included low water, so boats could not pass, and the winter freeze. If there was enough rain, the boats could pull full loads. If the winter freeze was late, the shipping season could gain extra revenue. In those years when nature did not cooperate, the tolls fell and the canal had difficulty making money. Another problem for those shipping south was the condition of the Illinois River. It often had low water levels

Barges pulled by mules on the I & M Canal. (Illustration courtesy of Lemont Historical Society)

due to silting and remained a navigational problem until the 1870s, when construction of two locks and dams on the river created a sufficient water flow.

With the canal finished, the township lost population. This fact is reflected in census figures for 1850 that lists Lemont Township as having 210, a number that seems small for the economic activity of the village. It is probable that village figures became confused with the township figures as the names of both the town and township were in the process of change at the time.[22]

The platted area of town was modest in size. It was bounded by River Road on the north side; there was no railroad then, only the bank of the Des Plaines River. On the east it was bounded by the end of Talcott Street. The western edge was State Street, and Illinois Street marked the southern limits. Visitors described the village as having only three homes and a few stores and taverns. This may not be a completly true picture, but the completion of the canal did cause many workers and their families to leave for other projects on the expanding frontier.

It was quite a change from the community that had as many as 3,000 residents five years before. In the year Lemont got its name, 1850, what we have of a census shows a number of remarkable things. First, of the recorded population over 50 percent were children under 16. Of those children, 27 percent had been born in Illinois (the oldest one was born in 1838), 16 percent had been born in Ireland, one percent had been born in Michigan, and six percent had been born in New York.

The average age of the rest of the adult population was 38, rather old for a frontier area. Of the adult population 45 percent had been born in Ireland, two percent in Vermont, three percent in Canada, 19 percent in New York, 24 percent in Illinois, two percent in Michigan, one percent in Scotland, and four percent in Germany. Young adults age 18 to 21 made up only five percent of the village, a very small number, which suggests that there was not enough work for them. California gold fields and the new frontier may have called them westward or they may have gone to more urban areas, such as Chicago and Joliet, for work.

The waterway presented a new problem to the previously isolated community of Lemont. Easy travel through the village opened the chances for transmission of communicable diseases. One of the most feared was cholera, and the late 1840s and early 1850s saw the disease take a pandemic course, traveling from India to Europe to New Orleans and finally, to Chicago. Since no one understood the mode of transmission, it was associated with ships and waterways. In July of 1849, it was reported that cholera was spreading down the waterways. John Miller wrote to his brother that:

> I here [sic] that today one canal boat came in this morning
> with the owner and three others dead on the boat. It is thought
> that business on the canal will be almost suspended . . . for
> fear that Cholera will not abate till coald [sic] wether [sic].[23]

Yet, in spite of such fears traffic on the I & M Canal continued at a brisk pace. James Putnam, in his book the *Illinois and Michigan Canal*, points out that there were three stages of economic influence for the I & M Canal. The first period came during the development and construction of the project from the 1830s to 1848. The second period ran from the canal opening to the completion of the Chicago, Alton, and St. Louis Railroad through town in 1858. The third, and final, period covered the years 1858 to 1910, the year when the I & M was closed from Chicago to Lockport in favor of the Sanitary Ship

Steam-powered stone boat on the I & M Canal in Lemont. (Photo courtesy Lemont Historical Society)

Canal. This last era was marked by competition for traffic between the canal and the railroads.

The finished I & M Canal ran from the Chicago River to LaSalle. There it ended in large basins created from the Illinois River. Canal boats reaching that point were towed by steamboats down the Illinois to points beyond. The canal had 17 locks, two at the Chicago River to lift the barges 13 feet over the ridge at the beginning of the canal. There was also the pumping station at Bridgeport designed to pump Chicago River water into the canal. Putman summarized the effect of the canal, "with improved facilities for transportation and with the rapid industrial development of the region influenced by these facilities, the traffic and earnings grew almost steadily throughout the period."[24]

ENDNOTES

[1]John Lamb, *A Corridor in Time* (Romeoville, IL: Lewis University, 1987), p. 13.

[2]A.T. Andreas, *History of Cook County* (Evansville: Unigraphics, 1976), p. 153. See also, Howard Conrad, "Western Real Estate Speculation Fifty Years Ago," *The National Magazine* (Chicago, 1887) for N.J. Brown's comments on the losses he incurred.

[3]N.J. Brown, Letter to Samuel Williams of New York, October 1, 1844, (Lemont: Brown Papers, Lemont Area Historical Society Collection).

[4]Named for the number of Irish from the County of Cork. It was one of the first church stations of Father Plunkett of Joliet. Rev. Norman Werling, *The First Catholic Church in Joliet, Illinois,* Surname Index by Nancy C. Thornton (Baltimore: Gateway Press, 1987) pp. 46-49. Reverend Werling writes that the Corktown Church was the old log church that stood at what is now State and Main streets in Lemont.

[5]A tradition that has been recently revived by our downtown merchants.

[6]Another family political connection was through brother Benjamin Brown who served in the Treasury Department in Washington under President Polk (1844-1848).

[7]Theodore Karamanski, *Brown Property Evaluation* (Chicago: Loyola University, 1986), app. B, p. 8.

[8]The feeling against the Mormons was strong in Illinois. Remember it was in our state that Joseph Smith, their founder, met his death at the hands of the militia while in jail. Such an event and its associations would not favor a town's name. There also was a small village named Palmyra in Macoupin County established in 1830. Perhaps they had gained a postal designation by 1850.

[9]The French word *Lamontee* can also mean "the climb," perhaps a reflection of our geography.

[10]James Putman, *The Illinois and Michigan Canal* (Chicago: University of Chicago Press, 1918), p. 99.

[11]*Ibid.*

[12]*Ibid.*, p. 100.

[13]Lamb, *A Corridor in Time*, p. 8.

[14]Robert was the only Lincoln child to live to adulthood. He died in 1926.

[15]E.O. Bossert, *The I & M Canal*, ed. Joan Bossert Morsicato (1993) p. D-5.

[16]Bessie Pierce, *A History of Chicago* (New York: Knopf, 1940), vol. 2, p. 35. On October 25, 1848 a steam locomotive was run on its first five miles of track and proposed to become The Galena and Chicago Union Rail Line.

[17]Andreas, *History of Cook County,* p. 154.

[18]The dimensions were about the size of a standard school bus, only longer.

[19]Lamb, *A Corridor in Time*, p. 19.

[20]Stephen Longstreet, *Chicago* (New York: David McKay and Company, 1973), p. 8.

[21]Lamb, *A Corridor in Time*, p. 19.

[22]Carrington Ward, "Staying on the Farm: Persistence, Growth, and Turnover in Lemont and Palos Townships, 1870-1880," *Looking For Lemont,* ed. Micheal Conzen and Carl Zimring (Chicago: University of Chicago, 1994), p. 47. Ward comments on his work with

the 19th Century census manuscripts and the problems these records present. He lists a number of factors that make these records unreliable.

[23]William Beatty, "When Cholera Scouraged Chicago," *Chicago History* (Chicago: Chicago Historical Society, Spring, 1982) p. 6.

[24]Putman, *The Illinois and Michigan Canal,* p. 100.

U.S. HISTORY

1840: *2816 Miles of Railroad Tracks in U.S.*

1841: *William Harrison, President, Dies After One Month in Office — John Tyler Becomes President — Population of U.S. at 17 Million — First University Degrees Offered for Women.*

1842: *Boston and Albany Connected by Railroad.*

1843: *John Fremont Crosses Rocky Mountains to California — First Telegraph Line, Washington D.C. to Baltimore.*

1844: *James Polk is Elected President.*

1845: *Texas and Florida Become States — U.S. Naval Academy Opens.*

1846: *War with Mexico — Iowa Becomes a State — Many Mormons Leave Illinois for the Great Salt Lake Area — Deere Plow Comes into General Use — Sewing Machine Invented by Howe.*

1847: *U.S. Forces Capture Mexico City — Evaporated Milk Developed — Gold Discovered in California, Many Go West.*

1848: *Mexican War Ends; U.S. Gets Texas, New Mexico, California, Utah, Nevada, Wyoming, Arizona and Colorado Territories — Wisconsin Becomes a State.*

1849: *Zachary Taylor Becomes President.*

LEMONT HISTORY

1840: *Depression on the I & M Canal, Workers Laid Off — A.S. Sherman Buys Quarry Land in Athens [Lemont] — John Roosevelt Postmaster of Keepataw, the P.O. Designation — Population of Athens: 1,662 — Population of Des Plaines [Lemont Township]: 445 — St. Patrick's Parish Established — First St. Patrick's Day Parade in Lemont.*

1841: *First Divorce: Forbes Miner vs. Cornelia Miner — Private Subscription Schools: Mr. Lamb by the Stone Kiln on Bluff Road, Miss King at Slavin & Mclaughin, and Mrs. Flannigan on the East Side of the Village — Lemuel Brown is Justice of the Peace.*

1842: *60th Regiment of the Illinois Militia Forms at McKay's Tavern in Athens — Most Work on the I & M Stops for Two Years, Deficit of Four Million Dollars — Many Leave Area.*

1843: *Lemuel Brown Becomes Postmaster — A.S. Sherman, Lemont Quarry Owner, Becomes Mayor of Chicago — Lemont Farmers Form the "Illinois Fishing Colony" at Rock Island in Door County, Wisconsin.*

1844: *Money Voted to Finish Canal — Joel Wells is Engineer for the Canal; He Builds First Stone House in Lemont, Now Part of the St. James Academy Building on Illinois Street.*

1846: *Population of Athens for the Draft for the Mexican War is 543, Subject for Duty 125. Des Plaines [Lemont] Population is 999, Subject for Duty 276 — William Scott Brown Serves in the Mexican War — Cattle Shipped from Lemont Worth 8,900 Dollars — First Stone Quarry for N.J. Brown — Alex Reid and James Tripp Arrive in Town — H.M. Singer Working As Rod Man on the I&M Canal.*

1848: *I & M Canal Opens — Population of Township: 3,000 — 1st Train Goes to Riverside — Cholera in Chicago and Lemont: 300+ Die — Lime Made from Lemont Quarries Given Away Free As Disinfectant — N.J. Brown Opens Three Quarries — Dan Skelly Opens a Quarry.*

1849: *Mancell Talcott Goes to the Gold Fields — Old Pioneer Jeremiah Luther Also Goes and Dies Along the Way — St. Patrick's Cemetery Formed — Big Flood on Des Plaines River.*

CHAPTER TEN

STONE AND GRAIN TRADE
ON THE I & M CANAL

During the first years of the I & M Canal, grain was the main export while lumber was the main import. Local grain trade flourished even before the canal was completed. Grain exports to the East from the Chicago area climbed from 586,907 bushels in 1842 to 1,974,304 bushels in 1847,[1] so there was a market for this product even before cheaper inland water transportation was available.

After 1848, grain trade became so important to the local economy that the Chicago Board of Trade was established to oversee the industry;[2] as a result there developed a need for storage to hold grain off the market to control prices. This led to the creation of grain elevators in communities along transportation corridors. What was unique about these new elevators was the fact that machinery and not human labor was used to move the grain in and out of the buildings. The grain came in on a power belt, moved to the top of the building, and then was fed by gravity to holding bins in the warehouse. Early elevators were horse powered. The first steam powered grain elevator in Chicago was built in 1848, influenced by the anticipated trade from the completed canal and future rail lines.[3]

Most of the rural towns along the canal built grain elevators and feed mills. Lemont had two. One was located along the south side of the canal on the old Tedens property 102

S.W. Norton's store and grain elevator. The elevator is on the left. (Photo courtesy of the Lemont Historical Society)

(Stephens Street) and the other, part of the large Norton family holdings from Chicago to Lockport, was where the Strand (103 Stephens Street) parking lot now stands. These elevators became a form of bank in the early community, but one that did not pay interest.[4] When the farmer deposited his corn or wheat with the elevator, he was given a receipt. This receipt represented collateral for the farmer and receipts could be used like banknotes, "Elevators effectively created a new form of money, secured not by gold but by grain."[5] This way the product of the farm became one of the important sources of capital in our community.

At first the major grain grown and shipped was wheat, but this soon changed to oats and corn. Attempts to grow winter wheat in the township met with poor harvests in the 1840s and 1850s due to bad weather and insect infestation. So our local farmers turned to corn, useful for fattening livestock, and oats, useful for horse feed.

By 1860, the agricultural census for our township listed 96 farm units on 31 percent of the land. This means that a good deal of the land was in other use, some as quarry lands, some still wooded, some for grazing, and some remaining fallow. Most of the farms listed practiced general farming, raising grain for sale and for livestock feed. Along with cattle and swine, they produced eggs, milk, butter, and cheese. A few of the smaller holdings began specialization with orchards, bee-keeping, sheep for wool, and horse breeding. Another interesting crop was potatoes; in 1860 Lemont produced 9,598 bushels for the market. Our farmers also experienced a short period of "sorghum fever" that developed when the Civil War cut off sugar supplies from the South. Many invested in expensive equipment to

N.J. Brown standing on the left. The workers are transporting rough stone tailings. Photo circa 1880. (Photo courtesy of Lemont Historical Society)

process sorghum which was touted as the wonder crop that offered molasses, dye, fiber for paper, and even rum, if one had the proper machinery. However, the fad soon passed as processing was complicated and the syrup had an unpleasant taste.

Along with the farm products, building materials became a major portion of the canal trade. Lumber was needed for homes on the treeless prairies of central Illinois and it was easy to ship pine from Michigan and Wisconsin to Chicago and through the canal. In the early days, land along the canal route was dotted with lumber yards. Such companies as Tedens and Thormahlen, J. S. Luther, S. Norton, S. L. Derby, and J. Helbig, soon made a name in the trade.

S. L. Derby, a pioneer of the area, had a yard on Talcott Avenue along the south side of the canal. He invested in timber land and milling interests in Michigan and Wisconsin. Derby was active in the organizational affairs of the industry and served as president of the Illinois Retail Lumber Dealers Association in the 1890s. N.J. Brown and his brothers also kept timber lands in Wisconsin and Michigan during this boom period for building. Lemont had six families and family enterprises involved in the early lumber trade.

However, the opening of the canal was a major boost for what was to be the most active and interesting industry of the Des Plaines Valley, the stone trade.[6] Lemont has been associated with stone and the quarries of the Des Plaines Valley from its earliest days. Discovered during the building of the canal, the Dolomite stone of our valley became the major economic force in our area for over 80 years. The need to have unskilled labor to quarry our stone brought groups of immigrants to the town, adding to the unique ethnic mixture we see in Lemont today.

Some contractors building the I & M Canal, such as N.J. Brown, came from New England. They recognized that the limestone bedrock that they had to remove appeared similar to the native limestone of the New York/New England countryside. So, one of the first uses of this stone was to shore up the sides of the canal in sections through Lemont. Consequently, we still have some of the finest portions of the I & M Canal here. Water and time have not destroyed the stone walls and from them we can get a glimpse of how the canal looked in 1848.

The economic potential of the stone did not escape the smart Yankees who, stuck with canal script payable only in land, suddenly developed an interest in getting valley bottom lands and stony bluffs. Lemuel Brown, N.J. Brown's brother, entered the stone business here in an unusual way. In the 1850 census he is listed as a stone cutter with an early stone company. He apparently not only eventually owned stone lands, but also worked as a skilled mason.

New farmers coming to our township looking for flat, rich soil could not understand why anyone would want to buy or preempt land that had a topsoil of one to two inches resting on solid bedrock. It made little sense to them. It took vision to see the future of the cut stone trade because at first the stone was sold mainly for foundations and small outbuildings. People were reluctant to build with untested materials, although Woodruff reports a successful three story dolomite building in Joliet as early as 1835.[7]

Some early investors were interested in the stone not as much for building as for its chemical worth. In the 1800s, lime produced from limestone was second only to sulfuric acid as the most widely used chemical in industry. If stone had a high enough calcium content, lime could be obtained by burning the stone in kilns. The product of this burning then was used for plaster, mortar, whitewash, as a feed supplement for livestock and poultry, for sweetening the soil, and for a disinfectant.

In the quicklime form it could be sold for outhouses to hasten decay. During the terrible cholera year of 1854, when five percent of the Chicagoland population died, free lime was given out from the quarries as a preventive measure against contagion.[8] It was believed that if one washed the home with a lime solution and put quicklime on the dead it would halt the spread of the disease.[9]

However, most of the stone in our valley turned out to be of a hard type not easy to burn into lime. The stone land owners were disappointed at first on discovering that they had a grade of stone not easy to change into lime and lime products. This fact required a different marketing approach — the stone could be sold as cut stone for building if the public would accept it.

Stone not up to cut stone grade could be crushed and sold for railroad ballast. This was a valuable product during the railroad building era that swept the nation by mid-century. It is no coincidence that most of the smaller quarries were opened at the time the Chicago and Alton Railroad was constructed through Lemont and the Des Plaines Valley.

Larger dolomite pieces could be used for fill and for road building; and, finally, those pieces not thick enough for dimension stone but found in large flat "flags" could be sold for sidewalks and retaining walls. This major industry of cut and dimension stone, which had a modest beginning, would create at least seven millionaires out of Lemont's early quarry owners.

At first there was no great demand for stone buildings in the 1850s. Population expansion in Chicago was so rapid that the typical buildings were of the quick wooden balloon frame construction. This building style replaced the older grid and joist method with close light studs, joists, roof rafters and purlins "joined by simple nailing . . . [this was] covered with clapboard siding nailed to the studs."[10] Most buildings were unpainted, and unsubstantial, but filled the ever increasing need for housing.

Nevertheless, there were those with capital who wished the city to have less of a frontier look and they began to build with local brick and imported stone. A.S. Sherman, who had the quarry lands in Lemont producing lime and tombstones, got the idea to veneer his Merchants and Mechanics Bank in Chicago with sawn "Athens Marble." Soon buildings owned by F.S. Sherman, William Ogden and other business men began to copy the fashion.[11]

The facing technique was a quick way to upgrade a wooden structure, although through the 1850s the stone was not widely used for weight-bearing walls. Local contractors and the public had to be convinced that the stone was durable. Once the fashion of using Athens Marble for facing caught on in the commercial areas of Chicago, it became popular with residential builders who had money. Only those with money could afford such buildings because the cost of the stone was much higher than wood and required the skills of trained stone masons.

Lemont Stone is another part of the interesting geography and geology of our special valley and township. Stone deposits such as ours occur all over the world but only in certain places are they suitable for cut stone — Lemont and the Des Plaines Valley are two of those places. Most bedrock here contains limestone, sandstone, and shale on top of granite. The limestone on the upper layers of our bedrock is called Niagara Limestone because it runs under the Great Lakes eastward to reappear at the ledge of hard rock that forms the tip of Niagara Falls. Our section of that limestone is known by geologists as the Sugar Run Formation and is exposed at the surface here, in Kankakee, and along the Fox River in Kane County.[12]

The layer is from 200 to 450 feet deep in our area, and limestone bedrock makes an excellent aquifer providing water for many wells in the Lemont and Chicagoland area. It is for this reason that scientists and conservation groups become concerned when attempts are made to use the quarries for dumping waste. There is no way to predict where water in the quarries will move as it follows the natural joints and cracks in the stone bed.[13]

The stone layer of our valley is covered in most places with soil and ground-up rock called glacial drift, debris left from glaciers, running from a few inches to a hundred or more feet deep. An excellent visual example of the top height of this drift

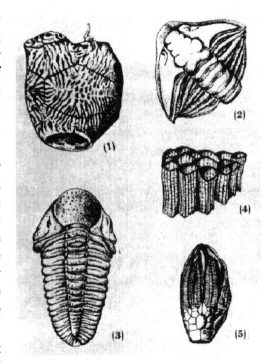

A few examples of local Silurian fossils. (Illustration courtesy of the Chicago Academy of Science)

is at Mount Forest Island, the ridge on which St. James of the Sag Church stands. On that ridge one can see the results of the glacial forces that shaped our valley. The glacial melt waters that washed out the valley took so much of the topsoil and drift that the limestone bedrock was left exposed on the bluffs and cliffs and near the surface of the valley floor.[14]

Limestone is a sedimentary rock, formed over millions of years. It is defined as a stone containing at least fifty percent calcium carbonate created from fossils, older limestone, marine animals, algae, coral, and some land debris. That means most of it was formed from shells of marine animals that settled in layers over hundreds of millions of years. Thousands of years were required to build a single inch of this rock monument to prehistoric creatures.

In Lemont, the upper layer of limestone, the newest in terms of age, is rough-grained and contains visible fossil bodies. There are places in the valley where one can see 400 million year-old fossils, beautiful examples of crinoids, brachiopods, corals, cephalopods, and trilobites, creatures that once ruled the world of Lemont. This upper layer limestone, though not of great commercial value, was the layer that meant the most to the Indians since it contains chert, the hard gray material used for arrowheads and cutting tools. The Mohs hardness scale rates most limestone at a three, dolomite at a four, and chert at seven — as hard as quartz.[15]

About 18 feet into our limestone layer the fossils disappear due to pressure and chemical changes. The calcium carbonate begins to be replaced by magnesium carbonate, called dolomite crystals, and when the magnesium carbonate reaches 30 to 45 percent it is called Niagaran Dolomite. Dolomite is harder and finer grained than ordinary limestone and preferred for building stone. When our stone land speculators recognized that the limestone they had was difficult to process into lime, they requested that the stone be evaluated by the Smithsonian as part of the Western survey for minerals and resources. The stone was graded and reported as containing: 41 percent carbonate of magnesia, 36 perecent carbonate of calcium, 17 percent silica and clay, and the remainder aluminum, iron, and alkalies. The same survey tested the crushing force, an important factor if the stone was to be sold for weight-bearing walls instead of use for veneer only. The report was favorable. The greatest force it could bear was 22,300 pounds per square inch. There could be no doubt that it was a commercially viable weight-bearing stone when taken from the right beds.[16]

The best stone for building has the highest magnesium content. Stone with a high calcium content is too soft and deteriorates when exposed to the elements. Some quarry beds, especially those that had been coral reefs, contain both limestone and dolomite in a loose matrix. Drive around Lemont and see proof of uneven weathering in this stone. Garden after garden has on display our "holey" rocks, those limestone boulders that look like sponges. What has happened is that the stones contained pockets of magnesium carbonate and pockets of calcium carbonate. Over the years the calcium has dissolved,[17] leaving magnesium carbonate.

Once the stone trade was established and the canal available for transportation, the stone was marketed from the Des Plaines Valley under several names. Here it was Lemont Stone or Athens Marble, Joliet sold it as Joliet Stone and Lockport as Lockport Stone. The early architect William Boyington used dolomite in the Illinois State Penitentiary building at Joliet in 1858. In 1869, he used stone from the Walker Quarry in Lemont, along with Ed Walker of our village as construction supervisor, to build the Chicago Watertower, the famous Chicago symbol that Oscar Wilde attacked as, "a castelled monstrosity with pepper boxes stuck all over it. I am amazed that any people could so abuse Gothic art, and make a structure look, not like a water tower, but like the tower of a medieval castle."[18]

With the opening of quarries, workers and their families concentrated in the Lemont-Sag area and Joliet because that was where the best grades of stone were located due to the geology of our section. Vincent Michael reports:

> Because of the gentle northeast tilting of the bedrock, the quality rock that occurs above the river level in the bluffs at Joliet is located at a lower elevation around Lemont. Many of the quarries in the river bed south of Lemont to Joliet produced poor building stone.[19]

The commercial names Joliet Limestone and Athens Marble were used for many years, but in reality there was little difference in the quality of the rock from these two areas since they came from the same beds. The fact that Lemont was closer to Chicago, and the cost of shipping cheaper, accounts for the reason that Lemont Stone was preferred in Chicago.[20]

Cut, or dimension stone, which the stonemasons used, had to meet certain standards to be asthetically acceptable. It had to be free from visible fossil bodies that would mar a smooth appearance, have a fine grain, be hard with a high dolomite content, occur in layers thick enough to cut into blocks, and have a standard color without streaks. Lemont Stone met all the above criteria, and it had a pale buff color that aged beautifully. The shade of the stone was so popular in its time that the Sears Catalogue for 1908 listed as a color for an expensive brand of paint, Lemont Stone (order no. 30k0207).[21]

The process of quarrying[22] the stone varied. Sometimes cliff formations and ledges could be hammered off, but this was usually done on a poorer grade of stone. Stone obtained this way often went for foundation stones for frame houses. One way to date an older home in Lemont is by looking at the foundation. Homes in the 80 to 100 year range usually used Lemont stone for the foundation. Some homes have plastered or cemented over the stone on the outside to cover the limestone but this leaves a rough textured wall that reveals its true origin.

The quality stone that we see in important buildings was found in deep beds. Stone in these beds have natural partings called joints. If the joints are closely spaced, the rock is valueless for stone blocks, but can be crushed or used for the other commercial applications. For good cut stone the vertical joints should be four or more feet apart, while the horizontal layers should run from six inches to five or more feet

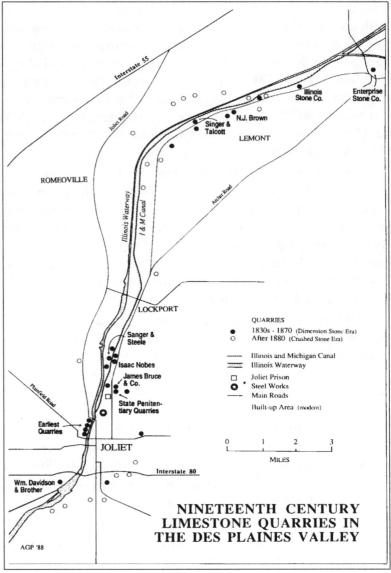

Quarries in the Des Plaines Valley. (Map courtesy of Professor Michael Conzen, University of Chicago Committee on Geographical Studies)

apart. Our quarries usually had horizontal layers of six inches to three feet. The last quarry to produce very large blocks was the Great Lakes Dredge and Dock in 1908; many of its pieces can be seen on the Chicago lakefront at 31st Street where it is used as a breakwater.

When a limestone deposit was located, the topsoil would be stripped off, exposing the layer. Then the rock would be separated from its parent ledge. For dimension stone, this could never be done with strong explosives as the stone would shatter. Blasting was done only when the stone was useful for crushed or rip-rap sales. The first cut for dimension stone was a channel to separate the block from the solid bed. Then the stone was cut by drilling holes and gently forcing the slabs apart with wedges, called the "plug and feather" method. We can still see these vertical drill holes on quarry walls around Lemont and on some stone blocks on buildings. Sometimes holes would be drilled, but the slab rejected because it did not meet standards. On a large stone ledge on the east side of the Sag quarry in the Cook County Forest Preserve there are examples of drill holes on rejected slabs. These holes, perhaps over 80 years old, now support little tufts of grass and weeds that have managed to grow in these drilled depressions on the stone ledge.

A visit to the quarries can reveal so much about the force and beauty of nature and its process of change. The stone blocks that were cut could sometimes be as large as 80 to 100 feet long, three to eight feet high, and four or more feet wide. Imagine the dangers involved in handling such massive stones, especially in the early days before steam power. The large blocks were subdivided into smaller sizes and shaped and sized. At first largely hand power and some water power was used to help with the shaping, but by the 1870s and 1880s steam power replaced much of the hand labor finishing. The introduction of steam power for finishing reduced the price of the stone and increased its use. There was a direct relationship between the introduction of steam power in the quarries and the peak years of the dolomite industry. Horace Singer, of the Singer and Talcott Quarries, is credited with the introduction of steam derricks for stone handling, steam-driven stone lathes, planers, and the first steam-powered canal stone boats.[23]

It is hard to locate the names of all the quarry companies that operated from 1830 to the 1900s. Many were small operations that soon ran out of stone, while others were bought and sold so that the names of the companies changed. Lemonters numbered the quarries in the early days, so that everyone knew where Quarry 1 or 2 was located. Today we have a different names for each quarry. We can tell how long someone has lived in the area by the names they give the quarries. For many the "cat lady quarry," the "icebox quarry," or the "Ludwig Quarry" are unfamiliar names. Each new generation seems to find their own names for the special quarry of their childhood, that secret place for fishing or spending time with friends.

Michael reports fifty quarries recorded in the Des Plaines River Valley between Sag Bridge and Joliet. Others existed but have been lost by urban expansion.[24] Some of our local quarries were: Brown's in 1848; Roughnot in the Sag in 1850; Illinois Stone and Lime owned by A. S. Sherman in 1851; Horace Singer Quarry in 1852, joined by Mancell Talcott in 1854; and D. Skelly's Quarry in 1854. Later operations included the Walker Quarry in the 1860s; Chicago and Lemont Stone Company in 1879; Bodenshatz and Earnshaw in 1872; Boyer and Corneau in 1870; Excelsior and Riordan in the 1880s; Kirby and Howe in 1878; Clowery and Reid in 1878; and Morrison in 1878.

The number of quarries continued to increase until the beginning of the 1880s when an era of mergers created larger companies. The main syndicate occurred in 1889 when the Singer and Talcott Company and five other firms were absorbed by Martin Madden into the giant Western Stone Company. The stone industry, like much of American industry in this period, became a monopoly to control labor and prices.[25]

No one has the exact figures on the economic value of the quarries over the years. A.T. Andreas wrote that in 1884 the estimated output of stone per year was 2,500,000 dollars and the number of men employed was over 2,000.[26] This number excludes those working as masons or barge men transporting the stone. Multiply that year over the 80 years of major quarry operations and one can understand how so many men became very wealthy from the stone trade. Few, however, were workers.

ENDNOTES

[1]Bessie Pierce, *A History of Chicago* (New York: Knopf, 1940), vol.1, p. 128.

[2]William Cronon, *Nature's Metropolis: Chicago and the Great West* (New York: W.W. Norton & Company, 1991), p. 114.

[3]*Ibid.*, p. 111.

[4]*Ibid*, p. 120.

[5]*Ibid.*, p. 120.

[6]Vincent Michael & Deborah Slayton, *Joliet-Lemont Limestone* (Chicago: Landmarks Preservation Society, 1988), p. 2.

[7]George Woodruff, *A History of Will County* (Evansville: Unigraphics, 1976), p. 436.

[8]Michael & Slayton, *Joliet-Lemont Limestone*, p. 6.

[9]Charles Rosenburg, *The Cholera Years* (Chicago: University of Chicago, 1962), p. 205.

[10]Carl Condit, *The Chicago School of Architecture* (Chicago: University of Chicago, 1973), p. 8. Augustine Taylor is credited with developing this vernacular form in 1833. He used it in building the first St. Mary's Church in Chicago. A form of it is still the basic home building style in the Midwest.

[11]Pierce, *A History of Chicago,* vol. 1, p. 147; A.T. Andreas, *History of Cook County Illinois: 1885* (Evansville: Unigraphics, 1976), p. 337.

[12]Michael & Slayton, *Joliet-Lemont Limestone*, p. 4. The stone is also known as Waukesha Dolomite. See Amy D. Alberts, "The Rise and Fall of a Building Stone," *Looking For Lemont*, ed. Michael Conzen and Carl Zimring (Chicago: University of Chicago, 1994), pp. 51-65.

[13]J. E. Lamar, *Handbook on Limestone and Dolomite For Illinois Quarry Operators* (Springfield: State Geological Survey, 1967), pp. 49-52. This handbook presents the problems that quarry owners face in dealing with water flow and illustrates the extent of waterflow systems in limestone bedrock.

[14]Sonia Kallick, *Lemont Stone* (Lemont: Lemont Area Historical Society, 1975)

[15]Lamar, *Handbook on Limestone,* p. 89. The author relates the problems that chert nodules present when using limestone for concrete aggregate.

[16]A.T. Andreas, *History of Cook County* (Evansville: Unigraphics, 1976), p. 850.

[17]The process is happening faster today because of acid rain in our environment.

[18]Harry Hansen, *Rivers of America: The Chicago* (New York: Rinehart & Company, 1942), pp. 298-299.

[19]Michael & Slayton, *Joliet-Lemont Limestone*, p. 6.

[20]*Ibid*.

[21]Kallick, *Lemont Stone.* See *Sears Roebuck and Co.* Fall 1900, reproduction (Northfield, IL: Digest Books Inc., 1970), p. 13.

[22]The origin of the word quarry is from old French *quarriere* meaning a squared stone.

[23]Andreas, *History of Cook County,* p. 851.

[24]Michael & Slayton, *Joliet-Lemont Limestone*, p. 6.

[25]*Ibid.*, p. 5.

[26]Andreas, *History of Cook County,* p. 851.

PARTIAL LIST OF STRUCTURES CONSTRUCTED WITH DES PLAINES VALLEY DOLOMITE

Chicago

St. James Episcopal Church 1857
First Presbyterian Church 1857
Old University Of Chicago 1857–1865
Holy Family Catholic Church 1860
Chicago Water Tower 1869
First Congregational Church 1869
First K. A. M. Temple 1891
Holy Name Cathedral 1875
Union Stockyards Gate
Breakwater, Lake Shore Drive & 31st Street
Freight House, Illinois Central 1855,1872
Central Music Hall 1879

Evanston

Northwestern University First Building 1855

Springfield

State Capitol Building

East Lansing, Michigan

State Capitol Building

Joliet

Joliet Public Library
Illinois State Penitentiary 1858
St. Mary Carmelite Catholic Church 1882
St. Peter's Lutheran Church 1884

Christ Episcopal Church 1886

Auditorium Building 1891

Joliet Township High School East Side 1900

All Saints Greek Orthodox Church 1918

Lockport

Gaylord Building 1838–1859

Congregational Church 1870

Milne House 1842

Norton Building 1855

Methodist Church 1855

St. John's Episcopal Church 1873

Central School 1898

St. Dennis Catholic Church

Alton Train Station 1858

Lemont

St. James Of The Sag 1859

Old Methodist Church 1861

Old Central School 1869–1896

Village Hall 1893

St. Matthew's Lutheran 1887

Bethany Lutheran 1895

St. Patrick's Catholic Church 1895

Lemont Water Works 1891

Alton Station 1858

St. James Academy 1885

111 Stephens Street

107 Stephens Street

101 Stephens Street

102 Stephens Street

Brown Barn at Rock Creek Center 1840

Home at Lemont and Lockport Streets

John Kettering Home 1859

CHAPTER ELEVEN

THE QUARRY WORKER AND THE LABOR MOVEMENT

1850-1882

When the quarry trade began in the 1850s, wages for labor were $1.25 a day for a 12-hour day, a modest but adequate pay for the cost of living then. With a slow but steady demand for the stone, the working conditions were hard but not harsh. Often the owner would work along with his men in a paternalistic arrangement, so there was little labor unrest. If a worker did not like quarry work, he could find work elsewhere as jobs were plentiful.

As Athens Marble became fashionable, other quarries opened and a greater demand was put on the local labor force to produce more at a faster rate. However, the workers available were few, and they were independent. Those with their own farms were not eager to put up with the demands of the owners without a pay increase. The economic conditions at the time were so good that the *Weekly Daily Democrat* for October of 1853 could suggest:

> Let the starving thousands of our eastern cities whom poverty is driving to crime and the almshouse, swarm and scatter over the busy teeming West.[1]

This lack of a competitive labor force led the Lemont quarry workers to form a loose local union as early as 1854 to standardize wages. They asked for a raise from $1.25 a day to $1.50 a day. In response, the quarry owners, many ex-canal contractors, resorted to the old methods they had used to get workers for the I & M Canal. They recruited the poor from the East and foreign immigrants, who had been coming to America in increasing numbers since the 1850s. These newer groups included more Irish and German along with Scandinavians, English, Scots, Welsh, Dutch, Poles, Czechs, Bohemians, and Austrians. They came willing to take any job at any wage. For those who did not speak English, quarry work was ideal because language skills were not necessary to learn the trade.

As newcomers were hired, at a lower wage, the older workers were laid off and violence and intimidation became a tool for preventing production. Quarry employers who continued to hire men unacceptable to local workers often found their quarries disrupted by strikers. In June of 1854, when seasoned Lemont quarry workers beat up and drove out those who had replaced them, the situation became so tense that the sheriff with a "sufficient retinue thoroughly armed and provided with cords, handcuffs, and other implements were called to the scene of the disturbance."[2] The quarries affected were those of Singer and Talcott, David Skelley, and the Illinois Stone and Lime Company.

A quarry worker. Detail of a mural at Canal and Stephens Streets. Mural done by Caryl Yasko as part of the Bicentennial Celebration of 1976. (Illustration courtesy of Lemont Historical Society and the artist)

The presence of the police stopped the disturbance and only those wishing to work for the lower wage returned to the quarries. Some leaders of the strike were blacklisted by the local owners, since they were known to everyone in a small town like Lemont. They were not allowed to work again for any of the local companies.

The year 1854 was only the prelude to a constant social and labor struggle that would continue in Lemont, and the country, through the remainder of the century. Tension became worse in a short time. By 1857, the nation went into another cyclic financial decline and economic conditions forced quarry owners to lay off many immigrants they had encouraged to come to Lemont. Wages were again lowered and Lemont's national groups began fighting to control the ethnic makeup of certain quarries. The owners did not try to stop this ethnic infighting; in fact, they indirectly encouraged it. By dividing the various quarry sites and placing them under the control of the Irish, Swedes, Germans, or Poles, the owners could break up any effective collective action by the workers.

Those were years when the Lemont quarry workers spent as much time hating and distrusting their own neighbors as the quarry owners. Our village developed stronger ethnic enclaves than had existed before: there was a Polish section, a German section, a Scandinavian section, a Yankee-English section, and an Irish section. Naturally, some of this separation came about because of language, cultural, and religious differences, but much of it was economic in origin, based on the quarry industry.[3] As early as 1850, these residential patterns show up in the census. Lemont then was a small community of about 200 people, yet there are five Irish families living next to each other, two German families together, and the native born Americans in a separate section.

Besides dividing on ethnic lines, the village also divided itself on social lines. This is true, of course, of most towns even today. In early Lemont the social division of the town was based on our geography. Those with more money moved to the higher parts of town. Lemont's development was on three geographical levels. The "flats,"[4] the canal, and the railroad became the section of commercial stores, industry, banking, saloons, stables, and hotels. The middle section, south of the railroad, became the site of early homes, schools, churches, and government institutions. Finally, the upper level became mainly residential except for a few churches and schools.[5]

Most quarry workers lived in town in the small worker cottages we still see today. Others lived in boarding homes, while others stayed at the quarry sites in dormitory housing, or in simple cabins rented to the workers by the companies. Life for the quarry worker was hard and seasonal. Weather was a factor in the amount of money that could be earned, so on good days, quarry workers were willing to put in 12 hours a day. All quarries closed for the winter months,[6] so they were glad to have days when they could work.

Quarry workers. (Photo courtesy of Lemont Historical Society)

There was no pay for rainy days and there were a number of bad years, such as 1873, when the season did not last more than five months.

Workers and their families had to have other jobs to tide them over the lean months. Those who owned land could farm, but most of the second wave of immigrants to Lemont could not afford to buy land. For the men, winter often meant working at odd jobs in the community. Many women did piece-work sewing to bring in income and, as a result, Lemont developed small garment shops and became known as a needle town. Over the years there were a number of local shops that made vests and pants for the ready-to-wear trade. These shops originated as an extension of the simple cottage industry of sewing by lamplight, after the children were in bed, by tired women trying to add to the meager incomes of their quarry worker husbands.

The quarry worker continued to work a ten to 12 hour day for $1.25 until the immediate post-Civil War period when pay was raised to $1.75 for a short time. This daily routine continued without complaint, although the years from the 1850s to the 1870s were years of tremendous upheaval in America and Lemont. The demands of the Civil War had industrialized the North and had changed manufacturing from simple small shops to large product-intensive companies. As a result, tensions developed between labor and capital that were, in part, a direct result of the push to produce for the war effort.

This pressure extended to the quarries toward the end of the war as construction increased in the Chicago area. Meanwhile, the cost of living also increased, much faster than the workers' wages. Clothing costs went up 100 percent, fuel from 80 to 122 percent, and some foodstuffs rose as much as 133 percent.[7] Conditions were so difficult that many workers joined the Union Army, most out of a conviction for the cause, but some as bounty men to serve for others, either to collect the bounty money or for the steady Army pay. For example, Lemont's set enlistment quota for 1864 was 33, but 273 men enlisted.

It was because of these conditions and the ethnic divisions in the community that little was done in the way of collective organizing by the quarry workers during the 1860s. After the war, the returning veterans added to the labor pool and began demands for an eight-hour day. This led to passage of legislation in Illinois in 1867 to establish such a limit on the work day, but employers got around the law by beginning to pay by the hour rather than the day. This action to bypass state law caused some labor groups to unify over the issue. Bessie Pierce writes that fear of this unity of purpose caused employers to defend their action by claiming they objected to the eight-hour law on the ground that shorter hours mean a lower standard of living, "They suggested that under the plan work-men and capitalists must suffer a diminution of wealth in the same proportion."[8]

Some Lemont quarry owners worked together to control wages. Edwin Walker, Singer and Talcott, and Illinois Stone and Lime tried to get around the law by offering to raise wages from a new high of $1.75 for an eight-hour day to $2.25 for a volunteer 10-hour day.[9]

On May 1, 1867, thousands of laborers marched in Chicago to celebrate the passage of the eight-hour law and as a warning to all those employers who planned to violate the law. Many went out on strike as the industrialists generally ignored the ruling, but the quarry workers agreed to the owners' conditions and continued to work.

The general strike failed within a week and organized labor suffered a serious blow. However, the eight-hour a day issue was not dead. It would return to Lemont, Chicago, and the nation.

There were many positive economic factors in Lemont during the first years following the Civil War, up to the panic of 1873. Construction in Chicagoland rebounded and much of it was built of Athens Marble, which added to the popularity of our stone. The economic boom in the trade led to expansion. It was reported that at this time:

> The quarry firms began the general pattern of American business expansion . . . Singer and Talcott had grown from its modest beginnings in 1852 to one of the largest in the region with some 800 acres of quarries and excellent transportation facilities on the new Chicago and Alton Railroad as well as the I & M Canal. Using rapidly advancing technology and management skills, the firm was an industry leader in the 1870s. It had yards and offices in two locations in Chicago and regularly carried a large stock of smooth, sawn, and dressed dimension limestone, as well as curbing, coping, and paving blocks.[10]

The Chicago Fire of 1871 helped the quarry trade. There was some post-fire rumbling that limestone was not able to hold up under high temperatures since the new Court House was destroyed by flames. However, it soon became evident that no known material could have withstood the holocaust. Dolomite stone was in great demand for rebuilding the portion of the city that burned. This was due to post-fire pressure to develop fireproof regulations for Chicago's city center by banning wooden buildings and sidewalks.[11]

The Cook County section of the Chicago Court House was rebuilt with Athens Marble facing from the Walker Quarry, a huge contract that offered work for many Lemont quarrymen. Interestingly, the city section of the courthouse was built with limestone from Bedford, Indiana, instead of the Des Plaines Valley quarries, a decision that foreshadowed future economic problems for the Illinois limestone industry.[12]

In spite of increased sales and expansion, the lot of the quarry workers did not change because by the time conditions were reflected in the workers' pay, the national economy again went into a severe depression, so that by 1873 "the growth of industry, which had been stimulated by the city's rebuilding stopped dead in its tracks. Closing banks swept away the savings of thrifty thousands and even the rich were touched."[13] Those who were employed had a choice between taking a lower wage or striking for the same pay. The strikes generally failed because there was always someone willing to work for the lower wage. So the Lemont quarry workers continued under the existing conditions without any attempt at organization or concerted action.

The worst time in Chicago was in 1877 when Eastern rail workers went on strike for higher wages and halted almost all rail traffic. Rail workers in Lemont joined in the action. The size of this movement forced the public to recognize the potential power that organized labor could have on the nation's economy. A review of the economic impact of the 1877 walkout on Illinois pointed out that if each of the 68,244 rail employees in the state had a family of three, about one-twelfth of the state's population was directly cut off from an income.[14] Rioting broke out in the East and many became afraid of violence. The situation brought together the radical labor elements of Chicagoland such as Albert Parsons, George Schilling, and August Spies. They took advantage of the strike to push for a socialistic approach to labor/capital relations.

Parsons was a good speaker who could move a crowd with his attacks on the "capitalist press." To a meeting of strikers in 1877 he said:

> If the proprietor has a right to fix the wages and say what labor is worth . . . then we are bound hand and foot slaves, and we should be perfectly happy; content with a bowl of rice and a rat a week apiece . . . For the sake of our wives and children and our self respect, let us wait no longer! Organize at once.[15]

Newspapers warned of "civil war" in Chicago and the Illinois Militia and police were put on alert. Industries and store owners hired armed guards to protect their property. Fear was so rampant that Field, Leiter & Company[16] even armed their employees. When the Chicago rail men marched it resulted in two confrontations, both near railyards, one at 16th and Halsted and the other at Archer and Halsted. The result was 13 dead and scores injured, but the trains began to roll again.

The most important result of this strike in Lemont and the nation was that it divided the worker from the employer and the conservative middle class from the striker. It began a philosophical struggle within the labor movement itself, and it convinced many citizens that the militia and police should be increased to protect both public and property from mob action.

In Lemont there were few radical labor men, mainly the older Irish and German workers. All that most quarry workers wanted was to make a living and have some security, and this was not easy as owners sometimes withheld money due them. In 1878, the *Chicago Tribune* reported that:

> Walker, the County Courthouse contractor, is again in trouble. He has had a serious time getting money from the county. He [finally] got 30,000 dollars a few days ago, however his . . . employees at Lemont are having a hard time getting him to pay them. They struck Monday and threaten to do all manner of ugly things unless they get their pay. Walker claims that he went down and paid them on Tuesday night, but those who know Walker, also know the many uses he has for the money . . . What has Walker done with the $30,000?[17]

In spite of the social and labor agitation around them, it would take from the 1854 strike to 1882 for the Lemont quarry workers to join across ethnic lines in an action against the owners.

In April of 1882, with the opening of the quarries many workers, dissatisfied with their pay that had returned to the old wage of $1.50 for a 10-hour day, demanded $2.00 a day. This was not an unreasonable request as inflation was, again, a serious problem. Between 1879 and 1881 food prices rose from 50 to 100 percent and all other living costs from 15 to 40 percent.[18]

Without a pay increase, the workers found themselves losing ground in an attempt to feed their families. The only grim alternatives open were either to work harder and longer, or eat less food and wear less clothing.[19]

The quarry owners ignored their request, so a small group of workers decided to walk out. The first quarry affected was the Walker Quarry, but within four days all quarrying in town was halted, with 800 to 1,000 men joining the original group. It was their intention to return in ten days, feeling that they could make the point with a simple walkout. The Illinois Department of Labor summarized the event:

> In fact they reduced their demand to $1.75 per day before the strike became general, but this was refused by the employers on the ground that it was premature, and that they would pay that sum on the 1st of May, in any event. The 10th of April was pay day, and the men drew only from 20 to 30 dollars, all that was coming to them for the month . . . The employers supposed that the men were too poor to stand a strike or walkout any length of time. Indeed it was said that the bosses were glad for the strike as the weather was unfavorable.[20]

The strikers avoided any violence, although some leaders were singled out and taken to Chicago for trial, charged with damage to property and inciting to riot. All were acquitted. As the strike dragged on, organizers from the Joliet *Knights of Labor* came to town and signed up workers into the order. The Knights were founded in 1869 as an attempt to put all workers, regardless of trade, into one big union. It was an organization with rituals loosely based on Freemasonry. They believed the workers could escape from the wage system with the producer's cooperation, popular education, and a union of all workers.[21] The only professions who could not belong were lawyers, physicians, bankers, saloonkeepers, gamblers, and stockbrokers.

Many in Lemont joined under the impression that they would get moral and financial support from the organization. Nothing came of this, however, as the Knights were a con-

Edwin Walker's home, Woodland Park, circa 1860s. The house was torn down during the 1990s, after tornado damage. (Photo courtesy of Lemont Historical Society)

servative group that did not support militant unionism. Still, the Lemont quarry owners feared the *Knights of Labor* and refused to hire anyone who remained in the organization. Some workers, loyal to the idea of collective action but who needed money, quit the quarries and went to work for the Chicago and Alton Railroad for $1.35 a day. Some others found work in the Joliet and Lockport quarries. Even with the hardships brought on by the strike, it must be said that very few of the men who joined the Knights resumed work in the quarries. They continued the strike because they felt a need to remain together in a brotherhood against the quarry owners.

As the days passed without any stone being cut or shipped, the owners decided to break the strike. "By great efforts the 'bosses' got Italians and other non-union men to go to work; but, many of these quit after they became aware that they were brought to take the places of men on strike."[22]

Edwin Walker went out of his way to try to keep the strike breakers working. He even housed them in tents and shacks on his estate, Woodland Park, on Main Street. Still, most left, a number going to the Romeo and Lockport quarries where they were hiring, since the Lemont quarries were down.[23] Although the owners had trouble finding replacements for the workers, it was the workers who weakened first. They had no way to support themselves and found it necessary to return. "By the 1st of May the strike was over. They had made a strong and orderly fight, but hunger compelled them to succumb."[24]

When the strike ended, the owners of the quarries affected — Walker, Singer & Talcott, Illinois Stone Company, Earnshaw and Bodenschatz, and Boyer and Corneau — decided to allow old workers to come back only if they dropped their membership in the Knights. Surprisingly, some 500 to 600 workers held out against this intimidation and went elsewhere, a tremendous loss to Lemont. This was a sad situation, as the 1883 Illinois Labor Report states, "the difference in wage controversy was only 25 cents a day, while it was well known that the employers doubled their own profit on each man who worked."[25]

The 30-day strike of 1882 caused several changes, some immediate, others that would affect the community in the years to come. First, there was the loss of wages to the strikers and the community. Secondly, it forced many experienced workers and their families to leave. Also, it brought in a new group of immigrants from Europe to fill the vacant jobs left in the quarries. Finally, it did lead most workers to understand that they could organize and work together.

However, this battle was lost, for when it was all over those who remained or were new hires returned to the old pay of $1.50 a day. The owners had won.

There remains the question of how much support the strikers in 1882 received from the community at large. The village administration was headed by D.C. Norton, whose family had extensive quarry holdings here and in Lockport. The village attorneys were William Brown, of the Brown family with its stone connections, and W. Skelly, who also was connected to quarry holdings. These town leaders apparently did little to interfere. However, since most of the stone lands were within the legal jurisdiction of the sheriff of Cook County, controlling the strike probably fell outside the town authorities' jurisdiction.

The community at large was divided in their support. Since so much of the middle class service economy depended on the worker in the stone trade, they too suffered. Some businesses offered credit and support, others did not. The English speaking Protestant church gave little encouragement to the strikers, as most of its powerful members were quarry owners. The non-Anglo speaking Protestant churches had real divisions in their congregations, as some Germans and Scandinavians were shopkeepers and tradesmen, while others were quarry workers. Catholic church members tended to support the strike as many strike leaders were Irish, Polish, or German. In any case it was a painful time in Lemont for all involved. The quarry worker still needed a decent wage and $1.50 a day was not a decent wage.

ENDNOTES

[1] Bessie Pierce, *A History of Chicago* (New York: Knopf, 1940), vol. 2, p. 150.

[2] *Ibid.*, p. 168.

[3] The question of how housing segregation begins can be traced to the natural "pull" of groups to be with those they know and understand. However, under social and economic pressures this pattern soon becomes a "push" to keep others out of the neighborhood.

[4] The area along the river was called the "Flats."

[5] George F. Kaye, "Growth and Development of The Townsite," *Looking For Lemont: People and Places in an Illinois Canal Town*, ed. Michael Conzen and Carl Zimring (Chicago: University of Chicago, 1994), pp. 111-120. This article also has a description of the development of the downtown and its unusual layout.

[6] Some quarry men were able to make money during the winter by cutting ice on the quarries. Ice was an important commodity for summer use. It also gained larger economic importance when the Chicago meat packers developed railroad ice cars for transporting meat.

[7] Pierce, *A History of Chicago*, vol. 2, p. 157.

[8] *Ibid.*, p. 178.

[9] *Ibid.*

[10]Vincent Michael and Deborah Slayton, *Joliet-Lemont Limestone* (Chicago: Landmarks Preservation Society, 1986), p. 8.

[11]Pierce, *A History of Chicago,* vol. 2, p. 308.

[12]Michael and Slayton, *Joliet-Lemont Limestone,* p. 8.

[13]Pierce, *A History of Chicago,* vol. 2, p. 240.

[14]*Ibid*, vol. 2, p. 245.

[15]*Ibid.*, p. 246.

[16]Present Marshall Field's store.

[17]*Chicago Tribune*, June 6, 1878. The *Tribune* had a campaign going about the cost overruns on the courthouse, and much of their displeasure was directed at the contractors.

[18]Pierce, *A History of Chicago,* vol. 2, p. 240.

[19]*Ibid*.

[20]*Illinois Labor Report For 1882* (Springfield: Labor Division, 1883), p. 266.

[21]Samuel Morison, *The Oxford History of the American People* (New York: New American Library, 1972), vol. 3, pp. 80-82.

[22]*Illinois Labor Report,* p. 266.

[23]This group was part of the beginning of the Italian community in Lockport today.

[24]*Illinois Labor Report,* p. 266.

[25]*Ibid*.

U.S. HISTORY

1850: President Zachary Taylor Dies — Millard Fillmore Takes over — California Becomes a State — U.S. Population at 23 Million; of That Number 3.2 Million are Slaves.

1851: Chicago Streets Lighted with Gas.

1852: Wells-Fargo Company Founded — Franklin Pierce is President.

1853: Commodore Perry Arrives in Japan to Try to Open Japanese Ports to U.S. Shipping.

1854: War for "Bleeding Kansas" Struggle between Slave and Free States — Republican Party Forms — Chicago Has 60,652 People.

1855: Western Survey of the Smithsonian Tests Lemont Stone and Declares It Valuable — Cholera Again in Area, 1,424 Die; Many are Taken from Chicago and Buried in St. Patrick's Cemetery in Lemont.

1856: James Buchanan is President — Proslavery Forces Attack the Town of Lawrence, Kansas.

1857: Trans-Atlantic Cable Attempted — Financial Panic in Country, Many Unemployed.

1858: Minnesota Becomes a State — Lincoln-Douglas Debates in Illinois Attract National Attention.

1859: Oregon Becomes a State — John Brown's Raid on Harper's Ferry — First Oil Well in U.S. in Pennsylvania.

LEMONT HISTORY

1850: Downtown Listed As Three Houses and a Few Stores and Taverns — Population of Township Now 210, Some Workers Have Left — Fifty Percent of the Population Children under 16; Place of Birth Listed As: Forty-Five Percent in Ireland, Two Percent in Vermont, Three Percent in Canada, Nineteen Percent New York, Twenty-Four Percent Illinois, Two Percent Michigan, One Percent Scotland and Four Percent Germany — Township Formed This Year: First Called Palmyra, Then Athens, Then Lemont — The Post Office Designation for the Village Went from Keepataw, to Palmyra, to Lemont — Township Supervisor Kettering — Chicago and Alton Survey for Rail Line is Done — Area North of Lemont Active in Underground Railway.

1852: Stage Coach Service Ends — Canal Takes over — Rail Service Will Soon Follow — the Merchants and Mechanics Bank in Chicago is Faced with Lemont Stone — Fad Starts for "Athens Marble" for Facing Buildings — St. James of the Sag Stone Church Construction Begins.

1853: *Alton Station Finished before Tracks Are Laid, Used by Methodists As a Meeting House.*

1854: *Lemont's Second Big Strike; Quarry Workers Want $1.50 a Day instead of $1.25, They Lose — H.S. Hall is Supervisor — H.M. Singer is Postmaster.*

1856: *T. Bracken is Supervisor — D.C. Skelly Made Captain of the Emmet Guards — 1.5 Million Dollars of Stone Shipped from Lemont.*

1858: *Alton Runs First Train to Joliet — Methodists Formally Organize.*

1859: *S.W. Norton's Founded in Front of the Family Grain Warehouse on Stephens Street — Six Canal Boats List Lemont as Home Port.*

CHAPTER TWELVE

TRANSPORTATION IN LEMONT
THE RAILROAD ARRIVES
THE CHICAGO AND ALTON RAILROAD

Local historians like to point out that as early as 1836, when construction began on the I & M Canal, plans were being made to form a rail company between Galena and Chicago. The idea was to use the line to bring farm products and Galena lead ore to the city. It had a shaky start but the first miles of that rail line were laid by 1848. The line ran from Chicago due west to the Des Plaines River.

The advantage of the railroad for delivering goods to the city soon became clear to farmers not located near water systems. Local roads were often muddy or dusty and it took time away from farm chores to carry goods to market. Businessmen of that time observed that it took a farmer on the Rock River five days just to bring an average sized wagon load of thirty bushels of wheat to market, so the cost of the journey "took off nearly all of the profits. Along the way there could be rain and unbridged streams . . . often resulting in grain that was dirty and damaged when it reached the market."[1]

From 1850 to 1860, over 25,000 miles of track were laid in the United States. By 1860 there were over 2,500 miles of rail in Illinois. The first line through Lemont was where the Main Street Metra Station stands. This landmark depot was built of our local stone in the middle 1850s, making it one of the oldest railroad stations in continuous use in the Chicago area. The building is a simple vernacular structure with the only design elements the wooden bracket decorations under the roof. Completed even before the rail line reached Lemont, the building was first used by the young Methodist Congregation as a meeting house before they built their own church on Lemont Street in 1861.

The Chicago, Alton and St. Louis line was constructed from 1847 to 1858. Built by Captain Benjamin Godfrey, it was started in Alton in 1852 and ran to Springfield. By 1853, tracks were laid to Bloomington with stations planned every ten miles whether or not towns existed along the route. It mattered little that some stations were built in unsettled areas because the presence of a rail stop meant a town would soon spring up.

After a good deal of political infighting, since railroad franchises were a big business, the Alton was allowed to build and operate a line from Bloomington to Chicago by 1854. This rail went through Joliet and Will County, bypassing the Des Plaines Valley. Here in our section there was political and economic pressure both for and against the railroad entering the valley. Canal interests had developed shipping markets along the route and were not eager to share them with the train lines. The I & M Canal Commissioners even suggested that the canal receive compensation for freight lost to the railroad. However, the courts ruled that the right of eminent domain could not be exercised in the case of

The Chicago and Alton Railroad, looking east, circa 1900. (Photo courtesy of Lemont Historical Society)

land already granted for public use, as with the canal. The railroad was successful in condemnation proceedings for the right to construct their road through canal lands without payment of tolls.[2]

Those who favored canal and rail competition in the Des Plaines Valley felt it would lower the cost of shipping and open the area to new manufacturing. The Alton line would be another means of delivering coal, an important energy source, from the newly developed mines in the LaSalle-Peru area — coal that could be shipped through the winter months for gas plants, since Chicago had gas lighting by 1851. Coal was also needed for steam power and heat. Economic pressure worked and the rail interests won. A line extension was built paralleling the I & M Canal through the Des Plaines Valley.

The first train through Lemont was on January 1, 1858, and the presence of the railroad did lead to strong competition with the canal. It offered a better and faster means of transportation for passengers and freight and also became a source of jobs for townspeople. Lumber contracts were let for wood used for construction of the ties and for engine fuel, until coal came into general use. Our local oak and hickory woods were a good source of income, as demonstrated by Lemont's 1850 census which lists seven townsmen as sawyers.[3] Much of Lemont's forested area was cut not only to supply lumber for homes but also for the railroad. Cutting our local timber also opened more land for farming. For example, William Derby, one of the township's first settlers, cut 20 acres of timber land in his section for a profit of $3,000 which was a great deal of money at the time. He then sold the land for farming at $12.50 an acre, considerably more than the going price of uncleared land, which was $2.00 to $6.00 an acre.

The Chicago and Alton line also influenced the economy by buying limestone for the railbeds, hiring telegraph operators, ticket agents, freight handlers, and work crews to repair the track. William Cronon writes in *Nature's Metropolis* that the railroad changed time, space, and capital investment. Time changed as Lemonters could now travel to Chicago in an hour and the city became a place to purchase goods and services not available in town. Space changed with the connections between cities and the rural areas. Railroads installed telegraphs and our local operator in the Alton Station was in touch with events in other parts of the nation, so that the news of the country became immediately available to the community. Capital investment changed with the development of huge corporations needed to raise money to build railroads. It was clear that "by 1860, the total investment in canals, which had been the largest comparable corporate enterprises, was still less than $200 million . . . while [the] railroad investment . . . had already passed $1.1 billion."[4]

The completion of the railroad led to a second economic boom in Lemont, the first being the completion of the I & M Canal. Our population tripled in size and new commercial and service ventures began. The Alton Line became a major route for shipping farm produce from the Des Plaines Valley, and Lemont became a center for such shipments. Downers Grove Township and West Lemont Township developed an important dairy industry that depended on fast delivery to Chicago. The township *Agriculture Census for 1860* shows the need for good transportation facilities to bring our local products to market. The canal alone could not have carried the volume of both stone and farm products produced. In 1860, our area farms raised 20,429 bushels of corn, 10,410 bushels of oats, and 1,694 bushels of wheat. Add to this production the cattle, sheep, and hogs, and it is evident the railroad filled a position in the economy of the town.[5]

The effect of having two transportation corridors can be seen in the number of new businesses and trades developed between 1850 and 1860. In 1850, the township tradesmen include 25 farmers, eight laborers, seven sawyers, one merchant, and one carpenter. We also had seven lawyers, a sign that there was active legal work in land acquisitions and disputes.[6] By 1860 Lemont had two agricultural implement dealers, one baker, four blacksmiths, and four boot and shoe manufacturers and dealers. There also were three butchers, three clothing stores, one retail and three wholesale druggists, two flour and grain dealers, one freight agent, two retail grocers, and three hotels. Added to the list for 1860 were one lawyer, one machinist, two physicians, one plow maker, two produce and commission merchants, two real estate agents, one storage and commission merchant, and three wheelwrights. The population growth in turn triggered the development of the building trades in Lemont. There were four architects, nine carpenters, two nail dealers, one house painter, one paint dealer, one glass dealer, and one sash, door and blind company.[7]

With the coming of the railroad, the Alton Station area became the center of commercial, political, and social activity, moving much of the main business of the community from the canal on Stephens Street to the junction of State and Main and along Main Street. Aside from the attraction of the railroad, another reason for moving activity away from the I & M Canal was the condition of its waters. During periods when the flow was sluggish, the stench of the water often became overpowering.

The biggest appeal of the railroad in Lemont and outlying towns was for passenger travel. To try to compete, the I & M lowered tolls, but in doing so lost revenue needed to maintain the canal banks. The railroad station became the place to see friends, get news, or simply get the sense of life flowing by. Train travel also developed a new type of profession, the Drummer, a traveling salesman who represented a product, a retail establishment, or his own goods. If he worked for a company, he was paid a commission based on sales orders. If he owned his own stock, he often carried his goods with him.

The Drummer was transient, unlike the traditional door-to-door salesmen who made regular rounds selling notions and household items. Traditional salesmen traveled the same routes for years and would work the area until they acquired enough capital to become independent. Salim Forzley did just that, arriving in Lemont in 1912, first selling from a backpack, then buying a wagon and finally establishing his own store in 1926.[8]

The Drummer was part of the new unattached world of commerce. They "scoured the landscape using every conceivable hard-sell technique to gain orders for themselves, or their firms . . . so successful were the Chicago wholesalers in dominating the market that the Eastern Drummers gradually withdrew from the field. One could recognize them instantly in any rail station with a grip sack and a sample case in hand."[9] These Drummers were important to merchants in the larger cities because they represented the big business that sent them. Our Lemont merchants were upset with their presence because they could offer products at a cheaper price and sometimes sold goods directly to the public. What the Drummer did represent was "big city ways." He wore fashionable clothes and was part of the adventure of travel. He knew the latest gossip along the train line and had a stock of jokes, many risque. He became part of American culture. Part of the legacy remains in the old familiar opening line, "Did you hear this one? There was a farmer's daughter and a traveling salesman, [you fill in the rest]."

Lemont learned a bit about this trade in the spring of 1897. As the train approached town a Drummer sat and glanced at his flashing reflection in the window of the Chicago and Alton coach. He was dressed in the fashion of the day, a jacket of striped wool, brown vest with a gold watch and chain, a stiff shirt, linen cuffs, and highly polished shoes. He knew one of the first requirements of a good salesman was fine clothes; the other, harder to come by, was a sense of self confidence. He had traveled the Alton Railroad towns trying to peddle fancy silk pongee ties at $1.50 each. Economic times were such that $1.50 was a day's wage for unskilled labor. Besides that, the ties, although silk, were of colors and patterns that would not sell in more sophisticated towns. He needed a plan.

When the train pulled into the station he glanced down Main Street and saw the usual Saturday crowd at Lemont and Main, in front of Otzenburger's Hall. The smooth Drummer approached the Lemonters. His soft hands drew out a 50-cent piece and addressing the crowd he began, "Who will buy this 50 cents for a quarter?" Silence greeted his opening, but he had their attention. "Come on. No one wants 50 cents for a quarter?"

A farmer jokingly produced a quarter. The Drummer took it and handed over the 50-cent piece. The farmer examined it carefully. It was genuine. The crowd circled. What was this salesman up to? More eager hands pressed money on him. He made a few transactions. The next step was easy. He pulled out a bill. "Who will buy this dollar for 50 cents?" Many more responded and he made two sales of a dollar for 50 cents. Now came the "decisive moment." He opened his case of garish ties. As he held a "genuine pongee silk tie" in one hand, he pulled out a 10-dollar bill, a week's wage for a quarry worker. He rolled the bill and placed it in the folds of the tie. The crowd listened as his voice rose and fell. "Now, friends, I place a bill in this tie. Who will give me $2.50 for the necktie?"

Two dollars and fifty cents for ten, they scrambled to buy the ties. Those who failed to get the great bargain begged for the same deal. So the Drummer folded more money, very swiftly, into more ties as customers bought them feeling the folds for the familiar crinkle. A few peeked into the folds, looked puzzled, but remained silent as they watched friends and neighbors purchase the "bargain ties." The Drummer sold out just in time to catch the next Chicago bound train. The new tie owners soon discovered what some knew already, but did not reveal for fear of feeling foolish. The money in the fold was only one dollar, not the expected 10 dollars. Those who recalled the Drummer's words remembered he had said, "a bill." They had failed to listen carefully in their eagerness to gain something for nothing. The *Lemont Observer* could not resist commenting on the event by saying that "very high fashion for this spring in Lemont consists of very silly looks and garish pongee silk ties."

In the early days travel on trains was not comfortable. The strap iron rails often became unspiked and curled up. Called "snakeheads," these rails could puncture the floor of the cars and cause serious injury. Sometimes trains running through rural areas would derail because the tracks had been stolen, since iron was scarce and expensive and the rail straps were useful on the farm. Riding on the strap iron rails was bumpy and cars swayed a good deal. The ride was finally improved with the introduction of steel rails in 1865. This steel needed for the rail tracks added to the economy of our valley with the creation of the Joliet Iron and Steel Company in 1873. The company was formed in the Des Plaines Valley because transportation routes brought ores from Lake Superior, coal from the Illinois Valley, and limestone from our quarries.[10]

Living near the railroad was not pleasant. Soot, smoke, and noise created problems. The term "the other side of the tracks" certainly held true for any area near the rail line. This led many Lemonters with money to move away from the downtown to the bluffs above town. Land near the track also became important for commerce, thus driving out residential housing. Early Lemont newspapers write of frequent grass fires started by hot cinders and ashes from passing trains. In 1897, cinders actually set fire to a building that backed up to the tracks on Canal Street.

Rail crossings were real hazards. Unguarded tracks in rural areas had many serious accidents. Horses often bolted when trains approached. Most villages had gatekeepers to prevent such disasters. Lemont had a crossing guard and gate stationed at Stephens and Canal Streets, but that arrangement did not always stop death and injury from speeding trains.

An interesting thing about the operation of the early trains was the fact that rates were often set by the station manager. It was in his power to decide the costs for shipping. In the summer and spring freight rates were kept artificially low because of competition with the canal tolls. When winter arrived and canals could not operate, the price for shipping by rail was increased. Before the railroad, all products from Lemont were shipped on the canal, or by wagon, including grains, produce, livestock, and stone. Grains would be stored at Norton's or Teden's and shipped when the canal rates were low. However, the long narrow barges were not built to hold huge volumes like freight cars. Thus, the total amount of grain that could be moved on the canal sometimes did not offset increased rail rates. There is no question that the tolls on the canal were cheaper — in 1870 during the navigation season corn could be shipped from Henry, 130 miles from Chicago, for five cents a bushel. Over the Rock Island Railroad, it was seven cents a bushel and after the close of the season on the canal it rose to ten cents. In places without water transportation, the price was eleven to fourteen cents a bushel.

A clue to the shift in agriculture development in Lemont by the 1870s and 1880s lies in the fact that were no grain storage facilities built in town along the Chicago and Alton Road. By that time many of our farmers had switched to cattle and hog production, using most of their grain to feed the livestock. To accommodate these animals, the railroad built large holding pens stretching westward from the station.

While most livestock and farm produce in Lemont shifted to the railroad, the I & M Canal here continued shipping stone. The canal ran along most of our major quarries and it took only one loading and unloading of the cut stone to get it to the yards in Chicago. It can be said that the canal that led to the discovery of dolomite in the valley created the very industry that helped prolonged the life of the I & M Canal as a vital part of the commerce of our region.

Because the Alton Railroad station became an economic center of town, it has been the focal point of many historic events in Lemont history. From there our Lemont men went off to fight the Civil War, the Spanish-American War, and World War I. One sad moment took place May 2, 1865, when Abraham Lincoln passed through Lemont. Around 11:10 p.m., a new Pullman car train approached town from the east traveling at 20 mph, but slowed as torches and lanterns of the people at the crossings appeared along the tracks. Lemonters, old and young, rich and poor, stood silently in the rain and mud. Some tossed spring flowers on the track. All came to bid farewell to their slain president as his funeral train passed the Alton Station on his last trip home to Springfield.

In spite of the early success of the railroads, many lines were overbuilt and under-capitalized. The westward expansion of trackage grew faster than the volume of goods that could be drawn from the prairie farms. Eastern lines did well, as they had a populated region and moved goods to their own markets. Most of the capital for lines west of Chicago came from money men in the East. When they did not get the fast return expected, they often sold out and consolidated with other lines. The Chicago and Alton ran into financial difficulties early and the line was sold to Samuel Tilden.[11] Tilden's group also had problems raising money and this prevented further expansion and improvement on the line. As a result, the route from Chicago to Joliet through the Des Plaines Valley was not improved after its opening and fifteen years later still consisted of only one main track and several smaller side tracks. This situation led to the "Wreck of '73," an early tragedy of railroading.

August 16, 1873, was a foggy Saturday evening, the type of thick ground fog that clings to our valley on cool summer evenings. Lemont's station agent was concerned about the weather and went to check the track before returning to the depot to visit with the dispatcher. The telegraph was silent as they gossiped to pass the evening.

Meanwhile, in Joliet, Edward Beane, the freight conductor of Engine No. 122, guided his train of coal cars out of the station. He glanced at his engineer, Joseph Mitchey, an experienced trainman from Jerseyville. Experienced trainmen were hard to find because the economic difficulties of the 1870s caused the railroad to hire cheap labor and men unfamiliar with the route. This night there were two new brakemen, Jacob Claussner and John Metzger. Neither man had worked the Chicago and Alton route before.

Conductor Beane assumed all this responsibility for three dollars a trip. On good months, with enough trips, he could make 90 dollars a month. He and his fellow trainmen were unhappy with the pay, the poor condition of the equipment, and the dirty hotels rented for their layovers, yet, there was little they could do about the situation as jobs were hard to get. The freight moved northward to Chicago at 20 mph, as there were only a few patches of fog in the Joliet-Lockport part of the valley.

In Chicago, conductor Henry Russell of the night express train No. 4, pulled out of his station a bit after 9:00 p.m. The train had one engine, one sleeper, two baggage cars, two regular coaches, an express car, and a smoking car. The smoker was at the front of the train and many male passengers moved to the smoker as they boarded, for it was a fine place to relax on the trip home after a day in Chicago. Russell also had new help. His engineer, Joshua Puffenberger, had just transferred from another rail line and this was his first Chicago to Joliet run.

The night express was delayed pulling out of the downtown station, so on the run to Willow Springs, the conductor had the engineer build up speed to 35 mph. However, the train was delayed again. This time, at the "Springs," coupling the Pullman sleeper took too long. Conductor Russell realized that he was already six minutes late. Taking no chances, he stepped into the Willow Springs office and told the dispatcher to telegraph ahead to all stations that he was behind schedule and to order all other trains to sidetrack until he passed. Puffenburger and Russell then climbed back on board for Sag Bridge. At the Sag, Puffenburger saw the "GO" signal and headed the train down the valley toward Lemont. Later evidence would show that what he had seen was the signal to stop to take on water.

When the message that No. 4 was late was received at the Lemont depot, the dispatcher told the station agent to go out and flag the freight. The message was clear; the freight was to sidetrack in Lemont until No. 4 passed. Meanwhile, the coal train slowed as it approached the Lemont station from the west. Fog had rolled in and it was hard to see the platform. The conductor did not acknowledge the agent's signal, and the train passed before the agent could get anyone's attention in the cab. Racing down the platform the agent yelled at the brakemen at the end of the train, "Do you have orders against No. 4?" One of the brakemen managed to shout that he did not know as he was new to the route. The train then disappeared into the fog. The Lemont agent ran into the station screaming, "Can we signal the coal train somehow?"

The reply was, "No." It was now 10:00 p.m. The dispatcher did what he could. He telegraphed the office of the Alton line and they began putting together a hospital train even before the fatal crash. In a suspended moment, all the two Lemont station men could do was sit and wait for the tragedy.

Because of the fog, the conductors did not see the headlights until they were in front of each other. There was no time for a warning whistle for the firemen in the back of the engine — only the conductors had time to leap. The trains met east of Lemont, near Walker Road and Main Street. The force was so great that the earth shook and people for miles around heard the explosion. Express No. 4 rushed up into the coal train, taking the baggage, express, and smoking cars with it. The boiler of Engine No. 143 exploded, spraying scalding steam on the passengers in the smoking car. Metal flew everywhere. A five by 12 foot piece of boiler plate was found later a hundred yards from the wreck, buried three feet in the ground.

As with all disasters, it took a while for aid to come, especially in such an isolated area. However, when Lemonters realized what had happened, they came to offer help. A reporter for the *Joliet Signal* arrived on the scene within an hour. He recorded the event as, "Horrible, so bad it paralyzed the bravest hearts with agony."[12] Shaken but alive, Conductor Russell stared at the track in disbelief. On seeing Conductor Beane, he asked to compare watches to check the time schedule. Beane claimed that his timepiece had stopped in the wreck. Confused and upset, Beane mumbled repeatedly that he had forgotten the No. 4 Express that had the right of way. Beane then wandered off, disappearing to become the object of a long manhunt. He was not seen again until September 2, when his best friend, Simon Miller of Monee, turned him into the police for a 6,000 dollar reward.[13]

The final total was 23 dead and 40 injured. The dead included the two brakemen, the fireman, and engineer from the coal train. On the No. 4 Express, the dead consisted of its fireman and many passengers including, Major John Smith, Warden of the Joliet Prison;[14] J.K. Ferely, purchasing agent for the prison; and James O'Neal, a well-known storekeeper in Joliet.

Since trains were a newer means of transportation, the Lemont crash received a good deal of publicity. The *Joliet Signal* headlined the story with such emotional prose as: "Twenty Persons Ushered Into Eternity Without a Moment's Premonition of Their Terrible Doom."[15] As an aftermath, instigated by the *Signal*, the public called for an investigation of the wreck. The newspaper played up the event:

> The Lemont Wreck of No. 4 eclipses anything in the catalogue of American railroad holocausts . . . as to the massacre of railroad employees and passengers and extensive destruction of railroad property.[16]

Future years would bring greater disasters; still, the Lemont wreck made the public aware of the need for more safety and supervision in the rail industry. The public and the media fixed the blame on the hiring of cheap untrained labor, because the railroad wanted to break the new labor unions. Concern was also raised about the lack of a double line through the valley. Beane and Puffenburger were arrested but acquitted of any fault in the disaster.

Most revealing of all was that on September 16, one month after the crash, the Chicago and Alton announced that they were building a double track as rapidly as possible between Summit and Wilmington. No longer would the schedule depend upon sidetracking trains on a single line. Lemont's tragedy led to the improvement of rail safety on the Chicago and Alton.

Accidents like this one also helped to create the powerful Brotherhood of Railway Workers. Workers were forced to form benevolent societies to care for their own sick and injured, since railroads refused to offer such compensation. The locomotive engineers had organized in 1863, but the other groups were slow in forming. It took incidents like the Lemont wreck to drive them to organize. From these societies — The Brotherhood of Firemen formed in 1881, The Order of Conductors formed in 1883, and The Brotherhood of Brakemen formed in 1884 — grew the militant American Railway Union headed by Eugene Debs, a union that would influence labor history in the 19th Century.

ENDNOTES

[1]William Cronon, *Nature's Metropolis: Chicago and the Great West* (New York: W.W. Norton & Company, 1991), p. 59.

[2]James Putman, *The Illinois And Michigan Canal* (Chicago: University of Chicago Press, 1918), pp. 109-111.

[3]Dennis Preshlock, "Peopling the Lemont Area to 1860," *Looking For Lemont*, ed. Michael Conzen and Carl Zimring (Chicago: University of Chicago, 1994), p. 21.

[4]Cronon, *Nature's Metropolis,* p. 80.

[5]Preshlock, "Peopling the Lemont Area to 1860," p. 30.

[6]The lawyers were John Bones, William Brown, W.C. Jillet, Isaac La Pant, Peter Quinn, John Reid, and Joseph Sturdevant.

[7]Historic American Buildings Survey (HABS), *An Inventory of Historic Structures Within the Illinois & Michigan Canal Heritage Corridor, Lemont* (Washington, DC: National Park Service, 1987).

[8]Barbara Bushman, ed., *Lemont, Illinois: Its History In Commemoration Of The Centennial Of Its Incorporation* (Des Plaines, IL: King/Mann Yearbook, 1973), p. 184.

[9]Cronon, *Nature's Metropolis,* p. 329.

[10]Lemont still has a vestige of steel production with the Austeel Corporation.

[11]Tilden was the losing presidential candidate in 1876.

[12]*Joliet Signal*, August 17-20, 1873.

[13]*Ibid.*, September 3, 1873.

[14]Major Smith was a reform warden who began a system of humane treatment for the Joliet prisoners. He opposed the practice of leasing out convicts for labor and developed programs to teach the convicts skills for their return to society.

[15]*Ibid.*, August 17-20, 1873.

[16]*Ibid.*

BUSINESSES IN LEMONT IN 1868*

Agriculture Implements: A. Friedley
Barber: Elihu Mayhew
Blacksmith: Charles Lutz, Fred Mathy, Philip Stein
Boots & Shoes: J. Barrett, J.H. Tedens & Co.
Clothing: John Volt
Drugs And Medicines: Geo. H. Hall
Dry Goods: A.W. Borland & Co., S.W. Norton, J.H. Tedens
Express Companies: American & Merchants, Mr. Parsons
Furniture: J. Gerharz
Groceries: A.W. Borland & Co., S.W. Norton, J.H. Tedens
Hardware: A. Friedley
Hotel: J. Halleck, Halleck House
Insurance: Geo. Hall
Meat Market: Joseph Frank
Notary Public: Geo. Hall
Plow Manufacturer: Jacob Miller
Post Office: Geo. Hall
Rail Agent: Mr. Parsons
Saloons: Anthony Dutter, D.B. Murphy, Wm. Smith
Stoves & Tinware: A. Friedley
Telegraph Operator: Mr. Parsons
Wagon Makers: D.H. George, Wm. Shuy
Stone Yards: Singer & Talcott, E. Walker

*These do not represent all businesses, but only those that were listed with *H.C. Chandler's Railway Guide for 1868*.

CHAPTER THIRTEEN

LEMONT AND THE CIVIL WAR

The years between 1850 and 1860 saw growth because of our transportation capacity and the development of the quarries. By 1860, Lemont had an official population of 1,389. This figure could be incorrect since the total four-year enlistment for the Civil War from our town amounted to 800 men. Several factors could have caused this discrepancy. First, perhaps quarry workers housed in dormitories and boarding homes were not counted as part of the population. Secondly, men may have enlisted in Lemont from other counties, as Cook County offered larger bounties for enlisting toward the end of the war.

It is hard to recreate the political climate in Lemont as the Civil War approached, since we have few records. However, it is safe to say that the town was divided in its attitude toward states rights and slavery. The New England Protestants, our oldest pioneers, tended to support abolition. Most became strong Republicans even before the election of 1860. As evidence, we have a Fremont Street named for John Fremont, the first Republican candidate for president of the new party and a strong opponent of slavery. There also is the local tradition that N.J. Brown's farm was a stop on the Underground Railway. On the other side of the issue, many Irish and German workers opposed freeing the slaves as they feared the economic competition that could come from such an action. Many simply felt that southern secession was not worth a war.

Here in Lemont, political passions ran high. After all, two of the four candidates in the 1860 election for president were from Illinois. Those Irish Democrats who had supported Douglas considered Lincoln's election and the possible resulting conflict dangerous and foolish, so Lincoln did not carry Lemont. In fact, the combined national total of votes for the presidential candidates tallied a million more votes than Lincoln received.[1] Lemont had a fair share of Copperheads, a fact reported by Robert Strong, a private in the 105th Illinois Infantry, who lived in Downers Township. In 1865, after the war was over and while waiting in Chicago to be discharged, Private Strong decided to visit home:

> That night, as I had no one to go to for a pass, I took the matter into my own hands . . . got a ticket for Lemont, and started home. From Lemont I started to foot it . . . a man in a wagon passed me with a load of empty milk cans. I asked for a ride. It was a bright night and he could see my uniform. He refused to let me ride and swore at me for a damned thieving bluecoat. At that I made a rush for him. He whipped his horses and drove away from me.[2]

With the election of Lincoln in the fall of 1860, before Fort Sumter, many held the belief that secession could occur without bloodshed. Some Chicagoans and Lemonters even welcomed the loss of the South. They felt that if the South left the Union, the Northwest and the Chicago area would become a ruling economic power. They envisioned the possibility of Chicago becoming "the Capital of the New Republic."[3] However, after the attack on Sumter, April 12, all chance at compromise was lost.

Those Republicans who supported the new president considered the war a holy struggle to keep the Union. Much of the pro-war sentiment in Lemont centered on the newly built Methodist church, now the Old Stone Church Historical Society Museum. In fact, the first wedding held in the building in 1861, between Mattie Jones and John Wells, saw the groom off to the war right after the ceremony. There is an old legend that General Grant visited the church on a recruiting drive. Records to support that story have never been located, but the Methodist Church certainly was a center for recruiting.

For example, the 55th Illinois Regiment was filled by Methodist ministers who preached and recruited through Cook, DuPage, and Kane counties. The historian for that regiment tells how the ministers traveled the circuit displaying Colt revolving rifles and saber bayonets to entice the young men "with this new ingenious and complicated instru-

The Old Methodist Church built in 1861. It is now the home of the Lemont Historical Society. The small frame house on the right was the home of Lemuel Brown. (Photo courtesy of Lemont Historical Society)

ment of death." When the 55th was finally armed, the guns they received were not those promised but poorly made imitations and soon "all the glorious dreams of romantic sharpshooting disappeared . . . and a feeling of intense disgust . . . swept through the regiment. The whole length of the barracks was continually echoing with cries of, 'Here's your d---d sanctified Methodist revolver!'"[4]

Whatever the politics or religion, in the end Lemont supplied many men for the effort. As late as 1864, when the country was disillusioned and tired of war, Lemont was given a quota of 33 men and she sent 293 into battle, this although many Northerners were so unhappy with the war that this parody to the tune of "The Battle Hymn of the Republic" was popular:

> Tell Abe Lincoln of Antietam's bloody dell,
> Tell Abe Lincoln where a thousand heroes fell,
> Tell Abe Lincoln and his gang to go to hell
> and we'll go marching home.

For the four years between Fort Sumter in 1861 and the end of the war in 1865, 259,092 Illinois men served. Of that number 35,000 died, some in battle, others in hospitals and prisons.[5] According to official state records Lemont, in the four years, sent 11 percent of its population and seven percent of those never returned to Lemont. Not all these were fatalities, since some may have deserted, while others may have begun life in new communities.

Finis Farr reports the typical Chicagoland soldier was a young clerk, student, workingman, or farmer. His officer was usually a plant superintendent, teacher, small businessman, or professional. Most of the soldiers were volunteers, the majority between 18 and 25. However, Illinois also sent five 13 year-olds and at least 237 were 50 years or older.[6]

One older volunteer was Lemont's Daniel Skelly. Born in Ireland in 1814, he was one of our early quarry owners. Since he served as the Captain of the Emmet Guards, a local militia, he felt it necessary to offer his services, although he was 47. He enlisted as a private in Company B, 23rd Regiment Illinois Infantry (known as the Irish Brigade), and was soon commissioned a First Lieutenant of Company G. He fought in Missouri with the famed Col. Mulligan and was taken prisoner. After release his health failed and he returned to Lemont, retired, and sold his quarries to Edwin Walker.[7] Other prominent Lemonters who served in the war included, Joseph Rood, M.D., with Company A of the 138th Illinois Volunteers; James Tripp with Company H of the 30th Illinois Infantry, who was part of General Sherman's "March to the Sea"; Lorenz Valentin with Company C of the 13th Illinois at Little Rock; Mathew Warner with the Chicago Mercantile Battery at Vicksburg; Jacob Meyer with the 92nd Mounted Infantry, also on Sherman's March; and Thomas Huston with the 58th Illinois Infantry at Shiloh, Fort Donaldson, and Libby Prison.[8]

Soldiers who returned to Lemont and are buried in our local cemeteries are:

Fairmont: A.T. Perry

St. James: Charles Arkins; Dennis Hurley; Frank McMahon; Daniel McMahon with Company H 89th Illinois; Peter Schmidt; Peter McQuire; Fred Hertzog; James Fitzpatrick with Company A 69th New York; Dennis Fitzpatrick; James Gleason; Bernard McKenna; John Rullo with Company K, 48th Indiana; Edward Cox with Company A, 31st Illinois; John Hickey with Company K, 65th Illinois; Michael Flood with the U.S. Navy; Patrick Dowd with Company L, 2nd Illinois Art.; James Kelley; Michael Hughes with Company E, Doles Battery; John Maroney with Company C, 140th Indiana; Daniel Gaffney; Geo. Stevans with Company A, 134th New York Infantry; Francis Kent with Company C, 2nd Illinois; James Woodman with Company G, 2nd Ohio Infantry; James Donohue with Company G, 96th Illinois; and John Schermer with Company E, 44th New York Infantry

St. Matthew's: Peter Brackin and Fredrick Simon, both in Company D of the 147th Illinois Volunteers; and Peter Blesch and Ludwig Lau

St. Patrick's: Patrick Cogger; Patrick McDonald; James Noonan; Dennis Noonan; Jas. Scott; Cornelius Talty; John Redman; and Patrick Barrett

St. Alphonsus: Charles Freehauf with Company E, 8th Illinois Cavalry who was in the unit that searched for John Wilkes Booth and escorted the Lincoln funeral train; Peter Germande; Michael Heinz; Christ Hettinger; Anthony Hesserich; Johan Stamm; Batis Shummer; and Peter Heinz

Odd Fellows: P. Peiffer and Lyman Depue

Cass Cemetery: Joseph Cobb with Company K of the 19th Illinois; Abraham Heartt with Company B of the 1st Illinois; George Heartt with Company B of the 33d Illinois; Clark Madden; and John Valleam with Company K of the 28th Michigan.[9]

The passions of that war are hard to imagine now, but are reflected in a sentimental poem written by Josephine Smart Madden, that describes the sad goodbyes at our Alton Station:

> The boys of Illinois heard the loud cry.
> "We're coming, Abe Lincoln, to do or die." Lemont,
> Downers Grove, Barbers Corners, Old Cass
> Responding to the call, turned out in mass.
>
> The six horse teams, girls all in white,
> 'Neath waving flags and flowers so bright,
> Young men on horseback, proud and brave,
> Fathers and mothers, serious and grave.
>
> Higher and higher excitement ran,
> Louder and clearer the war songs they sang;
> Then that other cry, "Young men, enlist,
> Our country's in danger, will you assist?"
>
> In innocent bravery their names they enroll,
> To those young men it was manhood's goal.
> Then in place of joy, it was grief ran high,
> For in a few short weeks, Oh! the sad good-bye.
>
> The tenth of September, the hardest time came,
> When all went to Lemont where they took the train,
> Fathers, mothers, sisters, Oh! I see it yet,
> Mothers hugging their sons, their darlings their pets.
>
> Forever it seemed, we were saying good-bye
> To Fathers and sons who answered the cry:
> "To arms, to arms! Your country to save
> From the disrupted Union and disgrace of the slave."[10]

Throughout the war both women and men worked to support the troops. Women in Lemont and the nation labored at raising money for the families of the enlisted men and for widows and orphans of the conflict. A favorite method of fundraising was through bazaars and fairs. Our churches sponsored sewing circles that made clothing, lint, and bandages for the war effort. Fresh and canned food[11] was sent to the soldiers, along with Bibles and religious tracts. One favorite item of the men was a handmade small sewing kit called "the homemaker." These contained sewing supplies and buttons and were often accompanied with letters from the young women who made them. Many a romantic pen pal developed from this tradition.

It is not easy to describe war since most of its truth rests with the individual experience. It is simpler to tell one story to represent all others, that of a Congressional Medal of Honor winner from Lemont, John Warden. The Medal of Honor is the highest award a nation can give for bravery and was established by an act of Congress in 1862; its requirements are as follows:

> The deed must have two eyewitnesses and must be so out-
> standing that the action is above and beyond the call of duty.
> The deed must involve a risk of life and must be the type of
> act that if not done, would not have subjected the individual
> to any criticism.

John Warden's father, Peter, came to the new Illinois frontier in the 1830s. Here he found life good and full of opportunities. He wrote glowing letters to his family in England about the rich, free, and full life available to anyone willing to work in the growing Chicagoland area. As a pioneer, Peter Warden became an important part of the community of Chicago, especially in its religious and political life. He was a devout Baptist and helped establish the First Baptist Church in Chicago. His name, along with fourteen others, appears on the first charter of the church established in 1833. Eight of those signers were soldiers in the garrison at Fort Dearborn. The organization was small but dedicated. Baptisms were performed in Lake Michigan, summer and winter.[12]

This group formed an alliance with a group of Baptists living in DuPage Township and, along with others in the Northwest, they established the Northwest Baptist Association. Peter Warden was involved with both groups. Politics began to touch daily life by the 1840s as the nation took sides on the issue of slavery. The murder of Elijah P. Lovejoy, abolitionist editor of Alton, brought the struggle to the Illinois frontier and the emotions generated pervaded the churches. Peter Warden was anti-slavery; he could not accept the idea that one man had a right to own another. Feelings became so heated that in 1843, Peter and 61 other members of the church who advocated abolition, left to form the Tabernacle Baptist Church. Their group was so opposed to slavery that they refused to receive anyone in communion or as a preacher who "would advocate or justify from civil policy or the Bible the principles or practice of slavery."[13]

Peter Warden's six sons grew up in this militant abolitionist atmosphere and when the family moved to the Lemont area to farm, they settled north of the village near a community of German farmers who also were abolitionists. Therefore, there was no question where the Warden family stood on that April day in 1861, when Fort Sumter fell and the Civil War began. Lincoln made his first call for troops on April 15, and men, young and old, rushed out to enlist.

All six of the Warden sons would eventually serve in the Union forces, but the first two to go were John and Moses. Eager to have the glory of a cause behind them, they rode to enlist when they heard the news. But the quota for Illinois was already filled, largely by militia and semi-military drill clubs, such as the Emmet Guards. These militia men, already trained, signed up for the original enlistment of three months with the feeling that the war would soon be over.

However, as the war dragged on through the summer months, the need for soldiers became apparent and John and Moses were able to join a company by the late fall. They were assigned as privates in the 55th Illinois Infantry, Company E, which was mustered in on December 1, 1861, at Camp Douglas in Chicago and ordered to Benton Barracks, Missouri. There they were placed under the command of General Sherman, nicknamed "Crazy Sherman," because of his devotion to the Union cause and because he had the peculiar habit of talking to himself.

The two young, eager soldiers were then shipped to Paducah, Kentucky. On that trip, both got a foretaste of what military service would be like — little glory and much suffering. Some of this suffering was the result of careless management and stupidity. The steamboat that shipped the 55th became frozen in the ice between St. Louis and Cairo. It had left port with only two days of rations, yet the ship remained ice bound for eleven days. The young recruits found themselves cold and hungry for over a week. The experience introduced them to the ways of the military. The ship carried some women, one of whom cooked up a vile whiskey she sold for a dollar a cup. The result was a drunken brawl that lasted well into the night. After the recruits grew tired of fighting with each other, they turned on the hated "Methodist" smooth bore guns and threw many of them overboard before they were stopped.[14]

When they finally arrived in Paducah, it was decided to reorganize the whole company and join it with others to form a brigade. Civil War companies were formed in peculiar ways. Anyone who recruited men would be given a commission and was often voted officer by those he recruited. Because of this system, the recruits usually were from the same area and often related. In fact, the 55th was known as "the Regiment of Brothers." The companies and groups thus formed had deep loyalties and powerful politics, and these bonds lasted long after the war.

This reorganization upset many, and several elected line officers resigned even before they had faced an enemy. The commander of their regiment was Colonel David Stuart. Stuart entered the service under the cloud of a notorious divorce case. He raised the regiment partly to redeem his character. This fact put his actions and the work of the 55th under a strain. The regiment soon earned the reputation of being tough but hard to handle, and Stuart's command inept.[15] Moses and John were disturbed by the turmoil, but were not concerned with officers. They were young and eager to fight for the Union; what they wanted was a taste of battle. Lemont's Warden brothers soon had two minor skirmishes, including the capture of Columbus, Kentucky, but their first real test came at Shiloh.

At Shiloh, the 55th was part of Sherman's Fifth Division. Somehow the brigade, including John and Moses' Company E, was detached from the main body and placed three miles from the general and a chain of command. Therefore, on the first day of battle the 55th found itself on the extreme left of the Union line. Here Col. Stuart displayed his lack of battle expertise. "He attempted to form the unit into a hollow square, an antiquated maneuver dating back to 1776."[16] Next to their line was the Ohio 71st and 54th. The 71st Ohio group, new to battle, took flight at the first volley of bullets, but the Warden brothers and their brigade held their ground.

Because of their isolated position, Company E and the 55th had no cavalry or artillery support and no one in power to order a retreat. By this time the regiment had lost all respect for Stuart and largely ignored his commands, and instead began to take orders from the chaplain, Milton Haney. Known as the "Fighting Chaplain," Haney was one of two chaplains to win the Congressional Medal of Honor.[17] The regiment fought, holding the position until all others on the left flank could retreat and regroup. Then, only after two-thirds of their number were dead or wounded and all ammunition gone, did they give up their stand. Of the 944 men of the 55th, 612 participated in the battle. At the next roll call only 215 could muster. John and Moses Warden were there, now seasoned veterans of the Army of the Western Front. John was named Corporal. Yet, as heroic as the battle was, it was not "above and beyond the call of duty." It was simply a small part of the larger campaign to open the Mississippi.

The West was important to the war effort. Lincoln and his generals saw that it was necessary to clear the Mississippi and thus cut off the Southwest from the rest of the Confederacy. It was also essential to open the Mississippi from the Gulf to the North for transportation and supplies. So the 55th Illinois Regiment was assigned to spend most of

1862 along the Mississippi River, moving back and forth, engaged in small battles. As the weeks passed, the three-month enlistees were forced to reenlist since not enough trained reinforcements were available.

Life in the army was a struggle. Food and supplies were often scarce. Troops were not paid on any reasonable schedule; it was not uncommon for men to go five or six months without pay. The pay was meager, only 13 dollars a month for privates, and it was not raised until near the end of the war, and then only to 16 dollars.[18] This caused a burden on families back home and drove many soldiers to desert. However, John and his brother remained without any complaint. They had been raised to view the war as a moral crusade, but John and Moses, like many common soldiers, realized that if the army had moved on to Vicksburg right after Shiloh, the city probably could have been taken with relative ease. By 1862, the Mississippi was open except at Vicksburg and Port Hudson. The problem was that the longer the Western armies moved around, the more time Vicksburg had to prepare its defenses.[19]

By October of 1862, Grant asked permission from Chief of Staff Halleck to attack Vicksburg but permission was not given until December. And, when the orders did come, they were confusing. It was not clear whether Grant, Sherman, or McClernand had orders to capture the town. It seems that McClernand, an Illinois political general, visited Washington that fall and had given a plan he developed to Lincoln designed to capture Vicksburg. Lincoln awarded him some form of command because he was a Southern Illinois Democrat and Lincoln felt it necessary to keep the Southern Illinois Democrats loyal to the Union. Too many Democrats were tiring of the war and some were actively working against the Union cause.

Whatever the actual orders were, McClernand left Washington with the belief that he had an independent commission to capture Vicksburg, although the area was under Grant's command. General-in-Chief Halleck was never informed of any new orders and Grant learned of McClernand's proposed plan from the newspapers.

There was a good deal of in-fighting among the generals of the war, both North and South. Many saw the war as a future route for a military or political career. This glory seeking did not help the common soldier who was often sacrificed in needless small skirmishes to gain power and fame for his commander. While McClernand made his plans, Grant and Sherman, along with the 55th, ignored the contradictions in orders and finally began a movement against Vicksburg. The first attempt, to take the town from the rear, was a failure. Grant then moved his army across the Mississippi and south of Vicksburg. From that position he ferried part of the army back and worked swiftly to separate two units of the Rebel army in the area. To do this, he had to move his men away from their base of supply and march them as rapidly as possible. Sherman and his forces, including the Illinois 55th, caught up with Grant on May 1, 1863, and all of the soldiers began a remarkable march under terrible conditions.

The terrain that the 55th had to cover was wooded and marked with gullies and swamps. John and Moses Warden were familiar with that type of ground, having hunted and explored our Des Plaines Valley as young men. However, many other Midwestern boys from the prairie lands found the enforced march exhausting. All suffered from the heat and humidity of the South. Mississippi was not like Illinois, and added to its heat and dust were many insects. The struggle uphill with packs and cartridges was hard, but coming downhill was just as difficult. A complete knapsack and haversack totaled around 50 pounds.[20] Most experienced soldiers quickly eliminated items they considered useless. This action created a secondary army of peddlers that followed the men picking up items for resale.

When the dust on the march became unbearable, the company prayed for rain. But when it rained, mud became an even worse problem than the dust, for then the tents and blankets could not be dried out and had to be rolled up wet and carried on the march. The water added extra weight as the tents were made of a heavy grade canvas. The rain also made walking especially difficult for those men who followed the wagons. The weight of the transport and artillery wagons created ruts in the roads forcing the foot soldiers to tuck their pants into the tops of their stockings and tie them with string, but even so, the mud usually worked its way into the boots.[21]

Under such conditions there was little time for washing and the troops soon became infected with lice. A soldier described his encounter with the creatures jokingly called the "friend of man":

> They would get into the seams of our shirts and pants and drawers and when not engaged in laying eggs would sally out and forage off our defenseless bodies . . . At every leisure moment the boys would pull off their shirts and such a cracking of thumbnails [they can be killed by crushing them] never took place anywhere but in our army.[22]

The rations were also short, as the march began with only a four-day supply, and it took careful conservation to make the food last. Coffee was a special delight to the tired men and each man guarded his personal supply very closely. All issued rations were carried in the haversack. Under marching conditions, flour, salt and salted meat tended to mix together and to avoid ruining the coffee, it was kept in a special bag within the haversack. The men in Company E had been around long enough to know how to brew coffee as quickly as possible. The grounds and the sugar ration were mixed so the coffee could be prepared when the water was hot. For a tired soldier nothing tasted so fine as a good cup of coffee.[23]

Coffee call. (From a contemporary lithograph)

On their forced march, even in hot weather, the four days supply of coffee soon disappeared and fatigue set in and Company E found it hard to keep going. As for hunger it could be tolerated as long as the hardtack held out. Hardtack was a plain flour and water biscuit measuring about three inches by three inches. The small ones were issued fifteen to a man for the day's ration. There was a larger version measuring about six inches by six inches and four of these made a day's ration. The men joked about them, as the biscuits were so hard as to be able to withstand any type of weather condition. The larger ones were made in Boston and had the letters "BC" stamped on them. To the soldiers that meant that they were so hard because they were made Before Christ.[24]

Through the days, while in pursuit of the Confederate forces, men had little sleep. Reveille was usually at 3:00 a.m. and marching began around 6:00 a.m. The soldiers did not stop until late evening and by then almost all fell exhausted without concern for food. All they wanted was to catch up with the Rebels they had been pursuing for so long. Finally on May 16, the tired troops of the Illinois 55th Company E met a Confederate force at Champion Hill and, in spite of hunger and fatigue, drove them back toward Vicksburg. Meanwhile, the other part of Grant's Army defeated a group at the Big Black River. With these two victories, the Union forces felt that taking Vicksburg would be easy. The battle cry of the soldiers was "On to Vicksburg." John and Moses felt it would all be over in a short while. How wrong they were.

As the Confederates retreated to town they developed an elaborate trench and earthwork system to defend their city. General Pemberton, the Confederate commander, was under orders from Jefferson Davis to hold Vicksburg at all cost.

The two days before the first attack were quiet. Military supplies had not caught up with the army, so they could sleep, wash and boil clothes to kill lice, write home, and attend religious services held by the many preachers in the service. John Warden and his brother rested and tried not to think of food, for everyone was hungry. The carefully conserved rations ran out during the forced march and there was nothing to forage as the local farmers were near starvation. However, the army was proud of what they had done. They had marched 200 miles in 18 days over rough terrain and had taken part in one large battle and many skirmishes, while outnumbered, on enemy territory, and without a supply line.

On May 19, 1863, the armies of Grant, Sherman, and McClernand began their first attack on the Vicksburg fortifications. It was a test of Union power and Confederate defense. The Union Army met stiff resistance with volley after volley of shot from the well-protected trenches and earthworks. After several aborted attempts to scale the defenses, the Union forces retreated and began digging fortifications of their own.

The first small assault had cost the Army of the West 262 killed or wounded. The effect on the Confederate defenders was minimal. Yet, the Union generals still believed that the fortifications could be stormed with a direct frontal attack, although the common soldiers who had experienced the overpowering barrage had doubts.

On the 21st, the generals spent the day laying their attack plans while the soldiers began writing letters that might be their last messages to the folks back home. Mess cooks, who had caught up with the army but were still short of food, spent their day in an usual, painful, pre-battle ritual. The cooks did not fight, and therefore were entrusted with those personal effects that soldiers wanted sent back home should they die: a tintype of a loved one, a lock of hair, watches, letters, or a few dollars saved from their small pay — mementos that represent life and links to home. It was the same before each battle. The cooks and chaplains would take the objects and reassure each man that he would be back to collect his things afterwards.[25]

The mood was strange in Company E that afternoon, as it was throughout the encampment. There was a foreboding that was new to this hardened Western army. They were unsure of the attack plans and still hungry. As General Grant, who was a great favorite with the troops, passed by a line of men, he heard a noise, a kind of whispered chant. The chant grew louder as each soldier he passed bravely took up the cry. They were calling repeatedly, "Hardtack, hardtack." Grant did not acknowledge this military breach, but went to his headquarters and ordered that full rations, known as the "cracker line," be broken out for the troops.[26]

Before the first assault both Union and Confederate soldiers were stationed within close range. At one guard post, the issue of extra coffee to the Union side prompted a Confederate guard, cut off from supplies, to call out: "Lend us some coffee for supper won't you. We will pay you when Johnston comes to relieve us." The Union reply was, "Never mind the coffee. Grant will take dinner in Vicksburg tomorrow."

The point of attack selected was south of a Confederate fort situated atop a bluff. On the afternoon of May 21, each regimental commander asked for volunteers to lead the assault and prepare the way for the real attack. No married men were allowed to volunteer due to the risk involved. John Warden was one of those to volunteer.

The attack on the Vicksburg fortifications began the next day at 10:00 a.m. Grant had all the commanders synchronize their watches so that the soldiers along the line could move at once. It was the first use of a synchronized attack in military history. It was not really a battle that day at Vicksburg, it was a slaughter. The Confederates held their protected superior positions and wave after wave of Union forces could not scale the earthworks or cross the open ditches without being fired upon.

Even today, visiting the now lush green battlefield at Vicksburg and tracing out the position of the Illinois 55th, it becomes clear that any attempt at a frontal attack was foolish.

There were many heroes, a number dying vainly trying to plant their regimental flags on a high point along the line. The smoke and noise was dreadful. It has been estimated that it took at least a man's weight in lead to kill a single soldier in battle because Civil War weapons and marksmen were so inaccurate. The amount of shot that flew on that May morning must have been unbelievable to inflict the damage it did, for over 4,000 men were killed or injured during the assault.

Many brigades and companies were pinned down under constant fire, while others rushed behind them only to find themselves caught and unable to move. There they had to remain, not able to charge and not able to retreat. The 55th, John and Moses' regiment, was assigned to the Second Division and were faced with a defensive trench twelve feet wide and six feet deep. The only way to mount a charge across the ditch was to bridge it. It was the duty of those earlier selected volunteers to carry tools and timber to build a bridge while under constant fire. One hundred and fifty men, including John, went forward in spite of the danger.

They moved quickly, carrying timbers and equipment. They worked with two men to a log, dashing to lay the groundwork for the bridge. Others carried lumber to lay across the bridge while the last men carried scaling ladders. As the Union soldiers reached the ditch, the Confederates would open with full fire. When one man went down another would take his place to try to finish the bridge. While the rest of the division watched helpless, one man after another fell trying to complete the task. In the noise and confusion Moses could not see his brother; he had no idea if he had been killed or was still vainly attempting to bridge the trench. When half the men had fallen, those that remained realized they could not complete the job and took shelter in the ditch and began returning fire. Those few who remained of the original volunteer company piled the dead around for protection and out of anger and desperation continued to fight until nightfall. They were still firing long after the rest of the Union forces had pulled back. No one came to their aid.[27]

Only after it was too dark for the Confederates to continue firing did the remaining few return to the Union lines. Of one hundred and fifty men only fifty-three survived and every survivor was wounded. John was shot in both knees but did recover. For their action these volunteers were awarded a new medal, the Medal of Honor, created by an act of Congress in 1861. The bridge was never built. The idea of a frontal assault on Vicksburg was foolish from the start. Vicksburg finally did fall, but only because the Union forces laid siege to the town; cut off from supplies it surrendered within a month.

When the war ended there was a victory parade through Washington D.C. The soldiers from the East and West marched on two different days. It was here at this moment that one could see a new psychological division in the country. Not North versus South, but East versus West. The Eastern troops were all spit and polish while the Western men were an individualistic, proud, poorly dressed group. Both sides made fun of each other and their world view, a sectional conflict that would play itself out in the 1890s with William Jennings Bryan's campaign for president.

John finished the war and was mustered out as late as August 14, 1865, having spent time after the conflict camped near Little Rock. During his term of service with the 55th Illinois the unit had marched on foot 3,340 miles, traveled 2,875 miles by railroad, and sailed a distance of 5,850 miles. During his service, John rose through the ranks from private to first lieutenant, but the years in the service made him bitter and disillusioned with war and politics. He never applied for the medal. It was not until 1893 that he was requested to come and receive the honor. Much to the dismay of his family, John Warden told them and the government that he would not accept any medal especially from President Cleveland, whom he considered a "bum." Cleveland never served in the war because he had purchased a substitute. Furthermore, in an economy move, he had cut Civil War pensions. To John Warden, soldiers did not need medals but pensions, especially those who suffered wounds and disabilities.

It was John's cousin, Lemont's Chicago alderman, Martin Madden, who finally convinced Warden to accept the medal, in spite of his feelings for the President. Madden, active in Republican politics, realized that a family member with the Medal of Honor would help him politically. So, John agreed to accept to please Martin.

On September 2, 1893, 30 years after that day at Vicksburg, John Warden received his Medal of Honor. It read, "For gallantry in the charge of the volunteer storming party — May 22, 1863."

In 1916, the government reviewed all the Medal of Honor winners in an attempt to purge the rolls of those acts not above and beyond duty. Nine hundred and eleven were stricken from the Honor Roll. John Warden was one whose outstanding bravery merited remaining among the honored men. It is a select group as only 3,400 men have received the Medal of Honor from 1861 to 1993.

John Warden died in 1906 in Sumner, Washington, and is buried in the Orting Cemetery, in Orting, Washington.

ENDNOTES

[1]The final national total was Lincoln: 1,866,452; Douglas: 1,376,957; Breckinridge: 849,781; Bell: 588,879. Lincoln won with an electoral vote of 180.

[2]Robert Strong, *A Yankee Private's Civil War*, ed. Ashley Halsey (Chicago: Henry Regnery Company, 1961), p. 217.

[3]Bessie Pierce, *A History of Chicago* (New York: Knopf, 1940), vol. 2., p. 250.

[4]Edwin C. Bearss, ed., *The 55th Illinois: 1861-1865*, (Huntington, W.V.: Blue Acorn Press, 1993), pp. 41-42.

[5]Victor Hicken, *Illinois in the Civil War* (Urbana: University of Illinois Press, 1991), p. ix.

[6]Finis Farr, *Chicago* (New Rochelle: Arlington House, 1973), p. 74

[7]A.T. Andreas, *History of Cook County* (Evansville: Unigraphics, 1976), p. 854.

[8]Huston suffered physically and mentally after the war. When he committed suicide, 30 years later, the family blamed his ordeal in Libby Prison. *Lemont Observer*, Feb. 20, 1897.

[9]Listing from Lemont American Legion Post 243 published in *The Lemonter*, May 28, 1936. Other names from *History and Cookbook of Saint James At The Sag* (1983), p. 217. Some of these men did not enlist from Lemont but were buried here.

[10]Sonia Kallick, "Views of Old Lemont," *The Lemont Metropolitan*, May 1, 1980. The poem came from a private collection of poems by Josephine Madden, wife of the congressman from Illinois.

[11]The lint was to stop wounds from bleeding.

[12]Andreas, *History of Cook County,* p. 246.

[13]Bessie Pierce, *A History of Chicago*, vol. 1. p. 249.

[14]Bearss, *The 55th Illinois,* pp. 43-45.

[15]Hicken, *Illinois in the Civil War,* p. xvii.

[16]*Ibid*.

[17]*Ibid*.

[18]Bell Irvin Wiley, *The Life of Billy Yank* (Baton Rouge: Louisiana State University Press), 1992, p. 49.

[19]Kallick, "Views of Old Lemont," May 8, 1980.

[20]Wiley, *The Life of Billy Yank,* p. 64.

[21]Strong, *A Yankee Private's Civil War*, p. 24.

[22]*Ibid*.

[23]*Ibid*., p. 132.

[24]*Ibid*, p. 102.

[25]Hicken, *Illinois in the Civil War,* p. 169.

[26]Ulysses Grant, "Vicksburg Campaign," *Battles and Leaders of the Civil War* (New York: Century Company, 1888) vol. 3, p. 518.

[27]Bearss, *The 55th Illinois,* pp. 242-245.

U.S. HISTORY

1860: *Abraham Lincoln Elected President — South Carolina Says It Will Secede — 424,000 People Come to America from England between 1850-1860; 914,000 Come from Ireland in the Same Period — First Pony Express.*

1861: *Civil War Begins — Ft. Sumter Falls — U.S. Population at 32 Million — Kansas Becomes a State — Battle at Bull Run.*

1862: *Union Forces Capture Ft. Henry, Ft. Donelson, Jacksonville, and New Orleans — They are Defeated at Second Bull Run and Fredricksburg — Homestead Act Gives Public Free Lands of 160 Acres If Conditions are Met.*

1863: *Emancipation Proclamation — Arizona and Idaho Become U.S. Territories — West Virginia Becomes a State of the Union — Battles at Vicksburg, Gettysburg, and Chattanooga — Gettysburg Address by Lincoln — Free City Mail Delivery Begins — Roller Skating Fad Sweeps Country.*

1864: *Grant Becomes Commander of the Union Forces — Sherman's March to the Sea — Lincoln Reelected — Nevada Becomes the 36th State — Sand Creek Massacre of Indians.*

1865: *Civil War Ends April 9th — Lincoln Assassinated April 14 — 13th Amendment Passes.*

1866: *14th Amendment Passes — National Labor Union Forms, Lasts Only Six Years.*

1867: *Alaska Purchased October 18 — Nebraska 37th State — University of Illinois Founded.*

1868: *Impeachment Proceedings against President Johnson.*

1869: *General U.S. Grant Elected President — Transcontinental Railway Completed.*

LEMONT HISTORY

1860: *Population at 1,389 — N.J. Brown Supervisor — S.L. Derby Builds Home on 131st and Derby — Smokey Row Begins on North Side of I & M Canal, One of the Most Notorious Places is Peter Schlapp's "Dutch Gardens" — St. Patrick's Church Built on Hill at the Top of Stephens Street, Renamed St. Mary's.*

1861: *Lemont Boys Enlist in the Armed Services — Methodist Old Stone Church is Built, First Marriage in the Church, the Groom John Wells Leaves for the Army Right After the Wedding — John Warden of Lemont Enlists in the 55th Infantry, Will Become a Congressional Medal of Honor Winner — J.H. Tedens Arrives from Mokena to Start a Store North of the I & M Canal Near the Present Post Office.*

1862: *Thormahlen Joins Tedens in the General Store — Gerharz Has Furniture and Undertaking Business at 266 Main Street.*

1863: *Lemont School Principal is George Plant — Union Hotel Operating in Town — War Slows Stone Quarry Work — Farming and Grain Production Does Very Well — Farm Acreage in Township 3,774 Acres of Improved Land — Value $12 Per Acre.*

1864: *Lemont's Draft Quota Based on Population is 33, Number Who Enlist is 293.*

1865: *Lemont Stone for Union Stockyards Gate — I & M Canal Deepening and Improvement Begins, Will Cost 3 Million Dollars — George Hall is Postmaster — Lincoln's Funeral Train Passes through Lemont.*

1866: *I & M Deep Cut Project Continues to Bring Money to Town.*

1867: *Mat Borland Postmaster — Village of Lemont Plat Sold to H.M. Singer for Back Taxes — St. Alphonsus Formed.*

1868: *Walker Mansion Built [Now Gone] — Pete Boyle, Owner of Saloon on Smokey Row, Kills "Con" Brown, a Bounty Jumper.*

1869: *H. Martin Has Store on Canal Street — Bolton Bottle Works Begin — Old Central School, Rear Section Dedicated — B. Van Buren Postmaster — Wm. Dugall, M.D. Works in Town and Marries Daughter of Edwin Walker — Jas. Rood, M.D. Also in Town.*

CHAPTER FOURTEEN

LEMONT VILLAGE INCORPORATES
Post-Civil War Growth: 1865–1885

The years of the Civil War were profitable for those who did not serve and some of our wealthy leaders bought substitutes to take their place. The conflict created a labor shortage and, as a result, the country had another influx of laborers from Europe, many of whom settled in Lemont. Our population increased to 3,575 with the township's economy based on agriculture, transportation, quarrying, and all the services those industries required. Most of the new immigrants were in their 30s and half were unmarried. There were 30 saloons in town to serve this young population, almost one saloon for every 120 people. A number of these establishments were located near the I & M Canal, along Smokey Row.

One project that brought money and work into the community during this period was the deepening and repair of the I & M Canal. Those who believed in water transportation had continued the fight for improvements on the I & M Canal. As Bessie Pierce reports in her *History of Chicago*:

> The demand . . . for an improved water route was not surprising in a day when it was customary to think of water carriage as affording relief from hardships inflicted by the railroads. Then, too, transport by lake and river had been, for a long time the way to market.[1]

In 1862, a bill was introduced in Congress to enlarge and deepen the canal and improve the Illinois River channel. It was presented as a military necessity, not for the Civil War then raging, but as a protection against possible action against America by England on the Great Lakes.[2] However, the cost of the Civil War made any action on the bill impossible. This was a problem because low water levels, combined with a fouled Chicago River, created stagnant water in the canal. This water had a terrible odor which was so bad that the Joliet *True Democrat* reported that the smell coming from the canal was "enough to make a horse sick." To Lemonters the canal was not just a source of an unpleasant stench, but was a threat because of the widespread belief that bad odors caused disease.[3]

Finally in 1865, after the war, money was let for this work and the project ran until 1871 because digging had to be done in the winter off-season. The idea was to deepen the canal to reverse the flow of water from the Chicago River that had become a human and industrial cesspool.[4] This increased flow was supposed to help purify the canal and keep the Chicago River from contaminating the lake. Construction cost three million dollars and offered jobs and money for the community. The work in Lemont was supervised by Dewitt Clinton Norton,[5] whose Republican connections gained him the contract.

Because of this "deep cut" the pumping station at Bridgeport was eliminated and the Chicago River began to flow directly into the I & M Canal. Hopeful that this meant a new life for the canal, completion of the project was cause for a large celebration. Optimism ran high as "within three or four days the water from Lake Michigan filled the canal at Lockport and was thrown off there over the rocks almost as clear and blue as the falls at Niagara."[6]

The deep cut was dedicated in the dry summer of 1871, a year that would prove so disastrous to Chicago. On July 25, a crowd of notables filled four large canal boats with one thousand people and set off for Lockport in the early morning. The first part of the trip was boring as spoil banks were piled so high that any view of the countryside was impossible. As a result the dignitaries took to "liquid refreshments." These were ample and liberally dispensed. Progress on the boats was slow and the party did not reach Lemont until 5:00 p.m. Here many of the imbibing notables developed "seasickness" and decided to catch the evening train back to Chicago. Lockport, decked in bunting, awaited the arrival of the party, only to learn that most had returned to the city. However, Governor Palmer, General Sheridan, Chicago's Mayor Mason, and Senator Judd did go on to Lockport to see that the deep cut was properly dedicated.

In a time when all events were celebrated in poetry, this day, too, was memorialized by a local poet known only as H.R.:

> The waters now have met again,
> Lake Michigan meets the Des Plaines
> The Illinois joins its refrain, with onward flow;
> Old Mississippi takes the bride,
> Escorts her to the ocean tide,
> Joining the groom in wedding ride,
> To sea they go.[7]

However, within a year after completion of the project, the flow slowed again and returned to its stagnant condition. It would take a much larger project to deal with Chicago's waste.

From the occupations listed on the 1870 census, we get a picture of the town's work force at the time: 84 percent of those counted were reported as unskilled workers, the majority of these quarry workers; 11³/₅ percent were recorded as skilled laborers, this included such occupations as bartender, blacksmith, butcher, carpenter, grocer, and cobbler; 3²/₅ percent were listed as merchants and professionals; and only one percent were listed as farmers.[8] The low number of farmers represents three possibilities: that the census takers failed to reach everyone in the township, that the Homestead Act of 1862 had attracted many pioneer Lemont farmers to sell and move west for free land, or that pressure of township and village growth had raised the price of farm land so that only those with money, or farmers with large holdings, could afford to buy land and continue farming.

The principal grain crops in the township remained corn, oats, and some wheat, and barley.[9] The sections of our township that were not good for crops because of topography were given over to orchards and grazing land. Lemont, and Downers Grove Township in DuPage, had large dairy and cheese operations. During the Civil War, many farms ran sheep for wool, as wool was in large demand for uniforms. Some sheep raising continued for a number of years after the war. The war also encouraged increased mule and horse

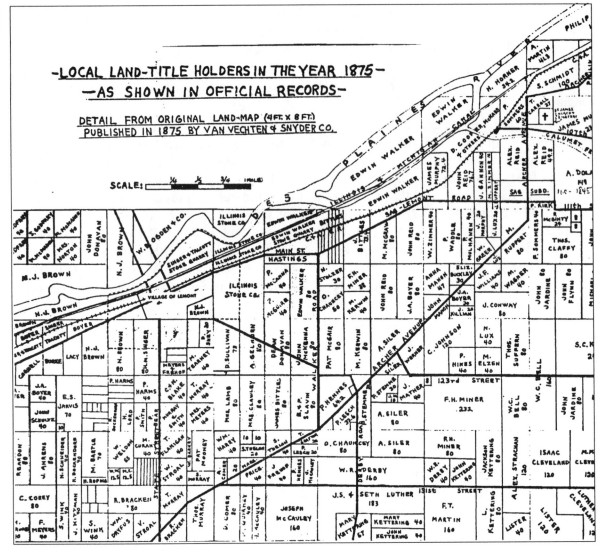

Lemont Township local land title holders in 1875. Detail from original land map. (Illustration courtesy of Lemont Historical Society)

breeding and some lands in our southwest sections was used for that purpose. Horses, of course, were essential for transportation and farm work. They continued to be an important commodity through the early years of the 20th Century.

During this post-war period of 1865 through the 1880s, we see the beginnings of small industry in town. The Civil War hastened the economic change from an agrarian to an industrial society. Tedens and Thormahlen operated a leather goods company as part of their general store where they produced boots and harnesses, employing ten men. Joseph Bresin had a cheese factory and John Bolton had a soda and beer manufacturing and bottling plant. O'Neil and Sheuy made farm wagons, while the Lindgren Brothers operated the Lemont Brick and Tile Company that employed nine men, and Jacob Miller made steel plows. The Gerharz family built furniture and had a funeral parlor business on Main Street, evidence that the community had reached the level where death and the events

The Martin Hogan, *a stone boat on the I & M Canal. (Photo courtesy of Lemont Historical Society)*

surrounding it could be removed from the front parlor at home and attended in a more formal setting.[10]

Transportation on the canal and the railroad also offered work. Between 1860 and 1870, there were seven canal boats that listed Lemont as home port; Captain Osborn of the *Rescue*, Hawkins and Reinhart of the *Sir John Franklin*, Allison of the *Terror*, and Cleveland of the *Resolute*. Captain Hogan owned two boats, *Col. Stearns* and the S. F. Gale, while the *Lady Franklin* was manned by four masters, Locks, Davis, Rockwell, and Wardell. These were independent of the boats owned and operated by the quarry owners.[11]

The main industry, however, remained Lemont's quarries, for they offered a place for the immigrant without special skills. Of our unskilled laborers, 80 percent were foreign born.

The Irish, as mentioned before, came for economic and political reasons as early as 1836. By 1870 many were first generation Americans who still were listed as Irish on the census. Some of these families had been joined by relatives eager to earn a living in this country.

Germans continued to arrive for economic and political reasons. At first it was those associated with the politically liberal movements that swept France and Germany in the late 1840s and 1850s. However, not all Germans who came later were political refugees. Crop failures throughout the 1840s and 1850s and land confiscation also brought conservative rural peasants seeking farm land. America also attracted German shopkeepers from small communities who followed their neighbors to the New World.

Scandinavians came to Illinois as early as the 1830s, but the largest wave of immigration, especially Swedish, did not peak until after the mid-1850s. The Swedes came to Lemont to farm, to work as artisans, blacksmiths, stone masons, and carpenters. They also came for work on the railroad and in the quarries. Many began life here as hired farm hands and domestics. In the 1860s and 1870s common farm labor in Sweden was paid the equivalent of 66 cents a day in summer and 46 cents a day in winter, while here in the States, common farm labor could earn one dollar and 34 cents a day in the summer and 97 cents a day in the winter. Mechanics and skilled labor did even better; pay for blacksmiths and carpenters was 80 cents a day in Sweden and $2.90 in Illinois.

The Polish community in Lemont developed mainly after 1871 when Bismarck enforced the "Germanization" of the Polish provinces. Oppressed and brutalized, they came for religious freedom and economic freedom, for *za chlebem* ("for bread").

This period in Lemont history was part of the pattern of community building. Our post-war population increase and a solid economic base led to the desire to organize. Most of our permanent

Old Saint Alphonsus Church (Photo courtesy of Lemont Historical Society)

institutions have their beginning around the twenty-year period from 1865 to 1885. Consider the following: the Methodist Episcopal Church had a building by 1861 and the second St. Patrick's Church was built in 1862 on the hill now east of Central School to accommodate the growing Irish community. It was dedicated on August 15, and renamed St. Mary's Church.[12] By 1867, the Redemptorist Fathers organized the start of St. Alphonsus to serve German-speaking Lemonters, many from Luxembourg and Alsace-Lorraine.[13] It was established so the newly arrived Germans and German-speaking Poles could offer confession and hear parts of the mass in their own language. The first German mass was held in the public school on Main Street and by the end of that year that community had their own frame church.[14]

Old SS. Cyril's and Methodius Church. (Photo courtesy of Lemont Historical Society)

As early as 1871, Rev. Adolph Baranowski, of St. Stanislaus Kosta in Chicago, came to Lemont to offer mass to the increasing Polish population. By 1882, Archbishop Feehan authorized Rev. Leopold Moczygemba, who was serving at St. Alphonsus, to form a Polish parish in Lemont.

From this was born Saints Cyril's and Methodius Church, completed in 1884.[15] Moczygemba had the church designed after his home church in Pluznica, Poland.

Between 1870 and 1873, both the German Lutheran St. Matthew's and the Swedish Lutheran Bethany organized churches and developed parochial schools as part of the sense of ethnic community within the village.[16]

Along with the church, an ordered community needs schools. Concern for education developed as early as 1841, with the formation of subscription schools to serve the children of the canal and quarry workers. Mrs. Lamb held school by the old lime kiln on the east side and Mrs. Flannigan

A view of Singer's Private School, circa 1913. At this time, it was part of the St. Matthew Lutheran Church complex. Also note the steeple on St. Matthew's, which was destroyed in a fire in 1918 and not replaced.

offered classes at the Slavin & Laughlin site.[17] Shortly after, the township began to support education with the creation of public ungraded rural and village grammar schools: Derby, at the corner of Derby and Archer Road; Bell School at Bell and Parker Roads; Hastings at Walker and Main; Sag School at Sag Bridge; and the Bracken School on 127th Street about one-half mile east of State Street. All rural schools were located with the idea that the pupils should be within walking distance, usually one to one and a half miles. These country schools offered classes through the eight grades, but many students left after the age of ten. Teachers for these schools were hired by each local school board and,

in the early days, anyone who had completed some extra schooling could present himself or herself as a teacher. The quality of the candidates was as varied as their background. Some of the teachers worked only a few years using teaching as a way to earn money while reading for the bar or studying business.

By the 1870s and 1880s, education in Lemont, and the nation, became so important that there developed several private and parochial schools. One private institution, in Lemont, was Horace Singer's school for male students. This tuition school was open to those of middle class background, mostly children of the stone companies' administrative staffs and children of the village professionals. This was probably a reflection on the physical condition of the village school and an attempt to separate the middle class students from the large number of immigrant children.

The village, having more pupils, established a graded school on Main Street by the 1850s.

The 1869 Lemont Public School, also known as the "Madden School." (Photo courtesy of the Lemont Historical Society)

Graded schools separated students according to their educational level and those who taught in town had extra qualifications or experience. Our first recorded school superintendent was George Plant. A native of Boston, he trained in Milwaukee and took law courses at the Chicago Law Institute. His skills at organizing and teaching were so remarkable that by 1873 he was elected superintendent of all Cook County Schools. One other early teacher was Professor John McCarthy.[18] Students spoke of him as a very tough but fair man. He had lost his right arm serving in the British Army, however, he was more than able to handle any discipline, which was often corporal, with his left arm. By 1869 the voters recognized a need for a modern village public school and built the fine stone building that stands today. It was completed in 1870 and Singer's private school soon closed.

Life for students in the new public school was not as idealistic as we like to picture. The class and ethnic divisions that motivated the adults were reflected in their children. One student, Horace Singer Norton, recalled this fact when telling of his school days in 1875. Son of Dewitt Clinton Norton,[19] Horace grew up in strict but comfortable circumstances. He even had a nurse-nanny, Mary Dee, from Ireland. She filled his early life with love, worldly advice, and superstition. Horace said, "I became infected with her Irish superstitions at an early age and to this day can see Druids dancing on the hearth, or looking at a full moon find an Irishman up there chopping wood."[20]

When Horace was seven, he started school. Mary Dee dressed him in clothes befitting the son of one of Lemont's leading citizens and he climbed up the hill to the new Central School to enroll in first grade.[21] Trouble started immediately. Horace had barely reached the first grade classroom when Paddy Goodman, the tyrant of the upper grades, spotted him. Dressed in velvet and lace with new shoes, Horace was the perfect target for Paddy's brand of terror. Many of the school's students came from poor families and some had fathers who worked the Norton quarries. Young Horace, looking like a page from a fashion magazine, stood out. So, in the days that followed, school became a terror. Each day Horace tried to devise a new route to take from school to his home on Illinois Street to avoid Paddy and his gang. If they saw him, they would pelt him with hedge apples, rotten fruit, or mudballs.

He did not tell his family but kept his fears secret. Mary, wise to the ways of the world, was not unaware of his problem. He sometimes came home with a bloody nose or blackened eyes. One day as she was helping him dress, Mary took a small scissors from her sewing basket. She removed the center screw and took half of the scissors and tied it to a ribbon and placed it around Horace's neck. Mary then told him, "When the big boys pick on you and you are outnumbered, use this weapon Mary has made for you. There is not a bully in town so big as can disdain the bite of it."[22]

Horace reported that he wore that weapon like an amulet, with some inner peace. He became secure in the knowledge that he had protection if he needed it. That day soon arrived. Coming home from school one afternoon, Horace was followed by Paddy and his gang into a barn where they cornered him. There they began to take turns teasing and beating him. When Paddy began to close in, Horace pulled out the homemade knife and lunged at Paddy. Paddy fell moaning and everyone ran away — including Horace.

Mary was in the kitchen when Horace came home. He told his dreadful tale to her and Mary told him to go to his father with the whole story. Mr. Norton was on the front porch. Horace ran to see him, but who should be there but Mrs. Goodman. She was crying and through her sobs Horace could hear such words as, "attacked my poor Paddy." At that

Horace took off for the stable. There all kinds of ideas ran through his mind. He considered running away and wanted to take Mary with him. His fears were interrupted by Mary's call to dinner. Deciding to eat his last meal, he crept into the dining room and toyed with his food.

After a long silence his father spoke, "How did you fare in school today, Bub?"

Horace looked up, his heart racing and replied, "Oh, all right." He thought he saw a faint smile on his father's face. Nothing more was said. The next day, he went off to school fearing the worst. To his surprise Paddy was in school and not dead. Paddy smiled and said, "Hello." So did his gang. There were no more insults and jeers, Horace was now a member of the group. His tough school years at Central did not hurt him. He went on to become vice-president of U.S. Steel in Gary, Indiana, and helped to develop and lay out the town while serving as the land agent for U.S. Steel.[23]

For those parents who wanted an alternative to public school, Lemont developed a parochial education system. St. Alphonsus had a school by 1880 which was run by the Sisters of St. Agnes; St. Patrick's had a select school, St. James Academy, begun in 1883 under the Sisters of Providence; and SS. Cyril's and Methodius had a school by 1884 served by the Franciscan Sisters. SS. Cyril's offered classes only through the fourth grade until the early 1900s. The German Lutherans at St. Matthew's developed a day school in 1888 and the Swedish Lutherans at Bethany had a school by 1875.

This interest in education reflected the growing change in society. It was clear to parents that the new industrial age demanded more education. In response, the Central School made an outreach at this time by developing a post-eighth grade program, the forerunner of our Lemont High school, offering advanced courses as early as 1885.[24] Enrollment in this program had as many as 53 students by 1887. The idea of education for all children and adults was reinforced by a campaign in the local paper, the *Lemont Press*, for the establishment of a public library in the community.[25]

The beginnings of social organization, apart from the church and school, also started with the formation of the International Order of Odd Fellows Marble City Lodge in 1870.[26] Its membership list included William Case, Archibald Ingraham, J.B. Neil, D.H. George, L. M. De Pue and Horace Singer. In 1873, the A.F.& A.M.[27] Lodge joined the ranks of secret societies in Lemont with such men as T.J. Huston, A.W. Irwin, J.C. Thorpe, J.S. Shattuck, L.W. Parks, James Box, B. Van Buren, J.W., Coombs, John Brooks, and George Briffet. Social societies were not limited to those in town. Farmers in Lemont and Homer joined the Grange. A positive value of the Grange was that it recognized "the importance of the farm wife and steered away from the 'men only' tenets of some more urban secret societies."[28] Dues and fees were low and both men and women were eligible for seven degrees patterned after other secret societies. The value of the Grange was that it served as an organization that gave farmers a collective voice, economically and politically.

As the community grew, there developed a movement to form a village government. Up to the 1870s, Lemont was governed under township and county rule. The township supervisor was the governmental head and directed the health and safety concerns of the public. Law was enforced by the township constable, the Cook County sheriff and local justices of the peace. Road maintenance, tax collection, and public welfare was also part of his role. When the State Constitutional Convention met in 1869 in Springfield, they paved the way for the state legislature to pass laws to encourage municipal incorporation and the community of Lemont responded.

On June 9, 1873, a special election was held to decide if the settlement of Lemont wanted to become a village. The vote was 243 for incorporation and none against. Clearly, the people of the community wanted to take charge of their own affairs. The village boundaries were established as follows:

> Commencing at the SE corner of Section 20, running thence East 80 rods, thence North to the South bank of the Des Plaines River, thence in a Westerly direction along the south bank of the said river to the West line of Section 20, thence south said Section line to the SW corner of said Section 20, thence south 80 rods, then East 240 rods, thence North 80 rods, thence East to the place of the beginning; all of the territory being situated in Township 27 North, Range 11 East.

The first trustees for the village were Joel A. Wells, who was superintendent of the Lemont Stone Company; Stephen Keough, a saloon keeper and township supervisor;[29] Nicholas New, who had a dry goods and saloon business; Dr. Wm. Pierce, a physician; Daniel B. Murphy, who owned a general store; and John W. Tedens, who operated Tedens and Thormahlen's Store. In those days, the procedure was for the board of trustees to select the president, or mayor, who served for a one-year term. After 1894, mayors were directly elected by the public for a one-year term. Later this was changed to a four-year term.

After Wells, others who served during the 19th and early 20th Century were: L. W. Park, 1876; A. Ingraham, 1877; D. B. Murphy, 1878; Stephen Keough, 1879; James Noonan, 1880; Nicholas New, 1881; D. C. Norton, 1881 to 1891; James Hennebry, 1892; John McCarthy, 1893 to 1896; Daniel B. Murphy, 1897 to 1899; Peter Fischbach, 1900 to 1901 (died in office); P. A. Nelson, 1901 to 1902; Otto Earnshaw, 1903; Tim Sullivan, 1904 to 1908; and Francis Keough, 1909 to1910.[30]

The Township Hall then was a wooden structure at the present site on Main Street. The village shared offices in the building. It served until the 1890s, when it was replaced by the building that stands there now. The act of incorporation was an addition to the town and its early leaders were eager to attract both business and residential development. Stephen Keough, who served both as mayor and town supervisor, was one of Lemont's biggest boosters. He invited the editor of the *Joliet News* to tour the town in 1874. The result was a glowing report to its readers:

> We made a short visit to Lemont the other day and found it one of the liveliest towns in this section of the country, except Joliet. The stone quarries there, particularly that of J. A. Boyer and that of the Illinois Stone Company under Hon. J. A. Wells are working a full force of men. We were favored with a ride about the burgh and its surroundings by our friend S. Keough Esq., the popular and efficient supervisor of the town, after his blooded pacer. We must say we enjoyed the scenery and its improvements and everything except the speed which his fast nag jerked us along. It was rather faster than we decided to ride. Lemont has doubled its population and business in the last five years and is destined at a not very distant day to become one of the most flourishing and prosperous of our inland towns.[31]

Horse and buggy, circa 1900. Note the droppings on the roadway. (Photo courtesy of Lemont Historical Society)

When a community organizes into a governmental structure, it must be assumed that there are certain problems that need to be addressed. That was as true then as it is today. Those needs include the health and safety of the village. One of the first problems that needed action was the control and regulation of animals within the village. The horse was everywhere because it was an important economic factor in community life. Teams and wagons moved along the streets to bring people to shop or to deliver goods from the farms, the canal and the train. Services for the horse included watering troughs, feed stores, harness makers (Tedens and Thormahlen's had three full-time harness makers in their employ), saddle shops, patent medicines, veterinarians, wagon makers, wheel wrights, farriers, blacksmiths, and farmers to supply hay and feed.

Lemont's streets were rutted by the constant flow of wagon wheels and marked by the endless droppings and inevitable flies.[32] The average horse produces 20 to 25 pounds of manure a day and if one estimates one horse for each eight Lemonters in 1870, that could mean as much as 10,000 pounds of manure ground into the dirt streets daily. Clearly, street cleaning and control of stables became an important part of village responsibility. In 1879, 830 dollars of the total village budget of 1,450 dollars was directed to streets, bridges, and sanitation.[33] With unpaved streets, mud was also a problem as this local newspaper verse recounts:

A SONG FROM THE DOWNTOWN STREETS

My name is mud, alias street,
My home is Lemont tis true.

I am not quite so swell perhaps
As others known to you.
In seasons dry, I'm dust galore,
In seasons wet, I'm slush.
In seasons known as half and half,
I'm better known as mush.
"Progressive Citizen" is my Dad.
He loves me cause I'm cheap.
Improvement causes him to groan,
And Taxes make him weep.
So wade and wallow in the dirt,
And choke with dust and sneeze.
I'm full of microbes and when I'm dry
I'll toss them in the breeze.

Not only was the private horse a problem but the volume of waste produced by the livery stables needed some control. Lemont's main stable in the 1870s, Brandt & Wagner, was located on Canal and Lemont Streets along the Alton Railroad track. It was used by people who could not or chose not to own their own horse or rig. It also rented equipment for special events. Horses were boarded there during poor weather, so stable owners looked forward to cold or rainy days as a time to make money. Horses were also stabled at the livery when their owners took the train to Chicago or Joliet.

The livery stable, along with the general store, was often the center of town activity. The stable was a masculine place where one could gossip and pass the time of day. It was not a spot where a "well-bred" woman would linger, and it was generally forbidden to

Farm animals in the village, 1890s. (Photo courtesy of Lemont Historical Society)

children. It was dangerous and often a haven for loafers and transients. It was also a place where drinking, gambling, and smoking were common. Mothers, of course, did not want their children exposed to such evils. There was also the possibility that stud services were offered and children of the village, not used to farm ways, were to be sheltered from such animal knowledge. Yet, these were the very reasons that there was no more fascinating place for a child to spend an afternoon.[34] Men would sit outside on warm days as the smell of the stable with its urine soaked straw was often overpowering, even for those raised with animals. Here they would talk town politics, while children ran through the barn.

Advertising by John Bourg in 1896 newspaper. (Illustration courtesy of Lemont Historical Society)

Customers, mostly local people, were responsible for treating the stable horses kindly and properly. Lemonters recognized local horses on sight, so any improper handling was reported. The rural society looked down on anyone who mistreated animals. Each horse was a living thing, with those special quirks that living creatures develop, which endeared some horses to their owners and to the community. Favorite horses were often those who would run fast and would not let anyone pass them on the road, or were fast enough for a race, with a few side bets, on the Des Plaines River Flats. In contrast, there were the steady loyal work animals such as the ice or milk delivery horses, who often knew the route better than the driver, stopping and moving on their own from customer to customer.

The stables and horses were not the only sanitary problem that the early village government faced. The transition from a rural community to a village did not come by vote alone. Most town people still wanted to keep chickens, pigs, and a milk cow or two on their own lot. These animals were not always supervised as they should have been. For example, as late as 1901, Mrs. Augusta Forkel was brought to court by Mrs. John Lavrentz over a rooster. It seems that Mrs. Forkel's rooster's crowing had caused the women to argue. Mrs. Laverntz accused Mrs. Forkel of throwing a stone at her. In response Mrs. Forkel replied that there were no stones in her front yard for she had the best front yard in Lemont. The jury found Mrs. Forkel innocent. What happened to the rooster is not recorded.

Another problem presented to the board was that of free roaming pigs. They were a rural tradition as they did clean up a good deal of the garbage and waste discarded by the citizens. But by 1879, residents appeared before the village board asking them to enforce the ordinance against the "running at large of swine."[35]

Even more dangerous to the health of the community was the difficulty presented at the August village meeting of the same year. Doctors W. P. Pierce, M. T. O'Cleary, and J. M. Rood asked the board to take action against the butcher shop of John Bourg at what would now be near 117 Stephen Street. According to the physicians, there were "offensive and unhealthy odors emanating from the shop." They went on to report that "experience and medical science teach that decaying annimal [sic] matter is the cause of many dangerous diseases, a fact we fear may soon be verified by an increase of sickness and mortality."[36]

They wanted enforcement of the ordinance that prohibited the killing of animals and the rendering of tallow within the corporate limits. They also requested that "all the decomposing blood and offal now sweltering in the sun or soaking in the soil about the place be thoroughly removed to a place outside the corporate limits."[37]

Lemont water works, built in the 1880s. (Photo courtesy of Lemont Historical Society)

Contagious diseases were common and mostly endemic. However, the village did suffer several epidemics. In 1881, a smallpox epidemic broke out and the village called a special meeting to handle the problem. Most of the cases were in the immigrant communities and the village fathers paid men two dollars a day to guard anyone from leaving homes with smallpox victims. Unable to confine the disease, within a month the village requested 200 vaccination points.[38] Although vaccination had proven effective before and during the Civil War and after the Chicago Fire, some were fearful of it, feeling that the vaccinations themselves caused disease. Therefore, many in the community were unprotected.

As Lemont began to address health and safety in the community, regulations were developed to control business and collect revenue. Saloons were licensed and in 1881 the village collected almost 2,000 dollars in revenue, an impressive sum in those days.[39] They passed an ordinance that made it unlawful for druggists to sell liquor without a license, therefore restricting its sale for medicinal use only. To meet the moral issue of the tem-

Marble City House, at the corner of Main and State Streets. (Photo courtesy of Lemont Historical Society)

perance movement they passed an ordinance that prohibited the sale of liquor to any drunkard, or to any person whose wife or relative requested in writing that liquor dealers not sell to such a person. It is not known if that ordinance was enforced.

By 1884, it was clear the village needed its own water supply and Martin Sauber built a reservoir and laid pipes in the main part of the village. A bond issue was passed to complete the system. Charges varied from ten dollars a year for saloons to six dollars a year for private homes. Many chose to keep their own private shallow wells, but the water was useful for large businesses and for fire protection.

By 1885, the community had developed into a structured village. Kerosene street lights were added that year, and the Chicago Telephone Company had an office on Canal Street and was stringing lines to those who wanted the service. Downtown Lemont in 1885 included three boarding houses and three hotels. The hotels were the Union near Main and Stephens, the American House on Canal across from the livery stable, and the Marble City Hotel by the Alton Station. There were 30 various stores and services plus 30 saloons, two billiard parlors, one dance hall, one roller-skating rink, two candy stores, a wagon maker, a cigar factory, a soda factory, two lumber yards, a coal yard, a window and sash shop, the Shering Beer Depot, a photographer, two grain elevators, one public central school, five parochial schools, and six churches.[40] Still there was some frontier left, as the county was paying a five dollar bounty for any wolves killed.

Lemont was a growing community with much of its growth based on the canal, the railroad, and the quarries with their unskilled immigrant labor force. They were underpaid and overworked; this was the dark side of the town's prosperity, a force doomed to erupt again.

ENDNOTES

[1]Bessie Pierce, *A History of Chicago* (New York: Knopf, 1940), vol. 2, p. 67.

[2]The war and other political developments within Canada created considerable paranoia between the North and the Canadian authorities. Some Confederate soldiers had used Canada as a base for raids into the North.

[3]*Joliet True Democrat*, June 7, 1862.

[4]Lemont and the other towns along the canal were quick to lay all the blame on Chicago. This was not true since waste water from all towns was washed into the I & M Canal. The problem became acute as the Chicagoland area and the Des Plaines Valley grew in population.

[5]D.C. Norton served as mayor of Lemont for ten years from 1881.

[6]Pierce, *A History of Chicago*, vol. 2, p. 157.

[7]George Woodruff, *A History of Will County* (Evansville: Unigraphics, 1973), p. 304.

[8]James E. Bourne, "Occupation and Ethnicity in Lemont, 1870-1880," *Looking For Lemont*, ed. Michael Conzen and Carl Zimring, (Chicago: University of Chicago, 1994), pp. 209-213.

[9]U.S. Agricultural Census, 1860, Lemont Township, Cook County, Illinois.

[10]*The Chicago and Alton Directory*, (Chicago: Chicago and Alton Railroad, 1860).

[11]Mary Ellen Gifford, "Lemont and the I & M Canal," *Where the Trails Cross* (South Holland: South Suburban Geneological Society, Spring 1977), vol. 7:3, p. 97.

[12]The church was later renamed St. Patrick's in 1880 by Rev. James Hogan.

[13]We have a Luxemburg Street honoring those early pioneers.

[14]Barbara Bushman, ed., *Lemont, Illinois: Its History In Commemoration Of The Centennial Of Its Incorporation* (Des Plaines: King/Mann Yearbook, 1973), p. 86.

[15]Archbishop Feehan was in favor of national parishes to keep the faith of non-English speaking Catholics. This is the reason that a community as small as Lemont had national parishes. The idea helped support the new immigrants but it also kept the Catholics in our community separated from one another.

[16]Bushman, *Lemont, Illinois,* pp. 88, 105.

[17]Subscription schools operated on a tuition basis. Parents paid the teacher what they could to have their children learn fundamental reading and math skills.

[18]Not related to the John McCarthy who served as mayor.

[19]D.C. Norton was mayor for ten years, a quarry owner, a contractor, and part of the Norton family enterprises.

[20]*The Lemonter*, December 15, 1938.

[21]The D.C. Norton home was on the southeast corner of Illinois and Fremont Streets.

[22]*The Lemonter*, December 15, 1938.

[23]*Ibid*. Interview on his retirement from U.S.Steel. Important as he was to the founding of Gary, he did remain tough in his dealings with people. See James Lane, *City of the Century* (Bloomington: Indiana University Press, 1978), p. 206. Commenting on the lack of people at Norton's funeral in Gary, one of his pallbearers said, "You could have sprayed that chapel with a machine gun and wouldn't have hit 17 people."

[24]*Lemont Press*, May 1887.

[25]This was completed by 1887 with contributions by N.J. Brown and Mrs. Mancel Talcott. See *Lemont Press*, March 1887.

[26]Lemont's Independent Order of Odd Fellows had their own cemetery on 127th Street. It is now part of St. Matthew's complex.

[27]Ancient Free & Accepted Masons.

[28]John Keiser, *Building For The Centuries: Illinois 1865-1898* (Urbana: University of Illinois Press, 1977), pp. 141-142.

[29]Keough's presence as the township supervisor and as trustee of the newly incorporated village made the governmental transition a smooth process. It seems that co-operation between the bodies was remarkable. Joel Wells was the father of John Wells, who went off to the Civil War right after his marriage.

[30]Francis Keough, son of Stephen Keough, went on to serve Lemont for 17 more years.

[31]*Joliet News*, July 9, 1874.

[32]Sonia Kallick, *Lemont Walking Tour, Site 30* (Lemont: Lemont Historical Society, 1975).

[33]Bushman, *Lemont, Illinois,* p. 23.

[34]Keiser, *Building For The Centuries,* p. 2.

[35]Lemont Village Council Meeting Minutes, vol. 1, May 14, 1879, p. 6.

[36]Lemont Village Board Minutes, vol. 1, August 16, 1879, p. 33.

[37]*Ibid.*, p. 33-34.

[38]Bushman, *Lemont, Illinois,* p. 23.

[39]*Ibid*.

[40]Sandborn Fire Insurance Map of Lemont, Cook County, 1884.

U.S. HISTORY

1870: *Standard Oil Company Formed — U.S. Population at 39 Million — First Subway Line, New York.*

1871: *Chicago Fire; 250⁺ Die, 200 Million in Property Damage — Pneumatic Rock Drill Invented, Will Change Quarry Work — Peshtigo Fire, 1000⁺ Die.*

1872: *Amnesty Act Pardons Most Ex-Confederates — Brooklyn Bridge Opens — Montgomery Ward Mail Order House Begins.*

1873: *Financial Panic in the East — First Color Photography — Silver Discovered in Nevada.*

1874: *Pressure Cooker Developed for Home Use — Women's Christian Temperance Union Forms.*

1875: *The Dynamo Invented — Luther Burbank Begins His Plant and Fruit Experiments.*

1876: *U.S. Centennial in Philadelphia — Colorado Becomes a State — Result of Presidential Election Unclear Goes to Congress and Hayes is Made the 19th President — Telephone Invented.*

1877: *Railroad Strikes Throughout the Nation — Federal Troops are Withdrawn from the Southern States — Edison Invents the "Talking Machine."*

1878: *First Bicycles in America — Edison Announces the Incandescent Lamp — Yellow Fever Epidemic in Country.*

1879: *Woolworth Opens First 5 & 10 Cent Store, Beginning of Chain Stores — Art Institute of Chicago Founded.*

LEMONT HISTORY

1870: *Population at 3,575, Almost Equal Parts Irish, German, Swedish, Danish, and "Yankee" Settlers — H.M. Singer Closes His Private School — Marble City I.O.O.F. Lodge Forms.*

1871: *I & M Canal Debt Paid Off — Martin Madden Working for Walker Quarry — Norton's Store Built — Ralph Paine Born in Lemont, Author and Newspaper Reporter.*

1872: *Bethany Church Organized — Lemuel Brown Returns to Lemont to Work in Family Business — Serious Contagious Horse Disease Affects Transportation in Town and the Country.*

1873: *Lemont Organized As a Village on April 10 — First Mayor Joel Wells — $5.00 Bounty for Wolves — St. Patrick's Present Rectory Built by S. L. Derby — House on 503 Singer Also Built by Derby — Great Train Wreck East of Town August 16, 23 Killed — Lemont A.F. & A.M. Formed.*

1874: *Boyer Stone Quarry Has 150 Men Working — St. Matthew's Formed.*

1875: *L.W. Park Mayor of Town — S. Keough Supervisor — Bethany Has a Parochial School.*

1876: *Town Hears of Custer's Last Stand.*

1877: *A. Ingraham Mayor — Third Major Strike in Lemont Quarries — Workers Go Out in Sympathy with National Rail Strike.*

1878: *D. B. Murphy Mayor — Martin Madden, Future Congressman, Marries Elizabeth Smart from Cass — Mancell Talcott, Quarry Owner, Dies.*

1879: *John Doolin Teacher at Sag School, He Teaches Lemont Children into the 1930s — Three Doctors in Town, W.P. Pierce, M.T. O'Cleary, and J.M. Rood — Law Passed Making Unlawful for Druggist to Sell Liquor Without License — Des Plaines River Bridge Repaired — Law against Killing Animals in Village — Lemont Jail Has Two Cells, Police Constable Wants More.*

BUSINESSES IN LEMONT IN 1878*

John Alden: *Meat Market*

Frank Bartz: *Mason*

John Baury: *Meat Market*

Joshua Bell: *Harnessmaker*

W. Bevington: *Lumber*

G. A. Bodenschatz: *Druggist*

John Bolton: *Soda Manufacturer*

L. L. Brown: *Coal*

John Collins: *Saloon*

B. Conrad: *Saloon & Shoemaker*

F. C. Copp: *Saloon*

P. Dockendorf: *Saloon*

Henry Dorre: *Baker*

Thomas Driscoll: *Saloon*

Anthony Dutter: *Saloon*

Frank Eckert: *Saloon*

Nicholas Eulert: *Carpenter & Hardware*

A. Friedley: *Hardware*

J. Gerharz: *Furniture*

Helbig & Hanson: *Hotel*

C. Hettinger: *Shoemaker*

Geo. Hettinger: *Saloon & Confectioner*

Patrick Hunt: *Saloon*

Illinois Stone Quarry

A. Ingraham: *Blacksmith*

Benjamin U. Jacobs: *Druggist*

Ellen Jennings: *News & Confectionery*

John Kearney: *Hotel*

Michael Keldon: *Saloon*

Kirby & Howe: *Stone Quarry*

Miss Lee: *Milliner*

J. S. Luther & Son: *Lumber*

Chas. Lutz: *Blacksmith*

H. Martin & Son: *General Store*

D. B. Murphy: *General Store*

M. New: *Saloon*

S. W. Norton: *General Store*

Peter Pitts: *Saloon*

Roebuck & Perriolet: *General Store*

Herbert Sauber: *Saloon*

H. Schmeltzer: *Boots & Shoes*

John Schneider: *Saloon*

Singer & Talcott: *Stone Quarry*

Frank Slavin: *Grocery & Saloon*

William Slavin: *Saloon*

Samuel Spence: *Saloon*

J. H. Tedens: *General Store*

Ferdinand Toussing: *Cigar Manufacturer*

L. Valentine: *Barber*

Ed. Walker: *Stone Quarry*

Ward & Daniels: *Butter & Cheese Factory*

Geo. Weimer: *Blacksmith*

SAG BRIDGE BUSINESSES IN 1878*

Clowery & Reid: *Stone Quarry*

James Falvey: *Station Agent*

John Gannon: *Justice of the Peace*

Jacob Hush: *Wagonmaker*

Mathias Hush: *Blacksmith*

Patrick Kirk: *Hotel*

Mathias Maltby: *Boots & Shoes*

T. Moranski: *Boots & Shoes*

Ezekiel Morrison: *Stone Quarry*

Alexander Reid: *General Store And Postmaster*

Wm. Richard: *Butcher*

John Ruppert: *Saloon & Hotel*

*From the *Illinois State Gazetteer & Business Directory* (Detroit, MI: R. L. Polk & Co., 1878). Note the increase in the number of saloons from the 1868 business directory. This probably means a larger working population present in town and more through traffic on the railroad and the I & M Canal.

CHAPTER FIFTEEN

THE LEMONT MASSACRE OF 1885
Lemont Makes Labor History

In spite of a stronger economy, conditions in Lemont did not favor any action by quarry workers against the owners. The 1882 walkout failed to gain more money or better working conditions. It was not that the men were happy with the situation; it was simply that they had little power or passion for another fight. It seemed that there was always someone more desperate and willing to take their jobs. As immigration from Europe increased, more people became part of the Des Plaines Valley labor pool that was available for work.

The next strike, in 1885, did not begin in Lemont, although Lemont paid the price. It began early in the morning, April 1, 1885, when a "stubborn Swede" at the Joliet Stone Company Quarry laid down his tools and refused to work any longer for the traditional wage of $1.50 a day. History does not record his name, but his actions were like a wave that ebbed and flowed down the Des Plaines Valley, slowly at first, then increasing in force until it ended violently in Lemont.

Because the Swede refused to work, the others at the quarry suddenly found strength and walked out. As a group they went to the Bissel Quarry and persuaded those workers to come out with them. By noon they numbered 150 and they spread out to Lemont and Lockport. Along the way the strikers stopped at each quarry to convince others to walk out. Almost all the quarrymen did, some out of a heady sense of brotherhood and unity, some out of fear of the men. When the army of strikers reached Lemont, along the I & M towpath, it was late afternoon.

> Which side are you on—boys
> Which side are you on?[1]

At the Lemont quarries the workers were toiling away in the spring evening when they looked up to see well over 300 men surrounding the area. To Lemont's newly immigrated Polish, Swedish, and German stone workers, this group looked like a mob out to lynch them or to take away their jobs. They grabbed picks and shovels and began to fight, yelling and cursing in a Babel of languages. After some tense moments the Lemonters were disarmed, not an easy thing to do, and the Joliet and Lockport workers explained their reason for being there. This was not simple, since Lockport and Joliet leaders spoke mostly Swedish and most of the Lemont workers Polish and German. After a long conference, translated from one language to another, the Joliet and Lockport workers failed to get the Lemonters to walk out. A few did but, most stayed in the quarries.[2]

Some remained because they did not understand the language. Some, mostly Poles, remained because they did not trust the Swedes for historical reasons. Sweden had invaded Poland in the 1600s and was a historical and religious enemy of Poland. Others stayed because they were poor and feared losing their jobs. Still others remembered that they had not been supported by the Joliet and Lockport workers in 1882. Finally, many no longer believed that group action would work, since they had lost against the owners too often.

Failure to get the Lemont workers to come out disappointed the Joliet and Lockport men, because Lemont was the center of the stone industry and the key to the price paid to quarry workers throughout the area. The Lemont stone trade employed over 2,000 men. The strikers returned to Joliet and Lockport that evening still determined to hold out in spite of the Lemont workers.

> Don't scab for the bosses,
> Don't listen to their lies,
> Us poor folk haven't a chance,
> Unless we organize.

The Lockport and Joliet quarries remained shut, while Lemont operations continued. This state of affairs gave the Lemont owners the false idea that their workers were loyal to the companies that employed them. So on April 3, the Lemont quarry owners notified Joliet owners that they would send 500 of their men to break the strike. This announcement incensed our local workers. They might be willing to work for $1.50, or $1.25 a day, but they were not ready to take anyone's job, or expose themselves to the dangers of strike breaking for the sake of the quarry owners.

> Oh, workers, can you stand it?
> Oh, tell me how you can.
> Will you be a lousy scab or,
> Will you be a man?

They refused to go. In fact, the tactics suggested for breaking the strike in Lockport and Joliet angered so many Lemonters that they began to walk out. On April 8, all of the workers at the Walker Quarry left. They were the toughest, most militant group, and by the ninth they convinced all other local quarries to shut down.

With all the Des Plaines Valley quarries out, the major action was to keep up unity and to prevent others from scabbing. Workers marched up and down the valley from Joliet to the Sag checking on the quarries to see that they were not in operation. Those waves of marchers during the first weeks were cheerful, funny, and yet poignant. The strength in their numbers convinced them that this time they could win. It was spring and there was a demand for stone. Most of the stone stored in the Chicago yards since the previous fall had been sold. The workers believed that if they all held out, the owners would come to terms.

The quarry workers themselves were a visible demonstration to the nativist pioneers of the valley of the effect of open immigration on their society. To many, these foreigners were strange and fearsome. For example, there was a unity parade from Joliet to Lockport led by a Swedish worker playing an ancient Norwegian lovesong on the mouth organ. At his side was a black Senegambian who worked in the Sanger Quarry. The Senegambian sang and danced for the crowds who turned out to stare at the strange demonstrations that looked lighthearted, but were deadly serious.

The Lemont workers also held parades through town. The *Joliet News* reported one large march that had a Polish worker carrying the Stars and Stripes, joined by others from all the ethnic groups in the quarries. The flag was a symbol of freedom and the right to have their petition heard. Finally, the group grew so large that Town Marshall Russell went out to break it up. Instead, the workers forced him to lead the demonstration by having a "big Swede apply pressure to his backside with a fence board."[3]

As the days passed the situation became difficult. Strikers' families began to face hunger and added pressure from owners, who attempted to hire strikebreakers from Chicago. The strike also began to lose what little support it may have had from the local merchants and shopkeepers. The quarries contributed a daily payroll of 3,000 dollars a day for Lemont alone[4] and the middle-class merchants could only survive because of the stone trade. When the payroll was not there, they suffered, too.

> Which side are you on, boys?
> Which side are you on?

The strike that began at the Joliet and Lockport quarries on the 1st of April continued as a general strike of all quarry workers in the Des Plaines Valley. So on April 11, quarry owners decided to take concerted action. The strike had affected sale of Dolomite Stone for spring construction. Builders and contractors under deadlines would switch to other materials if the supply of Des Plaines Valley Dolomite Stone was in doubt, so a meeting was held in the office of the Excelsior Stone Company in Chicago. Lemont quarry owners took charge since they were the larger companies and had economic control of the local industry. Lemont stone was shipped at cheaper rates because the quarries were closer to Chicago and because they had their own docks on the I & M Canal. Cut mill blocks of Athens Marble (Lemont Stone) sold at 20 cents a foot and, as a result, the Joliet and Lockport quarries could barely make a profit selling to the Chicago market. They relied more on local sales. One other factor made the Lemont owners the leaders in the industry — most of the men had strong Chicago political connections.[5] Much of this influence developed because Lemont is in Cook County and the large number of Lemont quarry workers were a voting block that carried a good deal of weight with the political powers.

After a long meeting the owners issued the following statement:

> The Lemont and Joliet Stone trade is in a depressed condition, especially competing with Indiana and Iowa quarries where labor is cheaper, and since there are a large number of men available in the area who are willing to work for the wages offered, no concessions will be made.

The statement was signed by the following quarry owners:

> *Bodenshatz and Earnshaw*, Lemont, George Bodenschatz; *Illinois Stone Company*, Lemont, J. McGinnis; *Excelsior Stone Company*, Lemont, S.W. Norton; *Singer & Talcott*, Lemont, E.F. Singer; *Boyer & Corneau*, Lemont, J.A. Boyer; *Enterprize*, Lemont, Martin Madden; *Chicago and Lemont Stone*, Lemont, E. Walker; *Wm. Davidson & Bres.*, Joliet, Wm. Davidson; *Joliet & Chicago Stone*, Joliet, A. Keltie; *Sanger and Moody*, Joliet, M. Sanger; *Joliet Stone*, Joliet, G. Campbell; *Bissell Quarry*, Joliet, Wm. Kronmeyer; *Cresent Stone*; and *Porter & Waters*.[6]

The strikers were effective in keeping the quarries closed and the owners, fearful of competition from other outside quarries, were eager to have them re-open. They offered to take the workers back without reprisals if they returned in 24 hours at the original wage of $1.50 a day.

> Strike for your altars and for your fires,
> Strike for your dollar-seventy five desires.
> Strike for the reward your toil requires.[7]

The *Chicago Tribune* reported that the firms of *Werberg & Company, Werner Brothers,* and *Erickson, Kraker, & Company* refused to attend the conference. They were paying $1.75 and felt that some larger stone companies had instigated the strike to freeze out smaller quarries paying a better wage.[8]

Others workers soon became involved as the strike dragged on. Among the groups that rallied to the quarrymen's cause were the Chicago Bricklayers and Masons. That group refused to lay any Lemont or Joliet Stone until the strike was settled. This action put pressure on the owners who now would lose contracts to the Indiana and Iowa quarries. As days passed and tensions grew, Joliet strike leaders began to waver. By the second week some men returned to work under private subcontracting deals and some began to scab for a wage of $1.25 a day. The great wave of unity and brotherhood that had swept the valley was breaking, but not in Lemont.

Once committed to the fight, the Lemonters grew stronger each day in their determination to hold out for better wages and the eight-hour day. The idea of unity had taken hold. The feeling was so strong that when they heard, on April 25, that some Joliet men had returned to work, a march was formed. This time it was from Lemont to Joliet. A group of over 300 men, led by a Lemonter carrying the American flag and accompanied by a worker with a concertina, went to Joliet. Shouting "no man shall work" and "on to Joliet," they were joined by other workers at Lockport.[9]

The march started peacefully but when they reached the quarries at Joliet, a pitched battle began. Strikers and non-strikers went at each other with fists, bottles, and quarry tools. The battle at Sanger & Moody was a donnybrook, but no one was seriously injured. When the Will County sheriff's police arrived the strikers scattered and headed down the valley for home.

Now it was the Lemont workers who were blamed for starting the strike. A spokesman for the Joliet quarrymen told the *Joliet News* and the police:

> The Lemont men control the matter. If we work here they
> will come and drive us out. THEY ARE AWFUL ROUGH MEN,
> THEM LEMONTERS, AND WE DON'T WANT THEM TO COME
> HERE.[10]

The Joliet papers began a campaign against the Lemont strikers and Lemont itself. In order to downgrade the town, the *Joliet Daily News* reported that the village had a voracious appetite for liquor, saying that one firm alone had sold over 60,000 dollars worth of lager beer in Lemont. A Lockport quarryman was also quoted as threatening the Joliet strike breakers with the following:

> You go back to work and the Lemont strikers will be down
> here and they'll show you fellows what is what![11]

The threats and counter threats reached such a pitch, largely encouraged by the media, that Governor Oglesby reinforced the state militia already stationed in Joliet. They assembled on the 29th of April. No one really felt that any more than simple police security action would be needed to end the strike by "those stubborn foreign Lemont quarry workers." They had little understanding of the deeper forces at work. One tent was reported to have a large banner across its flap reading, "Swede Hunters at Work."

During the week, Horace A. Singer of the Singer & Talcott quarry returned from Denver. He was deeply upset by the continuing strike and the inability of the quarry owners and supervisors including his son, Edward, to deal with it. On April 30, he traveled to Joliet and conferred with officials. What was discussed at that conference was unknown, but Horace Singer announced that he was hiring all new workers and that they would be protected by Pinkerton men.

The situation remained quiet until May 3, at Kracker Hill in Joliet. There another confrontation occurred between Joliet scab workers and Lemont strikers. The battle went on for some time.

The sheriff called the militia and they forced the men back home. Thirty-six Lemonters were caught and held in the Joliet Armory.

Horace Singer. (Illustration courtesy of Lemont Historical Society)

In the morning Sheriff Reitz released 32 strikers outside Joliet and told them to "get back home and not come back under penalty of arrest."[12] Four were held in jail as leaders of the march. They were Frank Peroaeke, A. Swanson, A. Lundgamen, and Frank Peterjaska.[13] One of the Lemonters arrested told the police, "Kill us if you want, we would as soon be shot as work for starvation wages."[14]

Ideas like that frightened the police. The governor was notified of the situation. The police and the quarry owners pressed him to act. So at 4:00 a.m. Monday, May 4, 1885, he telegraphed orders to the militia to move into Lemont. They boarded the early train with four companies and a Gattling gun, under orders to protect life and property in Lemont.

The Lemont quarrymen arrested and released by the Joliet police Sunday night returned to town determined to prevent any worker from crossing the strikers' boycott. The conservative *Chicago Tribune* reported that these men had been "going around among the more ignorant element of the Polish and Swedish quarry workers and insisting that they turn out in force at daylight for the purpose of deterring two gangs of laborers from loading stone boats in Walker's and Singer & Talcott's quarries."[15]

The *Tribune,* perhaps trying to play on ethnic tensions to split the community, reported that the strike leaders were mainly Polish, Bohemian, and Swedish. The paper insisted that the Irish and German population of Lemont was opposed to the strike. The facts do not support the newspaper's position.[16]

Between 4:00 and 5:00 in the morning, strike leaders had nearly 800 strikers mustered together near the village hall. According to the *Chicago Tribune* "every one of them was armed either with an axe handle or a stout hickory club about four feet long."[17] There was no question that the men were upset and that they were milling about the town, but the danger perceived by the *Tribune* was distorted by the political views of the time. The men who gathered were quiet enough that Town Marshall John Russell only swore in eight extra deputies.

Meanwhile, upon receiving orders from General Vance, Monday morning May 4, the four companies — Company A of Streator, Captain Blanchard; Company B of Joliet, Captain Joskin; Company G of Bloomington, Major Hefferan and Captain Smith; and Battery D of Joliet — were placed under the command of Colonel Bennett of Joliet. Within an hour a force of 250 troops boarded a special train on the Alton Route to Lemont. They were held up for a short time as news of the activation was sent to the sheriff of Cook County, who dispatched Colonel Potter and two other deputies to town to report on the situation. The civil authorities were placed in an awkward position since they had little input with the state forces. When Colonel Potter arrived in town, he met first with Township Supervisor J.W. McCarthy and Marshall Russell. It is not clear why he told only the township officials that the village was about to be put under military rule, perhaps because most of the quarries were outside the village or perhaps the village officials, such as D.C. Norton, who was mayor and owner of a quarry, already knew this was the plan.

When informed of the police action that the governor was about to take, McCarthy and Russell became extremely angry. There had been no rioting and extra local men were on duty in case of any trouble. The strikers, unaware of the action planned, gathered in town and around the village hall, singing and parading to keep up a united front and to discourage anyone from returning to work at the old wage.

Around 7:30 a.m., Colonel Potter left the meeting with McCarthy and Russell and went down to the Post Office on Canal Street. The Post Office was then at the rear of 118 Stephens Street. There he saw a crowd of over 400 men and he decided to inform them that the militia was called to Lemont. He looked around and found a small box, stood on it and spoke to the assembly.

He told the workers that the militia was about to arrive and he went on to follow legal form by reading the Riot Act. He warned them that failure to disperse would constitute a violation of law.[18]

According to a reporter for *The Alarm* he also added, "Now, men, I warn you, that if you do not go to work at once for one dollar and fifty cents a day, the military will be sent here to compel you to do it."[19] Many townspeople did not understand English, much less the formal and legal implications of the Riot Act, but soldiers they understood. A number of immigrants hated the military. Experiences with military and political oppression and forced conscription in Europe had brought them here to America. Now this type of oppression, as they viewed it, was happening again only in their own town, Lemont.

Horace Singer, the quarry owner, arrived on the scene to tend to some postal business, or, as some have suggested, to see how the strikers were taking the news. His anger and frustration over the whole situation flared as he pushed a worker who was in his way and stormed into the hostile crowd.[20] Singer really could not understand how the relationship between employer and employee had changed over the years. He had contributed many projects for the community such as his private school and financial support for the

Methodist Church. He had taken a paternalistic view of his relationship with the workers. Now, they were turning on him like ungrateful children.

After Potter finished reading the Riot Act, he found the crowd growing in size as word spread through town. Afraid, he tried to get into the Post Office to telegraph the Cook County sheriff, but could not move as the crowd on Canal Street had grown too large. The townspeople grabbed what sticks and objects they could find and moved down to the Alton Station to await the militia train. The idea was to forcibly board the train and make the militia surrender their arms. When the crowd arrived at the depot, the station master, T.S. Huston, who was also the village magistrate, became fearful of a confrontation between the troops and the townspeople. He thought he could head off the situation, so he telegraphed a message to the troop train to disembark outside town rather than at the station. At 9:00 a.m. the regularly scheduled Joliet train arrived. By then the crowd at the station was estimated at 900 men, women, and children. The passengers on the train were confused and frightened as Lemonters forcibly boarded and ran through the cars looking for the militia. A reporter from Joliet, who was sent to cover the events in Lemont, took one look at the crowd and decided to stay on the train and get off at Sag Bridge. He later confessed that he valued his safety more than any story.

When it was discovered that the militia was not on the regular train, some of the crowd left. Others stayed awaiting the next train. Meanwhile, the militia arrived quietly west of town at the Will-Cook County line and disembarked. On hearing about the arrival, Marshall Russell, Colonel Potter, and Potter's two deputies went to report that the troops were not wanted in town and they would only aggravate an already tense situation which could lead to serious trouble. The troop commander, Colonel Bennett, refused to listen to the civilian authorities. He said his orders were clear. He was a soldier. He would occupy Lemont and nothing could stop him.[21]

Bennett ordered rifles loaded and the bayonets attached as if for major combat. Many of the young militia suddenly became afraid. None really believed that they would do more than guard the quarries so workers who wished might return to their jobs. Bennett ordered two military columns formed for the march. Companies A and B began the entry down old Main Street, which then entered near the Will-Cook County line and ran along the limestone bluffs where the old Brown property[22] is located. Company G and Battery D followed along the Alton tracks. Companies A and B, with Bennett in the lead, were the first to meet the townspeople. At Main and Lockport Streets a crowd of about 250 people stood silently in front of the line of marching troops.

Bennett ordered the people to move. No one did. He then drew his saber and ordered a bayonet charge. The Colonel himself went after four men with his sword.[23] Later stories would put Horace Singer and Mayor Norton in a buggy next to the Colonel in the front line of the charge, but this seems unlikely. At the charge, the crowd broke and began to run. Most ran across what is now Legion Park and to the rear of the advancing militia. They began to throw stones and rubble at the soldiers. Some missiles came from the upper floors and roofs of the houses and stores along the route. As the barrage increased the soldiers became upset and tense. One stone struck a member of Company B in the head and he fell to the ground, stunned. In the confusion a shot-like sound was heard and the militia turned and fired a volley into the crowd. Many were wounded, one fatally. Andrew Stelter, 21, fell dead at Lockport and Main Street.[24]

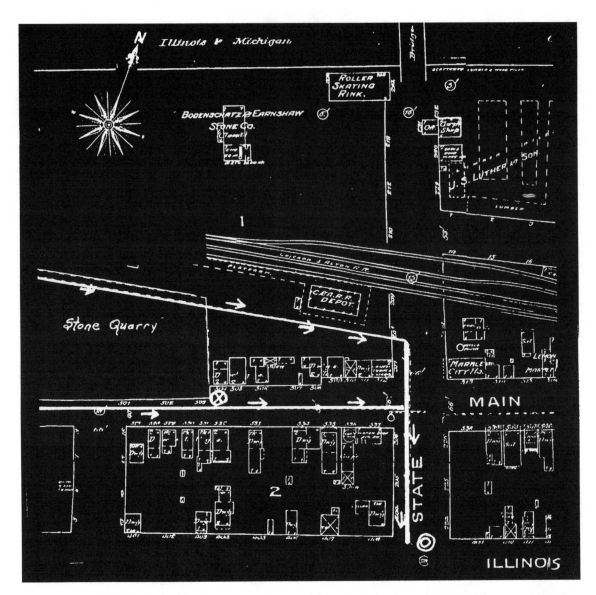

Lemont, 1885. The heavy lines show the route the two militia units took. The circled "X" is where A. Stetler was shot. The circled "O" is where J. Kujawa died. The buildings on the north side of the first block of Main Street are now Legion Park and the stone quarry on the west is where Totura's now stands. (Illustration courtesy of Lemont Historical Society and Sandburn Fire Maps)

After the initial confrontation between the Lemonters and the Illinois Militia and even after the first death, the crowd did not leave the area around the Alton Depot. It broke into small groups that continued to yell and taunt the soldiers with stones and curses in a number of European languages. These small skirmishes caused some members of the militia to break rank and go after individuals in the crowd. One soldier tried to get a Swede, John Ankerberg, to move. Ankerberg refused in spite of guns or force. He stubbornly told the military it was his property and no one could make him leave it.[25]

Finally, understanding the mood of the town, both columns of soldiers decided to join up at State and Main Streets and go on as a group to Illinois Street.[26] This maneuver enabled the crowd to circle the militia on three sides thus increasing their fears. The *Chicago Tribune* reported that the Lemont crowd numbered from 600 to 1,000 while the military only amounted to 75 to 80.[27]

At the corner of State and Illinois, 10 or 12 women attacked some soldiers with clubs and stones tied up in stockings. What happened is not clear, but one of the soldiers lost control and went after two women, listed as Mrs. Super and Mrs. Smach.[28] He either stabbed or hit them with his rifle. One escaped in spite of her injury while the other fell, unable to move. A young worker, John Kujawa, saw the situation and rushed to her rescue and was fatally shot. After that final bloodshed the crowd scattered.

Sadly, Kujawa's body lay on the street for well over an hour, a dreadful symbol in a suddenly deadly silent town. No one would remove it for fear of Battery D and their Gattling gun, which was deployed on the hill near Kujawa's body. Father James Hogan of St. Patrick's Church protested the bloody scene yelling, "You cold-blooded murders, lay down your arms. You have murdered the man."

To which an officer replied, "If you don't get inside the house, we'll drop you, too."[29] The priest ignored the threat and went to offer the death sacrament.[30]

After Kujawa's murder the militia continued its march to the east end of town. Here they met the authorities for the township, Supervisor J.W. McCarthy, and Marshall Russell, for the second time. The two, sick about what had happened, again asked the militia to leave town as the town could police itself. Colonel Bennett replied he was under orders from the Governor to remain in Lemont. He told them that the soldiers would encamp for the night on the hill overlooking the Singer & Talcott quarries.

Bennett did say he was sorry for the incident and that he had not intended to fire guns, but it was all the fault of the mob. There was nothing the town government could do to remove the hated militia now, so McCarthy, in a defiant gesture, walked back to State and Illinois Streets and, under the sight of the Gattling gun, picked up the body of Kujawa and carried it to undertaker Gerharz on Main Street.

Small angry groups gathered in homes and some churches as all taverns were closed by the village authorities. Many believed that it was Horace Singer who had the militia ordered to town because of his economic and political connections. There was talk of lynching him and burning down his home on Singer Avenue. The only thing that prevented more radical men from such retaliation was the presence of the militia and the fact that Mrs. Singer was a well-loved and respected woman. She had always displayed a social concern for the town and for education and health care for the workers. It may have been her good deeds and kind heart that saved her husband that night.

The next day, Tuesday, the 5th of May, the strikers gathered early to organize in groups to dissuade others from breaking the strike by returning to work. Their action was directed mainly at those who operated the stone boats, as there was a large supply of cut stone stored and available for delivery. If it reached the Chicago market the strike would be prolonged. Their action was successful as only a few returned to work.

With news of the shooting, reporters soon descended on the town. They came from Joliet and Chicago and hung around the Alton Station and the few saloons and cafes that were open. They interviewed anyone they could find. Everyone had their own version of the events. One reporter for the *Chicago Tribune* found Horace Singer, who told him that he had men working in his quarries already. Actually only 14 men showed up for work and all were supervisory personnel. Singer stated, "[that] none of his workmen were dissatisfied with their wages and that he was going to insist that handbills be posted that guaranteed protection to the non-strikers who wanted to work."[31]

Singer felt, as many capitalists did who were influenced by the writings of Spenser, that a worker made an individual contract with his employer and no third party had a right to dictate the terms of that agreement. The economic and political system of the country in the 1880s supported his view. Called a "theoretical liberty of contract" it offered the idea that each individual had "the right to sell his labor upon such terms as he deemed proper."[32] For the quarry owners this meant that they could pay any wage that an individual worker would agree to accept.

The promised handbills appeared by early Tuesday afternoon. The only problem was that they disappeared as soon as they were posted. The handbills proclaimed:

> Whereas, a large number of persons have unlawfully and riotously assembled in the town of Lemont, Cook County, Illinois, for the purpose of depriving owners and possessors of property of its lawful use and management and for the purpose of preventing other persons from working, or obtaining work at their lawful business on such terms as they see fit. Now, therefore I, S. F. Hanchett, Sheriff of Cook County, Illinois, by virtue of the power in me vested by the statues of the state do hereby, command all persons unlawfully and riotously assembled as aforesaid, do immediately and peaceably to disperse and in no way to interfere with any person or persons in pursuit of their lawful vocation . . . All persons desiring to work will be protected in their person, family, or property. All persons hereafter found unlawfully idling or loitering about the streets or other public places will be arrested and dealt with according to the law.[33]

At least half of the workers could not even read the notice. Many did not know enough English, while others were too poor to have even gone to a common school. Still, they understood the notice's purpose and intent.

The only "mob" that formed that day met the train from Chicago carrying Cook County Coroner Hertz. The strikers were fearful that the coroner would bring his own jury from Chicago, for, as usual, Lemont was getting bad press from the out-of-town newspapers. They portrayed the townspeople as a riotous mob dangerous to decent society. Naturally, there was talk of stringing up a few reporters along with Singer and Edwin Walker.

The county officials, however, understood the feelings of the townspeople and decided to select a coroner's jury from the community. Coroner Hertz met with the following officials: Town Police Magistrate, T.S. Huston; his aide, J.P. Clifford; and Township Supervisor, J.W. McCarthy. It is interesting that the village mayor, D.C. Norton, took no leadership role in this meeting. The burden of leadership seems to have fallen on Supervisor McCarthy.

The three men drew up a list of citizens, about 50 in all, who they felt were capable and objective people. From the list they chose six, the total still needed for a coroner's jury. The six were reluctant to serve. As businessmen, they all walked the middle line between the powerful quarry owners, who controlled the banks and money in town, and

Bodenschatz store on Canal Street. (Photo courtesy of Lemont Historical Society)

the workers, who were their customers. Marshall Russell and the deputy coroners were sent to get the men, but returned with the information that only one was willing to serve. To assure the appearance of the others, subpoenas were issued. Word spread through town and one prospective juror, J. Bodenschatz, a local druggist, managed to disappear before he was served. He was not found. His family had quarry holdings and perhaps he felt some guilt in the whole affair.

The completed jury consisted of Herbert Stauber, saloonkeeper; J.S. Tedens, dry goods store owner; Nicholas Eulert, hardware store owner; Mathew Warner, druggist; Emanuel Kline, dry goods store owner; and P.A. Nelson, general store owner. This list shows how society valued the small businessman as the foundation of the community in the 1880s. The townspeople felt that these men were capable of arriving at the facts of the shooting. The men of the final jury had lived in town for a number of years — Sauber had been in Lemont for 17 years; Warner for 30 years; Tedens for 24 years; Nelson for four years; Kline for five years; and Eulert for 28 years.

When the jury was convened, it was addressed by the coroner as to their duty and then, followed by a large crowd, viewed the sites involved in the incident and saw the victims. At Gerharz Funeral Home and Furniture Store, Kujawa's body had been packed in ice and was laid out for all to see. There had been a steady passage of viewers since early Tuesday morning. The group broke up to allow the jury to view his body. His skull was shattered and blood and brain tissue remained on his face.

From Gerharz, the jury went to the Stetler home, where Andrew Stetler lay in state. The militia bullet had also ripped through his skull. Their last stop, still followed by the quiet crowd, was at the home of John Polus, who was slowly dying of the injuries he had received in the initial shooting. He had no hope of recovery.

After the tour, the jury convened at three p.m. at the Village Hall. With over 200 people present there was not enough room for the Lemonters and the press, so most of the people were forced to wait outside for information. They wanted the coroner's jury to establish the guilt of the militia in the shooting. They also expected the jury to discover who had fired the fatal shots.

Testimony was hindered when it was revealed that Colonel Bennett refused to allow any of his soldiers to testify at the inquest. According to him, the militia was under military law and did not have to appear in any civil court. Coroner Hertz became angry and issued warrants for the soldiers to come before the inquest. He also sent a telegram to Governor Oglesby:

> I am holding an inquest over the quarry men said to be killed
> by the state militia. Have requested Bennett and other sol-
> diers to appear but they refused, and say, further, they will

> not appear at the inquisition if summoned or unless ordered
> to do so by military authorities. Please issue direction to Colo-
> nel Bennett and such soldiers as may be summoned to appear
> as witnesses at the inquest . . . answer immediately.
> > Henry L. Hertz, Coroner[34]

The telegram was of no avail, and the governor never answered and the militia never testified. Testimony was taken from the following people and it is from their viewpoint that some of the events can be pieced together: John Chojmacky, laborer; Patrick McCann, Justice of the Peace; John Ankerberg, laborer; Elis Nelson, laborer; John McGregor, laborer; Neil Corbett, plumber; Peter Dockendorf, capitalist; Peter Talty, saloonkeeper and village board member; T.S. Huston, police magistrate for Lemont and agent for the Alton Railroad; Thomas Godson, laborer; W.B. Cook, physician; Adolph Miller, shoemaker; Martin Lacey, teamster; Pete Dignan, tugboat captain; Dexter Nickerson, Deputy Sheriff; Colonel A.C. Potter, Deputy Sheriff; James Thorpe, physician; Valentine Kujawa, laborer; Ed. Clancy, canalman; and W. Smulski, editor of the *Polish Catholic Gazette,* who acted as interpreter.[35]

The witnesses represented a cross section of the town and its economic base. It is interesting that no women were called since there was considerable evidence that they were as active and angry as the men. The first day of the inquest, May 5, only two men offered their evidence. Valentine Kujawa, through the interpreter, said he was a laborer in the quarries. The dead man, Jacob Kujawa, was his nephew, and a laborer. He was 35 years old and had been employed in the Excelsior Quarry. Valentine told the court that he saw the riot but saw no stone throwing nor anyone but the soldiers shooting. He did not see his nephew that day until he saw him dead on the street.[36]

The other testimony came from John Chojnacky, who also spoke through the Polish interpreter. He testified about the other dead man, Andrew Stetler, who was his stepson. He was 21 years old and a native of Posen in what was then Prussia. John was present when his stepson was shot. He told the jury:

> I was standing about 100 feet from the depot and the deceased
> was standing by my side. I wanted to see the military come
> into town. I never saw military before. I was curious to see
> them. The military came from Joliet from Brown's [farm area].
> Mr Russell tried to stop the military but the gentleman with
> the gray beard marched right ahead. There was a crowd of
> women around. The soldiers pushed them back struck them
> with swords. Some of them had swords and some of them had
> guns. The men with swords struck the women and the women
> commenced to throw sand and stones. Then one soldier turned
> around and shot my stepson.[37]

The rest of his testimony, in answer to questioning, revealed that he did see six or seven women throw stones but could not tell the size of the stones. He heard no shots fired by anyone else before his stepson was shot. He took his stepson home where he died about two hours after the shooting. He did hear someone in uniform shout, "Fire," but could not tell who it was. He did not see any stone hit a soldier; in fact, Chojnacky claimed that there were only about 30 people around when Andrew was shot and that no one was in the street blocking the path of the soldiers.

After the testimony from the relatives of the deceased, the inquest was adjourned until the funerals for Stetler and Kujawa were over. On May 6 at 10:00 a.m. the funeral processions gathered in two locations. The Polish Benevolent Society assembled over 2,000 people, many coming from Lockport, Joliet, and Chicago. The first honor guard gathered at Stetler's cottage on Blue Hill, while the second group went down to Gerhartz's Undertaking establishment to accompany Kujawa's body. His honor guard was composed of 700 quarry workers, as he had been active in the strike movement.

Both processions moved to St. Cyril's for the funeral mass, slowly winding their way up the hill to the highest point in the village. SS. Cyril's and Methodius was then a year old and could hold only about 700 people. The rest had to stand along the walls or outside to hear as much of the service as they could. The presence of so many workers and labor organizers in town bound by a solidarity for the working man and the eight-hour day made the militia and the town authorities very nervous. There were rumors and threats of retaliation.[38]

As bells tolled, the two caskets, that of Kujawa and Stetler, were placed side by side outside the sanctuary railing with funeral torches on either side. There were few formal tributes out of fear that any emotional speeches might cause disturbances. The *Chicago Tribune* reported on the services:

> The church was crowded to suffocation, at least 1,000 persons being assembled in it. The solemn Mass of Requiem was sung by Fr. Moczygemba, founder of the parish, assisted by the Rev. Dr. McGovern of Lockport and Fr. Hogan of St. Patrick's as sub-deacon. After the mass, Dr. McGovern delivered a brief sermon in which he did not once refer to the riot of Monday, the strike, or the presence of the military in town. In the course of his remarks, however, he did say that for one body of workmen to attempt to coerce another [to] comply with the demands of others in the matter of selling their labor was nothing short of criminal and a disgrace upon the privileges of a free and peaceful community.[39]

Reverend McGovern's talk represented a conservative view of employee-employer relations. The idea of working together as a group to shut down a plant or quarry seemed to many in the middle class as contrary to the American concept of individual freedom. McGovern's other purpose for his temperate speech was to defuse the emotions of the day. He and Father Moczygemba had worked since Monday to calm the men to prevent further bloodshed. Father Hogan also helped by talking with the Irish workers, although he tended to agree strongly with the workers' action.

Of all the clergy who worked that week, Father Moczygemba of St. Cyril's was the most effective. He had a dominant personality and the ability to speak fluently in English, Polish, and German. Because of the efforts of these clergymen, no rioting or incidents occurred on that sad Wednesday as they escorted the two dead men to their final resting place in St. Alphonsus cemetery.[40]

Andrew Stelter's grave is located in row 6, section 1, block 2 of the cemetery. Strangely, there is no official record of Kujawa's grave in spite of the fact that they were buried at the same time. After the funeral the town remained quiet. Few men returned to work and the militia remained in town. The inquest continued that day with testimony from many people, mainly the civilian authorities who were partly responsible for the orders requesting the militia.

Deputy Sheriff Potter reported that he had warned the crowd not to oppose the entrance of the troops into town. He said that he was in front of the march and begged the crowd to make a passage, but they refused and began to throw stones. He added that a shot was fired by someone, either from or between the houses near Main Street and the depot. Potter claimed that he heard the whiz of a bullet.[41] It was at this point that the Second Company turned and fired into the crowd. Cross-examined by the coroner, Potter stated that he felt the soldiers were justified in shooting, as they were in danger from the mob.

Foreman Mathew Warner questioned who it was that had asked for protection in Lemont, a question that the townspeople wanted answered. Potter replied that a "committee whose names he did not know" had visited the sheriff's office. He had no written orders but was sent by the sheriff's office and that his badge constituted his authority, and the troops obeyed his orders. However, he stated that he did not give the orders to shoot.[42]

Warner continued his questioning, asking if Potter had any proven knowledge of property being destroyed or of mob action in Lemont. The only reply that Potter could give was that men were being prevented from working in the quarries by the strikers.

The jurors then requested a ruling on the law as they felt that the militia could not be called unless violence had been committed. The coroner explained that the law was written in such a manner that troops could be requested if there was a "probability of danger."

Other testimony centered on whether the troops overreacted to the situation and if there could have been notification of the township officials before the troops disembarked. Justice T. Huston testified that he had seen several hundred men in town carrying clubs or sticks with the intention of preventing others from going to work in the quarries. He stated that he was the one who telegraphed to have the troops detrain outside of town. As for the actions of the militia, he saw an officer strike John Ankerberg several times with his sword because the "old Swede" refused to move off his property for anyone.

The inquest then adjourned until the next day. On May 7, Albert Parsons, from Chicago, arrived in Lemont. He had been out of town or he would have involved himself in the turmoil long before. Parsons was the editor of *The Alarm* and a labor organizer with a following among the left and socialistic elements of the community. The events in Lemont were made for his attitude and philosophy about the condition of the working man in society. He was not about to let this opportunity pass.

Albert Parsons' arrival in town focused a larger audience on the events of the week. He was pushing for two ideas, collective bargaining and the eight-hour day. The detective, Allan Pinkerton,[43] who made a good living supplying private security forces for factories and mines, viewed Parsons as a threat to any community. He said of Parsons that he was a young man of flippant tongue, and was capable of making a speech that would inflame the blood of characterless rascals who are always standing ready to grasp society by the throat.[44]

Parsons came to town with copies of his paper which he sold for five cents each or gave away to those who could not afford the cost. He planned to use the shooting in

Albert Parsons. (Illustration courtesy of Lemont Historical Society)

Lemont as a basis for forming a union of quarry workers. The strike had been a spontaneous event without the formal sanction of any union or group. There were many who were Knights of Labor members in secret, but the Knights did not support strikes.

Parsons was recognized and welcomed by the workers. A *Tribune* reporter who followed Parsons around commented that he did not give his usual "Blood and Dynamite" speech on the streets and that he astonished the other reporters by "blossoming out in a clean shirt."[45] The tone of the report was clear. Parsons was to be feared by the good citizens of any community. To be sure, Parsons was not a moderate man. He was a political anarchist not opposed to bombing to gain labor's ends. His wife Lucy Parsons had written, "Dynamite! The Only Voice the Oppressors of the People Can Understand."[46] And talk of dynamite and bombing in a quarry town, where tons of dynamite and the experts to use it were freely available, made the owners of the quarries and the militia nervous.

Parsons spoke at three p.m. at Otzenburgers Hall at the northwest corner of Illinois and Lemont Streets. The building, which still stands today, was a social and Turner hall used by various German singing and gymnastic clubs. It was natural for Parsons to speak in such a hall, as many Germans were active in the early radical labor movement. Parsons was an organizer for the International Working Peoples Association, a group opposed to specialized trade unions. He was well known to Lemonters, and all Chicagoans for that matter. Only two weeks before he had threatened the Chicago police that he would use dynamite the next time that they interfered with one of his many labor marches. This outburst had been provoked by an attempt by the Chicago police to break up a march on the Chicago Board of Trade led by his wife Lucy.

J.W. McCarthy invited him and arranged the gathering. Tensions were high again in town as the third victim, John Polus, died early that morning. He was 48 years old, with a wife and six children. They were so destitute that the neighbors had to supply them with food to keep them from starving. A subscription list was circulated to bury him.[47]

The hall was crowded, but Parsons refused to address them until all the reporters except those from his paper and the German labor paper the *Arbeiter Zeitung* were thrown out of the room. The first to speak before the group was a striker. He stated the fears of the workers:

> We are assembled here to consider what to do. We have got
> the military in our town. We want the military to leave us
> alone. If we want to organize now, it will mean losing our
> bread forever and probably our lives besides.

At this point McCarthy introduced Parsons. Parsons spoke for over an hour. He gave his usual impassioned plea for unity in fighting the capitalistic interests. His talk was emotional and powerful. He told his famous fable about the farmer and the sheep:

A farmer had gathered his herd of sheep into a pen before shearing them of their wool. One sheep, bolder than the others, seeing the farmer with his shears asked:

"Pray sir why do you huddle us in this manner? Will you not let us out to play in the fields? It is hot and dry in these pens." Farmer: "Before I turn you out I must shear you of your wool." Sheep: "What harm have we done that you must take the covering from our backs, and leave us unprotected?" Farmer: "You ungrateful wretches! Have you no gratitude for the many favors I have given you? I furnish you with the pasture and by my generosity you soon supply yourselves with another coating."

The rest of the herd set up a "Hurrah" for their benefactor and all calmly submitted to the process of being "fleeced of their wool."[48]

The moral, according to Parsons, was when the "capitalists and their lying politicians" set themselves up as your benefactors and begin discourses on the harmony of capital and labor, you may be sure they are setting you up for a "fleecing." When he had finished, some workers, tired and discouraged by what had happened replied:

We can't organize. The bosses will break it up. They did before. It would not be allowed. They would starve us out and break it up.

Parsons then grew angry. "Then you are slaves-wage slaves — no better than the Negro slaves before the war."[49] A discouraged worker was quoted as replying, "Alas, sir it is too true." One young militant did speak up for some action saying, "As we have started and lived so far without bread, we must keep up the struggle against the bosses. We don't want those blue-jackets on the hill to have killed us for nothing."[50]

So in a last attempt, the workers decided to hold out while checking on the rumor that the Joliet men had given in and gone back to work for $1.50 a day and less. A committee was appointed to investigate and to meet with a Lemont quarry owner representative and report back before any other action by the strikers. The committee appointed to go to Joliet was a cross section of ethnic groups. Two Poles, two Swedes, two Germans, and two Irishmen were selected as a result of the meeting with Albert Parsons. Albert Morasky headed the delegation. They agreed to report to the strikers upon their return.

Word of the meeting at Otzenbergers and the presence of Parsons in town finally reached General Vance and he ordered Colonel Bennett to arrest Parsons on sight and to spirit him out of town. The militia, however, never found him. After the meeting Parsons spent the afternoon and the night hidden from the authorities by sympathetic Lemonters, including the township supervisor, McCarthy. The *Tribune,* eager for a story, accused McCarthy of taking the side of the strikers and encouraging them to hold out against the quarry owners.

When confronted by reporters, McCarthy denied that he had taken up with Parsons, but, there was little doubt in town that McCarthy, a Democrat, was supporting the workers. This was demonstrated by an event that caused some discomfort to the authorities; it was the issuance of a certificate of "good character" by McCarthy to Adolph Miller. A certificate of good character was a paper that authorized an individual to go to the community to obtain charity, the method used in the 1880s for an individual to obtain welfare. It was certified proof that the individual was in need and was an upstanding person. The problem was that Miller was one of those injured in the shooting and by issuing the certificate McCarthy established the position that those injured in the shooting action were not criminals who had provoked the attack but victims of a police action.[51]

The certificate would have presented no problem if Miller had gone to the charities and churches in town but he left McCarthy's office and headed straight for the militia encampment, after a short stop at a saloon, and began asking the soldiers for funds to help him until his wounds healed. He reasoned that since they had injured him they might wish to help. Many of the young men must have felt guilt about the whole affair, as he did collect a substantial sum until Colonel Bennett found him in camp and had him forcibly ejected.

Meanwhile, Parsons capitalized on the events in Lemont in his paper, *The Alarm*. He retold the strike from his point of view. To him the scene in town was one where, "the warm blood of the people bathed the flagstones of the sidewalks . . . the women, wives and daughters of working men, were bayoneted by the soldiers of capitalism: their only crime being that they do not wear sealskin dolmans and belong to the 'better classes.'"[52] As for the Alton Railroad, he blamed it for allowing the militia to travel on their line. He wrote, "The Chicago and Alton Railroad with that alacrity becoming in a fellow monopolist and labor exploiter, quickly placed a train at the disposal of the LABOR ROBBERS."[53]

He also faulted Tom Huston, the train agent and town Justice of the Peace, quoting Huston as saying to the crowd at the station, "Get away from here. Stand aside. It is an imposition on me and the company for you to stand around here. I am dependent on my wages for a living the same as you are, and the company holds me responsible for not ordering you away. I have always tried to treat you all well . . . You are in the way. Move on. Move on."[54]

Parsons named the incident the *Lemont Massacre* and it became a rallying cry for the radical labor movement. He spoke of the failure of the government to protect the working man in Lemont in speeches around the country. His wife Lucy called a special meeting of the International Working People's Association to condemn the events in Lemont. It was at this meeting that she made the famous statement that made her fearsome to society:

> Let every dirty, lousy tramp arm himself with a revolver or
> knife and lay in wait on the steps of the palaces of the rich
> and stab or shoot their owners as they come out. Let us kill
> them without mercy, and let this be a war of extermination
> and without pity. Let us devastate the avenues where the
> wealthy live as Sheridan devastated the beautiful Valley of
> the Shenandoah.[55]

The residents of Singer Hill did not rest easily for some time. One year from the time he was here in Lemont, Albert Parsons would stand accused of conspiracy in the death of eight Chicago Policemen during the infamous Haymarket Square Riot of 1886. In his defense he used the Lemont strike and the suppression of that action by the State of Illinois as a justification for violent actions to gain rights for the working man. He died on the gallows on November 11, 1887.

The Haymarket prisoners' cell before the hanging. In the cell are Albert Parsons, August Spies, Adolph Fisker, and George Engel. August Spies and Nina Van Zandt Spies appear on the cover because she fell in love with him at the trial and was married to him by proxy. (Illustration courtesy of the Chicago Historical Society)

As the week came to an end no one in Lemont was very radical anymore. The workers were hungry and defeated. They personally knew their capitalistic quarry owners. They were a stubborn group. The strike leaders reasoned that the militia would never leave town until the laborers returned to work, yet they held out hope that the committee sent to Joliet would come back with good news.

The Strikers Wage Committee returned from Joliet Friday morning. They were met at the Alton Station by a crowd of more than 500 who were eager to hear the results of the visit. They still held the hope that they could revitalize the sagging strike support in Joliet. Perhaps they felt the martyrdom of the three quarry workers would have a unifying effect throughout the valley. But, since the news was bad, the committee did not wish to make a public disclosure of their findings. Instead, they promised to meet with the quarry owners the next day and meanwhile conferred with their own leaders.

The committee found that almost all the Joliet and Lockport strikers were back to work and by the next week all the quarries in that part of the valley would be in full operation. The wage being paid was the pre-strike wage of $1.50 a day. What happened in Lemont did not rally the workers to action but, instead, convinced them that the strike was useless, if not dangerous.

The committee also reported that many men who had been active in the original April strike in Joliet had been blacklisted, unable to find jobs in any trade. This blacklisting extended to all quarries and even to some very skilled stone men. It appeared to the Lemonters that the strike in town would have to end soon.

By Friday the coroner's jury reached a verdict on Andrew Stelter's death after testimony from the other witnesses including Doctor Thorpe, who tended the wounded. No separate juries were impaneled for Kujawa or Polus. Coroner Hertz, at the request of the jury, again tried to get Colonel Bennett and certain members of the militia to testify, but to no avail. Hertz was of Danish heritage, active in Republican politics. He felt kinship with the strikers, especially the Scandinavians.[56] He told Parsons that the refusal was outrageous, "It has come to this pass, and it is true that there is no law for the poor. If you have money, if you are rich, it is all right with you then . . . According to the constitution the military was held in subject to the civil authorities, but there is no defense for the poor; the law protects the rich only."[57]

The governor finally sent a telegram to the jury that made his position clear in the case:

Henry Hertz, Coroner of Cook County

Replying to your telegram, I will state that when the State Militia, under orders to execute the law in cooperation with the civil authorities of the state, shall be in the performance of such duty they are not subject to a subpoena from the Coroner to appear as a witness before an inquest nor would it be proper for a governor to order them to obey such process.

Richard Oglesby.

Without the testimony of the soldiers there was nothing else that the coroner's jury could do, so they filed this report:

The said Andrew Stelter, now lying dead at Lemont in said town of Lemont, County of Cook, State of Illinois. Cause to his death on the 4th day of May 1885 A.D., from shock and hemorrhage produced by a wound caused by a gun or rifle shot fired by a soldier belonging to the state militia of the State of Illinois, his name we are unable to find.

The name was never found in spite of repeated requests. But, after the official cause of death was submitted, the jury of Lemonters bravely wrote and signed an additional statement about the whole action:

We the jury further find from the evidence before us that we are unable to determine what soldier or officer fired the shots that killed Jacob Kujawa and Andrew Stetler and Steven John Polack [sic]. We further find that the Sheriff of Cook County [Hanchett] was hasty in sending troops in our midst without previous warning and without asking the assistance of the town authorities to assist him in dispersing the men, women, and children. We further find that the Sheriff of Cook County should have asked the town officers to disperse all crowds of people in the streets . . . the said crowd gathered there from curiosity to see the soldiers and the officers in command should have used more discretion before firing into the crowd, and especially the soldiers clubbing with swords and bayonets our citizens before their doorsteps.

Signed: Mat. Warner, Herbert Sauber, John Tedens, Nicholas Eulert, P.A. Nelson, and E. Kline.[58]

The transcript and the testimony of the Lemont inquest was filed away but not forgotten. The description of the Lemont Massacre would be read eight years later by another Governor, John Peter Altgeld. The report of this jury would be part of the material Altgeld would use to help him make the monumental decision of his career. To get a background on the early labor struggles he would study it at the suggestion of his friend and Labor Director, George Shilling, who had been a friend of Albert Parsons and active in the movement. Reading the Lemont report would help to influence Altgeld to pardon the remaining Haymarket conspirators. It would help him to understand Lemont when he was faced with another strike in town in 1893.

After the coroner's report was released, Company G of Bloomington was sent home. The other three units remained. However, they were unable to stop an act of vandalism that night that resulted in the destruction of Singer and Talcott's 15,000 dollar steam shovel and their outbuildings. On the weekend, newly arrived immigrants from Bohemia were hired as strike breakers at the Enterprise quarry east of town. A group of Lemonters tried to go out to speak to them but were prevented from entering the property by the militia. The strikers now knew that if they did not return to work others would be hired in their place and protected by the militia. The strike was over.

No one declared it was over. Workers just began appearing at the quarries hopeful that they had not been blacklisted. The strike again left deep scars and divisions in town. Each ethnic group blamed the other for the outcome. The workers blamed the owners and the owners blamed the workers and businessmen who extended credit to the strikers. To punish the merchants, some owners developed company stores. From 1885, S.W. Norton's operated a system by which the wages of the quarry workers were deposited in accounts at the store and a discount was given to workers who only purchased from Norton's. This scheme made it possible to cut off credit if a worker went on strike. Remember, too, that four of the jurors on the inquest panel operated stores — Tedens, Nelson, Kline, and Eulert. Norton was not only punishing the workers, he also wanted to hurt his general store competition.

Labor troubles also made the owners unhappy with the town, so when Western Stone formed a conglomerate in the early 1890s, many sold out to the corporation and left the community. Despite the pain, suffering, and death, nothing was accomplished to better the lot of the quarry worker. Wages and working conditions remained the same and the failure of the action only served to divide the town rather than give it a sense of unity.

ENDNOTES

[1] Old labor song.

[2] See the *Joliet News,* and the *Chicago Tribune*, April 2 to May 12, 1885.

[3] *Joliet News*, April 11, 1885. The Joliet papers portrayed Lemont as the source of most of the labor ferment. They also made frequent ethnic references when describing the strike and walkout.

[4] Even at a rough estimation, the cost had to be $3,000 a day. Estimate 2,000 workers at $1.25 to $1.50 per day. This does not include the higher pay scale for those who worked as supervisors or ran the steam plants and stone milling shops.

[5] Horace Singer, Singer & Talcott, served as a member of the State General Assembly in 1866 and Cook County Commissioner in 1870. Edwin Walker, Walker Stone, was active in Democratic politics. William Brown, of the Brown family, served as City Clerk of Chicago in 1846. N. J. Brown's old partner, Augustus Garrett, ran for mayor of Chicago. D.C. Norton, superintendent of Singer & Talcott, was mayor of Lemont and active in Republican politics. Joel Wells, Illinois Stone Company, had been mayor and village trustee. Other partners in the stone trade included the Sherman family who had served as mayors of Chicago. The connections of money and politics to the stone trade and quarry industry were numerous.

[6] *Joliet News*, April 11, 1885.

[7] Labor strike chant from the 1880s.

[8] *Chicago Tribune*, May 4, 1885.

[9] *Chicago Tribune*, May 1, 1885.

[10] *Joliet News*, April 27, 1885.

[11] *Ibid*., April 26-27, 1885.

[12] *Chicago Tribune*, May 4, 1885.

[13] The newspapers of the time were not careful in recording names, especially those of the foreign born. The spellings here are probably incorrect. It does appear that the leaders at this march were Polish and Swedish. However, we do not have the names of those released by the sheriff.

[14] *Joliet News*, May 4, 1885.

[15] *Chicago Tribune*, May 5, 1885.

[16] See *The Alarm*, May 16, 1885. The committee that was sent to Joliet to check on the wages there was composed of men representing the Polish, German, Irish, and Swedish communities. Political support for the strikers came from J. McCarthy and John Doolin both Irish.

[17] *Chicago Tribune*, May 4, 1885. Since the paper did not support the idea of strikes, it tried to show that those involved were largely duped by the local leaders or fearful of them.

[18]*Chicago Tribune*, May 7, 1885.

[19]*The Alarm*, May 16, 1885. The "reporter" was probably Albert Parsons, who was not at the scene at the time but probably heard this from some of the strikers.

[20]*Ibid.*

[21]*Chicago Tribune*, May 5, 1885.

[22]The present site of Rock Creek Center (1996).

[23]*Chicago Tribune*, May 5, 1885.

[24]*Cook County Coroner's Inquest Proceedings*, testimony of John Chojuazki, stepfather of Andrew Stelter, May 5, 1885.

[25]*Ibid.*, May 8, 1885.

[26]The site is now part of the high rise bridge on State Street.

[27]This number is incorrect. The actual force was about 250 men.

[28]May not be their real names. Fearful of retaliation the participants often gave false names.

[29]*The Alarm*, May 16, 1885.

[30]*Ibid.*

[31]*Chicago Tribune*, May 6, 1885.

[32]Samuel Morison, *The Oxford History of the American People* (New York: New American Library, 1972), vol. 3, p. 85.

[33]*Chicago Tribune*, May 6, 1885.

[34]*Ibid.*

[35]*Ibid.*, May 7, 1885.

[36]*Ibid.*, May 6, 1885.

[37]*Cook County Coroner's Inquest Proceedings*, May 5, 1885.

[38]*Chicago Tribune*, May 6, 1885.

[39]*Ibid.*

[40]*Ibid.* The men were buried in St. Alphonsus Cemetery because St. Cyril's had not yet developed their own burial grounds.

[41]*Ibid.*, May 7, 1885.

[42]*Ibid.*

[43]Pinkerton first gained publicity by taking newly elected President Lincoln to Washington, D.C. by a secret way to foil an assassination plot on the President. During the Civil War, he had charge of spies and counterspies. See Finis Farr, *Chicago* (New Rochelle: Arlington House, 1973), p. 44.

[44]Allan Pinkerton, "Communism and the Riot in Chicago," *The Prairie State: Civil War to the Present*, ed. Robert Sutton (Grand Rapids: Eerdmans Publishing Co.,1976), p. 145.

[45]*Chicago Tribune*, May 8,1885.

[46]Carolyn Ashbaugh, *Lucy Parsons: American Revolutionary* (Chicago: Charles Kerr Publishing Company, 1976), p. 58.

[47]*The Alarm*, May 16, 1885.

[48]*Ibid.*

[49]*Ibid*.

[50]*Ibid*.

[51]*Chicago Tribune,* May 14, 1885.

[52]*The Alarm*, May 16, 1885.

[53]*Ibid*.

[54]*Ibid*.

[55]Ashbaugh, *Lucy Parsons,* pp.59-60.

[56]Odd S. Lovoll, *A Century of Urban Life: The Norwegians in Chicago Before 1930* (Champaign: University of Illinois Press/Norwegian-American Historical Association, 1988), p. 180.

[57]*The Alarm*, May 16, 1885.

[58]*Chicago Tribune,* May 9, 1885.

U.S. HISTORY

1880: *Garfield is Elected President — Bingo Becomes a Fad — Carnegie Builds First Steel Furnace — Canned Fruits and Meats in Stores — Railroad Mileage in U.S., 87,000 — Gold Discovered in Juneau, Alaska.*

1881: *Garfield is Assassinated — Chester Arthur Named President — Federation of Organized Trade and Labor Unions Formed — Severe Drug Abuse Problems Nationwide — "Billy the Kid" Bonner Dies — American Red Cross Founded by Clara Barton.*

1882: *U.S. Bans Chinese Immigration for Ten Years — First Hydroelectric Plant Built, Located in Wisconsin.*

1883: *First Skyscraper Built, 10 Stories High in Chicago — Civil Service Commission Forms.*

1884: *Grover Cleveland is Elected President — Washington National Monument Finished.*

1885: *Gas Mantle Invented — Golf Introduced to U.S. — Grant Dies.*

1886: *Statue of Liberty Installed — Chas. Hall Produces Aluminum by Electrolysis — Haymarket Riot in Chicago, Parsons and Three Others Hanged.*

1887: *Interstate Commerce Commission Formed — Dawes Act Gives U.S. Citizenship to Native Americans, Reservation Lands Broken into Individual Holdings.*

1888: *Benjamin Harrison Elected President — Tesla Constructs an Electric Motor — Kodak Patents Camera.*

1889: *North Dakota, South Dakota, Montana, and Washington Become States — Oklahoma Opened to Non-Indian Settlement.*

LEMONT HISTORY

1880: *Population: 3,793 for Township, Des Plaines [Lemont] 173, Lemont Village 2,108 — Trains Must Not Exceed 10 mph within Village — Fine for Letting Pigs Run at Large in Town $10 to $100 — Fire Laws Established for Town — Mayor Stephen Keough Dies, James Noonan Fills Out Mayor's Term.*

1881: *Village Health Office Created — 21 Saloons in Town — Union Telegraph Company Installs Poles on Main Street — Millwood Circus in Town — Smallpox Epidemic in Town, Guards Posted to Keep People in Their Homes — Mass Vaccination Program from the State — Mayor is Nicholas New.*

1882: *D.C. Norton is Mayor — Postmaster John Lee — Over One Million Tons of Shipping on the I & M Canal — Knights of Labor Organize in Town — Chicago Telephone Company Strings Lines in Town, Their Office is on Canal Street.*

1883: *Norton Reelected Mayor — St. James Academy Built.*

1884: *Waterworks on North Stephens Street Completed — Drug Store of B.V. Jacobs Purchased by John Bodenschatz — $3 to $200 Fine for Keeping or Patronizing a House of Prostitution — Water Tax for New Waterworks.*

1885: *Lemont Massacre — Fourth Major Strike — Three Workers Shot by Illinois Militia — Postmaster is Matthew Warner — Martin Madden Elected Director of Quarry Owners Association — Night Policeman is Alfred Lundholm — Fire Department Organized.*

1886: *Street Lights, Caretaker is N. Gleason — Indoor Roller Rink in Town along the Canal, Roller Skates Invented in Chicago in 1884 — T.F. Friedly Hardware at 311 Canal Street.*

1887: *Public Library in Town — President Cleveland Visits Lemont — St. Matthew's Church Built — Santa Fe Line Finished.*

1889: *T.J. Huston Police Magistrate — Western Stone Formed from Smaller Quarries.*

CHAPTER SIXTEEN

LEMONT AND
THE QUARRY OWNERS
The Capitalists

The plight of the working quarryman and his struggle for better wages and conditions gives the impression that the owners were "bad" men. That, really, was not always the case. It was simply that many had grown up on the frontier and by hard work and luck had carved out fortunes for themselves. Most came from modest backgrounds and few had little more than common schooling. The fact that they had become successful made it impossible for some of them to realize that economic conditions and population growth changed the world they pioneered. Most believed that anyone could repeat their success if they only applied themselves. That fact was no longer true by the 1870s, but most of these self-made men could not recognize that fact.

The list of quarry owners contains the stories of colorful men, many with qualities of adventure, risk taking, and determination. Their lives give an insight into the early industrialists of the frontier and their development of our area.

The contributions of the Brown Family to the building of the I & M Canal and land development in Lemont were discussed earlier. Although the family continued to hold quarry lands, they leased the operations so they were seldom directly involved with the labor conflicts of the community.[1] N.J. Brown lived until 1900 and was affectionately known as "Governor." His generosity to institutions and churches gave him a unique standing in the town. During the labor struggles he offered to donate land for a public library. He told *The Lemont News* that he was "willing to do anything to improve the condition of the working class — the men who make our town."[2] His devotion to Lemont was clear; at a meeting in his honor, he told friends that he had "been with them and would remain with them until the sands of the valley should roll down on his coffin."[3] His remains now rest in the Brown cemetery next to the Methodist Church on Custer Street, a site that overlooks his old homestead.

The largest quarries belonged to Singer and Talcott, two quite different men who formed a unique partnership. Mancel Talcott was born in Rome, New York, in 1817, the son of Mancel and Betsy Talcott. He had his common schooling in Oneida County, and when he was 17, he left for the West, like almost every young man in upstate New York.[4] The young were influenced by the nearness of the Erie Canal, the water route to the new Illinois frontier, and the adventure of making a fortune in the West. The family let him go because his brother Edward, an engineer, was already in Illinois working on plans for building the new I & M Canal.[5] Mancel sailed to Detroit and was supposed to remain on the ship until it reached Chicago, but the spirit of adventure and excitement so overwhelmed him that when the ship docked in Detroit, he got off and began walking to Chicago to see the new country for himself.

Talcott arrived in 1834, on foot, full of the wonders of the new land. He put money down on a farm in the present Park Ridge area, then called Bricktown,[6] and joined his brother in the Lemont-Lockport area to earn money to pay off his debt by working on the canal. The days of work in the Des Plaines Valley were pleasant for him. He had adequate housing and food since his brother was an engineer on the project and he came at a time when labor was scarce and wages high. Talcott did not have to suffer the lot of the immigrant Irish and German workers who followed, but he was aware of their plight. His experience on the canal was part of the reason that he became active in social and relief agencies throughout his life.

One of Talcott's friends among the children and relatives of the contractors was Horace Singer, the son of the Lockport division contractor, John Singer. They fished the Des Plaines River and climbed the bluffs and became good friends. Many marveled at their friendship since they were such different personalities. Talcott, the older of the two, was direct but not aggressive. He had simple and modest goals, to pay off the cost of his land and begin farming. Young Singer had a driving personality and a burning ambition to "make it big" and acquire a fortune. In this respect he was like his uncle, Isaac Singer, who also worked on the I & M Canal.

Isaac Singer developed a drill that helped to cut the time it took to remove stone from the canal beds. Isaac's ambition was such that he soon left canal work and went on to make a huge fortune by modifying Elias Howe's sewing machine through patent infringements. With aggressive marketing, he made the Singer sewing machine a household word.[7]

Mancel Talcott soon earned enough money to marry Mary H. Otis, pay off his farm debt, and settle down. Meanwhile, Horace Singer stayed with the canal, moving up in jobs and responsibility. When the bad times of the 1840s came and work stopped on most canal contracts, Talcott survived by trading food for services. Singer bought a team and began freighting between Chicago and points within a radius of 125 miles.[8] He returned to the canal when work started again and ultimately was promoted to superintendent of all repairs. Both men found themselves moderately successful on the new frontier.

As more people arrived after the completion of the I & M Canal, Talcott found himself being viewed as an "old man," one who had pioneered the region, although he was only in his 30s. Many newcomers were in their late teens and early 20s, the same age he was when he arrived, so to them he appeared as a venerable old pioneer. He was addressed as "Cap" or "Pop" Talcott and lines parted when he entered local stores or meetings. He began to get the feeling that the glory days of adventure were over.

There are times of crisis in human lives and the middle, mid-career crisis was as real 150 years ago as it is today. Mancel Talcott felt life slipping by and he wanted another adventure such as he had when he first came to our frontier. The opportunity soon presented itself. Gold was discovered in California and the fever to rush to the gold fields soon overwhelmed him. Mary Talcott was a calm and supportive wife, and whether or not she understood his need to go, she stayed and managed the farm in his absence. She joined the ever increasing ranks of Midwest women in the late 1840s and early 1850s known as "Gold Widows," wives whose husbands went to California for the gold and the adventure.[9]

Talcott was in California for two years. They must have been hard lonely years for Mary, but when he returned, Talcott had with him a modest fortune in gold; he was one of the few who came back from the West coast with money. He also had enough adventure to last the rest of his life. He settled on the farm and became active in politics in Maine Township. He was elected supervisor in 1853. Talcott wanted to invest his money in a business venture, but he felt inexperienced in most aspects of industry. Meanwhile, his friend, Horace Singer was having second thoughts about a career with the Canal. In 1853, a severe drought lowered the water level so that traffic could not move for most of the season. Added to that problem was the fact that the government, at the time, was indifferent to widening and deepening the canal. Finally, the Alton Railroad was opening a line in the Des Plaines Valley that would compete with the canal.

In 1853, Singer took a contract to construct a breakwater from 18th Street north along Lake Michigan. He used waste rip-rap stone left from canal construction and soon realized the potential for dolomite. Expanding Chicago was demanding cut stone, rip-rap fill, and gravel building supplies. The Des Plaines Valley had stone deposits available to supply that need and Singer had the mechanical knowledge to operate a quarry, but he lacked money. Talcott had the money and, in 1854, they formed the Talcott-Singer quarries.

The partnership prospered and each chance they had they purchased more stone lands, so that before long they operated most of the quarries in the Lemont area. Talcott and Singer continued to invest their money and made huge profits. When the state passed a law in 1863 supporting a national banking system, Talcott and Singer joined with a group to form The First National Bank of Chicago.[10] It was the second national bank in the country formed under the new law.[11] Talcott was asked to serve as a director and therefore moved to Chicago and into the social circle of Chicago's wealthy and powerful.

Because of his mechanical and organizational skills, Singer remained in Lemont in charge of the quarry operations. However, it was he who coveted power and social recognition, not Talcott, who was also made director of the newly formed Stockyards Bank, serving the new Union Stockyards.[12] Through this connection, the gateway to the stockyards, now a landmark,[13] was built of stone from the Talcott-Singer quarries.

Because of his power and prestige, Talcott was named a director of the South and West Division Railway companies and elected as alderman from the Ninth Ward of the city. He served in the council with such directness and honesty that his name was often suggested for mayor, but he preferred the quiet life. Talcott and his wife worked for many charities and did church work with the Redeemer Universalist Church.[14] Anyone could come to Mancel Talcott with his or her problems. He would introduce himself to strangers with the line, "You don't know me yet, but you will know me; I'm generally called 'Pop' Talcott." He was considered a benevolent employer who would listen and help. He and his wife had no children of their own but adopted and supported several orphans.

Mrs. Talcott was active in the Chicago Relief and Aid Society, which served the poor by offering food and employment, and the Home For the Friendless, an agency that gave aid to the indigent and established two vocational schools.[15] Many of Lemont's quarry workers' children were able to get vocational training through her good offices. She also worked with Mrs. Singer to establish the first library in Lemont located on the company property at the northeast corner of the I & M Canal and Stephen Street.[16]

With their service background, the Talcotts were called on to help Chicago during a time of great social and political upheaval. Crime became a very serious problem throughout the city and suburbs from the 1860s through the middle 1870s. By the year 1870, there were well over 100 unsolved murders and numerous robberies and assaults. The crime wave was a product of changes after the Civil War and the Chicago Fire. Chicago became known as "the wickedest city in the U.S."[17] During the War, Chicago had attracted both soldiers with army pay and enlistment bounties, and gamblers and con men to fleece them. Herbert Asbury, in his *Gem of the Prairie,* comments that the city was "filled with the scum of a hundred other cities including the lonely streetwalker, the sneak thief, and lordly gambler. So many that they overflowed into the suburbs, particularly Lemont where a collection of dives known as Smokey Row had been a municipal canker for almost 40 years."[18]

Chicago was also vulnerable after the fire. The need for reconstruction, new housing, and social services was more than the city budget could bear. Money poured in for relief, but it was used directly to aid the victims, not to provide services to the city. Naturally, little revenue could be generated in the city until businesses were rebuilt. This resulted in a cutback in police and law enforcement officials hired by the city.

The fire also added more disreputable characters who saw an opportunity to prey on a weakened town. Against this background, Joseph Medill, the editor of the *Chicago Tribune,* ran for mayor on a reform platform known as the "Fire-Proof-Union" ticket. Advocating reform in the building codes and more power for the mayor, he was elected. His first task was to improve the police department. He discharged two of the three commissioners and began a search for a Chief Police Commissioner, one who would serve during a short period of reform and help clean up the department. The individual had to be honest, strong, firm, and financially independent, so he would not be influenced by money or power. Mancel Talcott was the perfect choice.[19]

Talcott took the job and worked with great dedication, but Chicago, as usual, was not ready for reform. Before any great strides could be made, the whole question of crime and corruption became tied up with ethnic politics, temperance laws, and the Sunday saloon closing effort, but the real problem was a lack of manpower and trained police officers. Talcott tried to get money for a larger force, but to no avail, so he resigned in the winter of 1872. Two years later, Medill was defeated and the old police commissioners returned to office. However, a number of Talcott's ideas and reforms were carried out by later administrations.

Talcott spent his last days serving on the boards of various banks and charity organizations, until one night when he became the victim of the vicious crime he had tried to fight. Two young toughs entered his home in Chicago with the idea of burglarizing its contents. Talcott chased them off by wrestling with both of them. One slammed him into a gas fixture and injured his chest. He never fully recovered from the blow. His health continued to decline and he died June 6, 1878.

He died before the bloody days of the labor strife in Lemont, so his death was a sad blow to Lemonters who still looked on him as a paternalistic, benevolent, and kind employer. Upon his death, Horace Singer bought out all his quarry holdings and the name was rechartered as the Singer-Talcott quarries.

So, Horace Singer, by 1878, acquired one of the largest limestone producing companies in the world.[20] He had 800 acres of quarry land, a cut stone mill employing 30 men, boats for transportation, and over 400 men working for his company.[21]

Singer's story is unique because in his lifetime of 73 years, he managed to span the whole continent while following the Western frontier. He was bound up in the growth and expansion of not only our area, but also that of California. He was born in Schenectady, New York, on October 1, 1823, to John Singer and Ann Collins. His paternal grandparents had immigrated from Germany, changing their name from Reisinger to Singer. When he was a year old, his parents moved to Conneaut, Ohio, a port town on Lake Erie. His father was following the frontier down the Erie Canal and westward. Horace grew up in Conneaut and attended a rural school where he received only a common education, but he had inherited the family's remarkable mechanical ability, a valuable trait on the frontier.

When his father got the contract to build part of the new I & M Canal, the family sailed on a lake vessel from Ohio to Chicago. The trip to Lockport was made by wagon over the new Archer Road. In Lockport, he worked on the canal and formed his lasting friendship with Mancel Talcott. In 1847, he married Harriet A. Roberts of Lockport. They had three sons, Edward, Walter, and Charles. When he formed the partnership with Talcott in 1854, the technical and mechanical aspects of the quarrying operation fell on him because of his knowledge and talent. Singer invested in real estate in Lemont, along with the quarry industry, and subdivided a tract of land on the southwestern side of town. This part is still called Singer Hill and was considered at the time the "best" part of town.[22] As he became moderately wealthy and powerful, he built his family a fine home at 608 Singer Avenue.

Politically, he was a "Douglas Democrat" — a conservative for Union and willing to compromise on slavery. But as the Civil War drew near and Douglas lost the election, Horace Singer became a member of the new party of Abe Lincoln, a Republican.[23] The prewar and war years were good to businessmen. With industrial expansion, there was a need for building materials, especially gravel and rip-rap for roads and rail beds.

Living in Lemont, Singer had a local power base and was elected township supervisor in 1865. He enjoyed this introduction into politics, so in 1866 he ran as a Republican for the 28th Assembly of Illinois. Elected, he made many important friends while serving in Springfield, including Governor Richard Oglesby. While there, Horace Singer was part of an Illinois Legislature noted for their special interest bills. In that session public bills enacted filled only 205 printed pages, while the special interest bills favoring banking and corporations filled over 2,500 pages.[24]

By 1870, Singer returned to local politics and managing the quarry operation. He stated in his biographical sketch[25] that out of concern for the educational needs of the community, he built a private tuition school for male children in the 1860s at a cost of 2,500 dollars. It had good teachers and a fine library, which later became the nucleus of Lemont's first library. The interesting thing about this school is that Lemont already had a public school system in place beginning in the village by the 1850s, located near the corner of Main and State Streets.

Singer was elected to the Cook County Board of Commissioners in 1870. He picked the right time to return to county level government, for midway through his term Chicago experienced the Chicago fire. After the ashes cooled, there was a cry to set fireproof standards for all buildings in Chicago. The election of Mayor Joseph Medill was based on establishing rules for the use of less wood and more masonry buildings. For a while even Lemont stone was suspect about its ability to withstand fire. The story was spread that Athens Marble contained a high amount of coal oil and that was why buildings made of our stone also burned in the fire. The stone industry led by Singer, Talcott, and others conducted tests and published the results to stop such rumors. The survival of the Chicago Water Tower, built of Lemont Stone from the Walker Quarry, was the best testimony to the durability of the stone. Singer was selected building chairman for the rebuilding of the county courthouse. So, of course, it and many other public buildings were built or rebuilt using the stone of the Des Plaines Valley.[26] The quarry owners profited as Chicago began another building boom and, as the quarries grew, Lemont grew.

Singer was an important member of the community. He controlled a good deal of the economy of the town — he served as President of the Quarry Owners Association, participated in local affairs, attended the Methodist Church, and became an active member of the International Order of Odd Fellows, Lemont Marble City Lodge No.429. He was a powerful figure, distant, but somehow tied to the survival of Lemont.

However, when Talcott died, Singer was elected to the board of directors of The First National Bank and there found himself in the inner circle of Chicago wealth and power politics. He was named chairman of the Central Republican Committee and, for club fellowship, he joined the exclusive Calumet, Union, and Chicago Clubs, a far cry from the I.O.O.F Lemont Marble City Lodge. The Chicago Club operated on a policy of "no dogs, Democrats, women, or reporters."[27] Fellow club members included George Pullman, Marshall Field, Potter Palmer, General Phillip Sheridan, and Lyman Gage. The Calumet Club also held yearly parties honoring those members who pioneered the Chicago area, men who were here by 1840. Horace Singer could be counted in that small, elite number.

With social, political, and banking interests taking his time, Singer retired from active day-to-day involvement with his Lemont operations, leaving it to his son, Edward, to direct the company. However, he would not give his son full control and when the 1885 labor strike occurred in Lemont, Horace Singer returned from a vacation trip to Denver to take control and to direct the situation. It was he who called a meeting of all other operators and convinced them to hold firm against the strikers. He then traveled to Joliet to confer with Colonel Bennett of the militia. There is no proof that Singer requested the militia be sent to Lemont, but the orders came from his old political ally, Governor Richard Oglesby.

When the strike finally ended, Singer stood at the gate to his main quarries while the men who had held out begged to be allowed to return to work. He refused and had the leaders blacklisted for any other quarry jobs in the area.

After the Lemont Massacre of 1885, Singer became estranged from both Lemont and his wife of 32 years, Harriet Roberts Singer. He moved to Chicago, divorced Harriet, and at the age of 62 married a young widow, Emma Baker. That same year he showed another side to his complex personality by investing in a scheme proposed by his fellow Chicago Club member, Ferdinand Peck. Peck had plans to build[28] an auditorium complex for cultural events in Chicago. The building was to include not only an auditorium, but also a hotel and stores. There was little hope of great financial return, but Singer considered his investment a cultural contribution to Chicago. The beautiful Sullivan and Adler Auditorium building on the corner of Michigan and Congress stands today because of men with his vision.

In 1888, Singer retired from the First National Bank board of directors and by 1891 sold all of his stone holdings to Martin B. Madden of The Western Stone Conglomerate. He left the cut stone business because he could sense future developments and realized that stone would no longer be in such great demand for building. He only had to look at the new skyscraper architecture in Chicago to see the end of masonry, weight-bearing wall buildings in commercial centers. At the same time, styles in home and institution buildings were also changing. Lemont stone that had been popular for 40 years was beginning to show its age in some buildings. A 1891 publication stated:

> Limestone for front has properly gone out of use. The old smooth ashlar fronts to be seen on Washington Boulevard and Michigan Avenue are now considered out of date. In sawed ashlar the grain is exposed to weather and . . . soon shows the effect of such treatment. In the rock faced [rough style such as the front of Old Central] and trimming work that is now so generally used, the stone rests as it does in the quarry, which enables it to . . . resist exposure. Formerly, the number of quarries shipping stone to Chicago was very few, and the choice was . . . limited. This is the reason for the use of decaying stone, which is noticed in some of our buildings. At the present time, about 60 limestone and sandstone and many quartzite quarries are shipping here.[29]

Singer not only wanted to rid himself of the business, but he wanted to remove himself from dealing with the workers and foremen who ran the enterprise. Since they no longer looked on him as a good and generous employer after the 1885 strike, he rejected them. As for his own children, they apparently did not want to continue in the business or were not asked. Also, estranged from their father, his children left the area — Edward went East to New York, Walter went into shipping in Duluth, and Charles became a real estate broker in Chicago at 175 Dearborn Street.[30]

Like Mancel Talcott before him, Horace Singer then traveled to California. There was no gold then, but there was land and real estate development. It was still a new frontier and even at his age he wanted to be a part of it with his new wife. So he sold his home on Singer Avenue,[31] the one that Lucy Parsons wanted to burn down. Singer also left money for a stained glass window to memorialize his name in the Methodist Church,[32] and he purchased a plot in the Lockport cemetery — then he went west.

His first wife, Harriet, moved to a smaller home on the west side of town. Mrs. Singer did not brood about the loss of her husband, but continued to work on the library that she had organized from the collection that was in the Singer private school. At first a library for the workers, it became a public library called the Lemont Union Library. After Singer sold the quarries, the library lasted over ten years because of her strength and devotion. When she died, some books were transferred to Old Central School to become the nucleus of the public school library. There are still some old books in Lemont homes bearing the book plate of the Lemont Union Library.

Harriet Singer also helped to finance the present village hall. When a discussion arose in 1887[33] about the condition of the old wooden town hall, Mrs. Singer and Mrs. Talcott offered funds for a new structure if the village would contribute the rest and if the library could have space in the building. For those who remember the public library in the village hall, they know it remained there for years because of a promise to those two benefactors. The influence of these women who remained faithful to their community is also reflected in the fact that the architect of the village hall, Boehme, was a nephew by marriage of Mrs. Talcott. Mary Talcott did not live to see the village hall completed. She died in April of 1888.

Horace Singer settled out West in the new wealthy and growing suburb of Pasadena. Located on the Santa Fe line, it was a perfect area for winter and all-season homes. He began investing in the growth industry that had brought him across America — transportation. At 68, he began developing the newest form of transportation, the electric railway. Ever the mechanical mind, he became involved in a proposal to build an electric railway to Mount Echo, California, for recreational purposes.[34] It was the time of the electric railway and early investors made a great deal of money.

Singer invested over 100,000 dollars in the Pasadena and Mt. Lowe Railroad and helped to support the development. The railroad had an incline of over 62 percent, 127 curves, and 18 bridges. It was a spectacular ride, far better than any commercial roller coaster ride today, for it included beautiful scenery along the route. The history of this railway has been a favorite of electric railway buffs for years. It opened to the public on July 4, 1893, and never had a serious accident during its years of operation.[35]

In the five years he spent in California, Horace Singer became a leading citizen of that community. As he did in Lemont, he became involved in civic affairs. In Pasadena there were no quarries, nor laborers to accuse him of exploiting their sweat and pain to build his fortune. Instead he was a wealthy man of the world, open to new ideas and inventions and able to invest in those schemes he felt worthwhile. He, and his money, were honored in town. A park was named after him and businessmen courted him. He had found his golden West.

Horace Singer died on December 28, 1896, in the sanitarium hospital of Doctor J.S. Hodge, a homeopathic physician. Dr. Hodge founded Pasadena's first hospital and was well known in the community.[36] The death appeared to be a sudden event. The *Pasadena Daily Evening Star* reported on December 28, 1896:

> A shock was given the many friends of Mr. Horace Singer who had not heard of his dangerous illness by the news that he died about half past nine this morning. His last hours came as a result of a strain and a severe shock to his nervous system occasioned nearly four weeks ago in endeavoring to jump aboard a moving train. The nervous disarrangement passed to his brain and ended fatally in that part. For about three weeks prior to his death, Mr. Singer was given the best of care in Dr. Hodge's Hospital.[37]

The California funeral was held on January 4, 1897, and was attended by the notables of the community such as the president, directors, and secretary of the Pasadena Board of Trade, along with the mayor and two directors of the Bank of California. The service was conducted from his home at 200 West California Street by ministers from the Presbyterian and Congregational churches "and were of a character to deeply impress all present."[38]

The honorary pallbearers were Judge H. Cody, Wm. P. Gray, Richard Morgan, H.C. Durand, Dr. J.B. Talcott, and P. M. Green, "all intimate friends and all but the last named from Chicago."[39] None of his children attended.

Singer's will was probated by Charles Kimball[40] the day of the funeral, and his California assets were listed at 325,000 dollars, a sum that many back here thought was a deliberate underestimation. His body was prepared for shipment back to Lockport for internment in the tomb he had selected before he went West. Like the Chicago rail car manufacturer, George Pullman, Horace Singer feared that his body would be harmed by the angry laborers, so he had a mausoleum built to keep out the hate his last years of quarry ownership had created. However, in the end it was not the laborers but his own family that would not let the dead rest. Horace Singer, dead, would become the center of controversy.

After some delay the body was finally shipped to Lockport. The funeral train stopped in Lemont for those townspeople who wanted to see "Old Singer" put in his final resting place. Most of those who had suggested hanging him during the labor troubles were no longer interested in his last journey. Only a few boarded the train, including some who still held such deep hatred that they had to see him buried. Still, the train also included those who remembered his contributions in the early days; he was one of the pioneers who had built and developed Lemont. There was no question that without Singer the town would have been different. One group of mourners said the town would have been better off without him; others claimed that there might not have been a town without the Singer-Talcott quarries.[41]

The family trouble began in June when his son Edward went to Pasadena and began investigating the circumstances of his father's death, and by late June of 1897 managed to get an order to have his father's remains examined for poison. The *Chicago Tribune* reported, in a special dispatch from California, that "the son is convinced that the old man's death was hastened, if not actually brought about, by foul play. The disposition of the millionaire's property is the incentive for the investigation."[42]

The law firm representing the second Mrs. Singer, H. Cody and Sons,[43] released the following description of Horace Singer's death and illness in the hope it would forestall an autopsy:

> About December 1, 1896, Mr. Singer met with an accident trying to board a moving train; that was the beginning of his last illness. He assisted his wife and some ladies aboard, thus losing his chance and was obligated to catch the next car as it came along. He missed his step and hung clinging to the rail until he drew himself up. He was a heavy man and 73 years old and the strain he sustained was serious. He stated that he felt "some thing give away" in the left side of his chest. By the time he returned home on the 4th he was very ill and taken to the sanitarium. Mr. Singer's death occurred on December 28, as reported.[44]

As for the idea of an autopsy, the lawyers for the second Mrs. Singer were outraged that the body of such an important individual could be disturbed because of the "unfounded" suspicions of some family members. His lot and tomb he deeded to Mrs. Emma Singer, the second wife, giving her control of it during her life. The key was kept in her possession and when legal difficulties began over control of the body, she had guards posted at the tomb in the Lockport cemetery. They stood guard for three days and three nights until the coroner of Will County, accompanied by Mr. Chamberlain, a Lockport undertaker, produced a second key and opened the mausoleum.

On July 1, 1897 the *Chicago Tribune* reported on the autopsy:

Horace Singer's tomb in Lockport. (Photo courtesy of Lemont Historical Society)

> The body was removed from its sepulcher and taken to the rear shed of Chamberlain's undertaking establishment. Although the casket was a metal one and airtight, the spectators were not prepared to find the body in such a natural state of preservation . . . the face was calm and serene as if he had fallen asleep. But hardly had the lid been removed when the air striking the body caused a most wonderful change. Almost instantly the skin turned to an inky blackness and began to flake and fall from the body.

Horace was examined by the coroner Charles Downey and two specialists from Chicago. His vital organs were removed and taken by the independent doctors for analysis. The post mortem ended at 1:30 p.m. and everyone took off leaving the mutilated remains with Mr. Chamberlain. Horace's nightmare fears had been realized, not by the bitter strikers, but by his own bitter family. None of the children were present at the autopsy. They only awaited the results.[45]

The final report was presented the next day. It found that Mr. Singer had died of tuberculosis, heart problems, and Bright's disease, and not as a result of any poison or undue means. The trace of arsenic in his system was held to be a result of the embalming process.

So Horace Singer's remains were again returned to his honored spot, the safety of his tomb. It is a cold, gray mausoleum built, ironically, not of the stone that made him his fortune, but of Bedford Dolomite and granite. The only Des Plaines Dolomite visible is part of the foundation.

Over the years no one else has joined him in his lonely resting place, neither wives nor children. He remains alone in the town where he spent his youth, awaiting the judgement of history.

Some quarry owners, like Singer and Talcott, began life with financial backing. They arrived in the area early and had family that worked on contracts from the government, not that they did not go through bad times when the canal defaulted and cyclic downturns caused them economic hardships. Yet they began with advantages and could capitalize on those advantages.

This was not so for other quarry owners. One of the best examples of a man who worked the American dream from poverty to wealth and power was Martin B. Madden.[46]

Martin Madden was born March 20, 1855, in Darlington, England, the son of John and Elizabeth O'Neill Madden. He was the third child of seven born to the couple. Life was hard in Darlington. Unskilled and landless, his father had a tough time feeding the ever increasing family. The family also faced the unspoken social barrier of being Catholic and carrying an Irish name in England.

The days he remembered from his early life centered on a short school experience in a village called Castle Eden. He was so young and his few memories so joyful that the village became a special ideal to him, a memory that carried him through his bad times; so much so, that in later years he would name his estate at Cass for that small spot of England.

While the Maddens struggled in Darlington, Mrs. Madden received glowing letters from her sister and brother-in-law, Peter Warden, who had immigrated to the new frontier in Illinois several years before. They wrote of the small town they lived near, where there was land and work for all, a place called Lemont. Encouraged by the letters, the family left England and arrived in Lemont in 1860. Martin was only five years old, but he later recalled much of the adventure of the crossing, just as he always remembered his English childhood home.

The family arrived with great hopes, but America was not always the land of opportunity, and Martin's father continued his struggles with poverty. Conditions became so bad that when Martin was ten years old he realized that he had to quit school to find work to help support the family. It was not unusual in those days for students to leave school to begin work after the fifth grade. No doubt it hurt his parents to see their bright, capable boy forced to earn money to keep the family, yet few things discouraged Martin. It was in his nature to find opportunities, no matter what the circumstances. So Martin Madden went down to the Walker Quarry to apply for a job.

Edwin Walker had a hard time facing the constant stream of boys who came for work. There really was a limit to the number of water carriers he could use for his quarrying operation and he knew that all the applicants were in need. However, there was something in Martin's manner and maturity that captured Ed Walker's admiration and he hired him for 50 cents a day for a 12-hour day, the standard terms for a water boy.

In a short time, Martin fulfilled his promise. He became one of the brightest, quickest, and most likeable water carriers that the Walker quarry men had ever seen. No errand was too small or trivial. He was known for his quick response to the familiar cry of, "Boy water boy, water me now." He listened and obeyed cheerfully and openly. He was eager to learn anything and everything. When he left school to go to work, he promised his parents that he would continue his schooling when it was financially possible. So Martin looked upon the quarry and its workers and its operation as a kind of school. He soon realized that the men who worked the stone often were well educated but were unable to find work in other fields because of the language and social barriers that hindered new immigrants. Later in his life, Martin would credit much of his knowledge of Greek, Latin, engineering, and geology to the days spent working in the quarries of Lemont.[47]

The quarry workers were a mixture of men from all over the Western world and many befriended this curious, cheerful, and intelligent waterboy. One of his chief friends was a young African-American, John Buckner. There in the hot sun and rainy, cold days in the Walker quarries they developed a friendship that was to last a lifetime. Perhaps they recognized in each other that special drive to succeed and, although they did not know it then, the day would come when they would both need each other to rise in the world of politics and power.[48]

Madden's skill as a water boy soon earned him a position as time custodian, a job that required more responsibility. It also earned him a dollar a day. Once he started earning that sum, he began attending the night school offered by the Lemont Public School system for working boys. Although there is no official record of this school, Madden and others reported attending this special night school as early as 1867. If this is the case, those classes were offered by George D. Plant, the first superintendent of the grade school.[49] Madden also took correspondence courses for clerking, drafting, and bookkeeping. His teen years were spent working and studying. He developed a remarkable sense of confidence, so that when the plans for the 1869 Central School building were drawn up and taken down to the Walker Quarry for the stone estimate, the young Madden noticed them on the desk and he suggested a correction to enlarge the building interior by moving some supporting structures. The school board president realized that this 14 year-old was correct and he suggested that Madden sketch out his ideas and submit them to the school board for approval.

They were submitted and incorporated in the plan, much to the embarrassment of the contractor. The board then, jokingly, suggested that Madden send them a bill. The teenager did, one for 50 dollars. When he appeared for payment, one board member questioned the cost, remarking that it had taken only a half hour to change the plans. Madden replied that it may have taken a half hour to change the plans but it had taken him many months to learn the skills to do it. The bill was approved.[50] The landmark building that we see today at the rear of Old Central School was called "Madden's School" for many years afterward in recognition of the young man's drafting talents and his quick tongue in dealing with authority.

By the time Madden was 15, he was a veteran quarry man familiar with all the jobs and skills needed in a cut stone operation. At that young age he had five years of experience behind him. His wages were five dollars a week, almost a man's wage, and when Walker offered him a raise and a chance to work the barges running stone to Chicago, he grabbed the opportunity. That was only natural; it would be exciting to travel with the stone boats up and down the I & M Canal and be part of the economic life that centered on the waterway.

Looking at the weed-choked remains of the I & M today, it is hard to imagine the activity that surrounded the waterway. There were days in the boom times when barges of stone were strung in a line from Chicago to Lemont with barely a foot of water between them. All this was thrilling to young Madden, especially the layovers in Chicago. If he ever dreamed of one day being part of the glamor and power of Chicago's ruling class, he kept the dream to himself. In 1870, Chicago was growing and our stone was a favorite building material for facing buildings and as cut masonry blocks. The Walker barges, with Madden aboard, made many trips back and forth along the canal. He learned to manage with the tough bargemen. He worked hard, as he always did, yet with the reckless abandon of youth. The older men came to admire his energy and curiosity about everything around him.

However, barge work is dangerous. Madden had little fear of injury or death; he was, after all, only 15 years old. His previous experience was in the quarries and not on the boats, so he did not have the respect he should have had for the dangers involved in pushing large loads of stone.

One day, in the hot, dry summer of 1871, as he was lashing two barges, his foot slipped and his lower leg was crushed. In a heroic attempt to save Madden's life, the doctor was forced to amputate Martin's leg at the knee. Martin Madden hung between life and death for many days. When it finally appeared that he would survive, his parents began to assess what meager opportunities lay ahead for their son. He was 15 and seriously crippled. He had only five years of formal education and some night and correspondence school. Most of his work experience had been with heavy labor that he could no longer perform. To his parents, the future looked bleak. They feared that perhaps he would become a burden upon the already strained household. In those dark days it seemed that America and Lemont had not been the answer to their dreams. John Madden brooded about his troubles and let those who would listen know that he held Edwin Walker responsible for his son's injury.

Whether out of compassion or guilt, Walker came to the boy's bedside and persuaded him to accept an offer to begin work as a payroll clerk in the company office. If Madden had bad days because of his disability, he never showed it. When he recovered, he began his new career, with the same drive he had always had. He worked at the Lemont and Chicago offices of Walker's Stone Company and began attending Bryant and Stratton Business College, in Chicago, part-time. It soon became clear that Madden was as good at clerking, drafting, and managing as he had been at the unskilled hard quarry work.

The year of his injury was also the year of the great Chicago Fire and Walker won the contract to rebuild the Cook County portion of the courthouse. It was a lucrative contract awarded to the Lemont Stone industry largely through the political connections of Edwin Walker and Horace Singer. It was said, at the time, that Walker also got the contract because of his friendship with Mike McDonald, the gambling and political boss of Chicago.

The courthouse had two sections, city and county. The city side was built of Bedford Limestone from Indiana, a fact that hinted at the eventual decline our Des Plaines Valley quarries because "this combined use of Athens Marble and Indiana Limestone foreshadowed what was in store for the Illinois Limestone industry." Bedford stone was already competing for a share of the Chicago market.[51]

By 1875, Walker placed the 20 year-old Madden in a supervisory position on the courthouse construction. There he controlled every step of the operation, although it was sometimes hard for him to get around the site on his artificial leg.

While working, he took more business and law courses and when the project and his education were finished, Madden left Walker to join a rival stone company — Enterprise.

Madden quit Walker because Enterprise offered him the position of superintendent with full control of the company and because political fallout from the cost overruns on the courthouse were giving Walker and his company a bad name. The County Court House was even nicknamed the "thief's monument" by some newspapers.[52] Martin Madden was, at 22, a man who had worked his way up from waterboy to superintendent of a major stone company and he was just beginning his climb.

Romance entered Madden's life in 1878 on a ride out to the DuPage area known as Cass[53] to conduct business with a farmer-pioneer living in that section. Approaching the house he heard a voice singing so sweetly that, as he later claimed, he fell in love instantly. The voice belonged to Josephine Smart, the daughter of Elisha Smart. Josephine had been educated at Wheaton College, a rare accomplishment for a woman in those days. Madden was so taken with her that he began to visit the farm frequently and serenaded her with the popular song of the day, "Little Sweetheart." It worked.

The crippled, Irish-Catholic, self-made stone superintendent and the educated, refined Protestant daughter of a wealthy farmer were married under a large tree in the front yard of the Smart farm on May 16, 1878. It is not known if the families objected to the union, but it is interesting that the couple were married outside and not in the Cass Church that the Smarts founded and supported with land and money.

Josephine and Martin settled down to a happy life together in Lemont. Madden continued to serve at the Enterprise Stone Company even after Joliet Stone purchased a major share in the quarry in 1881. The only sad part of the comfortable life that Martin and Josephine Madden had in Lemont was that she developed an ear infection that slowly began to affect her hearing. She traveled to many specialists but none had a cure. The affliction became so severe that it limited their social life and, through the years, the couple seldom entertained. Most of their free time was spent with each other. Their only child, a daughter, was born in 1886. She had to learn sign language to communicate with her mother. In the isolation of deafness, Josephine took to writing poetry, mostly for her family, but she did publish a small book of verses.

The Quarry Strike of 1885 was a boon to Madden. The bad feelings and community upheaval that it created made many older quarry owners eager to get out of a business that was changing with the new social and economic forces at work. Because of his knowledge of the industry, Madden was able to arrange several small local mergers, which became the Joliet and Lemont Stone Company. He was recognized as a force in the industry by being elected the president of the Quarry Owners Association of the United States in 1885, and served in that position until 1889. He also was vice-president and director of the Builder's and Trader's Exchange of Chicago from 1886 to 1887.

By merging the stone companies, he could fire those employees considered labor agitators and begin shifting the quarrying to Joliet, where the union activity was weaker. This left most refining and cutting in his company in Lemont where the skilled stone cutters had not been a part of the strike movement. The company was successful and Madden became a vice-president of the firm.

Madden, like so many older capitalists, felt the need to show his new status by moving away from Lemont. The Maddens purchased a home in Chicago at 3563 Forest Avenue, in the old Fourth Ward of the city.

Madden realized the only way to control labor was for more of the stone companies to merge. By 1890, almost all private companies wanted to sell because they could not compete with the lower prices of the larger local companies and with the Indiana stone market. Madden represented a group of investors, headed by Noble P. Judah, which began purchasing smaller operations. Finally, Horace Singer's large Lemont holdings were added and Western Stone was born. Madden was named the new vice-president of the vast conglomerate. With this power he felt he needed a political base and he ran for alderman of his ward as a Democrat, but lost.

The new quarry owners had plans to make a fortune. They wanted a contract for the removal of stone from the site of the proposed Sanitary Canal. They planned to receive a double payment for the stone. First, the payment from the state and the Metropolitan Sanitary District for removing the stone, since they had equipment capable of such contracts, and a second payment for the sale of the stone that they removed for commercial purposes. It was a good scheme, one that had worked to make fortunes 60 years before, when the I & M Canal was built. To get the contracts, Western Stone needed political contacts.

So Madden turned again to the idea of running for alderman. After his previous defeat, he took a more studied approach to election and realized that he was in the wrong party for his ward, so he ran as a Republican. This time he was elected. He entered the Chicago City Council in 1889.

The Fourth Ward was a mixture of ethnic and racial groups, and Madden built a very strong local organization to support his power. To develop a relationship with the African-American voters in his ward, he called on his old childhood friend from the quarry days, John Buckner. Buckner had left the quarries and had begun working as a headwaiter for fashionable parties until he moved himself up to the management of a catering business.[54] Buckner lacked a formal education, but because of his work with the wealthy he had developed the "polish of the cultured class."[55]

With Buckner, Martin created a ward organization complete with African-American fife and drum groups to join with the various ethnic marching groups of the Fourth Ward. On special occasions, Martin Madden's black and white marching units would parade for Chicago events. To consolidate power, Madden helped to get Buckner appointed Deputy Collector of Internal Revenue for the First District of Illinois in 1890, and began grooming him to run for the state legislature. Ultimately, Buckner served the Fifth District in the 39th session of the state legislature.

By 1891, Madden's power, both economic and political, had grown so strong that he was elected president of the Chicago City Council. Martin Madden presided over one of the worst collections of political hacks that ever graced a city. The present Chicago City Council is tame compared to that of Martin's day. Newspapers and magazines called them the "gray wolves," eager and hungry for any graft that they could gather for themselves. It was a wild time but Madden, with his earthly Lemont experience and background, was able to make the best of it.

One major source of graft and bribery was associated with the franchise mania of the late 1800s. During that period, businessmen and speculators sought to be granted free, or cheap, franchise rights to operate transportation or communication lines within cities and towns. Holding a franchise gave a corporation the exclusive right to build or dig anywhere within the city limits. Many speculators paid bribes to obtain these rights for schemes they never planned to carry out. They would hold the rights until some legitimate business was forced to purchase those rights from them. A great deal of money could be made by simply getting franchise rights,[56] which were sold openly. An example of this kind of "boodle" was the Chicago Power Supply Company scheme. This company, supported by Madden, was granted the power to lay pipe in every street, alley, or public place for supplying compressed air to every home in Chicago.

Madden aligned himself with the businessmen who controlled the city. He was an ally of the transportation czar Charles Tyson Yerkes who came to Chicago in 1882 after serving time in a Philadelphia jail for a fund shortage in the sale of city bonds. Yerkes had a talent for convincing others that the shortage was a mistake, because he came to Chicago with money from Philadelphia bankers, money that was to be invested in Chicago transportation.

Before long he had built a fortune on subsidiary transportation, using companies watered and oversold to give him a large profit. Yerkes was quoted as saying, "Buy old junk, fix it up a little and unload it on the other fellow."[57] The present CTA and Loop "El" were established by Yerkes' companies.

When the west side loop of the "El" was built, the council, with Madden as their leader, voted a franchise for Yerkes that included a tax of 50 dollars a year for every car run 300 days of the year. Naturally, all of Yerkes' cars ran only 299 days a year. The city never received any revenue from Yerkes' company. During the years from 1889 to 1897, 116 ordinances favoring Yerkes' transportation line were introduced into the council. Madden opposed only five; it was a time when big business ran the city.

Madden was also active in other important events. He worked on several committees that planned the World Columbian Exposition of 1893. His power in the City Council was so great that he was one of those nominated to serve out Carter Harrison's term.[58] He missed being elected mayor pro tem of Chicago by six votes; it was a great disappointment to him that he did not get the nomination. The year 1893 was difficult for Madden in many ways — economic conditions began to erode his personal fortune as his investment in Western Stone was not returning a profit. In spite of his clout, the contract he wanted to dig stone for the Sanitary Ship Canal went to another company. So Madden took control of Western Stone and reorganized its structure. He was faced with a debt of 158,000 dollars. The assets consisted of the quarries, 150 boats, 500 team horses, and 2,700 men. Madden kept the boats and horses and fired 400 men; many of those fired had been active in union organizing.

Eager to get contracts, he used his influence in clever ways. When Madden and the city council became involved in an ordinance giving the Illinois Central Railroad the right-of-way along the south end of the lake shore, Madden opposed the plan, insisting that the Illinois Central had to elevate the trackage for safety reasons. Since any ordinance could not pass without Madden's approval, the issue was resolved with a compromise. If a retaining wall was built along the tracks, Madden would approve the plan. The wall was built, naturally, of Lemont stone from the Madden Western Stone quarries.

His company also held lucrative sidewalk flagging and curbing contracts. Newspapers and civic reform organizations pointed out this conflict of interest, but little was done, for Madden was a strong power. As for the Lemonters working the quarries, they considered Martin a smart man, since the contracts kept the quarries open. When Madden ran again for his seat in the Chicago City Council, in 1897, he was vigorously opposed by the Municipal Voters League. This watchdog group mounted a campaign against him based on his voting record. In a list of candidate recommendations sent out by the league, Madden was described as follows:

> His general disregard of public interests and his opposition to compensation for franchise condemn him as unfit for public service.

To which Madden, tough and aggressive, replied:

> [The committee contains] men whose morals are as rotten as a garbage heap. They stand for nothing in the community.[59]

Madden was for expansion of Chicago's boundaries and our local paper could not resist a comment on such an idea; it reported that Madden, the alderman, wanted to annex all of Cook County. "Just think of it, we will be Chicago's 269th Ward with paved streets, parks, boulevards, and gas meters and franchises at our very door."

In its eagerness for reform, the Voters League overlooked the positive contributions made by Madden. He served the city council as finance chairman, supported civil service reform for Chicago and Illinois, worked as an active member of the Republican party, and supported the creation of Provident Hospital in Chicago, introducing the ordinance supporting the creation of that pioneer, African-American training hospital.

The forces of reform continued to agitate against Madden and other members of the city council. This resulted in his defeat for Chicago alderman in 1897. Undaunted, he began a campaign to win nomination for the Senate while building his power base with the increasing black population of his ward. He supported his friend John Buckner, who pushed to create the Ninth Battalion of the State's National Guard, an all black organization. Buckner had himself named commander.[60] This support for civil rights helped Madden maintain his position in his district.

However, Madden's bid for the Senate nomination failed and he retired from seeking office for a few years. He spent the time in his business and consolidating his power base within the Republican party in anticipation of another try for office.

In 1901, all teachers and libraries in the state received a small book entitled, *Martin B. Madden: Public Servant*. Written by Edgar Brent, an author hired by Madden and published at Madden's expense, the book was designed to offset the negative publicity his candidacy had engendered in reform circles. The book tells, in glowing details, about Madden's early life and his struggle with poverty in Lemont. It is hard to say whether this public relations scheme worked to make the public aware of Martin Madden, but he did receive the Republican nomination for Congressional Representive in 1902.

The old charge of "boodling" (taking payoffs) came back to haunt him and the Voters League again conducted a campaign against him claiming that he was a friend of the two aldermanic vice-lords of Chicago, "Bathhouse" John Couglin and "Hinky Dink" Kenna. It was also charged that he had been involved in a conflict of interest while in the council. They were quick to point out that while Madden was the Republican leader of the council, 90 percent of all sidewalk contracts to the city went to Western Stone, Madden's company.

Those charges prompted an angry letter to the *Chicago Tribune* from George Walker, president of Lemont's Pure Aluminum Company and son of Madden's first employer, Edwin Walker. George suggested that all local reformers should stay out of the election as Madden was an able candidate worthy of anyone's support. But, Madden was defeated again.

It did not discourage Madden. He spent the next years giving political speeches, mostly in support of his pet project, the Isthmus Canal. His Central American Isthmus Canal speech was popular with audiences, and he gave it many times here in Lemont in the Tedens Opera house at 102 Stephen Street. It was his advocacy of the canal, a plan that could benefit shipping here and in the nation, that gave him a wider following than he had before. At the 1900 Republican convention, he wrote the platform plank that committed the United States to a canal in Panama or Nicaragua.

He also took time to build a home in the area, on the Smart Homestead.[61] Completed in 1903, it was built for Josephine as a 25th anniversary wedding gift, and named Castle

Castle Eden, now owned by the Society of Mount Carmel. (Photo courtesy of Lemont Historical Society)

Eden for his remembered England. The home is unique, as it was modeled after the original White House in Washington, D.C. Castle Eden remained his country home when he was not in Washington or in his Chicago District.

By the next Congressional election, Martin Madden was a familiar name to voters and far enough removed from the old days of the "gray wolves" to be elected. He went to the 59th session of Congress in March of 1905. In Washington, Madden served first on the Appropriation's Committee. As a member of that committee he sponsored hearings and made tours of the Panama Canal site. His interest and knowledge of canals and earth moving equipment came from his experience here in Lemont with the quarries, the I & M Canal, and the Sanitary Ship Canal. When Madden made a tour in 1907, he became one of the members of Congress supporting a canal built with locks instead of a sea level canal. The suggestion was accepted and the addition of locks helped to make the canal workable. His efforts for the canal were recognized by naming an impoundment lake along the canal, Lake Madden.

In Congress, Martin Madden lobbied for our local canals and waterways. He and Congressman Lorimer shared a boat called "Remirol"[62] that sailed the Chicago area and Illinois canals and waterways to promote the deep waterway system for Illinois. Their pioneer work is what made Lemont the inland seaport town it is today. Madden and Lormier envisioned a waterway that would allow products to be shipped worldwide from canal towns like Lemont.

In Washington, Madden worked hard and represented his district with great skill. Much of his early congressional interest was also centered on the postal service. He became the champion of the postal service workers and the department. Madden was often honored by postal groups and he was the first congressman they contacted for support for their needs. This support was important to his district back home, for the postal civil service was one area that did not discriminate against African-Americans. Spear writes in his book *Black Chicago*:

> By 1910 over 500 Negroes worked in the Chicago Post Office. Negroes rarely complained of discrimination in securing postal jobs. This was primarily the result of Congressman Madden's position on the House of Representatives Post Office Committee . . . The Postal Service provided Negroes with almost their only opportunity for clerical work and carried considerable prestige among Chicago Negroes. Several post office clerks became community leaders, and an organization of Negro postal employees, the Phalanx Forum, was a major political and social force in pre World War I Black Chicago.[63]

As a token of the affection the postal service had for Madden, his son-in-law, Paul Henderson, was named second assistant to the Postmaster General in the 1920s. Henderson was closely connected with the early development of the postal air service. In fact, Henderson entertained a number of the early air pioneers at Castle Eden, including Charles Lindberg.

Although a fiscally conservative Republican, in many ways Martin Madden was independent. He was probably the most progressive member of the Chicago delegation on the question of railroad rate regulation, working to increase the power of the Inter-State Commerce Commission, and trying to obtain a valuation on rail trackage to develop a fair rail charge. Madden's business background in Lemont influenced his view of the railroads. Lemont Stone could compete successfully with other building materials because of the cheaper cost of water transportation on the canals. If Western Stone had to rely on rail transportation alone, it would have been forced out of the construction market.

As his years in Congress continued, Martin became more involved with the fiscal and financial matters of government. He helped to frame the bill to create the Bureau of the Budget and, by the 67th Congress, Madden was elected chairman of the Appropriations Committee and became one of a long line of watchdogs of the treasury. This position gave him great power over government spending and earned for him a reputation of tough mindedness and fiscal restraint.

In 1915, when fear of war was gripping the country, Madden organized the first military training camp west of the Allegheny Mountains, at Fort Sheridan. He recruited men and served as a private in Company A, this in spite of his artificial leg from his childhood injury. When the United States entered World War I, Madden made trips to hospitals visiting the wounded and giving psychological support, especially to amputees.

As his work kept him in Washington, he was unable to keep up his business activities in Western Stone, and in 1915 he turned the operation of his company over to his son-in-law, Paul Henderson, who operated the stone company for a few years. Time and fashion had decreased the desire for stone and, in 1925, the company was dissolved by judicial order.

Madden did take time out to do some writing about his fiscal and political views. In 1925, he published two articles in *The Saturday Evening Post*, "Tax Reduction and the Public Debt," and "The Budget to Date." He was asked to accompany President Harding on his fatal trip to Alaska, but the press of Congressional business kept him in Washington. He worked hard and held many committee hearings, and it was at such a hearing on April 27, 1928, that Martin Madden, Lemont's greatest water boy, had a heart attack and died.

The *Chicago Tribune* ran a memorial sketch in his honor. Charles Dawes said the nation had lost its best fiscal mind. There were testimonials and praise from all over the country for his skills, his courage, and his determination. The loss of Madden was deeply felt by his party, by his district, by the postal workers, and by African-American groups, for Madden had remained a special friend to their needs. His political organization had trained many African-Americans in the political process and his death allowed them to finally exercise power in their own right. In all fairness, it must be said that Madden continued to represent his district long after the racial makeup had changed from mainly white to all black, but if the people in his district had wanted someone else they could have voted Madden out.

The *Chicago Defender* commented on Madden's death and mentioned his lifelong sincere effort to help blacks not only in his district, but also in all of the United States. The friendship born in the Walker Quarry between a poor waterboy and John Buckner, a young black from Kendall County, had paid off for the whole country.

Martin B. Madden was buried in Cass Community Cemetery close to his beloved Castle Eden. There he rests under a simple stone, a water boy who went from poverty to the halls of Congress.

Of the major quarry owners, Singer, Talcott, and Madden, all left Lemont as they gained money and power. Only N.J. Brown and Edwin Walker remained and saw the need to invest in manufacturing as the quarry industry began its decline. Edwin Walker came to this country in 1856 from Leeds, England.[64] He settled in Chicago by late 1857, and began work as a general contractor. As it was a time of growth for the area, he found his skills in great demand. His major interest was in large institutional contracts, and he soon developed a reputation as a fine stonemason contractor. To keep his crews together when there was no work he decided to acquire some stone quarries. This way, he could keep his men working and control the stone he used in construction. Walker found the quarries he wanted in Lemont by purchasing stone lands from Daniel Skelly, and moved to the town after the Civil War. His homestead was named Woodland Park and is now the site of the Franciscan Sisters Retirement Center.

Walker had many contacts in Chicago business and political circles and managed to get many major contracts let by the city and state. Two remain that are world famous — the original Chicago Water Tower and its adjoining buildings, and the upper section of the Illinois State Capitol building. Both are fine examples of good construction using dolomite limestone.

Walker's Chicago political connections included the honest and the shady. He was a friend of Mike McDonald, the gambling and patronage boss of the city for many years. It was claimed that Walker was awarded the lucrative contract for the Cook County Courthouse in part because of his friendship with McDonald. There could be some truth in the accusation, for when reform swept Chicago politics, for a brief time in the late 1880s, McDonald closed his gambling establishment and invested in Lemont stone land.[65]

Walker had unique ideas about stonemasonry construction. One was that the stone should be laid with mortar made from the same bed as the stone, which he could do because he owned the quarries. This concept made sense because the chemical composition of dolomite stone can vary from bed to bed and any mortar not compatible would eventually react with the stone.[66]

Of all the fine Walker buildings that have, in time, fallen to the wrecker's ball, one of the finest was the Central Music Hall located on the southeast corner of State and Randolph Streets in Chicago. The building was designed by Dankmar Adler and contracted to Walker in 1879. It was Adler's first independent commission and his most important work until 1881 when he and Louis Sullivan joined forces to create the Auditorium Building on Michigan Avenue. The building was of masonry and stone construction, except for iron in the theater portion. The exterior facing was of the finest dressed Lemont stone and, flanking the entrance to the building, were two granite columns over two stories tall.

Adler always felt that the Music Hall was the greatest achievement of his life and he wanted it to stand forever as a memorial to his work. Edwin Walker and Dankmar Adler became close friends working on the project. Marie Walker Polson, Edwin Walker's granddaughter, recalls her father speaking of Adler's visits to the family homestead. When the Central Music Hall building was sold to Marshall Field for demolition, Walker acted quickly and salvaged the two columns. One was erected over Adler's grave, and the other, all that was left of the once lovely building, Walker saved for his own family memorial.[67]

Walker worked the quarries from the peak of the industry to its slow decline. He saw that tastes were changing in building techniques, and by 1889 was willing to sell his holdings to his old employee Martin Madden. However, when Madden formed the Western Stone monopoly, the consolidation left many Lemonters out of work.[68]

This, along with a decrease in the demand for dolomite stone, made Lemont's civic leaders concerned about the economic base of the town. There was a fear that if the quarries closed the town would die, so the leaders began an active campaign to attract new industry to town.

In 1891, Lemuel Brown heard of two young men, Rounds and Ashton, from Cincinnati, who were looking for a site on which to build an aluminum factory. He arranged a meeting at the village hall where the two presented the products that they had already produced. They manufactured combs, hairpins, thimbles, and other sundry items.[69] Aluminum was a novelty then since it was the most modern of the common metals, and the civic leaders were eager to attract a manufacturing plant that would be part of the future. Aluminum was first isolated in 1825 and shown to the public in 1855 at the Paris Exposition, but could not be mass produced until 1886, when Hall in the United States and Heroult in France developed the electrolytic method.

At a meeting attended by J. Gerharz, J.W. Tedens, N. Eulert, J. Shattuck, L. Brown, E. Derby, and O. Earnshaw, it was agreed that the group would help the young men get started. Ed Walker soon joined the supporting team.[70] Earnshaw furnished the site for the factory at the corner of Holmes and Talcott Streets, and the Walker quarries supplied the laborers and the stone to construct a building. Payment to Walker for the labor and the stone was taken out in stock in the new corporation.

The operation began in August of 1892, but Rounds and Ashton overextended themselves in equipping the factory, and by the spring of 1893 were on the verge of failure. The

Illinois Pure Aluminum Company, Lemont. (Photo courtesy of Lemont Historical Society)

Illinois Pure Aluminum Co. office staff. (Photo courtesy of Lemont Historical Society)

dream of a new industry for Lemont was headed for disaster, and Walker saw his opportunity. Already holding much of the stock, he added more capital to the venture and appointed his son, George, to take part in the management. George Walker was elected president in June of 1893, and remained in that position until his death in 1947. He was followed by other Walker family members until the plant closed in the 1970s.[71]

The company exhibited combs, thimbles, and novelty items at the World Columbian Exhibition in Chicago. These items were not inexpensive, as aluminum was still so uncommon that the Czar of Russia had jewelry made from the metal. However, there was only a small market for the novelty items, and Edwin Walker realized that with proper marketing the company could make other objects out of the material. Under the direction of George Walker, the plant began producing tea kettles and drawn cookware. In fact, it was the first plant in the United States to produce aluminum cookware and Lemont became known as the "mother of aluminum cooking utensils."[72]

Aluminum makes excellent cookware because its properties are high thermal conductivity, light weight, and resistance to corrosion. The Lemont cookware became popular as a substitute for the older, heavy, uneven-burning, and rust-susceptible cast metal pots. The company became an important employer for those laid off from the quarries and for those who could no longer farm. Sons on the smaller farms of Lemont township would draw straws about who would go to town and work at Illinois Pure Aluminum and who would stay on the farm homestead. The one who could live and work in town was considered lucky.

Old timers explain that it was easy to recognize the IPA workers at the end of a work day because their hands and arms were covered with the dark stains of aluminum dust as they went home to dinner.

Not all the workers were engaged in manual labor. There was a large office staff, mostly female, and a large sales staff, as the company first began selling by marketing door-to-door. Lemont sent out "drummers" over the country offering Walker Ware. The practice of door to door selling stopped after World War I when the product was sold mainly to hardware jobbers and variety stores.[73]

In one of the early promotions, "customers were offered their choice of any one of ten cooking utensils at $1.00 each. When the offer was made through Jones Department Store in Kansas City, in 1920, police had to be called out to control the crowds of shoppers who bought more than 70,000 cookware pieces in a single day."[74]

The company also made canteens in World War I, and water pitchers, medical equipment, and food containers in World War II. Ed Walker's idea of a manufacturing plant in the community lasted over 80 years, about as long as the cut stone quarry industry. As times changed it, too, died. By the late 1970s the plant found itself unable to compete with aluminum ware coming from overseas and simply closed its doors. The building was razed and all we have to remind us of the company are some pots and pans and old photos.

Edwin Walker died in 1910. Of the major quarry owners who amassed a fortune, it must be said that only N.J. Brown and Edwin Walker remained in town and displayed a civic responsibility and concern for Lemont by living here and investing in the community.

Yet all these pioneers left a legacy that is part of the history of our town.

ENDNOTES

[1]A.T. Andreas, *History of Cook County* (Evansville: Unigraphics, 1976), p. 852.

[2]*Lemont News*, Aug. 13, 1887.

[3]Howard Conrad, "Western Real Estate Speculation: Nathaniel Brown," *The National Magazine* (Chicago: 1887), p. 676.

[4]Andreas, *History of Cook County*, p. 851.

[5]*Ibid.*, p. 152.

[6]*Ibid.*, pp. 490-491.

[7]Ralph Andrist, ed., *The American Heritage History of the Confident Years* (New York: American Heritage Publishing, 1973), p. 140.

[8]Andreas, *History of Cook County*, p. 854.

[9]*Ibid.*, p. 851.

[10]Up to 1863, banks were private free houses established by bankers who wished to profit by control of the various circulating notes. Most "money" was in the form of bank notes, warehouse receipts, county warrants, canal script, and even I.O.U's. See Bessie Pierce, *A History of Chicago* (New York: Knopf, 1940), vol. 2, p. 121.

[11]*Ibid.*, p. 131.

[12]Andreas, *History of Cook County*, p. 668.

[13]The gateway remains standing on empty land that was once the stockyards of Chicago fame.

[14]David Johnson, *Chicago Universalism* (Brookline, MA: Philomath Press, 1991), pp. 51, 99. Mary Talcott gave a gift of land to rebuild the Redeemer Church in 1886.

[15]Pierce, *A History of Chicago*, vol. 2, p. 447.

[16]They selected this site as a buffer against the "Smokey Row" that had developed along the I & M Canal east of the Stephens Street bridge.

[17]Herbert Asbury, *Gem of the Prairie* (New York: Knopf, 1940), pp. 61-62.

[18]*Ibid.*

[19]Andreas, *History of Cook County*, p. 854.

[20]Robin Selman, "A History of the Lemont Quarry Industry," *Looking For Lemont*, ed., Michael Conzen and Carl Zimring (Chicago: University of Chicago, 1994), p. 69.

[21]*Ibid.* See also Andreas, *History of Cook County*, p. 851

[22]Barbara Bushman, ed., *Lemont, Illinois: Its History In Commemmoration of the Centennial of Its Incorporation* (Des Plaines: King/Mann Yearbook, 1973), p. 6. The subdivision was in the area of Division and Custer Streets.

[23]Andreas, *History of Cook County*, p. 854.

[24]Robert Howard, *A History of the Prairie State* (Grand Rapids: Eerdmans, 1972), p. 329. As a director of The First National Bank of Chicago, it was in Singer's interest to see that bills were passed that supported banks.

[25]Andreas, *History of Cook County*, p. 834.

[26]Sonia Kallick, *Lemont History and Anecdotes* (Lemont: Lemont Area Historical Society 1984), p. 25.

[27]Finis Farr, *Chicago* (New Rochelle: Arlington House, 1973), p. 92.

[28]Emmett Dedmon, *Chicago: A Great City's History and People* (New York: Atheneum, 1981), p. 175.

[29]Vincent Michael and Deborah Slayton, *Joliet-Lemont Limestone* (Chicago: Landmarks Preservation Council, 1988), p. 9.

[30]Sonia Kallick, "Philanthropists With Vision Leave Their Legacies," *The Lemont Metropolitan*, May 25, 1989, p. 12.

[31]N.J. Brown purchased the home and then it was sold to D. C. Norton and Mathew Warner.

[32]You can still view the window at the Lemont Historical Society.

[33]*Lemont News*, August 13, 1887.

[34]*The Pasadena Daily Evening Star,* December 28, 1896, p. 1.

[35]Manuel Pineda, *Pasadena Area History* (Pasadena: 1972), p. 24. See also James Wharton, *Scenic Mt. Lowe. Echo Mountain* (Pasadena: 1898), pp. 25-33.

[36]Letter from the Pasadena Public Library, January 24, 1974, Daniel Hanne, Reference Department.

[37]*Pasadena Star*, 1896, p. 1.

[38]*Ibid.*, January 4, 1897, p. 3.

[39]*Ibid.*

[40]Kimball had served as treasurer and supervisor of the Singer-Talcott quarries when under Horace Singer's control.

[41]Sonia Kallick, "Views of Old Lemont," *The Lemont Metropolitan*, September 8, 1977, p. 5.

[42]*Chicago Tribune*, July 1, 1897.

[43]The same Hiram Cody who served as pallbearer for Singer's California funeral.

[44]*Joliet News*, July 15, 1897.

[45]*Ibid.*

[46]E.W. Brent, *Martin B. Madden* (Chicago: 1901). Much of this semi-autobiographical material comes from this book written and self-published to help Madden's candidacy for office.

[47]For Madden's view on his education in the quarries. see *Ibid.*

[48]Charles Branham, "Black Chicago," *Ethnic Chicago*, ed., Melvin Holli and Peter d'A. Jones (Grand Rapids; Eerdmans, 1984), p. 355.

[49]Plant later became superintendent of Schools in Cook County. See A.T. Andreas, *A History of Cook County* (Evansville: Unigraphics, 1976), p. 665.

[50]Sonia Kallick, "Views of Old Lemont," *The Lemont Metropolitan*, November 19, 1981, p. 6.

[51]Vincent Michaels and Deborah Slayton, *Joliet-Lemont Limestone* (Chicago: Landmarks Preservation Council, 1988), p. 8.

[52]Bessie Pierce, *A History of Chicago* (New York: Knopf, 1957), vol. 3, p. 348.

[53]The area is now called Darien.

[54]Branham, "Black Chicago," p. 227.

[55]*Ibid.*

[56]We have seen something similar when TV cable companies first began operations in local communities. Many were formed simply to hold the rights and then resold for profit.

[57]Emmett Dedmon, *Fabulous Chicago* (New York: Atheneum, 1981), p. 260.

[58]Mayor Carter Harrison had died from an assassin's bullet.

[59]Sonia Kallick, "Madden Pushed for the Panama Canal," *The Lemont Metropolitan,* October 27, 1977.

[60]Branham, "Black Chicago," p. 352.

[61]On the corner of Old Bailey Road and Frontage Road, in the area known as Cass, now Darien. It is familiar to many as it was a fixture along old Rt. 66. Today it belongs to the Carmelite Friars.

[62]Lorimer spelled backwards.

[63]Allan H. Spear, *Black Chicago: The Making of a Ghetto* (Chicago: University of Chicago, 1967), p. 36.

[64]Both the Maddens and the Walkers emmigrated from Northern England just before the Civil War. Economic conditions in that part of England forced many to come to America.

[65]Herbert Asbury, *Gem of the Prairie* (New York: Knopf, 1940), p. 152.

[66]Interview with Tracy Walker, May 20, 1979.

[67]Edwin's column is at Rosehill Cemetery and Dankmar Adler's is at Mount Maariv. The columns are rose-granite, Corinthian in style.

[68]Kevin B. Klowden, "Manufacturing in Lemont: The Fortuitous Rise of Industry in the Local Economy," *Looking For Lemont,* ed., Michael Conzen and Carl Zimring (Chicago: University of Chicago, 1994), p. 103.

[69]Sonia Kallick, *Lemont History and Ancedotes,* (Lemont: Lemont Historical Society, 1975), p. 278.

[70]Sonia Kallick, "Pure Aluminum Gets its Start in Lemont," *The Lemont Metropolitan,* March 27, 1979, p. 6.

[71]Barbara Bushman, ed., *Lemont, Illinois: Its History in Commemoration of the Centennial of its Incorporation* (Des Plaines: King/Mann, 1973), p. 185.

[72]Sonia Kallick, *The Lemont Metropolitan,* May 27, 1979.

[73]Bushman, *Lemont, Illinois,* pp. 184-185.

[74]*Ibid.,* p. 184.

CHAPTER SEVENTEEN

THE ROLE OF GOVERNMENT IN LEMONT: 1885-1910

Public Safety, Health and Morals

Probably the first concern of any community on the prairie was fire. Fire still ranks as one of man's biggest fears, especially in urban settings. Like most frontier communities, Lemont had an informal arrangement to fight its fires. When a fire was spotted, a general warning was sounded by tolling school and church bells. All who heard the alarm were required, by tradition, to drop what they were doing and bring buckets and equipment to help control the fire. Anyone refusing to come was subject to a local fine or, worse yet, social rejection by the community. A community built largely of wood could not afford to have anyone indifferent to the danger of fire.

In the very early days, although Lemont was a quarry town, few of the buildings were made of stone. The stone that our workers dug from the ground was far too expensive for local use.[1]

The Chicago Fire of 1871 made Lemonters aware that one small fire could engulf a whole town, so they began to demand better fire regulations, a better water supply, and an organized fire brigade. However, little could be done until the official formation of a village government in 1873, when a simple fire prevention ordinance was passed. This ordinance, upgraded in 1880, required that all stoves in homes be placed on bricks, and chimneys be built according to village standards and inspected twice a year. Also, the ordinance required that all hay and straw must be stored 60 feet away from a house and candles used in barns secured in a lantern.[2] These rules were designed for the safety of the whole community and were the beginning of the detailed laws and ordinances we have today.

Water mains were built between 1883 and 1885 to supply the village. The business section had six-inch pipes while the residential section was serviced with three-inch mains. The system was attached to a stone reservoir on North Stephen Street. In December, 1884, an ordinance to issue bonds for completing and maintaining the waterworks was passed, so the village then had adequate water for public use and to fight fires.

In 1885, the Board of Trustees authorized a committee composed of Joshua Bell, Jacob Meyer, and Joseph Gerharz to organize a hook and ladder company of 20 or more citizens of Lemont. This developed into two companies of 11 men each.[3] Company Number One was the hose company, and it had the duty of bringing the hose and pump to the fire and of directing the fire fighting. Company Number Two was the hook and ladder company. The name hook and ladder came from a special device called the Pompier ladder, a light-weight pole with cross rungs and a hook attached to one end so it could be fastened to an upper story window sill to rescue fire victims. The hook and ladder company was responsible for saving lives, and when possible, certain personal property.

There was more glory in the role of a life saver, so the hook and ladder firefighter held a slightly higher social role than a hose company member, but all volunteer firemen were held in high esteem by the community — they were exempt from jury duty, did not have to serve in the militia (unless there was a war), and did not have to pay local road taxes.

To get volunteers for Lemont's new fire company, sign up sheets were placed in J.G. Bodenschatz's drug store at Stephen and Canal Street. Naturally, the first one to sign up was Bodenschatz, who volunteered for the hose company. Ed Mitchell was next to sign for the hose company and became so involved with the idea that he signed up nine others: J.H. Tedens, George Losey, Frank Losey, R. Friedley, John Gerharz, Jerry Murphy, Louis Lott, John Dreigel, and Allison Kettering.[4] This company, Company One, in typical ethnic Lemont style became known not as the hose company but as the German Company, in spite of the fact it had a few Irishmen.

The Irish, not to be outdone, signed up for the hook and ladder company. The first was John. W. McCarthy and he enlisted James Bittles, John Hayes, Patrick Hennebry, Mr. Keegan, Mr. Russell, Mike Flavin, Will Muranan, along with the founders, Jake Meyer, and Joshua Bell. This became commonly known as the Irish Company.

At the first meeting of the volunteer fire department, the following officers were elected: President, J.W. McCarthy; Recording Secretary, Ed. Mitchell; Finance Secretary, Mike Flavin; Treasurer, John Hayes; and Sergeant at Arms, Will Muranan. Joseph Gerharz was appointed Fire Marshal and Jacob Meyers and Joshua Bell were named assistant chiefs.[5]

The village board provided 1,000 feet of hose stored in the town hall until a special shed could be found to hold it. A hose cart was ordered from Chicago and was shipped on the canal on a Singer and Talcott stone boat. The cart and hose were then kept in the Singer and Talcott barn on North Stephen Street opposite the village waterworks. The Singer-Talcott firm also sold their old bell, used to call each work shift, to the new company for a fire alarm.[6] Singer-Talcott had introduced steam power to its cutting equipment and therefore was calling shifts with a steam whistle and no longer needed the bell. Horace Singer's support for the new fire department was not entirely altruistic. Only one month before the formation of the department, his company lost 15,000 dollars worth of equipment and outbuildings to fire.[7]

The volunteer fire department established two stations, one on Singer Hill at State and Eureka, and the other downtown at the Village Hall. Lemont had no paved roads at the time and the firefighters pulled the hose cart and the pump by hand. They also had to pull a 40-gallon chemical wagon. Fire equipment was pulled because it took too long to hitch a team to the pumper and the cost of keeping a team ready was prohibitive. However, if anyone had a team harnessed at the time of a fire alarm, he could bring it to the department to pull the pumper. The standard pay for such a service was two dollars, paid by the village.

The department was formally incorporated on March 4, 1886. The volunteers free time was spent with practice alarms to keep in shape. They also worked at raising money for equipment. Their first 4th of July Fireman's Picnic was held in 1887. There a happy crowd consumed 164 dollars worth of beer and smoked 34 dollars and 80 cents worth of cigars.[8] One important order that year was the purchase of 12 brass spittoons for the fire stations.[9]

Not all went smoothly in the early years. Horace Norton, son of Mayor D.C. Norton, recalled a fire when he was a young man.

> There was this two-story brick building in town, the only brick structure in town at the time, that caught fire. The two companies, the Irish on the hook and ladder, and the Germans on the pumper and hose responded to the alarm. It was my first big fire. I was about ten years old. The flames had already made rapid headway by the time our international fire department got to the scene and began bringing up the ladders. When the two factions got to the roof, we could see something was wrong. Instead of fighting the fire, the Germans and Irish began fighting each other. The fight started because the Irish company got to the fire first. They teased the German company when it arrived and the tempers flared. In the excitement, John Bolton ran down to the Singer and Talcott barn to get the new hose cart. After he dragged it to the fire he discovered that he had forgotten the hose.[10]

The fighting firefighters got off the roof of the building just before it collapsed. All had a narrow escape and, of course, the building burned to the ground. The two companies learned their lesson. They had more at stake in their work than prideful quarrels.

However, there were few large fires in the first years, so as time passed, the company began to take on the aspects of a social club. They held dances and picnics to raise money and because firefighters were important members of the community, they were expected to attend parades and civic functions in full uniform. As a result, a good deal of their time began to be directed toward practicing marching drills for public events. The idea behind this activity was the belief that firemen who could obey marching drill commands could take commands at a fire. Many Lemonters saw it as a silly activity and openly questioned how effective their firefighters would be in a real emergency.

The first real test came on January 21, 1888. It was a cold Saturday night, with a stiff wind blowing from the east, one of those nights when the wind cuts through cloth and flesh. George Losey's saloon was a warm place, so John Gerharz and Mr. Keegan stopped by for a drink with their fellow firemen. Shortly before 9:00 p.m. a young girl ran into the saloon screaming that Klein's building next store was on fire. All three dashed out. Since the fire station was only a block away on Stephen Street, they ran and got the old hose cart and ladder truck and sounded the fire alarm bell. The three worked so fast that by 9:00 p.m. they had both the hose cart and the hook and ladder in front of the burning building. Other volunteer firemen quickly joined them, many without adequate clothing, since no one took the time to get protective covering. Clearly the blaze had a good start and was being fed by the east wind.

Mr. Klein, who had been away, arrived along with the rest of the equipment and began shouting, "My wife's inside. Get my wife. For God's sakes get my wife."[11]

The hook and ladder company responded by entering the burning building, expecting that the hose company would play water on them and the fire to give them time to find Mrs. Klein, but the hose company met unexpected problems. The new hydrant in front of Mrs. Jarvis' place was so important to the safety of the community that someone had covered it to prevent it from freezing. A fine idea, but the trouble was that they had used a pile of horse manure and that dung had such a high water content that it had frozen around the hydrant. The firefighters were forced to chip away frozen manure to expose the hose connection.[12]

Meanwhile, the hook and ladder men, unable to see in the heavy smoke, stumbled around upstairs looking for Mrs. Klein. To help clear the air they broke out the front windows. This created a huge backdraft and, without water support, the flames swept up the stairs in a fire sheet. At that point Mrs. Klein came running out of the crowd. She, too, had been away. Husband and wife embraced while the firefighters who had been looking for her barely escaped making it through the sheet of flames to the outside.

The hose company finally dug the hydrant out of the manure and then had to search for a wrench. The new one on the hose truck was missing. By 9:25 p.m. they had water on the fire but by then it was too late for the Klein Building, and, it soon became clear that the winds were feeding the flames toward the other buildings in the downtown. If not brought under control, the whole central commercial section of Lemont could be destroyed.[13]

Mayor Norton arrived on the scene at 9:30 p.m. and ordered the men to play water on all the wooden buildings in the rear of the Stephen Street stores so that the fire would not spread down Talcott or across to the west side of Stephen. But, by then the wind carried firebrands to Losey's Saloon, John Bourg's building, and Ries's Bankrupt Store[14] putting them in danger. Even more terrifying to the large crowd that gathered were huge fireballs of superheated gases that burst into the night sky, some with flames that licked across the I & M Canal toward the Singer-Talcott complex. Added to the spectacle was an intermittent shower of sparks and embers that rained across Stephen Street toward Main Street.

The fire companies fought bravely against what seemed losing odds. All were wet and covered with ice. They were joined by many non-firemen, all struggling with limited equipment to control the fire and prevent its spread. Some citizens were stationed across Stephen Street and the Canal to put out sparks and firebrands as they fell on McCarthy's building and Bodenschatz's Drug Store. Others worked Main Street to prevent the spread of flames across the Alton tracks. Losey, McCarthy, and Bodenschatz were all firemen, yet at this point none of them broke away from the main fire to save their own property. They showed true professionalism under difficult circumstances.

By 9:45 p.m., panic swept the onlookers. Little progress in striking the fire had occurred, and in fact it was gaining ground. Panic was also fed by the innocent actions of Mr. Ries and Mr. Losey. Because the stock in their stores could be lost, they opened the doors and encouraged people to help them by removing the goods to a safe place. Not all onlookers understood this and the sight of Lemonters carrying clothing and furniture down the red fire-washed streets made it appear as if evacuation had begun. The Chicago Fire of 1871 and its images was still a very real experience to many townspeople.[15]

Rumors and fear spread quickly and Mayor Norton, trying to help supervise the fire, found himself questioned about the safety and the future of the downtown. He, too, became alarmed that perhaps his volunteers and their simple equipment were outmatched, so he decided to telegraph to Joliet for help. Joliet replied that they would send assistance by special train. Joliet was the nearest source of aid, since neither Lockport nor Willow Springs had developed well-organized and equipped volunteer fire departments.[16]

Word was passed to the crowd that help would arrive within less than an hour and some panic subsided, but still the major fire fighting fell on Lemont's 20 volunteers and

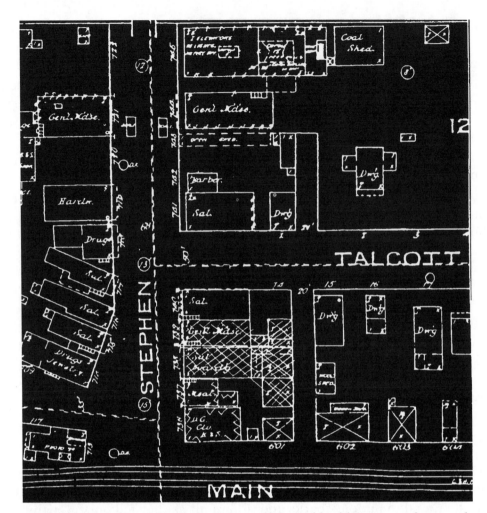

Site of the 1888 fire at Klein's store. Cross-hatched buildings were destroyed. The two buildings south of the destroyed buildings were damaged, but repairable. (Map courtesy of Lemont Historical Society)

the others who joined them. As the fire burned, Losey and Ries managed to empty their stores thanks to the ability of the firemen to keep the flames under some control. There were many eager hands willing to help Losey remove his whiskey and beer from the advancing fire; however, it must be said that many barrels rolled away from the fire that night were never seen again.

Time dragged on as the exhausted firefighters awaited relief from Joliet. They were finally able to control the fire but could not strike it. Each shift in the wind sent more sparks across town and the crowd began to fix on the idea that the arrival of the special train from Joliet would stop the fire. But, time passed and nothing appeared on the tracks. No train. No help.

After 45 minutes, Mayor Norton again telegraphed Joliet. He was then informed by the fire chief that Mayor Paige of Joliet had decided that he would not allow his equipment to be sent to Lemont. He was afraid to leave Joliet without "adequate fire protection."[17] When Lemonters heard the news, they were shocked. Their village was burning and Joliet had refused assistance.[18] The only ones who seemed unaffected were the local volunteer firemen who continued to work despite the odds and despite the general feeling that this social, picnicking, hometown organization was not up to the task. To most of the villagers it appeared that the fire would not be struck until the whole downtown was destroyed.

Mayor Norton also had little faith in his own firemen, so he telegraphed to Chicago for help. Chicago would have helped, except that they had a huge fire on the north side of town that night and all their equipment was in use. They offered to come when their own fire was out. There was no choice; it fell on Lemont's men to handle the fire as best they could. Without any extra help, the local volunteers continued the struggle past midnight and into the morning hours. Cold and wet, with ice forming on their thin coats, they were sustained with coffee and brandy from helpful citizens. With the morning hours, the wind began to die down and the firemen were finally able to do more than just contain the original blaze. By the time Chicago sent equipment and manpower, it was no longer needed. The fire was struck around 2:00 a.m.

The town had been saved from a massive economic disaster by its small but heroic volunteer fire department. Final damage included the loss of Klein's Building and Losey's Hotel and four frame buildings located to the rear of those stores. John Bourg's Meat Market, a Lemont stone building, sustained interior damage, as did Ries's Bankrupt Store. All other endangered buildings suffered only minor harm.

Losey and Ries both lost goods that were never returned after the fire. Losey estimated his loss at 500 dollars. He had little hope of recovery, considering how easy it was to dispose of liquor. Mr. Reis swore out a posse to search nine homes of persons that he suspected held some of his goods. His search was unsuccessful and engendered considerable controversy. Reis claimed that he lost at least 1,200 dollars worth of merchandise.

Sunday morning, January 22, was spent by Lemonters sightseeing the ruins and retelling the night of horror. In support of the Lemont firemen, the local paper commented that "no fire department on earth could have saved the buildings that were lost."[19] Lemont businessmen and townspeople were so impressed by the firemen that they collected 1,300 dollars for the department in two days and many who had expressed little interest in the group before willingly offered their services.

In Joliet, where they were eager to dispel the notion that the town had refused help to Lemont, Mayor Paige was quoted as saying that a special engine was ready at the Joliet Alton Station but he knew that Lemont would not need it, as they had a fine and experienced department. Lemonters did not buy his story, however, and the name Mayor Paige was a dirty word in town for years afterwards. Anyone not helping in an emergency became known as a "Mayor Paige."

What was more important, the fire brought home the need for better village fire ordinances and regulations, just as Chicago had done after its terrible fire of 1871. These regulations were not passed without difficulty, because some businessmen resented the idea of the village dictating how they could build or use their property. This was especially true of the downtown merchants. The village proposed a fire limit bill to regulate the type of construction in the town's central area patterned after Chicago's ordinance.

Mayor Norton pushed the issue and the village adopted the bill in March of 1888. It required that all new construction within the fire limits be of brick or stone, with only one story buildings that were used for homes exempted from the regulation. Wooden sheds over twelve feet were not allowed and all roofs had to be made of a non-combustible material.

The fire limit area covered the following blocks: the southeast corner of State and Illinois next to a line east of State to the I & M Canal, then south along the canal to Maxwell Street (Fremont), then the west side of Maxwell to Illinois Street, then west on Illinois to the beginning.[20]

There still are variations within this district after 109 years, but most of the frame buildings that stand now were grandfathered in, meaning that they, or some part of those buildings, existed before 1888. Controversy over this ordinance and the cost of a fire safety plan designed by Mayor Norton to extend the town water system to Singer Hill became a political issue. The aftermath of the "fire of '88" was a hot fight in the election that spring. The fire ordinances were perceived as an attack on the rights of the store owners. Led by J.H. Tedens,[21] a fire fighter who had fought the January blaze, the campaign was a test of the new village government and its power over individual businessmen and property rights. There was another issue related to fire protection that added controversy to the election, the proposed extension of the village water system to Singer Hill. The plan was expensive and Tedens came out against the project, which he viewed not as a plan for fire safety, but as a scheme to get water to a new subdivision carved out of Horace Singer's old estate on the west side of town. Just as water, sewers, and roads are the basis of growth and speculation today, so it was in the 1880s in Lemont. Tedens' suspicions were not without some basis, since the primary developers of that subdivision were Matt Warner and Mayor D.C. Norton.

Norton insisted that his only concern was for public safety, but Tedens insisted that it was all a plot to make a fast buck, especially since the fire department had water wagons that he considered more than adequate for fighting fires in that area. The disagreement raged with both sides using the recent fire as support for their views. Tedens and his supporters held that little could be done to prevent fires by regulations. The January fire

Lemont Volunteer Hook and Ladder Company. J.W. McCarthy, then mayor, sits in the center front row. (Photo courtesy of Lemont Historical Society)

had burned a stone building as well as wooden ones, and many famous buildings destroyed in the Chicago Fire of 1871 were of masonry, including our Lemont stone. Norton's side held that brick and stone buildings burn slower and even if they do catch fire, often most of the damage is to the interior. Also, brick and stone structures do not disperse embers like frame buildings.

Of course, both parties supported the "hero firemen" and their work. The main controversy revolved around two points: using tax money for fire protection, since so far the labor was volunteer and most of the equipment was donated or purchased after fund raising events; and the imposition of fire building regulations on private property. On election day, Lemonters let both sides know how they felt about the idea of offering fire protection to the citizens of the community — the final vote count was Norton, 382 and Tedens, six. The January fire was still very fresh in the public mind.

Over the years the department fought other major, memorable fires. In 1895, a small fire broke out at the Midway Theater, one of the Smokey Row entertainment halls, while a fancy masquerade ball was taking place at the Village Hall. Many volunteer firefighters reported to the scene still in outlandish costumes. Ironically, that same year a blaze destroyed the barn behind J.H. Tedens' store, a non-conforming barn that had been grandfathered in before the passage of the fire ordinance. The fire was so intense that it almost destroyed his store and opera house.

The professionalism of the department grew over the years, with a few lapses. When the Woods Store on the corner of Stephen and Illinois caught fire in 1897, the *Lemont Observer* reported that a fireman was sent upstairs to see that the Union Library[22] was safe. In his haste he broke out a window rather than raising it to report that there had been no damage. The editor added this comment:

> There should be a better understanding between the officers and the men of the fire department. Our department has capable men for officers and brave willing men for firemen, yet at almost every fire there are many who should be waiting for orders who are giving them, or working according to their own ideas.[23]

In 1894, the Sanborn Fire Map of Lemont, a map designed to list all buildings in commercial areas and their construction, reported the following manpower and equipment for the village: 37 volunteers, three hose carts with 3,500 feet of 2.5 inch hose, one chemical engine, and a water supply with nine miles of pipe and 50 hydrants.

The Lemont fire department helped Lockport when they had their great fire in 1895. Lemont made it a policy never to refuse a request after their own experience with Joliet. The Lockport fire began in August on the roof of the Phoenix building, east of Tenth and State. It then moved north and engulfed all the buildings between Hamilton and State, along with the Boyer barn and the grade school. Lemont sent men and the hose cart, but they could not bring their chemical wagon as the Alton rail line refused to couple the chemical tank on a train. The Alton later denied the refusal and some hard feelings resulted; probably the railroad wanted money to transport the equipment and no one was authorized to pay in an emergency. In any case, Lockport sent a check to our department for the services offered. More importantly they sent a delegation to Lemont to study our department to upgrade Lockport's fire safety program. While here, they viewed the new electric fire alarm installed in the Village Hall, the chemical pumper, Singer Hill station, and the waterworks.

The years between 1895 and 1898 were difficult years for the volunteer department. As the Sanitary Ship Canal workers moved on, Smokey Row began to fall on hard times. The shacks that housed the dives were abandoned and some were set on fire for the insurance or by vandals. In October of 1895, the firemen had to fight one such blaze at Peter Fischbach's Saloon. It spread rapidly and enveloped the entire structure. Yet, they were able to save the building and to prevent the fire from spreading. Within a few months there were other fires at Norton's warehouse and store and Peterson's Park on Singer Hill. The Norton fire at 103 Stephen was unique as it displayed the first use of the chemical engine by the fire company. Sanitary District engineers had an office on the second floor of the building and someone was careless in discarding a cigar butt, so that a fire resulted. With the chemical engine, the department could avoid the usual water-drenching that often caused excessive damage to property.[24]

On May 3, 1897, the department was called on to fight two fires in one night. The first one was at 9:00 p.m. in a vacant building east of Old Central School. The second alarm came at 12:30 a.m. at the Porter Brewing Company ice house next to the Alton Station. There was no doubt that the second fire was set because witnesses saw two men trying to accelerate the blaze by adding fuel. Shots were fired at them but they escaped. The *Observer* gave this warning, "It appears that the miscreants are some of Joliet's hard citizens, and it is safe to say that it will go hard with them should they be caught in Lemont."[25]

Other fires of note in the early years included: the Western Stone Company barn at Stephen and the I & M Canal in 1896, sending aid to Willow Springs in 1897, and the Polish School fire in 1898. It is an impressive and unique record. In 1898, on the thirteenth anniversary of the department the village gave diplomas of recognition to the following men: M.J. New, M.S. New, C.A. Talty, A.J. Helbig, Thos. Godson, Henry Tedens, John Gerharz, Jacob Meyers, J.G. Bodenschatz, J.W. McCarthy, Geo. Losey, Ed Mitchell, Wm. O'Neil, John Cummings, John Russell, J.H. Driscoll, H.J. Laughlin, Pat Driscoll, and Chas, Anderson. Three men served as chiefs in those formidable years from 1885 to 1910: Jacob Meyer, William O'Neil, and John Gerharz. It was from these willing volunteers that the model for our modern fire department began.

Another concern of society is police and law enforcement. When the area was first settled, crime was a small problem and usually solved frontier fashion. Before 1850, law was administered entirely by Cook County. The courts operated with elected Justices of the Peace who were helped by appointed constables. Citizens could be deputized in emergencies, such as during the canal workers riot of 1838. After 1850, with the establishment of townships, Lemont appointed her own constables. The first six to serve were I.A. Norton, J. Tripp, T. Kent, J. Barrows, W.C. Bell, and J. Roebuck. They worked with the Cook County sheriff to enforce the law.

With the incorporation of the village in 1873, another level of law administration was added. The town appointed a marshall, not only to police the village, but to try to control some of the wild activity along the I & M Canal strip. Village minutes record that the marshall received a yearly salary of 480 dollars, and that the town already had a two-cell jail.[26] Other minutes of the council from that period reveal law enforcement problems. On June 6, 1883, the council found it necessary to define larceny; by their standards anything less than 15 dollars would be classified as a misdemeanor. This may have been a response to some overzealous action by a local Justice of the Peace, who was allowed to keep some of the fines he levied. Since the larger the crime, the larger the fine, this was a practice that often led to abuse.

In June of 1883, the council proposed a law forbidding the sale of toy pistols to minors, a fact that suggests there were a lot of real sidearms carried by the local citizens.[27] Perhaps the board wished to prevent a tragic accident. By March of 1884, it was necessary for the town to pass an ordinance against prostitution within the village, and they set fines ranging from three dollars to 200 dollars for owning or patronizing such an establishment.[28] By 1885 there was enough crime in Lemont that a night policeman, Alfred Lundholm, was added to the force at 50 dollars a month.

Our officers apparently had some problems as the town had to offer a 50 dollar reward for the "apprehension and conviction of the party who broke into the Village Hall and liberated a prisoner."[29] There was another interesting rule established at the same time prohibiting members of the police force from entering a saloon while on duty, except in the line of duty.[30] The best our local officers could do was to try to control problems created by the saloons to a restricted area. The income in 1888 from these establishments amounted to 10,000 dollars, a tax revenue that the village fathers were not eager to give up.

Any attempt to control crime and public morality became even more difficult for Lemont law officers with the construction of the Sanitary Ship Canal beginning in 1892. The project doubled the village population in three years and most of it was composed of young male construction workers. Their presence created over 100 saloons, brothels, and gambling establishments that were impossible to patrol. Some help was offered with the formation of a separate police force called the Sanitary District Police, but even they were hard-pressed to keep law and order. Emil Wend, of Lemont, recalled those days of his childhood in an interview in 1973:

> There were more prostitutes than you could shake a stick at. The burglaries going on were terrible and there was a murder practically every Saturday night. The town was so wide open you couldn't walk down the sidewalk on Saturday. If you were a loner you might get held up. You always needed a couple of partners with you for protection. I recall several murders. One was when a drunk refused to pay for a sandwich and the owner, in anger, gave him a fatal blow to his head. Another involved a man killed in front of city hall over a woman. I remember him sitting there under a big elm still looking alive but his throat had been slit. It was common to find robbed bodies floating in the canal after payday night.[31]

Not all crime in Lemont during this era could be blamed on the Ship Canal construction, for after 1896 the Lemont portion of the project was completed and the village still had problems. The economic fact was that many young boys quit school at ten and 11 to work in the quarries and then, when there was no work, these children did not return to school but hung around in gangs. They were worldly-wise youngsters caught between childhood and manhood and trying to act important. After a nasty street corner fight that resulted in the death of canal worker and the imprisonment of a Lemont youth, the local paper observed, "Let us have a truant officer, at least 100 children who should be in school are not."[32]

The case also led the *Observer* to say:

> Young Hurley who murdered Mulvey last Saturday night is
> another example of the effect of allowing boys to get their
> early education on the streets . . . The school has saved many
> a young man from the gallows and the penitentiary; but the
> streets have been a direct route to such an end.[33]

The presence of these street children and their disruptive behavior so disturbed the editor, M.J. Hevenor, that he ran the following item encouraging the citizens to act:

> We can protect our wives, our sisters, and our daughters
> against the rude treatment of "dudes" and "loafers" who col-
> lect on street corners and insultingly leer upon every woman
> passer, indulging in remarks that no innocent girl should hear.
> The insult thus offered to the worthy and virtuous . . . is an
> insult to all womankind. It devolves on each citizen to give
> what aid he can to break up the crowd of street corner "dudes
> and loafers."[34]

During the spring of 1905, it was the "Hot Air Gang" that had its turn at pushing against the boundaries of proper social behavior. The gang varied in size, with as many as 20 young men at a time. Their main territory was the block from Lemont to State along Main Street, with the Anheuser-Busch Tavern at the southwest corner of Lemont and Main the center of their activity. Often they would play "Rushing the Growler."[35] One would get a bucket of beer, enough for five or six boys, at the cost of five cents. The bucket would be passed around and if anyone drinking left the handle down he had to buy the next round.[36] On idle spring days, before the quarries opened or when there was no work, they spent time talking and loitering along the block, crowding the sidewalk and forcing townspeople to walk around them into the muddy or dusty street.

The unofficial leader of this street corner society was Jacob Tomkowiak, a lively, outgoing youth who went by the nickname "Koover." The name "Hot Air Gang" came from their favorite pastime of insulting ladies and girls who dared to pass by the group. Watching the shocked reactions of the "fairer sex" was great fun for the immature youngsters and harmless as far as they were concerned, but soon the group began to dominate the block and became a disruption not only for Lemonters but also for the merchants. Businessmen began to pressure the new police officer, Pete Kane, to break up the gang. Joseph Gerharz, the undertaker on Main Street, found it especially hard to console the bereaved who, while in deep sorrow, had to run a barrage of insults and jeers to get to his establishment.

At first Officer Kane looked on the gang's behavior as youthful high jinks that would stop after the novelty wore off. He spoke to them, but they had become aware of the fuss they were causing and enjoyed the power they had achieved. In all fairness, they had little command over their own hard lives, having been rejected by the adult world and by middle-class school children their own age. The attention made them feel important, so that after his talk they did stop insulting people when Kane came on the block, but when he was gone they started again.

As days passed, the pressure increased to have Kane act. However, Officer Kane tried every means to avoid a confrontation in the hope that the foolishness would stop. The standoff lasted until Wednesday, April 26. As Officer Kane was making his rounds at 6:00 p.m., he approached the corner of State and Main. There he saw the gang loitering half a

Lemont police officer Peter Kane. (Photo courtesy of Lemont Historical Society)

block down Main Street. As he watched, two young girls began to walk past the boys. The girls began to walk faster, faces red and bowed as they tried to ignore the jeers and lewd remarks. Then someone in the gang added a new twist to the usual verbal insults and threw a stone at the girls. Other stones soon followed. This was too much for Kane. He ran down the street and spotting "Koover," he decided to place him under arrest.

Tomkowiak protested his innocence in the stone throwing, but Kane already had an audience of townspeople watching and demanding action. He could not avoid confrontation. Alone, he moved into the crowd with his night stick in hand. Tomkowiak grabbed the club and was about to strike as the gang encircled the struggle. None of the citizens watching went to Kane's aid, but just stood by, afraid to take on the gang. As Koover and Kane struggled, Kane reached for his gun to fire to disperse the crowd. In the struggle the gun went off.

First there was silence, and then the crowd parted. A stunned Tomkowiak, badly wounded, stepped forward clutching his stomach and fell to his knees. His brother Will and Pete Kane helped him to Dr. Leahy's office. That evening he was placed on the train to St. Joseph's Hospital in Joliet where he died at 12:20 a.m.

Saddened and upset, Officer Kane placed himself under arrest, turned in his gun and badge to Mayor Sullivan and went home to wait the results of the inquest. On May 4, the jury met and released the following statement:

> We the jury find that J. Tomkowiak came to his end by a gunshot wound inflicted by Officer Kane on April 26, 1905, and died of injuries April 27, 1905, at 12:20 a.m. at St. Joseph's Hospital, Joliet: and from evidence we believe that Officer Kane acted in self defense.
>
> Signed: John Kammerman, H. M. Lyford, Chas. A. Walters, Geo. McFarlane, Walter Wameck, and Matt Connors.

The "Hot Air Gang" never met again. Pete Kane was named chief of police in 1909 and served in that capacity for over 40 years.[37]

The other important agency needed by the newly incorporated village was a Board of Health. Although the town was forced to fight an epidemic of smallpox in 1881 with help from the state and a local physician, Doctor J. B. Rood, it took until 1885 for the council to create a formal board. Dr. Revera took the position established by Dr. Joseph Rood who had met an untimely death in 1884. Joseph Rood was a highly trained physician who attended Beloit College, the University of Michigan, and Rush Medical College. He formed a partnership in Lemont with his mentor, Dr. William Pierce, where they worked with local physicians to upgrade health conditions in the community. Rood also entered the social structure of Lemont by marrying Amelia Wells, daughter of Joel Wells, Lemont's first mayor. Rood was so highly regarded that he was appointed to the medical board of Cook County Hospital.[38]

On the night of October 24, a man came to his home asking the doctor to see his wife who was very ill. Dr. Rood got on his horse and rode off, never to be seen alive again. The next day men on their way to the quarries found a dead horse with Dr. Rood's body pinned underneath it. Apparently, something had happened to the horse and the doctor was killed in its fall. His wife memorialized her husband's last house call on his tombstone in the Cass Community Cemetery — it reads, "Joseph Rood, M.D., Cut down in the discharge of duty."

The foremost health concerns centered on childhood diseases, which were accepted as a reality that was able to kill and maim. Attempts at controlling these involved quarantine and disinfection. When the schools experienced many cases of scarlet fever, measles, polio, or diphtheria, they were closed, washed down, and fumigated. Families with sick children were restricted from contact with anyone until the disease was over. Other illnesses such as cholera, typhoid, and tuberculosis were harder to control, since they tended to occur in the adult population, a group less likely to obey quarantine restrictions. Added to the problem of these diseases was the fact that the village lacked any sewer system, depending on open ditches to carry away waste into the I & M Canal. The outhouse and privy vault were the only places for human excrement and they often contaminated shallow well water supplies, since not everyone was connected to the new village water system which was expensive and located downtown.

From pioneer days our area suffered waterborne diseases. A cholera epidemic in 1854 killed over five percent of the Chicagoland population.[39] In 1866, a similar epidemic caused such a shortage of burial space that some of Chicago's Irish victims were brought to Lemont's St. Patrick's Cemetery.[40] In 1880, the death rate for cholera was 68 percent, although medical science had already proved that the illness was contagious and controllable with sanitation, safe water, and good sewer systems; unfortunately, this information was not common knowledge. Old Lemont newspapers reveal sad tales of the effect of waterborne disease. In 1886, a family of seven moved into town to start a new life and within two weeks all had died of typhoid fever.

Without an understanding of germs, cholera and typhoid often affected the poor because of their housing locations. It was the poor Lemonter, the new immigrant, the quarry worker, and the canal worker who lived in small cottages at the base of Lemont's hills. As the affluent built above town, their waste contaminated the wells of those below. Many in the middle class blamed the victims since it was believed that the poor became ill because they lived in unclean conditions, were sinful, or intemperate. Only as scientific understanding increased did the public demand control and regulation of sewers and water. By the early 1890s, this knowledge would affect Lemont through the development of a plan to improve the drainage system of the Chicago area with the creation of the Sanitary Ship Canal.

Fear of contagious disease was significant and its presence in a town could cause economic and political consequences. Often communities would deny any difficulty existed. Lemont village authorities tried that strategy in November of 1903, when a small group of armed farmers from DuPage and Will Counties encircled Lemont and Lemont Township refusing to allow anyone to enter or leave on the area roads. The township was cordoned off while the farmers met residents from town and turned them back on threat of death. Only food and medical personnel were allowed to enter the village or township.

The farmers were unhappy with what they perceived was a lack of effective action by Lemont's local public health authorities. This drastic move was the only way they knew to control the spread of smallpox that had plagued Lemont from the middle of October.

Rumors and whispered fears started on October 20, when a worker at Quarry Number 6, who had been very ill, broke out in a rash. After visiting him, Dr. Fitzpatrick, who tended most of the quarry workers, had someone stationed in front of the patient's home allowing no one to leave or enter.[41]

Soon the frightening word smallpox began to creep into conversations. Dr. Fitzpatrick was evasive when his patients tried to get information, but he did review the symptoms of the disease for all who asked. He also added that isolation and vaccination were the best means to control the disease.

Mayor Otto Earnshaw discounted all the rumors. He felt that fear and anxiety were needless. To all who asked he said that it was only a case of the chickenpox and that the town was simply taking normal precautions. But soon, others became ill, developing a rash that appeared on the third or fourth day. The rash started with red spots that became raised then filled with a fluid and crusted over. When the crust came off, often a scar remained. The whole process from spots to the crust took about a week.[42] Nobody had to tell old timers the true nature of the illness. They knew all the signs of smallpox: rash in many areas of the body all at the same stage of development, high fever, more rash on the arms and legs than the trunk, rash on the soles of the feet and the palms, and a rash that took a week to crust. It certainly was not chickenpox.

As each day passed, more cases developed, so Mayor Earnshaw and the township supervisor, Joe Starshak, decided to place Dr. Fitzpatrick in charge of the "village health problem" and Dr. Leahy to oversee the "township health problem." The question of fees for their services was left to the doctors to bill after the emergency.

Dr. Fitzpatrick had the bulk of the work as the village was harder hit than the township. He demanded that all cases be strictly isolated with guards posted at the homes. He also requested that the Board of Health and the county authorities be notified of the epidemic. The mayor was reluctant to take such drastic measures. It would hurt business if word got out that Lemont was having a serious outbreak of smallpox. Farmers that shipped and bought goods in town would not come and that would hurt the economy of the village. He and Supervisor Starshak reasoned that the disease was fairly mild and the epidemic would probably end soon.

Their attitude angered Dr. Fitzpatrick who was frustrated and tired. In ten days he cared for 300 cases and could only see the outbreak as a major health problem. Unable to get the politicians to budge, he resigned his job as village health officer and returned to caring for his own patients. In his place, Dr. Leahy accepted full control of both the village and township cases. Dr. Leahy was willing to stand by the political decision that the epidemic was not a problem for outsiders coming into town.

But as news of the situation reached the farmers in DuPage and Will counties, they became fearful of its possible spread. Unable to make the Lemont authorities take steps to isolate the village, or to declare an emergency, they then organized the unusual army that laid siege to the town. This act finally brought the situation to the attention of the newspapers and county health authorities. The Cook County Board of Health sent medical help and 50 deputies to guard homes that were quarantined. The very things that Dr. Fitzpatrick had requested were done at last.

The siege lasted ten weeks through the coldest weather of the season. Strangely, no state or county authority attempted to intervene, perhaps because people could still move in and out of town by train. As weeks dragged on, some Lemonters became angry. It was suggested that the siege was a veiled attempt by DuPage and Will county towns to steal local farm shipments and trade. Still most of the townspeople understood the fear that kept armed men stationed night and day at the roads into Lemont.

The disease began to wane in late December and by the first week in January no new cases were reported. In all, about 450 people contracted the illness. Three hundred and fifty of the cases, ten percent of the town, occurred in the first three weeks.[43] No fatal cases were reported, but about half the victims had permanent scarring.

On January 7, 1904, the farmers, satisfied that the disease was under control, lifted the siege and commerce flowed in and out of Lemont again. At the January township and village meetings, Doctors Leahy and Fitzpatrick presented their bills. For ten days of constant work and 300 hundred patients Fitzpatrick charged 5,580 dollars. Leahy for eight weeks of work and one hundred patients charged 5,750 dollars. The total cost to the Lemont taxpayers was 11,600 dollars, largely because the officials at the start of the outbreak would not request outside free help from the state and county.

The bills were subject to much discussion, especially Dr. Leahy's bill which was considered exorbitant by the opposition. The payment of this bill and the handling of the epidemic became a campaign issue and, in April of 1905, the village and township boards were swept out of office by the voters. The winners were Timothy Sullivan for mayor and Pat Hennebry for supervisor. After hearing the results Starshak said, "Supper tonight will be humble pie and soup."[44]

Lemont had experienced a form of smallpox called Alastrim, a relatively mild form of the disease introduced into the state with the return of the troops from the Spanish-American War.[45] From 1899 through the spring of 1904, it was widespread throughout Illinois. Lemont was lucky, however, because in the fall of 1904 the character of the disease changed and returned to a more virulent type with a death rate of 22 percent for those affected. Ironically, Lemont's epidemic had the effect of naturally immunizing a large part of our unvaccinated population against the more serious form of the disease, because infection with Alastrim conferred the same immunity as if the patient had had the more virulent form of smallpox. The politicians who acted out of economic fear really did the community a strange favor. By letting the mild form of the disease spread they, in effect, protected the population from further epidemics of smallpox.

These stories detail not only the hard lessons that had to be learned by our early leaders but also represent the economic and political struggles that the newly incorporated village of Lemont had to face, taking on the responsibility for providing for the health and safety of its citizens. It was in these early years that the systems we now expect as part of our daily lives had their start.

ENDNOTES

[1]There were a few exceptions — two homes, a couple of stores and some church and institutional buildings. Benjamin Franklin is credited with forming the first fire company in the United States as early as 1736. Members of his volunteer company were required to furnish, at their own expense, six buckets and two strong linen bags.

[2]Lemont Village Council Meeting Notes, vol. 1, April 14, 1880.

[3]Lemont Village Council Meeting Notes, vol. 2, June 3, 1885.

[4]*The Lemonter*, November 30, 1933.

[5]Lemont Village Council Meeting Notes, vol. 2, July 22, 1885.

[6]*The Lemonter*, November 30, 1933.

[7]This fire was probably arson as a result of the intense feelings generated by the "Lemont Massacre" strike of May, 1885.

[8]Probably from Lemont's cigar factory owned by Henry Bodensick.

[9]Barbara Bushman,ed., *Lemont, Illinois: Its History in Commemoration of the Centennial of its Incorporation* (Des Plaines, IL: King/Mann Yearbook Center, 1973), p. 76.

[10]Interview with Horace Singer Norton, *The Lemonter*, December 15, 1938.

[11]*Lemont Press*, January 28, 1888.

[12]*Ibid.*

[13]*Ibid.*

[14]Ries offered new and used items for sale. Discount and resale stores are not a new merchandising practice.

[15]*Lemont Press*, January 28, 1888.

[16]Within ten years both towns would suffer major fires, partly due to this fact.

[17]*Lemont Press,* January 28, 1888.

[18]This was especially disturbing as J.D. Paige had been a volunteer fireman in Joliet from the 1870s.

[19]*Lemont Press*, January 28, 1888.

[20]Lemont Council Meeting Notes, March 1888.

[21]He owned the general store complex at 102 Stephen Street.

[22]Mrs. Singer's library project had been moved to a better location away from the canal.

[23]*Lemont Observer*, December 26, 1896.

[24]One of the engineers who worked out of the office spent considerable time in Lemont. He was Ed Kelly who went on to become Mayor of Chicago, from 1933 to 1944.

[25]*Lemont Observer*, May 8, 1897.

[26]Bushman, *Lemont, Illinois,* p. 66.

[27]Village Council Meeting Notes, June, 1883.

[28]*Ibid.*, March 12, 1884.

[29]Bushman, *Lemont, Illinois,* p. 66.

[30]Lemont Village Council Meeting Notes, October 28, 1885.

[31]Bushman, *Lemont, Illinois,* p. 26.

[32]Sonia Kallick, ed.,"The Good Old Days," *Lemont History and Anecdotes* (Lemont: Lemont Area Historical Society, 1975).

[33]*Lemont Observer*, July 23, 1897.

[34]*Lemont Observer*, March 13, 1897.

[35]A growler was a pitcher or pail used to carry beer home from the tavern. It also served as a dinner pail for workers.

[36]Nels Norden Papers, Lemont Historical Society collection.

[37]Sonia Kallick, "The Hot Air Gang," *Lemont History and Anecdotes* (Lemont: Lemont Area Historical Society, 1975).

[38]See A. T. Andreas, *History of Cook County: 1884* (Evansville: Unigraphics, 1976), p. 854.

[39]William K. Beatty, "When Cholera Scouraged Chicago," *Chicago History* (Chicago: Chicago Historical Society, Spring 1982), p. 10

[40]Bushman, *Lemont, Illinois,* p. 110.

[41]*Joliet News*, October 28, 1903.

[42]Gerald Mandell, R. Gordon Douglas, and John E. Bennett, *Principles and Practices of Infectious Diseases,* 3rd ed. (New York: Churchill Livingstone, 1990), p. 1137.

[43]*Chicago Inter-Ocean*, January 8, 1904.

[44]Sonia Kallick, "Views of Old Lemont," *The Lemont Metropolitan*, September 13, 1979.

[45]Mandell, *Principles and Practices of Infectious Diseases,* p. 1137

CHAPTER EIGHTEEN

TRANSPORTATION IN LEMONT: TWO NEW SCHEMES

The Santa Fe and
The Chicago & Joliet Electric

By the late 19th and early 20th Century, the railroad became the lifeline of our country, but because the government did not wish to undertake the cost of railway development, it was turned over to private developers. This was often done with the incentive of offering acres of free land adjoining the right-of-way of the railroads. Conservatives who objected to this approach said that the government was mortgaged to the railroad barons. However, the scheme worked, and so many rail lines were built that by 1900, there were more than 200,000 miles of railroads crossing our country. That equaled more than all of the tracks of Europe.[1]

Many entered the business of rail building with little skill or capital. As a result, numerous schemes went bankrupt or were consolidated into larger lines that developed into monopolies. These larger lines soon drove out smaller investors who had constructed rails to less populated areas, thus leaving many small towns and their dreams of progress and wealth to die.

Lemont, on the natural transportation corridor of the Des Plaines Valley, was unique because it had two rail lines serving the town. The Atchison, Topeka & Santa Fe (The Santa Fe) entered the Chicago market in the late 1880s, long after the main railroad building activity was over, but during a period of intense competition and reorganization. Other local rail lines did not like the idea of more expansion into what they considered their territory, and fought hard to exclude new lines from the area.

Yet, little could stop the aggressive Santa Fe owners who by 1883 had secretly surveyed and selected a straight line pathway from Kansas City to Chicago. The final route chosen ran through the Des Plaines Valley, to be in direct competition with the Chicago and Alton, the I & M Canal, and the planned development of a new ship canal.

Knowing that their application for permission to run a new line to Chicago would be denied, the Santa Fe made a clever move by quietly purchasing the old rusting and abandoned Chicago, LaSalle, and St. Louis Railroad. It was a double track that ran from Chicago, past Lemont, on the north side of the Des Plaines Valley, to Pekin where its funds and dream ended. The new plan was to have the track cross the valley and enter Lemont. A.T. Andreas in his *History of Cook County*, mentions this rail line as under construction in 1884 and calls it the Chicago, St. Louis, and Western Railroad.[2]

The rusting trackage was upgraded and attached to the rest of the railbed going west-ward to create the Atchison, Topeka and Santa Fe. To enter the Chicago market, the line began by offering to forego local passenger traffic and concentrate on express train service to the West. This was done to avoid litigation with rail lines in the local market and because the longer through-trains were more profitable.

This network of trains crossing our nation affected time in a very real way. Before the railroad, every town operated on local time. It was noon when the sun was at its highest point in the midday sky; as William Cronon points out:

> Every locale had a different noon . . . when it was noon in Chicago, it was 11:50 in St. Louis, 11:38 in St. Paul, 11:27 in Omaha, and 12:18 in Detroit. For companies to try to operate trains on such a schedule was a nightmare. Railroads around the country set their clocks on no fewer than fifty-three different standards — thereby creating a risk for anyone that rode them. And so, on November 18, 1883, the railroad companies carved up the continent into four time zones, in each of which all clocks would be set to exactly the same time. At noon Chicago [and Lemont] jewelers moved their clocks back nine minutes and thirty-three seconds to match the time of the ninetieth Meridian.[3]

It was a day that time really stood still for Lemont.

Service on the new Santa Fe line began in 1888, with deluxe appointments. Cars had carved mahogany interiors, electric lights, sofas, and settees. There were Pullman sleepers, and, of course, diners with food by Fred Harvey, whose name and service had become a standard for railroad food. His waitresses became famous as the "Harvey Girls."

In 1890, the route became part of newspaper and transportation history. Nellie Bly, a young, creative reporter for the *New York World*, set out to beat the imaginary record of Phileas Fogg, hero of Jules Verne's story, *Around The World in Eighty Days*. Starting from New York in November of 1889, she stopped in Paris and interviewed Verne, then proceeded to circle the world.

Each day, the newspaper carried articles about her trip, which were then carried in the local papers. A contest was held to guess the time when she would finish. Public interest was so great that the *World* received over one million entries. Nellie made the journey on ships, horses, rickshaws, burros, and trains. The final part of her journey was on a special Santa Fe train commissioned by the *New York World* to run from San Francisco to New York. Ever publicity minded, the railroad agreed without hesitation to take part. All along the way there were bands and fireworks. The trip to Chicago was made in record time, 69 hours. The division director of the Lemont section of the track, and all the other record-breaking sections, received from Nellie one quart of Mumms Extra Dry Champagne.

She made it back to New York in 72 days, six hours, 11 minutes and 14 seconds from the date she left, a time made possible because of the network of railroads then available throughout the world.

Her trip made the idea of distant train travel glamorous and the Santa Fe soon became part of the mystique, selling long-distance trips to the West and Southwest. The *Lemont*

Observer of 1896 and 1897 ran weekly ads headlined, "May I send you to California and back — Santa Fe?" There were even enticements for Lemonters to seek land owned by the Santa Fe. One ad offered:

Homes in Texas Coast Country

For full information regarding fruit, vegetables, and field crop farms located in the coast country of Texas apply to G.T. Nelson, Santa Fe railway, Chicago. Texas offers tempting inducements to the homeseeker. Investigate for yourself. Excursions rates via Santa Fe Route.[4]

When construction began on the Sanitary Ship Canal, the Santa Fe management decided that this was an opportunity to move their line to run near the newly created canal. This action then would put them along the proposed waterway, just as the Alton Railroad had done 40 years before when they laid out their route to compete with the I & M Canal. As the Des Plaines River was diverted from Lemont and channeled to its present site, the Santa Fe laid its trackage along the old river bed, using fill from the Ship Canal construction. They built the Santa Fe bridge over the Ship Canal, a swing bridge. It was listed at the time as the biggest ever made.[5] With use of the cheap fill, they elevated their trains and avoided a ground crossing in town. It did, however, require the cost of building the underpass we can still see today on Stephen Street, one that was not completed until 1899.

Santa Fe Depot. (Photo courtesy of Lemont Historical Society)

The rail line also built a small wooden passenger and freight station located on River Road on the north side near the present overhead bridge. The station was not designed for comfort, since the original intent of the Santa Fe was to compete for through traffic to the West. Nevertheless, it had an old western look and was unique. It was finally removed by the railroad in the early 1980s.

With two stations in town and an economic depression in the middle 1890s, competition grew intense between the Santa Fe and the Alton. The Santa Fe began to run local trains to pick up revenue. They also bid for postal train service, a development that had become highly profitable. In 1897, our town of 4,000 people had 11 commuter trains going to Chicago and nine returning. The Alton ran seven trains to Chicago and five back. The Santa Fe ran four to Chicago and four back. The result of this competition forced the Alton to merge with other railroads to survive, which pushed the Santa Fe to concentrate on their original market, the long distance traveler.

However, the Santa Fe did keep some interesting local trains for a period. One such train was the "Gamblers Special" in the years 1903 and 1904. These were trains that ran out three times a day with eight to ten cars to the Byrneville area, that section of land near Route 83, Kingery Road and the Ship Canal. For 25 cents, a gambler could avoid the rare political reform going on in Chicago at the time and come to our "no man's land" between the Sanitary District and DuPage County. There Big Jim O'Leary built himself a gambling resort that could not be raided.[6]

> He built a 150 by 120 foot frame building with a large main gambling room that took bets and posted action on five different race tracks. The building was surrounded by a fence interrupted by lookout houses; around all this was a 14-foot high solid wooden fence topped with spikes. The area between the two fences was patrolled by twenty to thirty snarling dogs. Western Union was more than willing to run telegraph lines and offer reports from the race tracks. Big Jim's immunity worked well in DuPage County which failed to notice either the building or the huge traffic of bettors that visited it daily.[7]

The *Chicago Journal* began a crusade against gambling and claimed that O'Leary was paying off DuPage officials to overlook his establishment. O'Leary replied that the place was on Sanitary District land and they were the only ones who had jurisdiction. The sheriff of DuPage went down to look at the fortress and reported that the place could only be closed down by a regiment of Japanese infantry with siege guns. Governor Deneen finally stopped the gambling by telling the Santa Fe to stop running trains to the Byrneville area and by forcing Western Union to cut their lines to the gambling joint.

The Santa Fe luxury trains ran twice a week to the West beginning in 1897, a practice that continues today under the Amtrack system. When the track was elevated through Lemont on the old Des Plaines riverbed, the engineers developed a graded curve from the steel bridge over the Ship Canal as it ran into town. This became known as Tedens Curve, as most of the land on which it was built had been in the Tedens family. This curve was the site of another Lemont train wreck, this one on August 3, 1905.

That evening it was the telegraph operator at the Santa Fe Station who was the first to hear and see the disaster. As he looked up to watch, the train *The Pride of San Francisco* began its pass through town. It was four minutes late and so it entered Tedens Curve at 50 miles per hour, slightly faster than the usual speed. Suddenly, the axle and wheels broke off the baggage car of the ten-car train. The baggage car, the smoker, and two filled Pullman cars left the track, tearing up chunks of ground and spraying cinders in all directions. When all the wood and steel finally came to a rest, the cars that had left the track were hanging dangerously over the side of the high embankment over Stephen Street.

In the freak accident, the engine remained on the track and the engineer, James Shea, and the fireman, Charles Paul, were not even aware of what had happened until they had traveled about a half mile past the station. Only on glancing backwards did they see what was left of their train strewn all over the track.

The Lemont telegraph operator sent an urgent message for aid. Looking at the tangled mess, he estimated the dead at 40 people or more. The noise and confusion were overwhelming. Passengers began climbing out of the toppled and crumbled cars. As they did so, the cars shifted, causing fear and panic that the rest of the train would fall off the side with the people still inside.

The passengers who escaped began looking for saws and crowbars to remove those trapped inside, but they found that the baggage car had fallen over on the railroad tool shed and no tools were available. Then suddenly a flame burst from one of the toppled cars casting an orange glow over downtown. The entrapped passengers became even more

Santa Fe wreck at Tedens Curve in Lemont, August 3, 1905. (Photo courtesy of Lemont Historical Society)

terrified for they were now facing either death by fire or being crushed as the train tumbled down the embankment. They needed help and, fortunately, fate had chosen the accident to happen on a Saturday night, which was a special time in downtown Lemont. The noise and fire brought hundreds of rescuers and the fire department to the scene as quickly as possible.

The volunteer firefighters quickly brought the blaze under control, while Lemonters organized a temporary hospital in the Santa Fe Station. Others got ladders and tools and helped to get passengers out of the dangling cars. If the same accident had happened further east in the valley near the canal, or on the bridge, the isolation of the train would have increased the number of dead and injured. As it turned out, the telegraph operator's estimate of the dead was wrong. Thanks to the townspeople and the fire department, only one man died and one was critically injured. Seven passengers had minor injuries and 15 had serious cuts and bruises.

Sadly, the dead man and many of the injured were from a group of newly immigrated Italian laborers who had been crowded together and sealed into one car on the train. They were part of a work force being shipped to Sunnyside, Utah, to work the mines as unskilled laborers in their new country.

Today this part of the line carries freight, no longer stopping to be part of Lemont's history. However, the land holdings the line acquired as part of the financial deals made to encourage rail building remains part of our local economy. The industrial park on North Lemont Road was part of the original land grant, and this area is still served by a spur running off the Santa Fe line.[8]

As we have seen, the growth and development of cities, towns, and villages in the United States are related to transportation. Lemont is unique because of a geography that has made it a natural corridor for transportation routes throughout its history. One could, on a small scale, view the village as if it were a town located along a mountain pass out West. By 1900, the Des Plaines River, the old Indian paths and trails, the Illinois and Michigan Canal, the Chicago and Alton Railroad, the Sanitary Ship Canal, and the Santa Fe Railroad all had brought goods and people to the area. Still, all known transportation designs were not complete, for the electric railway had yet to come to Lemont.

This new transportation technology swept the country around the turn of the century. Electric trolleys required less energy, the equipment was cheaper, and the trackage was easier to lay since it could be placed on already developed roads. Many electric railroads began along horsedrawn trolley lines. Two cities claim the first such systems: Montgomery, Alabama (1886), and Richmond, Virginia (1888). Like so many innovations at the time, soon everyone wanted to be a part of the electric trolley system. Franchises were sold by almost every village and hamlet in the United States, like the franchise mania of the Chicago street railways. Lemont also sold permission to trolley companies to operate within the village and township boundaries.

The turn of the century saw a great flurry of franchise speculation. Companies, who never had any intention of building, would obtain rights to a town or village and then sell those rights at a profit to serious builders. Many in the business were operating like the great railroad barons, but on a smaller scale. There was as much money to be made by holding franchises as there was in building the lines. Lemont was no exception to this pattern. Pressure was put on the village trustees to grant various franchise rights, and in 1898, the Chicago and Des Plaines Valley Electric Railway was granted the right to develop a line that ran between Lockport Street in Lemont to Carroll's Corner at Sag Bridge. The cost was five cents a ride.

Used mainly by the quarry workers and people shopping in downtown Lemont, the service was naturally limited. The original owners developed the small line to sell to the Chicago and Joliet Electric Company that was building a line on Archer Avenue. The Chicago and Joliet bought the line and expanded it out to Lemont in 1899, and to Joliet by 1901. The Lemont line then ran from Chicago, down Archer, then down Main Street to Lockport and Joliet, along this side of the Des Plaines Valley. It followed much of the route of today's New

Trolley on Main Street, looking east, circa 1900. Note the double track that leaves little room for horse and wagons, and the unsanitary conditions of the street. (Photo courtesy of Lemont Historical Society)

Avenue. The first trip was made on September 18, and the honor of this ride went to John Graff, who had been village clerk when the franchise was granted, and had been offered a job with the company. The *Joliet Daily Republican* could not let this fact pass when they commented that John Graff was "one of the leading politicians of the town made famous by Mayor McCarthy."[9]

The trip to downtown Chicago required a transfer to the Chicago Traction Company streetcars at Cicero and Archer Avenues. The passenger cars left every hour in the winter and every half-hour in the summer. Stops were made at Summit, Bethania Cemetery, Willow Springs, Lambert-Sag, Hastings, Lemont, Romeoville, Dellwood Park, Joliet State Penitentiary, and downtown Joliet. The trip from the Chicago city limits to Joliet took 85 minutes.[10]

Freight was also carried in special cars attached to the passenger cars so it was easy to receive packages and goods from Joliet or Chicago. Cars operated on electricity, supplied by an overhead hot wire which was charged by three power stations located in Joliet, Lemont, and Summit. Lemont's power station housed the stationmaster, a ticket office, and a waiting room in front for the passengers.

Electricity was supplied by large batteries over three feet tall, in rows of five, totaling over 100 in number. They were connected in a series to put out about 600 volts to the overhead line. The batteries had to be maintained around the clock, acid levels had to be checked, and the temperature of the solution controlled. Also, the generators had to be inspected frequently to see that there was a reliable source of power for the batteries. It was a difficult job. Mrs. Vera Austin Martin, whose father, Buel P. Austin, operated the station in 1903, recalled that the apartment for the family, the yard, and the station were attractive. She also remembered the other two shift men at the time, Mr. Vimpney and Mr. Endicavech.[11] On the west side of the power station was the repair barn, the only part of the station that remains today.

Although slower than a train, the trolleys had the advantage of a frequent schedule, cheaper prices, more stops, and operating closer to downtown stores and shops. The trolley offered more than just transportation. It was a nice ride, free from the noise and dirt of the steam train, so the trolley car was used for picnics and social and church gatherings. There were even funeral cars available to transport the casket and mourners to local cemeteries along the line.

An example of one social ride was one held by Lemont's Knights of Pythias in 1901. They rented two cars and started at 8:00 p.m. from the front of the Village Hall. Accompanied by a 20 piece band, the ride began with singing and blaring horns. Along the way they served refreshments and cheered themselves with this chant:

> Who are we?
> Who are we?
> Lemont 260 K of P,
> Kee - Kee - Kee po - po - taw Keepotaw,
> Keepotaw, Rah, Rah, Rah.

After visiting in Joliet with dinner at the Munroe Hotel and a return ride, the lodge brothers held a dance at the village hall that lasted until dawn.[12] This trip may have influenced the debate held at the lodge hall on Stephen Street that fall. The members debated the topic, "Resolved: That an electric street railway will be of greater benefit to Lemont in the next five years than the Drainage Canal."[13]

A trolley car ride was also considered good for health, and open air trolleys offered relief from hot summer days. A ride on the trolley was a cheap and popular way to court a young girl. There was a saying that "marriages based on streetcar courtships seemed to stick." True or not, such myths did much to popularize the electric railway. Each car carried a two-man crew: the conductor who collected the fares and saw passengers on and off safely, and the motorman who was in charge of the electric controller, air brakes, and horn.

A special feature of most electric railways was the development of a recreational park along the route. This park would then serve to attract passengers for the line. The idea was similar to the fancy resorts developed by the major railroads to attract customers, but with the electrics, the parks were created for the local trade.[14] They were working-class pleasure parks designed to be visited for a day's outing. The park for the Chicago and Joliet Line was Dellwood Park in Lockport. Admission was free, and it was not unusual for over 10,000 people to visit on a weekend. The park consisted of 70 acres, bubbling water fountains, a lake for boating, a bandstand, and a picnic area. The I & M Trail in Lockport ends in what remains of Dellwood Park, now a part of the Lockport Park District. Most of the amusement attractions are gone, but the site is still a lovely spot.

However, like the other transportation carriers, the electric railway had barely completed a year of service to Lemont before it had a major accident.

On March 28, 1902, Mrs. Mau watched as her husband put on his uniform. Some strange fear gnawed at her and she tried to find a way to express it. She finally settled on a simple plea for her husband to stay home and spend more time with her and the baby. The newspapers reported that John hesitated for just a moment, but then replied that he was going because he wanted 16 days on his paycheck, but promised her that on the next pay period he would lighten his schedule. Mau had nine years of service with the Chicago and Joliet Electric Company. He had begun at the organization even before all electric lines were completed, worked himself up to motorman, and was proud of his position and responsibility. This morning he was scheduled to take a trolley run into Chicago and return southbound on the 6:30 a.m. run in car 252.

Later that same morning, at the Lockport barn, a work crew employed by the Lockport Power and Light Company prepared a tripper car, number 257, to take to Willow Springs to complete a contract to put up electric poles to the Bridgeport Pumping Works. G.H. Hurley of Rockdale was in charge of the work crew, and George Barett of Lockport was in charge of the pole men. Mike McLaughlin of Joliet was selected to run the tripper. Before he left, he checked to see if there were any orders. He was not familiar with the schedule, especially the service on Main Street through Lemont, as service on that line had begun only six months before, in September. The only information he had was the fact that he had to use the east track at Sag Bridge as the west track was sinking from the heavy spring rains of that week.

John Mau reached Chicago on schedule and quickly turned the car around for the return trip on the east track. At that time of the morning he had only one passenger, Fred Mitz of Lemont. By the next stop, Willow Springs, he had picked up three more riders. At 7:00 a.m., outside Willow Springs, he passed the next scheduled Chicago-bound car and knew he had a clear track. He increased his speed to 30 miles an hour down the valley. Suddenly, at Sag Bridge he rode into dense, spring ground fog.

Meanwhile, McLaughlin, driving the tripper from Lockport, went through Lemont a little after 7:00 a.m. Since he believed the track was clear, he sped up after leaving town. George Barett, the foreman, liked riding on the front platform and he went out to join Mike at the very moment that they entered the same fog bank. Neither car could see ahead. The head-on collision occurred at 7:10 a.m. The bumper of Tripper 257 was torn up and the front end of the southbound 252 crushed. John Mau and George Barett were killed instantly. It took over an hour to remove their bodies. G.H. Hurley died later at the hospital. Mike McLaughlin's leg was crushed.

Local farmers helped the victims until the Chicago and Joliet Trolley Line sent a special car with the manager, Mr. Fiske. He directed the car to take the victims to St. Joseph's Hospital in Joliet. The dead were removed to Lemont. The wreckage of the "Unlucky 252" as it became known, was left scattered around the area. More than a few kids from town went out to collect scraps as souvenirs of the event.[15] Ironically, it was the very same area, Main and Parker Road, which had been the scene of another fog related collision 29 years before, the wreck of the Chicago and Alton No.4 that had killed 23 people.

The peak of electric intra-urban transportation occurred around 1917. In that year it was a four billion-dollar a year industry. This country had over 1,000 electric rail companies with 60,000 cars and 26,000 miles of track. There are many people who feel that this was one of the most energy efficient mass-transportation systems ever developed, but with the new century, electric trolley lines began to decline in popularity, due largely to the development of the private automobile and the passenger bus. While it lasted, the Chicago and Joliet Trolley line was a wonderful means of local transportation for Lemonters and Chicagoans alike.

ENDNOTES

[1]Samuel Morison, *The Oxford History of the American People.* (New York: New American Library, 1972), vol. 3, p. 50.

[2]A.T. Andreas, *History of Cook County, Illinois: 1885.* (Evansville: Unigraphics, 1976), p. 850

[3]William Cronon, *Nature's Metropolis: Chicago and the Great West.* (New York: W.W. Norton & Company, 1991), p. 79.

[4]*Lemont Observer*, January 30, 1897.

[5]*Lemont Ledger*, April 25, 1899. There is little evidence that the bridge was ever opened. The presence of this low bridge has been a problem for shipping on the canal.

[6]Son of Mrs. O'Leary of the Chicago Fire fame.

[7]Richard Griffin, "Big Jim O'Leary," *Chicago History Magazine* (Chicago: Chicago Historical Society, Spring 1977), p. 217.

[8]The recent Santa Fe merger still has considerable sections of valley land in control of the rail companies.

[9]*Joliet Daily Republican,* September 18,1901.

[10]Ben Williams, ed., *The Chicago and Interurban Trolley Guide* (Chicago: Norton & Co., 1908), p. 26.

[11]Don Witt, "The Electric Trolley," *Where the Trails Cross* (South Holland: South Suburban Genealogical Society, Spring 1977).

[12]*Lemont Ledger*, August 24, 1901.

[13]*Observer*, November 18, 1899.

[14]For a short period of time, the Chicago & Alton Railway sponsored a resort park in Lemont. Called Alton Park, it was located on property west of the Singer-Warner playground. It was sold in the 1890s and renamed Peterson's Park.

[15]See Barbara Bushman, ed., *Lemont, Illinois: Its History In Commemoration Of the Centennial Of Its Incorporation* (Des Plaines: King/Mann, 1973) p. 28. Walter Tedens recalled the crash when he was young, but had the date wrong. He said his brother John came home with a piece of the wreckage.

CHAPTER NINETEEN

TRANSPORTATION AND LEMONT: THE SECOND CANAL

The Sanitary Ship Canal: 1892-1900

Up to 1871, 23 years after the completion of the I & M Canal, the trustees worked to increase the traffic to pay off the canal debt.[1] The deeper cut in the canal in 1871 did help barge traffic for a time, but railroad competition continued to affect the amount of canal shipping. Rail construction was so rapid that by the late 1860s "no farm in Illinois was more than 50 miles from a railroad station and the average distance was seven miles."[2]

Still, the I & M Canal had its greatest tonnage years in the early 1880s and continued to offer a low cost alternative for non-first class freight until the turn of the century. Besides transportation, there was a secondary purpose to the I & M Canal deep cut, that of carrying the sewage and filth of the Chicago River away from Chicago's water supply, Lake Michigan. It was hoped that enough of a flow would be created to move pollution downstream to the Mississippi, thereby diluting it.

But the canal and river depended upon surface water runoff, and during dry cycles there was little flow. A large rainstorm in 1877 caused the river to flow back into the lake and "for several days the river emptied its filthy contents: sewage and putrid wastes from slaughterhouses into the source of Chicago's water supply. During this period, city water smelled bad, was nauseating to drink, and was wine colored."[3]

To increase the flow, lift pumps were installed at the junction of the river and the canal at Bridgeport. They helped for a short while, but were inadequate to solve the sanitation problems created by Chicago's rapid growth. Simultaneously, the public was beginning to understand the relationship between unsanitary conditions and disease. The early 1880s saw the development of germ theory, and with it the creation of public health systems in some major urban areas. Lemont had a Board of Health by 1885. Yet, as late as 1880, the death rate for cholera in Chicagoland area was 68 percent, a fact that led to the formation of a citizens' committee that year empowered to study the problem. The committee recommended that a canal or new river be dug to the headwaters of the Illinois River to increase the current in the stagnant Chicago River.[4] The idea won wide approval, but no one was willing to commit the huge funds needed for such a project until Mother Nature intervened.

On August 2, 1885, the Chicago area was hit with a six-inch rainfall. As a result, sewage and storm water ran into the lake and a major typhoid epidemic resulted. Meanwhile, the beaches were fouled with human, animal, and industrial waste. Many people fled the city in fear of disease. Mayor Carter Harrison, Sr. appointed a commission and, unlike so many commissions, this one actually produced a plan. It was composed of three far-sighted engineers: Rudolph Herring, Sam Artingstall, and Benezette Williams. They submitted their revolutionary project in a citizens' report in 1887. They had two suggestions. First, move the Des Plaines River to the northwest side of the valley. The river at this time fronted Lemont where River Road is today. Second, reverse the flow of the Chicago River by building a new canal from the river at Robey Street to the Des Plaines River at Lockport. The water was to be aerated to kill bacteria through oxygenation by having a flow of 24,000 cubic feet of water for each 100,000 people. To accomplish this flow, water was to be diverted from Lake Michigan. However, this part of the plan was never fully carried out since Canada and other Great Lakes cities objected to any lake water diversion.

On May 29, 1889, a bill creating the Sanitary District of Chicago passed the state legislature, subject to voter approval. This enabled an elected nine-member board of trustees to create, administer, and finance all the public utilities necessary to carry out the project. Lyman E. Cooley was selected as chief engineer. However, early planning of the project was subject to politics and pressure. "The trustees saw only the rising real estate values along the proposed canal route and were therefore eager to begin work immediately. They became increasingly demanding as Cooley became increasingly painstaking."[5] Cooley was criticized for making unauthorized surveys of private land for his view of a greater scheme, that of a waterway from Lake Michigan to the Gulf of Mexico.

Cooley made his first report on September 17, 1890, and the board fired him the following December.[6] This action set off a round of hirings and firings until Benezette Williams took the job in 1892.

After the Sanitary District, a canal zone of 185 square miles was approved by the voters; it remained a political issue, largely because it now was an autonomous taxing body that included most of Chicago and many western and southwestern suburbs. The election of trustees left a board divided over the size of the canal. Voters had approved a channel with a flow of 600,000 cubic feet per second, but some, perhaps with vested interests, held out for a smaller canal. The Democrats, who favored a larger canal, suspected that the Republicans wanted a smaller one to help "millionaire land speculators who had in mind the development of the Calumet harbor at government expense and who feared that the ship canal as proposed would draw traffic back to Chicago."[7] Later history proved their fears correct, for by 1905, the Sanitary District headed by the young heir of the Tribune's Medill-Patterson-McCormick family, Robert R. McCormick, laid plans for the development of the Cal-Sag Channel and the Calumet Harbor. This time, however, those in power won and renamed Lyman E. Cooley, an advocate of the larger ship canal, as chief engineer.

The official day for beginning the construction of the Chicago Sanitary and Ship Canal was September 3, 1892. Known as "Shovel Day," it was held on the Will-Cook County line in Lemont. Sensing the future importance of the waterway, the *Chicago Tribune* supported the idea of the canal and described the event as being as important as the driving of the golden spike in 1869 that united the transcontinental railroads.[8]

Contracts were let early and some construction had actually begun before the official dedication day. The *Joliet News* reported in August that, from Lockport to Willow Springs, work had begun. At the Romeo section, Mason, Hodge, & King and the King Brothers had already built shacks for housing. Part of their crew consisted of 700 African-Americans from West Virginia who had been working on the Norfolk and Northern Railroad Line. Their housing was deplorable, set in isolated clusters one mile apart from each other. The buildings supplied were loose and open, with no batting sealing the wooden walls, with some dormitories made only of corrugated iron sheets with shingle roofs.

At the Lemont section there were three small shacks and one large barracks. The Sag Bridge contract also housed animals, with 80 teams and plows ready to begin work. This work group came from Kansas and was under the supervision of Colonel R. Baske.[9]

It was reported that on Shovel Day "around 1200 people attended all in holiday attire, jubilant, and enthusiastic."[10] One thousand dignitaries were invited to the event, and a special train carried everyone who was anybody in Chicago to the site in the town of Lemont that was decorated for the occasion. The speakers' platform was draped with flags and bunting. It stood six feet "above the waves of drying September grasses of the Des Plaines Valley."[11] Next to the platform was a set of wooden seats for the dignitaries invited to attend the event.

In front of the platform, white lines had been painted to show where the canal was to be built. In the center of the two lines was a row of white flags marking the midline of the proposed canal. Vendors of all sorts took advantage of the crowds by selling ice cream, spruce beer, and red, white, and blue bags of peanuts and popcorn. Added to the vendors were people operating various games of chance ranging from a wheel of fortune to a ring toss. The gambling here was just a hint of what the construction years would bring to Lemont.

Above the crowd, two switchmen were stationed to signal when the train full of dignitaries arrived. The VIP train held the politicians of Cook County, state officials, the newly elected board of the Sanitary District, and two ex-mayors of Chicago, Carter Harrison and Dewitt Cregier.[12] Waiting in Lemont were our local representatives, the Lemont Band, Mayor Hennebry, Supervisor Matt Warner, Police Magistrate T. Huston, Postmaster J. Bodenschatz, Peter Nelson from the Board of Education, George Weimer of the Democratic Central Committee, Lemuel Brown, Horace Norton, Rev. Fr. Sixt, and J.W. McCarthy.

At noon the train arrived. The Lemont Band, consisting of eight horns, two drums, and a bass tympanum, began playing as the leader called out "number 42." Eagerly, the band proceeded to the platform cutting through the crowd. However, the dignitaries lingered over food and drank while our band marched ahead. They ended up at the platform alone. Finally, a messenger was sent to ask them to return to the train. One hour later, the band was given the signal to

The Lemont Band who played for the "Shovel Day" ceremonies. (Photo courtesy of Lemont Historical Society)

begin and this time the officials followed to the platform. There, Ferando Jones was introduced. He had been present in 1836 when the Illinois and Michigan Canal was dedicated in Bridgeport. Then came the ceremonial shovel used by Frank Winter of the Sanitary Board, followed by an authentic blasting cap set off by Engineer Cooley — all this to signify the beginning of the project that would take eight years to complete.[13]

There was considerable pressure to complete the work, for the typhoid death rate in 1891 was a still high: 174 persons per 100,000 population. The publicity surrounding this disease rate disturbed the promoters and boosters of the World's Columbian Exposition who felt that it might keep visitors away from the fair. There really was no way that the "Big Ditch" could be completed in one year, but the sponsors of the fair felt that the idea that Chicago was working on a sanitation project would be enough to calm any fears.

A working force of 8,500 men began the project that eventually removed 29 million cubic yards of soil and 12 million cubic yards of rock to create the Chicago to Lockport Canal. The canal is 28 miles long with an average width of 150 feet and a low water depth of 22 feet. From the Chicago River to Summit, the base was earth, and from Summit to Willow Springs, earth over a rock base; and, of course, from Willow Springs through Lemont and Lockport, solid dolomite rock.

The technological world had changed in the years from the construction of the I & M Canal to the Sanitary Ship Canal. No longer was the work done by hand in slow back-breaking fashion. Forty years had seen the development of steam power and compressed air mechanization, and this project concentrated all the mechanical skills that were available at the time. Many contractors developed their own equipment in a display of machinery never seen before. It was reported that "almost every type of steam shovel and digging apparatus known to American contractors was brought into use and according to the *Engineering News* 'nowhere at any time in the history of the world have so many novel and different machines for excavating and removing earth and rock been in operation in so small a territory.'"[14]

Among the amazing machines used was a grading machine pulled by 16 horses, which threw soil into a revolving drum that dumped it into wagons pulled alongside the grader. It must be added that many contractors, who respected the machine over the animal, were often cruel to their horses and mules. There are eyewitness reports of mounds of dead animals left to decay along the project sites. Willow Springs had a political struggle to fight off plans for an animal rendering plant that someone wanted to build to take advantage of the dead animals.

Louis Cain describes other marvelous earth moving equipment:

> Fifty steam shovels were used, one a dredge on wheels. Its boom — 23 feet wide and 50 feet long — operated a dipper with the capacity of 2 and a half yards. Excavated material was conveyed to the spoil banks [dump grounds] by a machine known as the "Heidenreich Incline." The frame of the incline was mounted on tracks laid perpendicular to the incline. The platform at the base held the engine, boiler, hoisting machinery, and an electrical generator. Later, engineers Christie & Lowe,[15] modified the incline to include a double track. Several other major earth moving machines were also used during construction. Mason and Hoover built a conveyer that spanned the channel with a cantilever arm over the spoil area.[16] The Bates conveyer had a hopper in which two cylinders containing intermeshed steel knives that separated clay fed in by one of the steam shovels.[17]

Because of the remarkable equipment and the complicated work involved in the digging of the canal, including the moving of the Des Plaines River and the reversing of the Chicago River with a lock system, the canal became known as "The Chicago School of Earth Moving." The machines and techniques developed helped to train people for the later construction of the Panama Canal. Still, a good deal of the work had to be done by hand. The men labored 10 hours a day and wages ran from 15 to 17½ cents an hour for laborers and teamsters. Drillers and train men were paid 17½ to 20 cents an hour. Boilermakers and stonemasons made 35 to 40 cents an hour. Overtime was paid on an hourly basis and these jobs were sought after, as the country was in another economic depression.

Conditions were so bad that the homeless roamed streets in Chicago and surrounding towns. Men and women slept in Chicago's City Hall on cold nights. William Stead wrote that the poor and hungry of the city would have starved had it not been for union labor help and saloons offering free lunches. For a five-cent glass of beer, the customer could eat as much as the tavernkeeper put out. It was calculated that the saloons fed over 60,000 free lunches every day.[18] Under such circumstances one can see how desperate men were for jobs on the project. The *Chicago Daily News* reported that "while food riots raged at relief stations," some lucky men got special work permit cards allowing them to report to the Alton Station for a 6:00 a.m. express train to Lemont.[19]

The problem was that the contracts were let like the old I & M Canal contracts. An individual or company formed for building would bid on a section of the canal to complete. The winner of the bid was responsible for the work, for working conditions, and the completion of his section. One of the problems with this arrangement was that many of the subcontractors were from out-of-state. It may have been political, or simply a situation that required accepting the lowest bid, but the result was that out-of state contractors

View of construction on the Sanitary Ship Canal. (Photo courtesy of Lemont Historical Society)

hired from their own area and not local workers. This caused hard feelings in Lemont and Chicago.

The desire for work created several crooked schemes that took advantage of the many immigrants arriving in Chicago. False employment agencies took money from men promising work along the canal. One such ring went as far as to:

> Link agents who clustered along Canal Street with cohorts among ten construction companies digging the Sanitary Ship Canal. In January of 1894 more than 2,000 men were bilked by collecting three dollars each and [taking advantage of their lack of English] by sending them to find a "Mr Watstodoe" [what's to do] at the canal. Other victims were charged an additional two dollars for transportation to work and then fired after a few hours of labor to make room for others They recovered none of their seven dollar fee.[20]

Dignitaries in large crane used on the Ship Canal project. (Photo courtesy of Lemont Historical Society)

Martin Madden, the Lemont water boy who went to Congress, was a Chicago alderman at this time, and he reported the long lines of men who each day took the Chicago and Alton out to Lemont and the other contract sites in an attempt to find work. He especially remembered a young Italian man who held up his new citizenship papers in the belief that these papers would offer him a special passport to work and to a future in America.[21]

As late as 1896, contractors were taking advantage of their employees. The Griffith & McDermott Company would pay workers on Saturday, then line the men up and ask if they boarded in company run camps. Those who did not were sent to the office for discharge.[22]

The building of the ship canal was such a unique project that the Chicago and Alton offered special excursion trains to the site at a reduced fare. John Geiger, a remarkable Lemont photographer, produced a booklet for the rail line with pictures of the canal and descriptions of the machines and the geography of the area. Those involved with the undertaking had a sense that they would be affecting the natural features of our valley. In the prose style of the 1890s, the brochure warned:

> The Urgent Importance of Not Delaying Your Inspection of The Chicago drainage Canal. The warning not to delay inspection can only be compared with the universal alarm which was sounded by the daily press throughout the country when The World's Columbian Exposition was about to close forever. Like the World's Fair the day will come [and] it is not far distant, when the "Big Ditch" will be no more. In place of the most stupendous and miraculous example of canal construction and channeling which the world has ever known, we shall see but a tranquilly flowing inland waterway, the bed and sides

of which with their transcendently interesting geological features will be hidden from human gaze forever.

The tours were conducted by Professor C.H. Ford, principal of the Calhoun School; the round trip cost 75 cents. One of the interesting items in this booklet is the mention of a section between Willow Springs and Lemont known as the "Gold Section," because a fragment of gold-bearing quartz was found there. It was a product of glacial action that moved it from the Lake Superior region. Digging in the valley also exposed some copper, iron, and silver ore in glacial rocks.

People on the tour of the "Big Ditch" were encouraged to get off the train and walk around the sites and machinery. They were informed that if they contacted the supervisors or workers there would be many fine examples of fossils available for purchase. There was an on-going business in fossils. Henry Norden, a young boy during the construction, told how he and his friends kept the best fossil areas secret so they then could sell the choicest fossils to visitors.[23] The guide book does not mention the Lemont sights of Smokey Row or Peterson's Park, but one can imagine that some tourists combined the educational tour with other more earthly pleasures.

Not only was the valley changed by the canal, but Lemont itself underwent an ethnic, physical, and spiritual change. The physical change included the removal of the Des Plaines River from our "frontyard" to its present channel north of town. The river was channeled for 13 miles parallel to the canal at a cost of one million dollars. We also had the addition of the elevated Santa Fe tracks cutting off the valley view from downtown. Older Lemonters told of the special scenic beauty that was Lemont when the Des Plaines River meandered where River Road is now. But, as always, the idea of progress and the money that the Ship Canal was to bring to town seemed, at the time, an economic gift to Lemont.

Moving the river was quite a feat. The ends of the river were dammed and a large section of the dolomite floor was channeled while the original river flow was diverted. This feat is clear when you go down to the river or view it from the high-rise bridge. Normal rivers meander as they flow, making a snakelike pattern. The Des Plaines River, in our area, is straight and lacks the heavy plant growth usually seen on Midwestern waterways. What vegetation is there has taken 100 years to gain a foothold.

If it seems now that the past leaders of Lemont were hasty in agreeing to the diversion of the river, it must be understood that there was a fear of floods. The Des Plaines was never deep, but it was wide, and at flood times could reach a flow of 800,000 cubic feet per minute. It spread across most of the valley floor surrounding three small islands. There were some bridges, but most of the year they were not needed, as it was possible to wade or drive across the water. However, as we have seen even recently, there are times in the spring and fall when all the watersheds flow into our valley. What most Lemonters feared was any flood that would wash into the I & M Canal. Since the river ran where River Road is now, any big storm would cause rainwater to mix with the sewage-contaminated canal water and spread through town. Fear of disease from such floods encouraged village officials to support diverting the river. One other factor was added to the economic promise for Lemont: the building of the Ship Canal offered the Santa Fe Railroad the opportunity to enter town on an elevated track using spoil bank material. This would eliminate a dangerous ground level crossing.

As before with the I & M Canal, Lemont saw an influx of laborers brought by the project. Lemont's population grew from 5,000 in 1890 to nearly 10,000 in 1895. This growth produced a very exciting time for Lemont, creating powerful social and political upheavals.

ENDNOTES

[1]James Putnam, *The Illinois and Michigan Canal: A Study in Economic History* (Chicago: University of Chicago Press, 1918), p. 62.

[2]Bessie Pierce, *A History of Chicago* (New York: Knopf, 1940) vol. 2, p. 75.

[3]F. Garvin Davenport, "The Sanitary Revolution in Chicago," *Journal of the Illinois Historical Society* (Springfield, IL: Illinois State Historical Society Autumn 1973), p. 310.

[4]*Ibid.*, p. 311.

[5]*Ibid.*, p. 313.

[6]*Ibid.*, p. 313.

[7]Bessie Pierce, *A History of Chicago* (New York: Knopf, 1957) vol. 3, pp. 371-372.

[8]*Chicago Tribune*, September 4,1892.

[9]*Joliet News*, August 26, 1892.

[10]*Ibid.*, September 4, 1892.

[11]*Chicago Tribune*, September 4, 1892.

[12]The mayor of Chicago, Washburne, did not attend; neither did Governor Fifer who was in a heated campaign against John Altgeld.

[13]Louis Cain, "The Creation of Chicago's Sanitary District and the Construction of the Sanitary Ship Canal," *Chicago History* (Chicago: Chicago Historical Society, Summer 1979), p. 103.

[14]Davenport, "The Sanitary Revolution in Chicago," p. 314.

[15]Christie had a hobby of taking photos of the construction process. He also took some photos of Lemont that are in the Historical Society collection.

[16]Mason and Hoover were from Baltimore and would become part of the events surrounding the shooting and Lemont strike of 1893.

[17]Cain, "The Creation of Chicago's Sanitary District," p. 104.

[18]William Stead, *If Christ Came to Chicago.* (Evansville: Unigraphics, 1978), p. 140.

[19]*Chicago Daily News*, September 6, 1893.

[20]Perry R. Duis, "Prey for Work," *Chicago History* (Chicago: Chicago Historical Society, Spring 1989).

[21]*Chicago Daily News*, September 9, 1893.

[22]*The Lemont Observer*, December 21, 1896.

[23]Henry Norden, *The Good Old Days*, interview by his daughter-in-law, 1962, Lemont Historical Area Papers.

CHAPTER TWENTY

THE SECOND CANAL: LABOR UNREST

The Strike of 1893

During the first week in June, 1893, labor troubles began again. Over the years since the 1885 strike, quarry men had gained a wage of $1.75 a day. This was largely because of the development of steam power equipment for the quarries, a fact that resulted in the replacement of some men by machinery. Those who remained working could get wage concessions. The introduction of steam-driven power was a major adjustment for many workers. The machines were considered "fearsome things," especially the Burley Drill used for crushed stone. John Doolin recalled those days:

> Working the pump hose in Quarry One was a man killing job. The big boilers supplied steam for all the "kid" drills through a six-inch pipeline strung over the quarry landscape. The company bought the cheapest grade of coal and one had to shovel almost a carload of that "duff coal" into the fireboxes for each shift. The boxes had to be cleaned several times a day and that was "hell." Those masses of white hot cinders seared everything within a dozen feet of them. Pete Kane worked that job for a while before he quit for the "peaceful work" of town Constable.[1]

When the quarries opened in the spring of 1893, workers found that their wages had been summarily cut to $1.50 a day. Quarry owners had reduced their wage because workmen on the Sanitary Ship Canal project in Lemont were also earning $1.50 a day. Since the only local unskilled jobs available were at the canal, the railroad, and the quarries, the quarry owners and the canal contractors decided to set the same wage scale. This would prevent a worker from moving from one job to a higher paying job.[2]

The quarry men responded with a strike, their first since the Lemont Massacre of 1885. Their strike was supported by men in Lockport and Joliet. Workers felt that they could get their old wages back if they could convince canal contractors to raise their pay scale, so they began a campaign to persuade Ship Canal workers to join the strike. This activity consisted of marching by the canal construction, speech making, and talking to the workers when they came to Lemont to visit the pleasures of Smokey Row and Canal Street.[3]

Many men working on the Ship Canal were new to the area because some contractors came from other parts of the country. For example, Mason & Hoges, on section 11, west of Lemont, was from the South. Their employees were a mixed group of whites and blacks.

Workers loading stone from the Ship Canal project. (Photo courtesy of Lemont Historical Society)

Smith and Company on section 10 was from Baltimore[4] and had recruited most of its workers from jobless men in the tough slums of the eastern cities.

The campaign to get the Ship Canal workers to walk out made the contractors uneasy, especially when some of their workers began to quit, so they requested the aid of the Will County sheriff to send deputies to prevent quarry strikers from talking to their men. Six deputies were stationed at the Will County line sections on June 7. However, the contractors felt that this was not enough manpower, so they armed some of their own workers and had them stand guard.

Friday, June 9, Frank Blachowski, a Lemont barber and strike leader, decided that Joliet, Lockport, and Lemont strikers would meet in Romeo to discuss if the men should return to work.[5] Because of economic conditions, many quarry workers were in no position for a prolonged strike. As the strikers walked to Romeo on the I & M Canal towpath, word reached the canal contractors' camps that a mob of Lemonters was approaching. Panic spread through the camps. Armed guards were reinforced and men with loaded rifles stationed themselves along the Ship Canal spoil banks.[6]

One group of workers reached Romeo without incident. There they were rounded up and arrested by the Will County Sheriff's police and taken to jail in Joliet. Around noon a second group tried to walk to Romeo past the Smith and Company camp. They were stopped by armed canal workers at the Norton Bridge.[7] Afraid, the workers turned back to return to town when the guards and the sheriff's deputies began firing. The Lemont men were peaceful, but the armed guards ran after the workers shooting at them for a mile down the road. The strikers were unarmed and had to take cover behind a spoil bank of the I & M canal.

After the shooting stopped, the Lemonters scattered, dragging their dead and wounded with them. By the time they reached the Alton train station, word of the incident had spread and a crowd began to gather to protest the violence. Fearful of the angry Lemont crowd, Sheriff Gilbert of Cook County and the sheriffs of Will and DuPage Counties joined to send a telegram to the newly elected governor, John Peter Altgeld. It falsely reported that there was rioting in Lemont and several men had been killed. They said that they were not able to maintain order and protect life and property, and that a mob of 5,000 was planning violence. They requested that the governor send the militia to Lemont.[8]

After receiving the telegram from the sheriffs, Governor Altgeld obtained a second telegram sent from Mayor John McCarthy and Supervisor Weimer of Lemont. It was short, "If requisition is made to you for state troops for Lemont, act cautiously. Probably not as bad as it might be represented."[9]

Illinois Governor John Peter Altgeld.

John Altgeld did act cautiously. He sent a telegram back to the three sheriffs asking just how many deputies were on duty and if anyone other than strikers had been hurt or killed. He received only a partial answer. He was informed that there were 120 deputies on duty and order still could not be maintained. Believing that the request for the militia came from the sheriffs of Cook, Dupage, and Will Counties, when in fact it had only come from Sheriff Hennebry of Joliet, Altgeld did what he felt was necessary. He called out the militia at 11:30 p.m. on June 9, 1893. The Second and Third Regiments from Chicago and Joliet were assigned to Lemont.

Meanwhile, in town, the dead and wounded from the towpath shooting were counted. The dead included John Kluga, age 17, a young man from a well-known local family, who was not involved in the strike, but was working as a section hand on the relocation of the Santa Fe trackage through town. He had just taken his lunch break, almost a mile from the shooting, when shots were heard and he tumbled over fatally wounded with a bullet in his brain. Also killed was Gregor Kisha, age 35, married with one child. He had been in the United States for only two weeks and had arrived in Lemont only a week before; he had just found a job. The third death was that of Ignatus Asche, unknown to any local people. He had been wounded and fell into the I & M Canal. The armed guards kept firing so he could not be rescued. It was not clear if his death had been from drowning or hemorrhaging.

The wounded included Mike Blackrowski, Frank Blackrowski, Mike Byer, Nelson Colson, Dan Kismich, Larry Lovenduski, Tom Merika, Mike Michelor, John Peterson, Joe Schmish, Chrismund Schodish, Mike Skolski, John Wojtanowski, Anton Wesolowski, and J. Jaskulski.[10]

When the word came that the militia was again going to subject Lemont to military rule, the townspeople became angry. Strikers had done nothing but march to Romeo and had taken to the streets only after the shooting. The father of John Kluga went to the police station and swore out a warrant for Mr. Locker of McCormick Construction, who was said to have fired the first shot. There was talk of a lynching if Mr. Locker was brought to town. After this incident no one from the construction camps west of town dared enter Lemont. Those working for Smith & Company were especially marked for revenge.

In Springfield, sometime in the early morning hours after he had ordered the militia to Lemont, Altgeld began to review the events of the day. He had responded to the situation in a traditional anti-labor way. Altgeld, "up to this point, had acted no differently from Governors Oglesby or Fifer under similar circumstances. He had been asked to control a mob, i.e., strikers, and he had sent the militia."[11]

Ironically, Altgeld knew about Lemont and its labor troubles from legal briefs and related material that he had been reading to review the trial of the remaining Haymarket

Militia in Lemont, June 10, 1893. The photo is fuzzy because it was taken in hiding by J. Geiger. (Photo courtesy of Lemont Historical Society)

conspirators. One of his readings on the troubled labor movement was the coroner's inquest titled: *The Quarrymen's Strike, Lemont Illinois, The shooting of Andrew Stetler and others by the State Militia May 4, 1885.*[12] Altgeld realized that his actions were no better than those before him. He had taken the word of the police authorities without investigating the matter. He had campaigned as a Populist, a friend of the farmer and the working man and now he had sent the militia to a town that hated them deeply. If the militia were to be present in Lemont, he had to go there and seek the truth of the shooting and assure the people that the militia would not act without direct orders from him.[13]

Altgeld left Springfield on the first Chicago and Alton train to Lemont. The train arrived at 3:30 p.m., June 10. Accompanying him was Brand Whitlock, his clerk,[14] and Lt. D. Baker, an aide. The troops had already encamped in town, much to the dismay of Lemonters. The total force included 550 men of the Second Regiment under Colonel Judd. The other regiment of 300 soldiers was stationed at Romeo. Altgeld had sent orders ahead not to allow that force into town, for they were under the command of none other than Colonel Bennett, the same Bennett who had commanded the militia in the 1885 Lemont Massacre. To avoid any confusion in orders for the troops, Altgeld appointed General Orendorff as the top commander of both regiments. Orendorff was to report directly to Altgeld.

The governor was met at the station by a large crowd of townspeople. The body of Gregor Kisha was on display in front of the Alton Station, now the area known as Legion

Park, for Altgeld to view. The scene was a moving one, so much so, that Altgeld's clerk,
Whitlock would write years later:

> The soldiers were just going into camp on the level rocks by a
> bridge across the canal to the Des Plaines River. The bridge,
> according to military scientists, was, I believe, considered,
> for some mysterious reason, to be a strategic point. The pic-
> ture was one for the brush of Remington, those blue-clad
> soldiers — I stood and gazed affected by the fascination there
> always is in the superficial military spectacle; and then sud-
> denly we were aware that there was another more dramatic
> point of interest, where a group stood about the body of a
> workman who had been shot in the riots . . . He was a for-
> eigner, the clothes he wore were doubtless those he had when
> he passed under the Statue of Liberty, coming to this land, to
> Lemont, with what hopes of freedom in his breast no one can
> know. The wife who had come with him was on her knees
> rocking back and forth in grief, dumb to any words in a strange
> land whose tongue she could not speak or understand. The
> man had reached Lemont only a few days before and had been
> happy in the job he had been promised. And now, there he
> lay, shot dead. An old newspaper friend looked at me and said,
> in deep irony, — "the Land of the free and the Home of the
> Brave."[15]

Altgeld then spoke to the crowd in English and German and reassured them that the
troops would not act without his personal order, and that he had come to find the truth of
the issue. The governor's next action was to go directly to the site of the shooting. It was
not an easy walk, so he rode a Santa Fe handcar operated by Ross Henberger, a section
boss on the rail line. The sight of the governor of Illinois sitting on the front of a handcar
with his legs dangling over the side amazed the workers, and Lemonters responded with
cheers as he passed by.

Altgeld examined the site, climbed up and down the spoil banks, and interviewed witnesses. He spent a long time with the Santa Fe workers, since they were in the area when
the shooting occurred and had not been involved in the conflict. When Altgeld returned
to town, he went directly to Mayor McCarthy's office, where he continued his investigation. All those who wished to testify were allowed to speak. The governor promised to
protect those who gave evidence and he questioned each person carefully.

Meanwhile, the governor's labor aide, George Schilling, went around town gathering
information and possible witnesses. He found that the Lemonters wanted the militia withdrawn from town; Altgeld then had the units move and camp near section 8 of the Ship
Canal. After completing interviews with the workers and townspeople, Altgeld sent for the
canal contractors. The foremen came, but not the contractors. Angered by the contractors' attitude, Altgeld sent for the following information: *How many Sanitary Ship
contracts were let to out-of-state companies? How were the contracts obtained? Was
there open bidding? How many local workers had been hired?* [16]

The questions troubled the contractors. There had been rumors of scandals in the
contract awarding process, and perhaps the new governor could do little about contracts

already let, but they were not sure. Altgeld then released to the newspapers this statement:

> I received a message last night sent from Mr. Gilbert's office in Cook County, stating that there was rioting and a number of men had been killed. I telegraphed asking how many deputies had been sworn in and whether anyone had been hurt other than the strikers. The sheriff of Will County said he had 120 deputies. I received no response from Mr. Gilbert until today. Believing the telegram signed by three sheriffs stated the correct facts, I ordered out the militia. By 2 p.m. the troops were here. They responded promptly.
>
> I arrived at 3:30 p.m. and have been making inquiries. I learned from the deputy sheriff of Cook County that yesterday and up until the time the telegram was sent NO deputy sheriffs were on duty. Twelve special and eleven regular were sent today. I have talked to the men who were disinterested, especially the railroad men. They gave me a full account. The information I got tends to show that there had been NO rioting or serious disturbance for a week before yesterday and THE ONLY VIOLENCE YESTERDAY WAS BY A NUMBER OF MEN, COLORED AND WHITE, WHO HAD BEEN BROUGHT BY ONE OF THE CONTRACTORS FROM THE SOUTH AND WHO WERE ARMED BY HIM WITH RIFLES. They opened fire on some strikers who were walking along the towpath of the old canal and were not making any demonstration. THEY OPENED FIRE ON THEM AND CONTINUED FIRING WHILE CHASING THEM FOR ONE MILE . . . In short the only men who seemed to have violated the law yesterday and that in COLD BLOOD, were the men who had been armed by the contractors and who did the shooting.
>
> I have been told by some gentlemen claiming to give the other side of the story that the contractors claim some of the strikers fired over them. This is not in harmony with the statement of the railroad people and NO contractor claims that there was any necessity of following the men who were running and shooting them after they had run a mile. I expect to do further inquiries and will do what I think the law requires. If I conclude that the law requires me to keep the troops here I will do so; if not, they will be taken off.[17]

The governor was angry! The police authorities and newspapers had distorted the situation. He had been tricked to get the military involved to break the quarry strike. If he had not made the trip to get the facts for himself the situation could have led to a greater disaster. He ordered the contractors to attend the meeting the next day along with representatives of the canal and quarry workers. Altgeld could not tolerate inaction; he wanted the strike arbitrated. He had expressed his personal views on getting a job done in his famous address to the graduates of the University of Illinois that spring:

> Let me tell you, if you are sent to bring something, bring it, and not an explanation. If you agree to do something, do it; don't come back with an explanation. Explanations as to how you came to fail are not worth two cents a ton. Nobody wants or cares for them. The fact you met with an accident and got your legs broken, or your neck twisted and your head smashed, is not equal to the delivery of the goods.[18]

All parties responded; clearly the new governor was not one to be trifled with. The meeting was held in McCarthy's office. Attending were the following contractors on the Sanitary Ship Canal: J. Jackson, E. Smith, H.B. Hanger, H. Mason, O. O'Sullivan-Burke, and the attorney for the Sanitary Canal, Mr. Carter. Strikers at the meeting included Joseph Ratoski, Michael Novatiki, Joseph Wrobleski, and John Swanson. Swanson was the only man who worked on the ship canal. The others were quarry workers.

The contractors agreed to listen to the complaints of their canal workers, but wanted Altgeld and the authorities to make the quarry men stop harassing their employees. Wrobleski said that the contractors had discriminated against hiring local help and that by importing laborers who worked for a lower wage, like Southern whites and blacks, the canal contractors had encouraged quarry owners to lower their pay scale. Swanson stated that the wage of 15 cents an hour was not enough money; for example it cost him 25 cents just to cash his paycheck at the local bank.

Under advice from Altgeld, who believed that the only way to stop trouble was to have everyone working, it was agreed that the canal workers who joined the quarrymen's strike would return to work Monday morning. A special meeting was then planned to work out problems with the quarry owners, since they were not at this conference. Finally, it was agreed that the militia would remain only until all men had returned to work under agreeable conditions.

The Polish community of Stanistawowo[19] in Chicago also responded to this crisis by sending a committee, including a Polish physician, Dr. Janczewski, to view the situation. His report to the Chicago Poles was bleak. Dr. Janczewski spoke of the dire poverty of the Lemont workers and the lack of medical attention for the wounded. He reported that Juskulski and Wojtanowski needed surgery and the operation could not be done in Lemont. He had them transferred to a Chicago hospital at committee expense and then called for community help to raise money for the Lemont workers.[20]

A meeting then was held at the parish school to protest the "cold-blooded attack on the Polish workers." Called to order by A. Rudnicki and J. Arkuszewski, Lemont sent a delegation including S. Markiewicz, K. Buszkiewicz, P. Maday[21], J. Katzkan, W. Grosziewicz, and J. Biniak. They brought a letter from Reverend Candid Kozlowski of St. Cyril's Parish supporting the assembly, but explaining that his duties in Lemont during the crises kept him from attending. The following resolution was adopted:

> Since the contractors, especially Locker & Bibb, gathered together an armed band who attacked innocent Poles, we demand justice; and since Governor Altgeld, in his first public discussion of the case, has exposed the exact state of affairs; thereby earning the acknowledgement of all justice loving citizens for his noble support of the truth; we having met June 25 at the school of St. Stanislaus Kosta's protest publicly

against the criminal violence, lawlessness and wrong doing perpetrated on innocent workingmen on June 9 of this year. We will do all in our power to have the guilty punished. We also give thanks to the governor for his noble and impartial investigation of this matter. A committee will be formed to publish our protest in the American papers.[22]

A collection of over 150 dollars was subscribed for the victims. At the end of the meeting Reverend V. Barzynski took the occasion to stress that legal action must prevail over force. He encouraged the idea of national solidarity and a union of the Polish in America to meet such social problems. He and Peter Kiolbassa[23] shared a vision of a Union of Polish Workers, but such an organization never developed.

In Lemont, a mass meeting was held Monday night in the Music Hall, a large wooden structure half a block north of the Alton Station along the I & M Canal. Two men from each major ethnic group were elected to the working committee; for the Polish it was Peter Maday and Joseph Wrobleski; for the Germans it was Matthew Seva and John Weber; for the Irish it was Tim Sullivan and James Ashe; for the Swedish it was John Solstrom and Alex Bertin; and for the Danish it was Matthew Rasmussen and Chris Paulson. After a long discussion, the committee offered to return for 17½ cents an hour, or $1.75 for a ten-hour day. The quarry owners accepted the offer and by Tuesday everyone was back to work. No blacklisting was allowed.[24]

Tuesday evening the troops left town. The quarry workers learned about labor arbitration and progressive government from Governor Altgeld, and the governor learned from Lemonters. An immigrant himself, the strikers reminded him of his own struggles with poverty and language in a new country. He went back to Springfield with a new resolve to do what he said was "only right."[25] Re-reading the transcripts of labor documents including the coroner's report on *The Lemont Massacre of 1885*, Altgeld began to write his review of the Haymarket trial.

He would not offer clemency for the remaining "conspirators"; he would give them a full pardon. His concern was justice and not mercy. Altgeld would admit in his review that authorities can abuse power and that our legal system, though the best in the world, can make mistakes. Two weeks after the Lemont strike, Altgeld pardoned the three remaining Haymarket prisoners, Michael Schwab, Sam Fielden, and Oscar Neebe. What pain that simple act of justice caused him!

> Tell me was Altgeld elected, and what did he do?
> Did they bring his head on a platter to a dancer,
> Or did he triumph for the people?[26]

His actions enraged most of the public and press. Altgeld was attacked from coast to coast. He was called "John Pardon Altgeld," an anarchist and demagogue. He was called socialist, foreigner, apologist for murder, and fomenter of lawlessness. The *Chicago Tribune* wrote:

> He has apparently not one drop of true American blood in his
> veins. He does not reason like an American, not feel like one,
> and consequently does not behave like one.[27]

The furor never died down. His act of pardon was political death. Altgeld was defeated for governor in 1896. The rest of his ticket went down, including William Jennings Bryan for President, and the young labor lawyer, Clarence Darrow for Congress. Others rejected Altgeld, but in Lemont he remained the hero of the workers. He died on March 11, 1902, in Joliet, while giving a speech against the Boer War. On a March afternoon, Altgeld made his final trip through Lemont on the 3:55 p.m. train bound for Chicago.

The Illinois poet Vachel Lindsay wrote of Altgeld:

> Sleep softly, eagle forgotten, under the stone
> Time has a way with you there and the day has its own.
> Sleep on, o brave-hearted, o wise man that kindled the flame.
> To live in mankind is far more than to live in a name.

Altgeld did not end Lemont's labor troubles. However, he did show that problems could be worked out in a reasonable manner. But, change can be slow, as proved by one of the last quarry strikes in town. Four years after the strike of 1893, organized labor was in disarray, frustrated by such events as the Lemont Massacre of 1885, the Haymarket Riot of 1886, the Homestead Strike of 1892, the Lemont strike of 1893, Altgeld's pardon of the Haymarket conspirators with its attending public outcry, the Pullman Strike of 1894, and hundreds of other failed labor uprisings. These events discouraged the Lemont wage earner from joining any group that might endanger his job or safety.

> Every morning around seven o'clock,
> There are four and twenty men-a drilling on the rock.
> Drill ye tarriers-drill.
> Oh you work all day for the sugar in your "tay"
> And you stand by your drill and you blast all day.[28]

In Lemont, by 1897, it required extraordinary measures to get the workers to act in concert again. Work was hard to get that summer as Ship Canal construction was completed in the Lemont section. Also, the local economy was badly damaged when Norton's store on Stephen went bankrupt in the spring. Many quarry workers had deposited their earnings with the store, drawing out goods against their savings. The failure left them without any protection for the winter months when the quarries closed.

John Doolin, who worked at Western Stone, described the hard daily routine of the quarry worker in the late 1890s:

> We would start work at four in the morning and work until nine at night. I left home at 3:30 a.m. Mom would be up and have coffee and a snack for me. About 8:00 a.m. my brother would bring breakfast to me in a tin dinner bucket. At noon he would show up again with the bucket [and] again about six. We worked 17 hours each day except Sunday when it was from 6:00 a.m. to 6:00 p.m. I recall, too, we worked every day until the 4th of July. The bosses wanted us to work that day too, but Pat Kane[29] said, "No sir Johnnie, we don't work on the fourth." And we didn't either. Working in the stone quarries was hot. Pat Kane sweated so hard that you could see a streak of salt along side his suspenders from his shoulders to his waist. I used to sweat "vinegar." Strange the little things that make such a lasting impression.[30]

The dissatisfaction started with small groups over the nightly beer in the saloons. It spread from there to the streets and churches. The men wanted a wage of $1.50, the old wage of 1885. They had started the season getting only $1.15, a long way from the pay settlement of $1.75 achieved for them by Altgeld. But Altgeld was gone, and the realities of the economy in Lemont had forced the men to accept $1.25 a day.

The *Lemont Observer* wrote that the $1.25 a day was the first money that many workers had seen since autumn. What was even worse was that there was little prospect for more jobs and at least 1,000 men in town were idle.[31]

As July ended, some unspoken determination began to join the workers into a unit — not a formal labor union, but a union of Lemont workers — Poles, Irish, Italians, Bohemians, Swedes, Germans, and others. On August 2, they dropped their drills, picks, and wheelbarrows and walked out, demanding $1.50 a day. It would be hard to imagine the apprehension in town that day. After all, the history of labor strikes in Lemont often led to violence against the workers. So it was a pleasant surprise when the workers found that the management of Western Stone agreed to meet with their representatives. The meeting lasted all day and into the evening. Then around nine p.m. there was yelling and screaming along Main Street. Fearful men grabbed weapons and rushed outside only to find John Sullivan screaming at the top of his lungs:

> Hear ye, Hear ye! We all go to work in the morning. The quarry
> owners recognize our right to bargain for wages. We will get
> $1.50 a day.[32]

What a glorious night that was with a victory so easy and painlessly won. It was true; the working man could gain his rights with peaceful action and reason. One week later Western Stone began paying $1.50 a day and began discharging men. Twenty were pink-slipped in the first week[33] and others followed all fall until the quarries were shut for the winter.

View of Lemont from State Street and the I & M Canal, circa 1898. (Photo courtesy of Lemont Historical Society)

On Labor Day, then a new national holiday, the *Observer* wondered, "will the quarries observe it as they usually do — by working?" The paper held out some hope for economic change with a rumor that there was to be a privately owned quarry opening in the spring. It reported that many Lemonters felt that the community's economic woes started when the private companies sold out to the Western Stone monopoly.

Next spring when the quarries were opened, the pay scale was one dollar a day and none of the vocal leaders of the strike could find work in the quarries. They had been blacklisted. The *Lemont Observer* said it all. "Here in 1898 the Lemont dogs wear tags — so do the men who work in the quarries." The quarry worker had become a victim of change. First, much of the old hand work was now done by machine; and, secondly, Lemont Stone was no longer the popular building material it had been for most of the 19th Century. As early as 1873, the use of concrete blocks, known as artificial stone, was replacing dolomite because its cost was one-fourth that of cut limestone.[34] The transition was so rapid that while in 1890 one-half of Illinois stone production was for cut stone, by 1910, 75 percent of Illinois stone was sold as crushed stone, mainly for concrete and road and rail beds.

The industry that supported Lemont for so many years has disappeared, but reminders of that stone trade are all around us, not only in the labor struggles, but in the beautiful buildings made of our stone; in the water-filled quarries that dot the landscape; and, most of all, in the children, grandchildren, and great-grandchildren of the people who worked those quarries and laid the stone.

ENDNOTES

[1]Nancy Thornton, ed., "Quarry Work Recalled in the Doolin Family," *Cornerstone Newsletter* (Lemont: Lemont Area Historical Society, August-September 1988),pp. 2-4.

[2]*Chicago Tribune*, June 10, 1893.

[3]*Ibid*.

[4]*Chicago Tribune*, June 11, 1893.

[5]It is interesting that a few strike leaders were not quarry or canal workers. This could be for a number of reasons. It might represent political activists committed to labor rights, or it could be that those men in the community who were bilingual were asked to represent their countrymen not fluent in English.

[6]*Chicago Tribune*, June 14, 1893.

[7]A temporary bridge across the I & M Canal west of town.

[8]*Chicago Tribune*, June 11, 1893.

[9]*Chicago Daily News*, June 13, 1893.

[10]Name spellings in these reports are unreliable. Reporters seldom took care to find the correct names and in some cases the victims gave false names to avoid being blacklisted.

[11]Harry Barnard, *Eagle Forgotten* (New Jersey: Lyle Stuart, 1973), p. 180.

[12]*Ibid.*, p. 209.

[13]*Ibid.*, p. 180.

[14]Whitlock would later become an author, politician, and ambassador. He also would serve as mayor of Toledo, Ohio.

[15]Brand Whitlock, *Forty Years of It* (New York: Appleton Century Co., 1914), p. 924.

[16]*Chicago Tribune*, June 11, 1893.

[17]*Ibid.*

[18]Ray Ginger, *Altgeld's America* (New York: New Viewpoints, 1973), p. 1. The address was delivered on June 7, 1893, only two days before the Lemont Strike.

[19]*Stanistawowo* means the village of St. Stanislus, a name the Polish pioneers of Chicago gave their first parish.

[20]*Dziewnik Chicagoski*, June 20, 1893.

[21]His name is also written as "Madaj" in our local records.

[22]*Dziewnik Chicagoski*, June 26, 1893.

[23]His second wife, after the death of his first, was the widow of the owner of Lemont's Otzenburger Hall.

[24]N.J. Brown owned the hall and he tried to collect rental from the workers after the strike was over.

[25]Barnard, *Eagle Forgotten*, p. 214.

[26]E.L. Masters.

[27]*Chicago Tribune*, June 27, 1893. This editorial shows a strong anti-immigrant attitude.

[28]Old labor song. A tarrier is one who delays or is slow working.

[29]Peter Kane's father.

[30]Thornton, "Quarry Work Recalled," pp. 2-4.

[31]*Lemont Observer*, May 8, 1897.

[32]*Ibid*, August 5, 1897.

[33]*Ibid*, August 12, 1897.

[34]Carl Condit, *The Chicago School of Architecture: Commercial Building 1875-1925* (Chicago: University of Chicago, 1964), pp. 28-29.

BUSINESSES IN LEMONT IN 1891*

Mrs. A. Burghardt: *American House*

Anderson, Otto: *Laundry*

Bartz, Nicholas: *Main Street Pharmacy*

Beermann, Frederick: *Barber*

Bethke, M.: *Saloon*

Bittles, James: *Dairyman*

Blanchowski, Frank: *Barber*

Bodenschatz, John G.: *Drugs, Books, Medicines, Postmaster*

Bodenschatz, Henry: *Cigar Manufacturer*

Boe, Christian: *Saloon*

Bourg, John: *Meats*

Boyer, Wladyslaw: *Confectioner*

Brackin, Patrick: *Superintendent, Illinois Stone Co.*

Brass, O.H.: *Dentist*

Brown, N.J.: *Capitalist*

Brown, William S.: *Lawyer*

Buerfeind, Rev. B.: *German Lutheran Church*

Buszkiewicz, Kasmir: *Saloon*

Christopherson, Nels: *Jeweler*

Claussen, Claus: *Hunter's Home Saloon*

Counter, Matt: *Carpenter*

Cummings, John: *Blacksmith*

Derby, Sylvester: *President, Retail Lumber Dealers of America; Dealer in Lumber, Construction Supplies, and Coal*

Dillman, Jacob: *Barber*

Egloff, Mrs. Margaret: *Milliner*

Engel, Andrew: *Grocer*

Eulert, Nicholas: *Hardware*

Farnsworth, Aaron: *Lumber*

Faser, Frank: *Hunter's Home Saloon*

Fernau, Philip: *Basketmaker*

Fiddyment, Walter: *Baker*

Fischbach, Peter: *Liquor and Cigar Dealer*

Fitzpatrick, J.A.: *Physician*

Forkel, Theodore: *Livery Stable, Carriage Maker, Agriculture Implements*

Forkel, Theo.: *Hardware*

Freed, James: *Chicago & Alton Agent*

Frelichowski, Frank: *Express Agent*

Frelichowski, Joseph: *General Store*

Frelichowski, Mrs. J.: *Saloon*

Friedley, Theodore F.: *Hardware*

Gerharz, Joseph: *Furniture and Undertaking, Chief of Fire Dept.*

Gregory, John J.: *Librarian of Union Library*

Grethan, Mrs. Hubert: *Grocer*

Hardlannert, George: *Barber*

Hassel, Fred: *Manufacturer and Dealer in Harness, Whips, Collars and Horse Furnishings*

A.G. Hawley: *Commercial Advertiser*

Helbig, Jacob: *Carpenter*

Helirich, Adam: *Blacksmith*

Hennebry, James: *Dealer in Fresh and Smoked Meats, Mayor of Lemont*

Hettinger, Miss Anna: *Milliner*

Hettinger, Chris: *General Store* (with John Mlodzik)

Hettinger, George: *Dray*

Hiss, Andrew: *Saloon*

Hoffman, Dr. E.C.: *Dental Surgeon*

Huston, Thomas: *Justice of the Peace, Collections, Real Estate*

T.J. Huston, Pres., C.G. Barth, Cashier: *Lemont State Bank (Capital $25,000)*

Ingraham, Archibald: *Blacksmith*

Herman Welk: *Agent, Interstate Building and Loan*

Johnson, Charles: *Shoemaker*

Kacbon, Joseph: *Shoemaker*

Kaminsky, Frank: *Tailor*

Keith, Andrew: *Tailor*

Kettering, Harris W.: *Blacksmith*

Klein & Wold: *Peter Klein and Edward Wold, Bottlers*

Konrad, Barthel: *Shoemaker*

Kozlowski, Rev. Kandyd: *SS. Cyril's & Methodius*

Lemont Valley Stone Quarries

Lindenau, Frederick: *Meat Market*

Lindgren, Oliver: *Brick Manufacturer*

Lindholm, Alfred: *Liquor and Cigar Dealer*

Losey, George: *Hotel and Saloon*

Lotscher, Joseph: *Baker*

Lutz, Charles: *Blacksmith*

McCarthy, John W.: *Lawyer*

Maday, Peter: *Dry Goods, Hats, Shoes, Groceries, Books & Pictures, Hardware, Steamship Passenger Agent*

Maguire, Edward: *Blacksmith*

Mathy, Fred: *Blacksmith*

Markiewicz, Peter: *Butcher, Dealer in Meats*

Markiewicz, Stanislaus: *Saloon*

Martin, Hylon: *General Store*

Martin, Henry: *General Store (with Father Listed above)*

Meyer, Jacob: *Manager, Fred Shering Brewing Company*

Mirkes, Theodore: *Shoemaker*

Mlodzik, John: *General Store*

Moritz, Charles: *General Store*

Mueller, Jacob: *Blacksmith*

Murphy, Dennis: *Clothing*

Nelson, Peter A.: *General Store*

New, Michael: *Chief of Police*

New, Mrs. Theresa: *Marble City House*

Norton, Herbert S.: *Dry Goods, Shoes, Groceries, Steamship Agent*

Norton, Samuel W.: *Banker*

Nylund, Victor: *Jeweler*

Oldfield, Jessie: *Livestock (Four Miles North)*

Ostenburger, Joseph: *Saloon*

O'Neill, Wm.: *Supt. Public Works*

Peiffer, Peter: *Drugs, Agriculture Implements, Insurance*

Peterson, Andrew: *Fresh and Salt Meats*

Piekarski, Simon: *Saloon*

Pinter, Nicholas: *General Store*

Rachyskowski, Stanislaus: *Shoemaker*

Ries, Moses: *Clothing*

Robbins, S. Volney: *School Principal*

Roberts, Mrs. Susan A.: *Physician*

St. Alphonsus School: *Sisters of St. Agnes*

SS. Cyril's & Methodius: *Sisters of St.Francis*

St. James Academy: *Dominican Sisters*

Sauber, Herbert: *Saloon*

Schmelzer, Mrs. Henry: *Boots and Shoes*

Schmitt, Mrs. Philip: *Saloon*

Schumers, Miss Regina: *Milliner*

Seiler, Joseph: *Farmers Home Saloon*

Seiler, John: *Farmers Home Saloon*

Sheuy, Miss Matilda: *Agent for Singer Sewing Machines*

Simmons, Fredrick: *Justice of the Peace*

Sixt, Rev. Francis: *German Catholic*

Skarin, John A.: *Grocer*

Skelly, Daniel: *Justice of the Peace*

Slavin, Wm.: *Grocer*

Spence, Supt. S.B.: *Western Stone Company:*

Tedens, J.H.: *Dry Goods, Clothing, Shoes, Flour & Feed, Coal & Lumber, Harnesses*

Thormahlen, John: *Partner with Tedens*

Theis, Michael: *General Store*

Thorpe, James: *Physician*

Valentien, Lorenz: *Barber*

Wagner, John B.: *Livery*

Wagner, Martin: *Livery (with brother listed above)*

Warger, Joseph: *Dealer in Liquor and Cigars*

Weimer, Andrew: *Saloon*

Weimer, George: *City Clerk and Notary Public*

Welk, Herman: *Lawyer, Justice of the Peace, Insurance, Real Estate, and Collections*

Wilder, Joseph: *Painter*

Wintlin, George: *Carpenter*

Woods, John: *General Store*

*The above do not represent all businesses in Lemont at the time. This list came from a professional directory, and persons and establishments listed probably paid a fee to be included. In such a case there are those who chose not to be listed.

CHAPTER TWENTY-ONE

THE SECOND CANAL: SOCIAL CHANGES

Smokey Row Days: 1893-1897

The Ship Canal construction brought more than labor problems to Lemont. It also brought social and moral change that divided the town and, as usual, became a political issue. The presence of many transient workers created a special labor pool similar to the Lemont I & M Canal community of 44 years before. It was mainly a rough, worldly group that spent their money in saloons. They did not create the red light district in Lemont, because there already was a Smokey Row[1] in Lemont, a strip that offered gambling, liquor, drugs, and women as early as the 1860s. Isolated as a small string of dives located along the northeast side of the I & M Canal, it was cut off from the main business section of town, so it remained largely "invisible" to the "honest" citizens of Lemont.

These dives existed mainly for the barge, quarry, and railroad men who were not a part of the community and was similar to a seaport city red light district.[2] From what few reports we do have, it was a tough, violent place. Most of the saloons were of the type known as a "bucket of blood." A bucket of blood is frequented by men who cannot, or will not, control their drinking. While most bartenders will cut off drinks to a patron who is visibly drunk, a bartender in a bucket of blood establishment will continue to serve as long as the customer will pay. Naturally, the atmosphere in such a place is charged, and patrons seldom know each other. People often go to such taverns just to fight or to see fights — it is an attraction to the violent side of humanity.

Murders in this small Smokey Row were common, but were seldom investigated since the operation was outside any meaningful legal control. There was no village police force until 1873, when the village was incorporated, and the elected township marshals had no desire to go into Smokey Row alone. The sin strip received little open publicity but was well known along the canal. Each year its character would change with the economic conditions and the volume of barge traffic. Nevertheless, through good or bad times, some liquor and gambling establishments remained from the 1860s through the 1880s.

When the construction of the Ship Canal began in 1892 with a huge labor force stationed in the area, it was natural that these taverns and saloons would expand. By 1895, it was estimated that well over 100 of these dives were in operation. The original dives of Smokey Row remained where they were and were thought of as "tame" compared to the new ones that opened on North Stephen's Street, River Road, the flats,[3] Main Street, and Canal Street. The expanded district also took on the name Smokey Row and, by virtue of its size and volume of business, it soon came to the attention of the Joliet and Chicago papers. The *Joliet News* reported the following:

The scenes and orgies, the crimes and revelries around Sag Bridge and Lemont would disgrace even frontier settlements. The saloons and dives are doing an immense business and probably 60 percent of the $600,000 paid each month goes into their hands. All along the channel are saloons which sell a brand of firewater called "Canal Tanglefoot." This drink tastes like a compound of blue vitriol and gunpowder; one sip of this concoction will either send a man on the warpath or render him unconscious. Outside the regular population of 7,000 the noisy places on Smokey Row have attractions for several thousand men who either work on the canal or make a living on those who do. Most of the good folk of the town lock their doors at night and pull the covers over their heads. Some few rake in the money.[4]

The places were as varied as men's tastes. *The Standard Club* had a three-piece band in a back room. To get to the room you had to pass through a huge barroom with a sawdust covered floor. Behind the bar sat a tough bouncer ready to toss out anyone who misbehaved. The charge for the entertainment was ten cents. As you entered you were greeted by a "lady" who shouted, "Beer, whiskey, and cigars, give me your order, this ain't no free joint."[5]

Many of the new dives that developed on Smokey Row were extensions of saloons from the Chicago Levee — Chicago's sin strip.[6] Chicago's strip had been booming with the visitors to the Columbian Exposition, but business fell off after the fair closed in the fall of 1893. This fact, coupled with an economic depression, had cut into the "resort" business, as it was known. Lemont, because of the canal construction, was one of the few areas in Chicagoland enjoying economic good times, so it was natural that many of the Chicago resorts would establish franchises on Lemont's Smokey Row. Newspapers from outside town eagerly reported that:

Lemont was receiving advertising of the undesirable kind, such as the Bowery of New York and the Levee of Chicago, and it is Lemont's Mayor McCarthy who is responsible for the affairs of the town.[7]

It is hard to list all the dives on Smokey Row during its height, many had so little class they were not even named. Adding to our lack of knowledge is the fact that it is not the kind of history a community records with great pride. However, some better-known establishments included *The Standard Club*, with a bar and dancing along with nude entertainment; *The Palace Saloon*, bar and gambling; *The King of Hearts*, an all black establishment for the workers who were African-American;[8] *Ted Boyle's Place*, featuring all nude dancing; *The Big Casino*, owned by Fred Lawler, whose wife shot and killed one of his "girls" in a fit of jealousy;[9] *The American House*, a brothel;[10] *The Big Four Palace*, offering gambling, liquor, women, and dancing; *Farmers Exchange*, liquor and women; *Jawoski's Place*, liquor, gambling, and women; *Mazzie's Place*, liquor and women; *Pete Shea's*, liquor and women; *Mrs. Priestly's Place*, a brothel; *The Silver Dollar*, owned by another Boyle, this one Henry; and *The Little Casino*, offering liquor and women.

Not all of the resorts were low class: for example, *Peterson's Park* was different; it was located away from Smokey Row on the outskirts of Lemont at the corner of Warner and

Logan. A summer open air gambling and drinking retreat, it was famous along the Alton Line and popular with townspeople. There young people could dance under the stars, or stroll the beautiful grounds covered with trees along cool, shaded ravines.

Canal paydays were the worst times for the town and the workers. The "female companions" of the resorts were extremely greedy. They would keep watch on payday and when the tops of the workers heads could be seen coming across the limestone flats they would rush out in all manner of dress and undress to entice workers to spend their money. This created fights as last week's girl sought some new sucker. The ordinary Lemonter certainly could not have been indifferent to having this display in the town's front yard.

We know little of the women who worked on Smokey Row. Their names changed as frequently as their clothes. Of the few we know, one favorite was a middle-aged woman who called herself Sarah Burnhardt. Arrested in one of the infrequent raids, she had a mob of over 100 men rush eagerly to jail to post her bond. Hattie Briggs also operated a place. Hattie was over six feet tall and weighed 250 pounds. The newspapers described her as, "black as a stick of licorice and as ugly as anyone could imagine." Hattie always wore a long red coat — it was her trademark.[11] Hattie had started with two places in Chicago, notorious dens that specialized in stealing from the customers. The cost of a prostitute in her place was only 25 cents, but few clients escaped without being robbed. There was no scheme involved in the robberies; Hattie just grabbed her victim, slammed him against the wall and threw him out. However, she managed to stay out of trouble by paying the officials for protection.

This worked until Hattie took up with William Smith. She set Smith up in the saloon part of her business and he soon became big-headed, walking around in colorful clothing and jewelry and giving orders to everyone. Hattie was proud of Smith and encouraged him. She claimed to be making so much money that she would buy all the saloons and brothels on the Levee and elect Smith as the mayor and abolish the police force.

Chicago officials finally tired of Hattie and began to raid her places day and night in a campaign to close her down. It worked, and within ten days of the first raid, Hattie packed up and headed to

Sanitary Ship Canal station along the canal. Note the display of weapons. (Photo courtesy of Lemont Historical Society)

Smokey Row in Lemont. There she set up another successful business robbing her clients. Hattie sent back word that there was money to be made in our town, and many of her friends on the Levee came to join her.[12] As a result, rents skyrocketed for stores and ramshackle buildings in downtown Lemont and several of our own upstanding citizens eagerly collected rents on the dives.

As the new and improved Smokey Row grew in notoriety, more people flocked to its dens. By early 1894, every night along the strip was wild and rough, with weekends a

Mayor John McCarthy (left) and J. Franklin Clancy (right). (Illustrations courtesy of the Chicago Tribune)

special nightmare. Murders and assaults averaged two a week and Lemont's small police force, along with the special Sanitary Canal police, were hard pressed to maintain order. Meanwhile, the owners of the dives were delighted with Lemont. Here they had an economic windfall. The canal payroll amounted to 600,000 dollars a month, and much of that money was spent on Smokey Row.

Ben Scott, who owned the *Little Casino*, a dive just over the Santa Fe tracks, was pleased when he told a reporter, "I was asleep in Coal City for over a year. This is the best location on the grandest street in America. Do you see that long row of houses? Every one is a bawdy house."[13]

As bad as it was, the crime and sin remained mostly within its own area and did not directly affect the life of the ordinary Lemonter. What the strip did do was contribute money to the village, money in terms of jobs, services, rentals, and taxes. License fees on Smokey Row establishments were collected as early as 1888, when the first dens contributed 10,000 dollars a year to the village. By 1894, the collection amounted to 500,000 dollars a year, a tremendous sum in those days. Village trustees found themselves torn between the money the dives brought into town and the lawlessness their presence caused. Our present Village Hall, better water, sewer and lighting systems, and the annex to Old Central School were built with Smokey Row monies.

Mayor John McCarthy was a pragmatic man. The saloons and dives provided revenue, and if Lemont did not tolerate the strip, another community would. He felt that when the Lemont portion of the canal was finished most of the saloons would close and move on to follow the construction. McCarthy loved the "sporting crowd." He liked to identify with the big spenders and the political powers of Chicago. He smoked strong, black cigars, had an occasional drink, and loved boxing — so much that he allowed illegal boxing matches in the saloons.

There probably never would have been any organized outcry against Smokey Row if it were not for Reverend J. Franklin Clancy. Reverend Clancy was assigned to the Lemont

Methodist Church in 1894.[14] When he arrived, he found a beautiful simple stone church and a deeply devoted, earnest congregation. The only flaw in this spiritual paradise was that from his quiet church he could look down the hill and see the taverns, Canal Street, and Smokey Row.

Clancy believed that the presence of the sin strip was affecting his congregation and the town. Many of his young people did not attend Sunday school or services as there were far more exciting pleasures down on the strip. Gambling and drinking was creating unhappy families and broken homes, since the strip attracted Lemonters as well as construction workers. Crime was rampant along the street and the local government did little to control it.

It was then that Reverend Clancy decided to campaign against Smokey Row. He took his plan of action from William Stead, an Englishman who had traveled to Chicago to visit the 1893 World's Fair. Stead had viewed Chicago's dives and saloons, assessing the moral climate of the city and published a book, *If Christ Came to Chicago*.[15] The book sold thousands of copies[16] and led to the formation of the Chicago Civic Federation. This federation was formed from leaders in business, religion, education, and labor, and it directed action toward closing down Chicago's Levee.

Patterning themselves after Chicago, a group of Lemonters formed their own Civic Federation to support Dr. Clancy. The first board of directors included S.W. Norton and J. Derby, both members of Clancy's congregation, and Patrick Brackin, superintendent of the Illinois Stone Company. Dr. Clancy began his assault with a series of temperance and prayer meetings in the stone church to find a moral direction for action. His next step was to take his prayer meetings down to the "sinners" on Smokey Row. There every Sunday afternoon at three p.m., in front of Tedens Store at 102-106 Stephen Street, he prayed for the souls of those he felt were lost and handed out small Bibles. He then made a tour of the saloons, stopping to kneel in prayer before the larger establishments. He always attracted a good crowd since he was a fine speaker, but few of the customers changed their ways. Many came to heckle him, as it was considered great sport.[17]

Meanwhile, Lemont Civic Federation members attended village board meetings demanding that village ordinances concerning saloon hours and health conditions be enforced. They reported violations to the local authorities, but little was done in response. Dr. Clancy and the Civic Federation began to feel they were losing the fight until word of their activities reached the editor of the *Cook County News,* and then to the Chicago papers. Reporters converged on Lemont. If ever there had been a chance for both sides to compromise, it was soon destroyed by a sensation-seeking media.

The moral fight divided along political lines. Modern historians who study this period point to political affiliations based on a moral-religious point of view. Those raised in a formal, highly-structured church tended to hold that morality could not be enforced with secular laws. Those raised in a less formal church, who held a more personal view of God, felt that morality could and should be enforced by laws. This pattern of beliefs still holds true today, except for a few issues advocated by direction of a formal church hierarchy.[18]

The liberal Democratic newspapers pictured Clancy as a fanatic temperance crusader and McCarthy as a practical politician — a friend of the working man and Lemont. The conservative Republican papers, mainly the *Chicago Tribune*, described Clancy as an idealistic young man and McCarthy as an evil corrupt official. This publicity, naturally, divided the town, as Lemonters felt it necessary to take sides.

The Civic Federation had two small victories during the early summer of 1894. One was an amateur raid on the *Big Casino* staged by federation members. Partly fascinated by sin and partly angered by its presence, the men of the Civic Federation eagerly participated. However, the ladies of the *Big Casino* had been forewarned and fled down the I & M Canal to the woods on the Brown property. The other small victory was picketing *Petersen's Park* and thereby cutting into his business.[19] Petersen complained about the picketing to a Joliet reporter:

> I have 50 percent less business. My business is not what it ought to be on account of that d---- preacher. He hurt my business and I propose to get even with him. I want you to understand I run a decent park and that turkey-legged editor of *The Cook County News* has no business to interfere. Clancy is no man at all. He runs down my park and injures my business when it is none of his business. I help keep up the city's expense more than any other man in town.[20]

As Reverend Clancy and the Civic Federation continued their pressure the community became polarized over the issue — it became political. What began as a crusade against sin and crime was translated, with the aid of the Chicago and Joliet newspapers, along party lines. In the late summer of 1894, the Civic Federation began a new campaign to enforce the Sunday closing laws on the village books. This action meant that those saloons that only served Lemonters would also have to close on Sundays. Since many Lemonters, especially the quarry workers and unskilled laborers, worked six days a week, Sunday was the only day left for socializing. Some townspeople, especially those of German heritage, felt the Sunday closing laws were directed against the immigrant groups in town who conducted their social life in family saloons. To some, the crusade against Smokey Row was a veiled crusade directed by the Anglo-Saxon Protestant "Singer Hill" crowd against the newcomers and their personal habits. It did not help matters when temperance minded N.J. Brown told the papers that "Lemont is the breathing place of Hell."[21] This attitude further divided the town.

Clancy was a man of great faith and certainty in his role and, therefore, was unable to understand the subtle social class factions at work in Lemont. All he could see was sin and evil occurring right in Lemont's own front yard.

The lack of any great overthrow of evil in the summer and fall of 1894 discouraged some Federation members and they dropped out of the activity. Meanwhile, some of Clancy's congregation began to put pressure on him to avoid town politics and to stick to church affairs like Sunday preaching, visiting the sick, and the Sunday school. However, undaunted and sure of his calling, Clancy continued his mission.

> And the whole congregation of the children of Israel assembled
> together at Shiloh and set up the tent of meeting there.
> *(Joshua 18:1)*

The publicity from the *Chicago Tribune* and the Joliet papers made Dr. Clancy the honored speaker at the New Lennox Methodist Camp meeting in the summer of 1895. There in the green woods of New Lennox he told the faithful about the corruption in our town:

> Alcohol is king in Lemont. It is the destroyer of our wealth,
> our city, our government, our community, and our boys and
> girls. It elected Mayor "The Whole Thing" McCarthy by fraud

and robbery, for I know he stole votes to make his majority.
You should see our book of ordinances. It is fine . . . no finer
in any city. They govern the saloons and dives. Do you know
that not one of the 100 saloons ever obeyed the ordinances
under the McCarthy administration? The Sunday closing law
is not enforced because of the profit. The wife of one saloon
keeper said her husband made $700 from one Saturday night
to Sunday night. Most of that $700 came from poor people.[22]

To the eager crowd Clancy told of corrupt money brought in by the saloons and dives.
He told of young women being degraded by sex and alcohol. He told of officials purchased
by sin money. He told of the village board that was indifferent to his efforts at reform:

I and the Civic Federation had, many times, fulfilled the law
in every way in regard to the issuing of warrants but we cannot put them through. The village police will do nothing and
the county sheriff claims he is too busy. On July 4, I saw a
father at the bedside of his dying wife. She got him to promise to quit drinking. A few weeks later I saw him, a little girl
on each side trying to hold him up. They said, "Come home
Papa." He would not. He sent them down the road crying. He
went to the saloon, and that saloon has destroyed that home,
killed that wife, ruined that man, and sent those children down
a long road. The saloon has destroyed government, home, and
society — and man itself — and is doing so today in Lemont.[23]

The camp meeting received wide publicity, and because of it, the *Tribune* again renewed interest in the McCarthy-Clancy feud. Eager for more circulation, the newspaper
offered financial and legal help for Lemont's Civic Federation. It was accepted. Vice and
sin make good reading. Infused with new support, the Civic Federation began making
plans while Reverend Clancy announced to the papers:

I am confident that a great change will soon take place here
and we will have one of the biggest revivals ever heard of. I
believe it is coming. I am not going to stop until it does come.
The walls of Jericho[24] must come down and we will march in
and take the city with Christ as our captain.

However, as the weeks passed with enthusiastic picketing and calls to reform, nothing
stopped the activity on Smokey Row. The village board did respond to the issue raised at
meetings by appointing McCarthy and two other board members to "examine the moral
condition of the village and to stamp out lawlessness,"[25] not the type of response the
reformers wanted. It was then that the Civic Federation, with the help of the Republican
Chicago Tribune, decided to entrap Mayor McCarthy. The editorial board of the paper
had a strong dislike for McCarthy, who had formed a strong alliance with Chicago Democrats. His association was so powerful that Lemont was considered a ward of Chicago
when it came to turning out Democratic votes and was, jokingly, called the 51st Ward of
Chicago. Added to that, McCarthy had friendships with Mike McDonald, the Democratic
patronage dispenser for the party, and Edwin Walker, who held construction contracts
under Democratic administrations for the city and county.

With the pivotal 1896 election coming, the paper could hardly resist an attempt to impugn McCarthy, and by association, the Democrats. So, a private detective, Robert Carter, was hired to report on the happenings on Smokey Row. He confirmed what Clancy and the Civic Federation had already told the editorial board:

> It is a spot of vilest debauchery and brazen Prostitution. Vice, well protected and paid for runs riot, and the town fattens on the proceeds . . . The "women" of the town boast of McCarthy's favors and protection. To be the mayor's friend is a distinction among the circles of vice.[26]

The detective's report convinced the *Tribune* to continue its investigative journalism. A reporter was sent with Carter to Lemont to sound McCarthy out about the possibility of opening a gambling wheel in one of the saloons. The two met with the mayor in his upstairs office in the village hall on August 27. The reporter, Stuart Wade, was introduced as a gambler by the name of James McDonnell. They reported their version of the conversation to the paper:

> Detective Carter introduced the reporter: "This is the friend I spoke of before, McDonnell of Chicago."
>
> "Pleased to meet you, Mr. Mayor." Wade and McCarthy shook hands.
>
> "You are the man, then who wants to open a game here?" asked McCarthy.
>
> "Yes, I think there is a possible chance for a little game. Things are quiet in Chicago."
>
> "I reckon things will open up in Chicago after a while," said McCarthy. "Were you running in Hopkins'[27] time? How much did you have to give them? John P. knew how to run things. He must have made a pile. Have you settled on any place you think you could run quietly?"
>
> "Yes," said Carter,"we think a game might go in the back of *Pete Shea's* saloon."

The mayor, according to the pair, then saw a serious objection:

> "I don't think you would last a week in Shea's place without being pulled. I'd hate to see your outfit broken up."
>
> "Do you know of any better place mayor?"
>
> "Yes, I do and I'll tell you of it. You see I hate to see your outfit smashed. I have saved several in times gone by. I can't bear to see good stuff destroyed. I had to work like h--- to save a fine double roulette wheel a while ago."
>
> "I want to be frank with you, Mr. Mayor," said the reporter. "We won't make any trouble for you for we know your position is a difficult one. Now if we can only get your protection and fix it with the police station so we can run it. How many policemen have you got, mayor? Shall we take care of them, or shall we just be good fellows to them?"

"Oh, I can't have you spoil my three policemen," replied McCarthy. "If you get 'playing' with them, I won't be able to control them. You can be good fellows to them. That is all that is necessary if everything is — all right."[28]

According to the reporter and the detective, the conversation went on to discuss the place for the operation. McCarthy told them to locate at *Talty and O'Neil's.*

"They have a better class of trade and run a quiet little bit of poker. That is the best place you can get . . . You ought not miss the next payday on the ditch. That's the time to make your harvest. At *Talty and O'Neil's* you would catch the best end of the crowd, the men who make good money and spend it well."

Reporter Wade then claimed he replied, "Then if I fix them [Talty and O'Neil][29] $50 a week for you and they say it is all right, there is no doubt about you protecting us?" Wade and Carter stated that McCarthy replied, "Not a doubt about it, sir."[30]

After the meeting, Wade and Carter hurried to tell Clancy and the Civic Federation the news. With Reverend Clancy, they traveled to Chicago to appear before Justice Martin to swear out warrants for the mayor; Chief of Police Francis Frelochowski; William O'Neil, a partner of C.A. Talty; C.A. Talty, president of the school board; and John Peterson and other saloon keepers and their "girls" to appear before Judge Neely and the grand jury. The reporter and Clancy could hardly contain themselves. Reverend Clancy would have the sin strip removed and the paper would have an exclusive story.

McCarthy did not suspect any plot. He had little fear of Clancy and the Civic Federation. He told a reporter two weeks before in the *Fischbach Saloon* on Canal Street, "I'm not afraid of anything that d---- Federation can do as long as S.W. Norton is president. He dare not turn his group to throw one straw in my way. If he does I'll put him in his place."[31]

However, on September 6, 1895, Smokey Row was raided. On that day warrants charging Mayor John McCarthy and 28 others were placed in the hands of 40 detectives from the Stanley Detective Agency. Those agents were dispatched on a ten-car train hired by the *Tribune* and the Civic Federation. The train left Chicago at 3:30 p.m. and arrived in Lemont at 4:30 p.m. There the ten cars were side-tracked on River Road while the detectives waited with warrants and billy clubs for the raid to begin.

The plan was to arrest McCarthy first and then begin the raid on Smokey Row, so two of the raiding detectives went directly to McCarthy's law office on Canal Street in the Fischbach Building, where they presented him with the warrant. McCarthy looked at it, quietly locked his roll top desk and went with the officers. The detectives were afraid that knowledge of McCarthy's arrest would tip off the habitues of the strip that a raid was in progress, so they took him by a round-about path across the I & M along the State Street footbridge to the train. All along the way, McCarthy declared his innocence. He spoke of the reforms he had established in Lemont and how money from the Row had been used for civic improvements. As McCarthy viewed it, his only enemies were the "Methodist Monster" Reverend Clancy, and the Civic Federation.

On the way to the depot, the mayor and the officers encountered a fellow Lemonter. McCarthy took advantage of the opportunity to send word about his situation. Before the officers could stop him, the mayor spoke out, "Ed, I'm under arrest and I want you to be sure that a bondsman is sent to Judge Neely's court in Chicago." The man had barely passed when the detectives realized that he was Ed Bohn, owner of two of the worst dives on the Row, the *Theater Comique* and the *Standard Theater*. They knew that there was a warrant for Bohn's arrest, but they were concerned with getting McCarthy to the train.

Once McCarthy was on board, the raid began in earnest. The Santa Fe Station hangers-on got the surprise of their life when the 40 officers bounded out of the train, clubs in hand. This Smokey Row army thundered along the plank sidewalks scattering rats and dust in all directions. Their first stop was the *Silver Dollar Saloon*. Caught off guard, the owner, Henry Boyle, was found tending bar. In the back room were four scant-ily-clad girls. All were promptly taken into custody and marched to the train.

Raid on the Standard Theater. (Illustration courtesy of the Chicago Tribune*)*

Word quickly spread that a raid was in progress. It was quite a sight. As detectives ran in, patrons ran out. McCarthy's chief of police, called "Rubber Neck" by the *Tribune*, weighed over 250 pounds. He ran to warn Lemonters in the dives who might find it diffi-cult to explain to family and friends why they were there. His warnings also served to tip off the normal patrons. Many acted on his warning and left the taverns by various escape routes. Most of these routes led to the I & M Canal towpath. From there they could escape into the town or the nearby Brown woods. The *Chicago Tribune* described the scene:

> This flight of the unfortunate was in some ways an amusing affair. At one time nearly 40 to 50 women in various stages of nudity were hurrying down the towpath in an effort to escape arrest, many of them awkwardly trying to dress themselves as they ran. Some of them carried shoes and stockings in their hands and ran bare-footed for nearly a mile.[32]

Word of the raid also reached town, and Lemonters came down to see the excitement. Young boys and men flocked the area to get glimpses of the evil sinners they had heard about. The raiders also hit *The Place*, a den kept by John Chandler. Chandler made his escape, but many patrons were arrested. The story was the same at *Ed Boyle's Place*; he was out, but some of his girls were slow in getting dressed and were arrested.

Ed Bohn was finally tracked down; he pleaded with deep emotion that his beloved wife was upstairs dying. His petition was so sincere that the raiding party decided to overlook the *Theater Comique* for the time. When the raiders reached the *Big Casino*, it was closed. The girls had been bundled up in a livery wagon and driven to the country for "fresh air." Those people finally rounded up were taken to the railroad station where the detectives read the warrants. Reporters noted that while standing on the platform, Township Constable Frelichowski and another officer, "fraternized with the women under arrest and sympathized with them in their temporary affliction."[33]

Before placing the prisoners on board the train an officer tried to take names from the women. According to the reporters:

> An old hag of 50 summers blushed beneath her paint and said she was known as Sarah Bernhardt. The next was more plebeian and admitted that Sarah Brown was good enough for her. The remainder gave the names of Grace Wood, Minnie Oliver, Lillie Smith, Maud Gray, Edith Johnson, and May Hall. The creatures were arranged in fantastic dresses which fairly outshone Joseph's celebrated coat of multi-colored hues . . . They had been planning to get protection from the mayor, but upon entering the train they discovered that he too had been arrested.[34]

McCarthy was not disturbed about spending his trip to Chicago with his Smokey Row friends. The reporters noted that he did not feel ill at ease with the crowd that kept referring to him as "The Man."

By six p.m. the train was filled and headed for the city. The "walls of Jericho" had been breached by Clancy and the Civic Federation. All of Smokey Row was quiet that afternoon. Well, almost all. As the train pulled out, the lights on the *Theater Comique* were turned on and two dingy canvas signs placed outside, "Big Show Tonight." After all, it was the only action in town. Meanwhile, Mrs. Bohn was still upstairs, dying.

The Santa Fe raiding train headed for Chicago while McCarthy's friends and those tavern keepers not arrested decided to catch the Alton night train to attend the court session in the morning. On board the raiding train, nervous detectives began to fear that there might be an attempt to free McCarthy when they slowed to enter the Santa Fe rail switching yard. This was based on McCarthy's known pro-labor stand. Somehow, they got the idea that rail workers would storm the car, a ridiculous notion, but it shows the depth of fear that had developed between labor and capitalist forces in the 1890s; because of this, they locked McCarthy in the baggage car.

Undaunted, the mayor puffed on one of his famous black cigars, telling the detectives that he wished to be back home by nine p.m. McCarthy planned to be met by his bondsmen, M.C. New and D.B. Murphy. He felt that the fuss would soon be over. It was then that the officers told him that bond might be posted, but he could not be released since his warrant was for Judge Neely's court which would not convene until Saturday morning. McCarthy was given his choice of overnight accommodations — county jail or the Saratoga hotel. He chose the hotel.

The prisoners were unloaded at 23d Street and Armour Avenue and transported to the courthouse from there. The Alton night train made much better time than the special Santa Fe raiding train, so the crowd from Lemont already had gathered to see the group processed. As the prisoners entered, someone in the Lemont crowd called out, "Is Sarah Bernhardt there?" Sarah waved to her fans. The final list of the Smokey Row inhabitants who were arrested was as follows:

> *American House*, A. Burkhardt and wife, inmates, two white women; *Casino*, Fred Lawler, inmates, six white women; *Big Four Palace*, S. J. Harris, inmates, two white and two colored

women; *Farmers Exchange*, H. Mazzer, inmates, six colored women; *Jawoski's Place*, H. Jawoski, inmates, four colored women; *King of Hearts*, P. Merkes, inmates, six white women; *Mazzie's Place*, M. Mazzie, inmates, five colored women; *Palace Saloon*, J. Chandler, inmates, sixteen colored women; *Pete Shea's Place*, P. Shea, inmates, two white women; *Mrs. Priestly's Place*, Mrs. Priestly, inmates, seven Black women; *The Silver Dollar*, H. Boyle, inmates, seven white women.[35]

MRS. A. W. BURGHARDT,
PROPRIETOR OF THE
AMERICAN HOUSE,
LEMONT, ILLINOIS.

FIRST-CLASS ACCOMMODATIONS IN EVERY RESPECT. TRAVELING TRADE SOLICITED.

Newspaper advertisement for the American House in the 1880s, before the canal construction. (Illustration courtesy of the Lemont Historical Society)

All of the above offenders were taken to Judge Martin's court where the seats were filled with interested Lemonters and Smokey Row characters. There was a great deal of laughing and joking until they found out that McCarthy was not going to be released. The mayor's attorney, Harry Coburn, complained about the unfair treatment of his client to anyone who would listen.

Justice Martin set bond for the saloon keepers and the inmates of the disorderly houses at 500 dollars each. Alderman Fischbach of Lemont offered to sign all the bonds, telling the reporters present that he was worth 100,000 dollars. So, bonds were posted for all the Smokey Row inhabitants and they were released within an hour. "By 1:00 a.m. every prisoner who had left Lemont involuntarily was back in Lemont again, and in no pleasant mood. At *The Standard* and *The Comique* theaters, a slim performance was given by those who returned from the woods."[36]

Still, every place on Smokey Row had extra parties through the night and into the next day. The *Tribune* commented that it seemed as if each inmate had brought a friend from the city.[37]

The streets were so crowded that it was impossible to pass. A man was shot in Ed Boyle's saloon, and a number of men complained of being robbed. Not all of the crime centered in the dives. A laborer from section ten entered Dillman's Barber shop and sat in the chair getting ready for a shave. Four men came in from the street, held a revolver to his head and forced him to give up all the money he had, seven dollars.

McCarthy's bondsmen, New and Murphy, and politically influential Edwin Walker, owner of Illinois Pure Aluminum factory, had to wait until the morning to hear testimony against the mayor.

> And afterward he read all the words of the law the blessing and the curse, according to all that is written in the book of the law. *(Joshua 8:34)*

Meanwhile Reverend Clancy, overwhelmed with his victory, told the papers how he worked to gain his great day, referring to *Joshua 8:34*. He went on to say:

> For several months I did my own detective work and sounded the depths of depravity on Smokey Row. When I had collected

sufficient evidence I laid it before some of the leading citizens of Lemont. The Civic Federation took up the matter and Mr. Norton and Mr. Barth[38] and I were appointed a committee of three to conduct the matter. Then we began to lay plans which culminated in the cleaning out of Smokey Row. The details you know. The *Chicago Tribune,* which has always taken the greatest interest in our efforts to purify Lemont, entered into the plan and because of its efforts much of the success of the raid is due.

In the future we are determined the town will be kept clean. No dweller on Smokey Row will be allowed to continue in business in Lemont. We have rid ourselves of them and we are determined they never again shall gain foothold in Lemont. As for Mayor McCarthy, we will impeach him and remove him from office. We may do more. He certainly will be prosecuted to the full extent of the law. I learned lately that he secured the office of mayor by the theft of 50 ballots cast for his opponent.[39]

The fight between McCarthy and Clancy was not a simple struggle between questions of public and personal morality. It may have begun that way, but other players had money and greed at stake. There was a real risk for Clancy, yet there was no question that Clancy was courageous. He had faced danger investigating Smokey Row. In fact, there had been three plots on his life and reputation, which did not succeed because someone revealed each plan. The first one was direct; it was to have him waylaid at night, beaten to death, and dumped into the spoil bank on the Ship Canal where his body would never be found.

The second plot was more subtle. Reverend Clancy was to be induced by his own desire to rescue sinners. If the Smokey Row prostitute involved had not told the plan, Clancy certainly would have fallen into a trap. The idea was to send someone to his home at night and tell him that one of the women on Smokey Row was dying and wanted to repent her many sins. When Clancy arrived, as the plotters reasoned he would, he would either be done away with or compromised in front of witnesses, but the young girl yelled out a warning as Clancy climbed the steps to her room.

The third plot was to excite his horse at the open air prayer meetings he held along the I & M Canal. The horse and buggy would be forced into the canal and it would look like a runaway accident. One actual shooting attempt did occur outside his parsonage. The plot failed because the cartridge did not explode. The would-be murderer escaped down an alley and into a wooded ravine that ran parallel to Lemont Street.

These plots led J.T. Derby, a Justice of the Peace and member of Clancy's congregation, to form a bodyguard for a period of time to protect their minister. It was a strange sight to see the Reverend greeting his parishioners on the steps of the Old Stone Church with Derby standing next to him holding a double barreled shotgun.

On the morning after the "Great Raid," J.W. McCarthy appeared in Judge Neely's court. The visitors seats were again packed with Lemonters. An amended complaint was entered against the mayor charging that he had received a 50 dollar bribe from the undercover *Tribune* reporter, Stuart Wade. Reverend Clancy was also in the courtroom to see his enemy brought before the bar of justice. Lemonters were divided between those supporting McCarthy and those supporting Clancy, and the Chicago reporters had a field day interviewing the opposing sides. The newspaper publicity painted a very unpleasant picture of our town and, therefore, Lemonters who had stayed out of the quarrel became uneasy about the news coverage. It was feared that Lemont would be viewed as a sin city and a dangerous place to live.

The *Tribune* ran a cartoon showing Lemont swept clean by a flood, entitled: *Some Results of the First Flood on the Drainage Canal*. At the bottom was this ditty:

> The Mayor went into the Gambler's den,
> The Gamblers played two by three.
> Play uppe, play uppe, my merry men,
> The game's for you — the rake-off for me.

Meanwhile in the courtroom, the complaint was read and preliminary testimony taken. Wade, the reporter, gave his story regarding the bribery incident. His information followed what had already been reported as an exclusive in the *Tribune*. Attorney Donohoe cross-examined Wade but failed to shake his testimony. Wade swore that he had never been in Lemont before the day of the alleged bribery incident and never intended to go again. Lawyer Donohoe attempted to show that the reporter was prejudiced against the town and therefore unreliable.

> Donohoe asked: "Did you carry a revolver when you were
> there?"
>
> "I did," said Wade, "as a preventive against a disease almost
> epidemic down there that is familiarly called *Lemont heart
> failure*."

Half the courtroom laughed, while the other half moaned in disbelief. After Wade's testimony, McCarthy was released on a 5,000 dollar bond. Indictments for McCarthy were under the provision of Chapter 23, article six, section eight of the Illinois statutes. These statutes offered punishment for "any member of the city council or board of trustees or any officer of the corporation who shall accept any gift or promise of money or undertaking to make the same under any agreement or understanding that his vote, opinion, judgment, or action, shall be influenced thereby."

McCarthy was officially indicted by a grand jury the week following the Big Raid, and his case was scheduled for trial in December. Back in Lemont, Smokey Row opened for the weekend to take advantage of the canal pay day, but many saloon keepers were uneasy.

Their uneasiness increased Sunday, September 8, when they could see, up the hill, vast crowds gathering at the Stone Church to hear Reverend Clancy speak. Clancy chose his text for that day from *Joshua 1:6-9*:

> Be strong and of good courage for thou shall cause this people
> to inherit the land which I swore unto their fathers to give
> them. Be strong and of good courage, be not affrightened, nei
> ther be thou dismayed, for the Lord thy God is with thee
> whither soever thou goest.

Addressing the overflow crowd, Clancy certainly did not preach the Sermon on the Mount. Instead it was an Old Testament clear call to arms and action. His voice carried across the congregation:

We have come to a point in our history as citizens of Lemont when the words of Joshua are especially fitting to us. We have met with many serious difficulties, but our real work is still before us. Courage, too, we need. Men with these qualities we must have for the taking of Lemont, for God. Our greatest battle lies before us. They say your mayor and his chief, that they are going to make it harder than ever for us. These men shall have their punishment. Your mayor walks the streets of this town a very large and important man, but if you could have seen him before the bar of justice you would have seen a different man. He is a coward and so are his minions. God helping us, giving us the courage and strength, we will take our rightful inheritance.[40]

After the sermon, the Civic Federation and Clancy continued to make plans. They realized that there had to be another way to attack the sin strip other than through constant, expensive raids. The raids only resulted in 500 dollar fines and business as usual the next day. It was decided that a campaign should be conducted against the saloon keepers. With the help of M. Rosenthal, the Assistant State's Attorney, letters were sent to each property owner informing them, if they did not know, of the type of activity occurring on their land and warning them that they could be subject to a 200 dollar a day fine for allowing illegal behavior on their property. Since most of the dives were rental property, this move exposed the true owners, who had, up to this point, kept their holdings secret through trusts and corporations. Needless to say, most of the land in the downtown area belonged to early pioneer settlers, and many owners were very important people in Lemont. Some were upright members of Clancy's own congregation's "Amen corner."[41]

Lemonters must have put some force on the Methodist organization because the papers reported that at the Rock River Conference that fall, Clancy's application to remain in Lemont was granted "in spite of pressure from some to have him removed."[42] The Conference recognized that Clancy was "the right man in the right place." They reported that it would be wrong to send any new minister into that "hell hole to take up Clancy's work."[43] Any change, as the ministers saw it, would only "encourage McCarthy and his gang and they would gain absolute control."

The policy of the Civic Federation against the landlords of Smokey Row proved successful, as some of Lemont's townspeople did not want it known that they owned the land and had profited from the dreadful dives. The threat to identify landowners helped to hasten the end of the sin strip, but it also helped to make more enemies for Clancy within his congregation. By December of 1895 the *Joliet News* reported:

Lemont has been purged and renovated to an unexpected degree but not completely. The number of saloons has been reduced to 25 in the last six months and the Civic Federation does not deserve all the credit; it is the completion of the canal near Lemont.

The once famous *Standard Theater* has its windows boarded up and it now only marks the place where several men were killed for paltry sums of money. *The Big Four* gambling den is closed with a "For Rent" sign. *McDonald's Saloon and Athletic Rooms* is closed and Mac no longer lives in town. Almost a whole block on Canal Street is closed with for rent signs and Smokey Row, once the toughest street in America is closed down. Some disorderly houses are still open. *The Big Casino* and the *Little Casino* openly defy laws and have some colored and white "ladies" as permanent inmates.

McCarthy's case, set for December of 1895, was also reviewed in the *Joliet News* with the usual bias the paper held for the town:

The trial of Lemont's chief executive will take place in a few days according to reports, but the probability is that it will never come up. It will not if the mayor can put up enough money for a bribe and it is generally believed that he has done this. A few dollars, especially in political affairs have great power and often outweigh justice. The mayor has been using strong influence to defeat the work of the Civic Federation and some Federation members feel the case will never come to trial. Reverend Clancy is positive, however, and feels McCarthy will spend one year in jail.[44]

With delays and appeals, J.W. McCarthy's final trial did start one year later in December of 1896. Then, in a surprise move, both Detective Carter and Stuart Wade claimed that they could not recall the events in McCarthy's office, so the case was dismissed by the state. Wade later acknowledged that he had used Reverend Clancy and the Civic Federation to get a story for his paper, but by then it did not matter — Smokey Row was gone.

The 1896 and 1897 issues of *The Lemont Observer* record the changes in the community. Most of those issues carried the following classified ads:

For Sale: The property known as *The Comique Theater* on North Stephen Street. A well built, large building will be sold on very reasonable terms as the owner has no further use for it.

For Rent: A house containing nine rooms two doors west of Marble City House. Inquire of C. Talty.

Instead of honors for his work and concern for Lemont, J. Franklin Clancy had become too political and controversial for his flock, so early in 1896 he was transferred to La Grange. His going away party was small. He had only a few friends who understood his zeal, devotion, and desire to represent God with political and social action.

McCarthy also grew tired of the fight, and he felt the political division created by the struggle over Smokey Row. He decided not to run again for mayor and left office in 1897.

In the years that followed only a few "houses" remained on Smokey Row. The *Observer* reported one incident in the spring of 1897 that occurred in Justice of the Peace Weimer's court. There a Lilly Jackson disrupted the session with "heart-rendering wails." It seems that she had been beaten by a patron of one of the few remaining brothels and appeared to swear out a warrant against the man. The newspaper described her as "one of the lilies of the field, she toils not neither does she spin." The editor suggested that it was time for a "general roundup of these disreputable remains of the drainage days. As a class they are shiftless, dirty, and criminal, and Lemont would be better rid of them."[45]

The last brothel was removed by Lemont's legendary policeman, Pete Kane. This house had continued to operate until 1906. It was so notorious that Kane was forced to raid it three times a week, but it would always reopen. The state and county refused to move against it and Kane got tired of the cycle of raid and reopen. So he approached the village board and asked for 25 dollars to clean out the place.

Pete's plan was as simple and direct as he was. He rented a dray and went over to the house. There he loaded up the keeper, her girls and their furnishings and drove out of town. He took his load to the vice district of Chicago, which was running wide open again, made police contacts for their protection and rented a nice place for them. He then tipped his hat, bid them farewell and drove back to Lemont. He spent only ten dollars of the appropriated money so he returned the rest to the village board along with his assurance that the "girls" were well settled in Chicago and would not be back in Lemont again.[46]

Both John McCarthy and J. Franklin Clancy continued in community service after the conflicts settled. McCarthy continued to practice law and served as a director of the Lemont State Bank; a vice-president of Illinois Pure Aluminum; Chief Deputy of the Probate Court of Cook County; village attorney from 1909-1923; a land developer east of the village; Representative of the 7th District through the 50th, 51st, 52nd and 53d sessions; a member of the Minuteman organization during World War I; and a major mover in the development of the hard road system of Illinois in the early 1920s. His efforts developed six miles of concrete road from the Sag to the Will-Cook County line through Lemont. McCarthy Road was named in his honor for his contributions, as was the bridge on Stephen Street over the I & M Canal.[47] John McCarthy died in his office on Canal Street on May 5, 1924, at a meeting of the *Lemont Good Roads Association.* His life certainly spanned some of the more colorful years of Lemont and his contributions were both remarkable and interesting.

And, what of Reverend Clancy? He was assigned to La Grange for a year and then sent to the Halsted Street Institutional Church in Chicago. Here again his reform spirit was fired. With the same concern he had for youth that had led him to Lemont, he saw that the ideas of the new settlement houses, such as the Hull House, could be applied to churches. If young people were offered recreational opportunities in the church they would not get into trouble in the streets. This idea was radical at the time as churches saw their sole role as offering formal services, Bible studies, and Sunday school. To develop the program he envisioned, Reverend Clancy did the impossible. He convinced Gustavus F. Swift, the meat packer, to finance his ideas.

Swift was notorious for his unwillingness to spend money without a visible return. Clancy used his gift of persuasion to get backing from a man, a millionaire, who continued to live for many years at the edge of the stockyards rather than build a new home. When Swift did consent to move, he refused to spend money on drapes or curtains. He was so cheap that he was widely quoted as saying, "No young man is rich enough to smoke 25 cent cigars." Whatever Clancy said, it worked. With Swift's aid, Clancy pioneered a recreational and social program at the Halstead Church. He built a gym, swimming pool, social hall, and a bowling alley, all in four years. At this point his health broke and he was sent for a brief rest to a small quiet Methodist Church in Blue Island.

However, Blue Island was not quiet. It was the site of a well-known horse fair, which had started in 1866, and by the early 1900s had developed a wild reputation. Men came each month to trade, drink, and gamble. The fair was a large money maker for the village, but it did bring in a criminal element. Clancy saw this and in his usual Joshua fashion began a crusade to clean up the fair. He saw it as an "ugly debauch." Through his efforts, he forced the town to supervise the fair more closely, thereby cutting down its popularity. This time it was the *Chicago Daily News* that took note of his work and coined a new word, "Clancyfied." Now both Lemont and Blue Island had been Clancyfied. He had to seek another church after purging Blue Island, so he went to LaSalle for two years.

In 1905, he was called back to a Chicago parish. At the Ada Street Methodist Church he pioneered another large social and recreational program for the youth. Support again came from the Swifts. Gustavus had died in 1903, but Mrs. Swift and her daughter helped Clancy's work in every way. By 1908, Clancy had the program organized, but again was exhausted physically and emotionally — J. Franklin Clancy could not do anything without full and total commitment. For rest, he served in Rock Falls from 1908 to 1911, and Sandwich from 1911 to 1916.

Meanwhile, the Swift family founded the Union Avenue Methodist Church in honor of Gustavus Swift. New and modern in concept, it had all the recreational facilities that Clancy had pioneered. There was only one person the family wanted to serve the congregation and that was J. Franklin Clancy. He began his service at the Union Church in 1916 and developed one of the most progressive family and community programs in the Chicagoland area. Dr. Clancy finally had found his place to work and serve, and he remained there until 1944. At his retirement dinner he was praised by all: the congregation, his family, his friends, and civic authorities. He was 82 when he retired, and lived to baptize his great-great-grandchild. He was a minister whose vision always went beyond his church walls to the community at large.

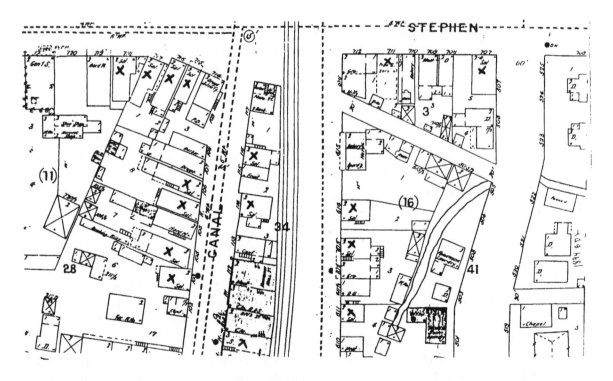

1894 Sandborn Fire Map showing a small portion of Lemont's downtown. All buildings marked with an "X" are saloons and/or dives. (Illustration courtesy of Lemont Historical Society)

As a final note it is only fair to report that although local oral history has Smokey Row a special isolated area, a study of the Sanborn Fire Maps of 1896 reveals that much of the downtown area was in the saloon or tavern business, so that not all the dives were isolated from the business section. In fact, 33 percent of the businesses in the area bounded by Illinois Street, Fremont Street, the I & M Canal, and State Street were saloons and gambling halls. The following is a list of some once notorious buildings that still stand today, though most have been remodeled and none resemble the dives they were.

29 Stephen Street, two story saloon connected to a dancehall.

35 Stephen Street, saloon and bordello.

39 Stephen Street, saloon.

100 Stephen Street, saloon and stage hall with nude dancers.

107 Stephen Street, saloon and second floor lodge hall.

112 Stephen Street, saloon.

111 Stephen Street, saloon

114 Stephen Street, saloon.

116 Stephen Street, saloon.

210 Main Street, saloon.

236 Main Street, saloon.

302 Main Street, saloon.

306 Main Street, saloon.

324 Main Street, saloon.

406 Main Street, saloon.

408 Main Street, saloon.

313 Canal Street, saloon and bordello.

309 Canal Street, saloon and bowling alley in 1894.

315 Canal Street, saloon and pool hall.

307 Canal Street, saloon in the rear.

ENDNOTES

[1]The name is spelled two ways, *Smoky* and *Smokey*. There is no source for a correct spelling. The correct spelling for the adjectival form of *smoke* is *smoky,* yet most papers and books used *smokey.*

[2]A unique fact about our town is that it is an inland port city. This part of our economy is visible along the banks of the Ship Canal, where one can go by water to the Gulf of Mexico or to the Alantic Ocean.

[3]The "flats" was the term used for the land between the I & M Canal and the Santa Fe tracks. It also included the road on the north side of the Santa Fe embankment, known today as Ceco Road.

[4]*Joliet News,* June, 1895.

[5]*Ibid.*

[6]The term "Levee" came from sin strips traditionally established along waterfronts.

[7]*Joliet News*, 1894.

[8]The presence of African-American entertainers as early as the 1870s probably was the source of the name Smokey Row.

[9]An act that neither the county nor village authorities prosecuted.

[10]This hotel is advertised in 1891, before canal construction, as having first-class accommodations in every respect.

[11]Herbert Asbury, *Gem of the Prairie* (New York: Knopf, 1940) pp. 110-111.

[12]*Ibid.*

[13]Sonia Kallick, "Walking Tour 20 and 21," (Lemont: Lemont Area Historical Society, 1976).

[14]Now the Lemont Area Historical Society building at 306 Lemont Street.

[15]William Stead, *If Christ Came to Chicago* (Evansville: Unigraphics, 1978). The original was published in 1894. Stead died on April 15, 1912, on the *Titanic*.

[16]Some cynics say it was because he gave the addresses of all the dives he located.

[17]Sonia Kallick, *Lemont Anecdotes* (Lemont: Lemont Area Historical Society, 1975) p. 167.

[18]An example of this direction from formal church structure today is the Catholic and Baptist position on the abortion issue.

[19]One of the Civic Federation's larger demonstrations occurred on September 15, when Petersen's staged a championship boxing match.

[20]Kallick, *Lemont Anecdotes.*

[21]*Joliet News*, August, 1895.

[22]*Chicago Tribune*, August, 1895.

[23]*Ibid.*

[24]Rev. Clancy's personal hero was Joshua. He felt himself a modern Joshua, storming the walls of Lemont's Jericho, Smokey Row.

[25]*Village Board Notes*, August 28, 1895. The other two appointees are not named, but four of the six trustees of the village were in the saloon or liquor business.

[26]*Chicago Tribune*, September 8, 1895.

[27]Mayor Hopkins was selected to run after the death of Mayor Carter Harrison. The election between Hopkins and the Republican George Swift was so close that court litigation over the results lasted two years.

[28]*Chicago Tribune*, September 14, 1895

[29]Talty was McCarthy's brother-in-law.

[30]*Chicago Tribune*, September 14, 1895.

[31]Kallick, *Lemont Anecdotes* .

[32]*Chicago Tribune*, September 8, 1895.

[33]*Ibid.*

[34]*Ibid.*

[35]*Ibid.*

[36]*Ibid.*

[37]*Ibid.*

[38]S.W. Norton and C.G. Barth were stockholders in the Lemont State Bank. Barth was the cashier.

[39]*Chicago Tribune*, September 8, 1895.

[40]*Chicago Tribune*, September 9,1895.

[41]The "Amen" corner of the Methodist Church was a section reserved for those members who contributed the most financial and spiritual support.

[42]*Chicago Tribune*, September 29, 1895.

[43]*Ibid.*

[44]*Joliet News*, December 23, 1895, editorial.

[45]*Lemont Observer*, April 10, 1897.

[46]*The Lemonter*, January 10, 1946.

[47]Dedicated as the McCarthy Bridge, the name is now forgotten.

U.S. HISTORY

1890: *Martin Madden Elected to Chicago City Council, He is Chairman of Illinois Republican Party and Writes Plank Advocating the Isthmus (Panama) Canal — Idaho and Wyoming Become States — First All-Steel Frame Building Constructed in Chicago.*

1891: *The Wireless Telegraph Invented — Naismith Invents Basketball.*

1892: *Grover Cleveland is Elected President — Chicago Population at 1,000,000 — University of Chicago Opens.*

1893: *World Columbian Exposition in Chicago — Henry Ford Begins Working on Inventing a Car — Mayor Carter Harrison of Chicago is Assassinated.*

1894: *Coxey's Army Marches on Washington — Edison Demonstrates His Kinescope, the First Motion Picture Machine — Pullman Strike.*

1895: *First Professional Football Game — Bryan Delivers His "Cross of Gold" Speech.*

1896: *Utah Becomes a State — McKinley Elected 25th President — First Olympic Games in Greece — Klondike Gold Rush Begins.*

1897: *Chicago Loop "El" Completed — First Photos with Artificial Light — Fitzsimmons Beats Corbett for Boxing Heavyweight Title.*

1898: *Battleship Maine Explodes in Cuba, War with Spain.*

1899: *First Sound Recordings — Carrie Nation Begins Smashing Saloons — Temperance Movement Strong.*

LEMONT HISTORY

1890: *Metropolitan Sanitary District Plans a New Ship Canal — Sam Markiewicz Opens Furniture and Undertaking Parlor at 212 Main Street — Knights of Pythias Active.*

1891: *Bath House on Canal Street Offers Hot Baths for 25 Cents — Smokey Row Continues to Grow with Construction Workers in Town.*

1892: *"Shovel Day" on the Ship Canal — Illinois Pure Aluminum Founded — James Hennebry Elected Mayor.*

1893: *Downtown Street Lights Changed to Electricity — Lemont Power Plant Opens — John McCarthy Elected Mayor — Major Strike and Shooting June 9, Three Killed, Governor Altgeld Comes to Lemont to Settle the Dispute — Village Hall Dedicated September 17 — James Noonan Postmaster — Social Organizations are Knights of Katzmercz, Independent Order of Foresters, German Benevolent Society, Lemont Polish Brass Band, and the Polish Holy Cross Society.*

1894: *Rev. Clancy of the Methodist Church Begins Crusade against Smokey Row and Mayor McCarthy — September 15, Jimmy Barry Wins American Bantamweight Crown in Lemont — Rev. Clancy and Members of Lemont's Civic Organization Try to Halt the Fight.*

1895: *Clancy's Crusade Gets Mayor McCarthy Indicted for Bribery Along with Other Town Officials — The Chicago Tribune Sponsors a Raiding Party on Smokey Row; the 100⁺ Taverns and Brothels are Open the Next Day — Present Bethany Stone Church Built — Cornerstone for St. Patrick's is Laid — Old Central School Annex is Built — The Lemont Light Artillery Group is Formed and So is the Handel Music Association — Fire at Peterson's Park.*

1896: *Norton's Fails, Many Lose Life Savings — The Sag Bridge Ghost is Seen for the First Time — William J. Bryan Speaks at the Alton Station in Lemont to Well over 5,000 — 102-106 Stephen Store Gets Limestone Front — Horace Singer Dies in California — D.B. Murphy Elected Mayor — The Turnverine Vorwaerts is Formed by the German Community.*

1897: *People on Talcott Street See an Airship or Flying Machine — Geo. Losey Postmaster — Quarry Workers Strike Again, Settled Quickly But All Leaders Fired — Willow Springs Has a Huge Fire — The Lemont Electric Light and Power Now Located in the Waterworks Building.*

1898: *St. Cyril's School Built — Underpass at Santa Fe on North Stephen is Built — Chicago and Des Plaines Electric Begins to Lay Tracks on Main Street.*

1899: *Polish National Alliance #465 Formed.*

CHAPTER TWENTY-TWO

THE SECOND CANAL: EVENTS AND POLITICS

Smokey Row Days: 1893-1897

The money from Smokey Row did bring physical changes to the town. Two buildings that dominate our landscape came from those heady days — Old Central School Annex and our Village Hall. The Village Hall was built in 1893, during the administration of John McCarthy. Shortly after he took office, he sold the wooden Village Hall and firehouse on the site. Charles Lutz bought the Hall for 255 dollars and A. Ingraham acquired the old firehouse for 205 dollars. McCarthy then contracted a stone structure measuring 40 by 100 feet. The cost was 13,319 dollars and the no-bid contract was let to his brother-in-law, C.A. Talty. When questioned about the contract, McCarthy answered that you can always trust relatives to do an honest job.

The architect was H. Boehme of Joliet. Boehme had designed a number of buildings in the area using stone from the Western Quarries where Talty had been a foreman. The completion date was set for December of 1893, with the dedication ceremonies scheduled for September 19. The date was selected in a grand gesture to coincide with elaborate ceremonies held in Washington, D.C., honoring the centennial of the laying of the cornerstone of our nation's Capitol.[1]

Lemont's ceremonies had a bit more of a frontier flavor. The village had to hire special guards to watch over the cornerstone before the ceremony, because there was a rumor that someone was out to steal the stone before it could be put in place. The day arrived with the guest of honor, Chicago's popular Mayor Carter Harrison, Sr., in attendance. He came to town on the Alton train and

Lemont Village Hall, 1893. (Photo courtesy of Lemont Historical Society)

was escorted from there by a parade of village officials, civic organizations, and fraternal groups. The parade was led by Mayor Harrison, Mayor McCarthy, and Major Jake Meyer, a Civil War hero, and, more importantly, the agent for Sehring Beer in Lemont. The event was crowded with Democrats and Republicans alike because Harrison was a political powerhouse and a colorful character who attracted attention wherever he went. Affectionately known as "our Carter," he was a five-term mayor of Chicago. His influence extended not only throughout Chicago and the state, but worldwide.

The World Columbian Exposition of 1893 had introduced "Our Carter" to an endless number of international dignitaries. Mayor Harrison filled the role of host with showmanship and style. It was a testimony to the political importance of Lemont and Mayor McCarthy that Harrison took time out from his busy schedule to attend the cornerstone ceremony. Both men shared a pro-labor view that caused them the enmity of the *Chicago Tribune*. Harrison had been mayor during the Haymarket Riot and its attendant social and political problems, while John McCarthy was Lemont's township supervisor during the 1885 Lemont quarry strike.

Mayor Carter Harrison, Sr. (Illustration courtesy of Lemont Historical Society)

Large crowds followed the parade in order to see Mayor Harrison and perhaps shake the hand that shook the hand of the Duke of Veragua, a descendant of Columbus.[2] The parade marched to the site of the unfinished hall where the cornerstone was still safely under guard. There, McCarthy introduced Mayor Harrison to the crowd. McCarthy's small son, Roy, stood enraptured by the whole event. The world of politics was so fixed in his mind that he would grow up to serve as mayor[3] in the very same building he saw dedicated that day. Harrison looked over the crowd and spoke in his usual direct style:

> I knew Lemont before I knew Chicago, when it was dignified with the name Athens. It was in 1855 that I was passing through Joliet on my way to Chicago when I first saw your city. As I remember, now, the thing that impressed me most was the fences which were built with slabs of stone instead of the wooden rails I was used to . . . The stone is important more important than wood . . . That is because large oaks can grow from small acorns and instead of Chicago swallowing Lemont, Lemont may well swallow Chicago . . . [cheers from the crowd]. Chicago thinks well of Lemont. We like your stone and we send you our "cologne water."[4] The latter service we are rendering you will not last much longer because the Drainage Ditch [Sanitary Ship Canal] will soon be completed.

With that the cornerstone was put in place and Mayor Harrison escorted back to the train. He promised to come back on the day the hall was completed, but that was not to be. The easily accessible Mayor Harrison was fatally wounded by a disgruntled office seeker a month later.[5] Mayor McCarthy only served three years in the hall he created, but as we have seen, they were a wild three years.

The other landmark left to us from the Smokey Row monies is the 1896 addition to Old Central School, designed by John Barnes of Joliet, in the Romanesque-Victorian style then considered modern. It was created to show a fortress-like stability and to tell the community that Lemont was dedicated to education, especially higher education.[6] Barnes was born in Will County and received special training in architecture at the University of Illinois between 1885-1889. While there he studied under Professor Nathan Ricker.[7]

Lemont Central School 1896 annex to the 1869 building. (Photo courtesy of the Lemont Historical Society)

He specialized in school buildings and worked for the Joliet school system, where he was responsible for Farragut High School, Grove Street Primary, and the Ridgewood School. It was at the Ridgewood school that he developed the tower plan that he repeated in Lemont's Old Central School of 1896, and Lockport's Central School, also built in 1896. The towers are slightly squared, supporting structures which bow out at the center to increase floor space and available light. Lighting and spacious classrooms became Barnes' trademark.

The clock tower on Old Central School is 80 feet high, and originally had a face on all four sides, visible to anyone in town. No student could have an excuse for being late based on not knowing the time. Twelve feet below the clock was the school bell taken from the 1869 building. The grayish stone columns and the cornerstone on the front are not Lemont stone, but Indiana Bedford Stone, a softer stone that takes well to carving. The new annex became such a proud symbol that other communities recognized its value.[8] The *Hinsdale Doings* of 1896 reported:

> Lemont is building a magnificent home for its high school and is laying a foundation for a school that will someday outshine Lyons Township High School.[9] It is to be constructed of stone and above the handsome structure will be an artistic clock tower. The rooms are conveniently arranged. Such a building may someday shelter Hinsdale's higher institution.

The completion of this annex was based on the belief that the school and adult population of Lemont would continue to grow at a rapid rate with the completion of the Ship Canal. Village trustees and townspeople thought the new canal would be an economic addition to Lemont in the same way that the I & M Canal had been 48 years before, but such growth did not happen from the Ship Canal partly because of its location away from town, and partly because much of the land adjoining the Ship Canal was under the control of the Metropolitan Sanitary District.

Because of the wide-open days of the Sanitary Canal construction, Lemont has a part in the annals of American boxing history. The presence of construction workers made an excellent audience for sporting events, and sports promoters recognized that fact.

At the Polk Street Station in Chicago on September 15, 1894, it was apparent to the waiting passengers that some unusual event was to occur that evening. The ticket seller sold hundreds of tickets to Lemont, and all of the purchases were made by men of the "sporting set." Mr. James Connelly, better known as "one-eyed Jimmy," walked around the depot complaining bitterly about the high cost of sporting entertainment. Jimmy, a friend of alderman "Bathhouse" Coughlin, was a notorious gate crasher who prided himself on his ability to avoid paying admission to any event.[10] This time, however, he had to pay in advance and the cost was ten dollars, a large sum in those days.

But neither cost nor the law, since boxing was illegal in Illinois in 1894, could discourage the crowd. They were going out to Lemont to see Chicago's own Jimmy Barry battle for the American bantamweight crown, and in Lemont they would be safe from a raid, since Mayor McCarthy supported and encouraged the fight. The only possible problem that could arise would be interference from Lemont's Civic Federation and the always crusading Reverend Clancy.

The fight was promoted by Charles "Parson" Davis[11] and Mike Jacobs. Both men collected admission at the station and saw that all the necessary supplies were on the train to Lemont. The train, filled with the rowdy crowd, including Mike McDonald, Harry Keller, Tom White, and Sol Van Praag, arrived in the early evening, and the excited fans surged up the hill to Peterson's Park at the corner of Warner and Logan. There a tent was erected while news of the fight was spread through town and along Smokey Row. Soon Peterson was doing a booming business in food and drink.[12] Reverend Clancy and company did show up at the gate, but were hooted down by the crowd.

The purse for the fight was 1,000 dollars, with 800 dollars going to the winner, plus any side bets. The promoters and the sporting set were concerned with the betting, as the odds swung back and forth. Barry was the local, sentimental favorite, while his opponent, Casper Leon, the Italian bantamweight champ, was the favorite of the Eastern sportsmen and a large group of Italians who traveled from Lockport to see the fight.

The ringside was lit by torches and lanterns held by the spectators as the fans moved as close as possible to see the action. However, they were forced to wait until the arrival of the guest of honor, Lemont's Mayor McCarthy. When McCarthy did appear, it set off a large round of cheers, and then opponents entered the ring. The fight referee was George

Proper boxing stance for the start of a fight in the 1890s. (Illustration courtesy of Lemont Historical Society)

Sieler, who was considered a fair man who would control the action. Leon was the larger of the two fighters, 5 feet, three inches and 112 pounds. Barry was 5 feet, two inches and 105 pounds. Leon's style of fighting was to crouch with his feet spread wide apart and his left shoulder uplifted, a stance that protected his head and neck, but opened him up to body blows. Jimmy's style was to play away, bob and weave, then come in on his opponent. The fans enjoyed his display of footwork which was new to the art of boxing, having only been recently introduced by the famous Bob Fitzsimmons.

The crowd hushed as the two men advanced to the scratch in the center of the ring. Both halted and assumed the pugilistic attitude of the day, with the left foot and arm half extended, right leg behind and the right arm protecting the body. To the delight of the crowd, Jimmy Barry began a flurry of jabs as soon as the bell rang.

Barry was born on Goose Island, that little spit of land in the Chicago River. It was said that from the moment Jimmy entered the world, the only time he stopped swinging his fists was when he was sleeping. That was not surprising, since he was the smallest kid around Goose Island, and the Island was a tough neighborhood. He was a true "street fighter." He loved to fight and he loved to win, and soon gained a reputation for his skills. No one dared to pick a fight with Mrs. Barry's kid.[13]

When he was 12 years old, Jimmy went down to McGurn's handball court, where he heard that they were giving formal boxing lessons and he signed up. Small and skinny, he weighed 90 pounds (only 15 pounds away from his adult fighting weight), but his fast speed and cleverness came to the attention of Harry Gilmore, a well-known featherweight boxer. Gilmore encouraged Jimmy, and soon Jimmy was boxing in amateur competition. By the time he was 23, he was a fine boxer who had never lost a fight. When his father died, Jimmy decided to earn extra money for the family by entering professional boxing. It was a quasi-legal business at that time, run by men like his promoter, Charles Davis. Boxers were paid small purses and side bets for illegal fights, usually held in bars and saloons. Smokey Row's establishments had fights every week that delighted the barge, quarry, ship canal, and rail workers. These bouts were often nothing more than bloody violent brawls between men desperate for a few dollars.

However, during the early 1890s, some states, though not Illinois, began to legalize and control boxing, therefore attracting champions from other countries who came to give exhibitions and to fight American contenders. As public interest in boxing increased, Gilmore, Davis, and Davis's friend, Mike Jacobs, saw an opportunity to make more money. They realized that Jimmy Barry was not just another saloon fighter, but that he had the skills and a special desire to win, and they began grooming him for the championship.

The bantamweight championship had been vacated by George Dixon, who could no longer make the weight requirement, and there were many would-be contenders. At first, Barry was an unknown and had a great deal of trouble getting bouts with acknowledged contenders. Finally, with money from backers, he got his first important fight with Springfield's Jimmy Connors. Barry beat Connors soundly and won a side bet of 1,500 dollars. After Connors, he met New York's Joe McGrath and New Orleans's Jimmy Gorman. He beat both of them. That left only the Italian champion, Casper Leon, who was touring the United States at the time. Leon accepted the challenge, not expecting too much difficulty in putting away an Irish-American Chicago "street fighter." The fight was a glove event that was to last until one contender could not get up to "toe the mark" in the center of the ring.[14]

From the beginning of the fight, Barry took the initiative; he pursued Casper Leon around the large ring. Leon resorted to frequent clinching in order to regain his breath and balance. The pace of the fight even at the start was almost unbearable, as both men jabbed and hit each other. Through the early rounds there was little wrestling or tripping as was common for fights in those days. These two opponents boxed. The early rounds ended with Leon clinching to gain his breath, and Jimmy appeared to be leading in points.

In the 11th round, Casper delivered a straight blow to Jimmy's eyes and head. As the crowd gasped, Barry staggered, but did not fall and soon regained his strength. Betting increased as the bout continued, the torches and lanterns burned down, and the fans voices grew hoarse. The lanterns were refueled and drinks served as the two continued their struggle. Through the 12th, 13th, 14th, 15th, and 16th rounds, Leon continued shifting and crouching waiting for a chance for another telling blow like the one he had delivered in the 11th round.

Barry continued pressing with his left jab and looking for an opening to deliver a body blow, one "on the mark." A blow "on the mark" is one aimed at the jugular at the neck, under the ear, between the eyes, or just above the stomach. As they continued fighting sweat poured out and attracted insects, which added to the difficulty of their struggle. By the time the 20th round arrived, the crowd began to realize that this was becoming a very special fight, and not just because the championship was on the line, but because both were out to win with all the skill and guts men can muster. They had given everything from the very beginning and were going on determination alone.

The pace never let up through the 21st, 22nd, 23d, and 24th rounds. Over an hour had passed, but no matter how tired or bloody the contenders were when the bell rang, for the next round both men "toed the line." Blood mingled with sweat as both men began to stumble or miss their timing. After one and a half hours, in the 28th round, Casper Leon let his guard slip. Barry was alert and let go a blow to the mark. It was a body blow above the stomach and the Italian fell unconscious to the canvas. Jimmy Barry, the Chicago street fighter, was big-time now. To the cheers of the crowd, Barry claimed the American bantamweight championship in Peterson's Park in Lemont.[15]

After Lemont, Jimmy Barry gained world fame and met a number of other fighters attempting to take the title from him. In 1895, a rematch was scheduled with Leon. It was a good fight but no title passed hands as the police learned of the fight and raided the place before the fight was finished. Barry began traveling to matches, and met and defeated the Australian title holder, Jim Antony, in San Francisco. Barry's fame was such that even though he had begun as a bare-knuckle fighter, by 1900, the Sears Catalogue offered a set of *Barry Pattern* boxing gloves for young sportsmen.[16]

It was clear to Barry and his backers that he was good enough to try for the world title held by Walter Croot of London. So, in 1897, Barry sailed for England with his trainer, manager, and two close Chicago sporting friends, Ted Sloan, a jockey, and Cap Anson of the Chicago White Stockings.

The match was held at the National Sporting Club. It was a world far removed from Lemont's Peterson's Park or the Smokey Row saloons. The ring was indoors and modern. There were even gentlemen with their ladies at this ring who had come to see the young American from Chicago. The lights were hot and the crowd hostile to the Irish-American.

Walter Croot was the same kind of fighter as Barry, tough and fast. Ted Sloan and Cap Anson had great confidence, but they had underestimated Croot's ability and endurance.

From the very beginning it was a difficult fight. The referees were partial to Croot, and their decisions, along with the hostile crowd, unnerved Barry. He began to lose his timing and had to go on the defensive. He fought hard but by the 19th round he was exhausted and behind in point scoring. Returning to his corner he found Sloan and Anson battling back tears of defeat; it was then that Barry realized how close he was to losing this important fight.

The Goose Island street fighter returned to Barry's soul and he charged out at the next bell. The minute he got an opening he began beating Croot about the head. He pounded at Croot until he fell to the canvas. Amid the boos and hisses of the crowd, Barry was declared the World bantamweight champ.

Croot did not move through all the noise and commotion. In fact Walter Croot never regained consciousness, and died shortly thereafter of a skull fracture. Barry was forced to remain in England while the authorities charged him with manslaughter. He was heartsick about the whole affair. The courts dismissed the charge, but it haunted him. Barry returned home to cheering crowds with the title now in American possession, but his joy of fighting had gone forever. Barry fought only one more professional fight in 1898, when he met Casper Leon, for old time's sake. They were still a good match. They fought 20 rounds to a draw.

After 1899, Barry vacated the title. He never fought again, with the exception of a training program he directed for soldiers in World War I. He spent the rest of his life quietly in the county clerk's office. When he died in 1943, the newspapers barely noticed his passing. Jimmy Barry's lifetime record was 36 professional fights; five knock-outs, 14 draws, and 17 wins. But those who know boxing history say his greatest fight was that memorable September evening in Lemont.[17]

The presence in Lemont in the middle 1890s of a large body of quarry and ship canal workers also drew that other great American passion, politics. Like the days of the I & M Canal, candidates came to Lemont to gain votes. The Alton train station was the center of town life and, as such, the station was often the platform for political events. Just such an event occurred on October 27, 1896, when William Jennings Bryan came to Lemont.

People began gathering early that October morning. Long before noon it was impossible for traffic to move in and out of the station, and by the train's arrival time, well over 5,000 people awaited the campaign special. Lemonters had come to hear the "Boy Orator of the Platte," the young crusader who had found the words to express the frustration and tension of the working and farming classes of the 1880s and 1890s. It had been a period of hard times with economic depression, crop failures, bank foreclosures, strikes, and civil unrest. Lemont understood bad times; there had been serious strikes, the quarries were closing and, finally, the Ship Canal construction and the Santa Fe extension work that had kept Lemont economically solvent was almost completed.

William Jennings Bryan had parlayed his skill as a speaker to win, as a dark horse candidate, the ultimate prize for a politician — nomination for President. The Democratic Party picked him on the strength of one speech, a speech he had perfected over the years leading to the 1896 convention in Chicago. It was a speech that offered a simple solution to the terrible social and economic problems of the time: free coinage of silver at a ratio of 16 to one.[18] He gathered various groups around this idea of inflated money that would bring prosperity to the common man. Monetary policies have always had two sides. One group is composed of people who want to preserve the purchasing value of the dollar, mainly the wealthy, who hold their savings in notes and bonds usually at a set interest rate. The other group benefits from some inflation, such as wage earners, small retailers who can raise prices, homeowners whose property values increase, and those in debt, because inflation makes it easier to repay debts. The money question became a struggle between the Midwestern Populists (pro-inflation) and the Eastern establishment (anti-inflation), or gold versus silver.[19] It was in this election that the new sectionalism of East versus West was manifested. Bryan identified with the common man, taking his text from Psalm 138: "For though the Lord is high, he regards the lowly; but the haughty he knows from afar."

Born in Illinois, Bryan was a good student with legendary skills in debate. This was a time when oratorical skills were considered a special mark of intelligence and ability. Communications were limited because a large part of the population could not read or write, and people were eager for ideas and political concepts which could be gained from public speakers. Therefore, the ability to make a convincing argument and to project your voice, in a time without microphone systems, was considered a great talent. Such students were marked for law, preaching, or politics. Bryan, in a sense, combined all three vocations during his career.

Bryan moved westward after finishing law school and settled in Nebraska. There he became a force in the local Democratic party. He went to Congress in 1891, where he had an opportunity to speak to a national audience. He made one speech; it was on the silver question, but the time was not right and it attracted little attention. Defeated in the next election, he then edited the *Omaha World Herald,* a bi-metal paper.[20] While editor, he lectured on the silver question throughout the United States. In small town Grange halls and churches he perfected, as he called it, "The Speech."

Meanwhile, Bryan paid his party dues by speaking in support of various candidates and organizing party affairs, all the while waiting for the chance to use "The Speech" before a national party convention. He knew he had to get the approval of Illinois Governor Altgeld to have a stage at the 1896 convention in Chicago. Altgeld was not impressed by the young lawyer, for he supported another candidate, Richard Bland, who had been active in the party for many years.

Bryan requested permission to speak on the issue of silver. Altgeld was hopeful that all the speeches had been assigned, thus leaving Bryan no opportunity to use his gifts.[21] It was not to be.

Bryan was given time to speak before the vote for the party platform plank on silver coinage. It was the perfect time for "The Speech." All the years of his debating and speaking skills were distilled into that moment.

On a warm July afternoon in the Chicago Coliseum, Bryan took the platform after two inferior speakers who could not be heard above the restless crowd. Bryan motioned for silence, posed with his head thrown back, one hand on the lectern, and took command.

The speech he was about to give would sweep the convention and the hearts of those who felt locked out of the economic system. He began:

> I have come to speak to you in defense of a cause as holy as
> the cause of liberty — the cause of humanity.

And thus began his Speech and the events that would lead Bryan to Lemont.

> With a zeal approaching the zeal which inspired the crusad-
> ers who followed Peter the Hermit, our silver Democrats went
> forth from victory to victory until they are now assembled
> not to discuss, not to debate, but to enter up judgement al-
> ready rendered by the plain people of the country. . .

Bryan went on to tell the Eastern interests and the Gold Democrats that business interests represent everyone in the economy — the farmer, the small town storekeeper, even:

> . . . the man who is employed for wages is as much a business-
> man as the corporation counsel in a great metropolis.

The magic of his voice and the poetry of his speech continued. He did not analyze the economic issue. He only spoke to the growing class division in the country — urban vs. rural, labor vs. management, East vs. West — that was becoming so much a part of the social pattern of the day.

> You tell us that the great cities are in favor of the Gold Stan-
> dard; we reply that the great cities rest upon our broad and
> fertile prairies. Burn down your cities and leave our farms
> and your cities will spring up again as if by magic, but destroy
> our farms and the grass will grow in the streets of every city
> in the country. . .

After the words for the farmer, he ended with labor and gave the catch phrase for the campaign to come:

> If they dare to come out in the open field and defend the Gold
> Standard as a good thing, we will fight them to the uttermost.
> Having behind us the producing masses of this nation and
> the world, supported by commercial interests, and labor in-
> terests, and toilers everywhere, we will answer their demand
> for a Gold Standard by saying to them: You shall not press
> down upon the brow of labor this crown of thorns, you shall
> not crucify mankind on a cross of gold!

As he said "crown of thorns" he raised his hands to the side of his head in a gesture of crowning and when he said "cross of gold" he flung his arms outward and paused for five seconds as if crucified.[22] He then lowered his arms and stepped off the stage. The crowd was silent, in that stunned silence that comes with an overwhelming performance. Then it went wild.

The next day the nominations for president were presented. After the fourth roll, Bryan, largely unknown until then, was nominated as the Democratic candidate for presi-dent. So began the campaign that would take him to Lemont and most of the country, in an election that would end up centering around Illinois and the governor who held a special place in Lemonter's hearts — Altgeld.

The campaign train was scheduled to arrive in town at 2:40 p.m. A small platform had been erected overlooking the site in front of the Alton Station, where three years before, Governor Altgeld spoke to Lemonters promising to solve the 1893 strike and had viewed the bodies of men shot in the disturbance, the very same spot where President Cleve-land[23] had stopped in 1887 with his new bride and, tongue in cheek, told the crowd that:

> Lemont is a charming city that always held a warm place in
> my affection . . . You will readily believe when I tell you it was
> in honor of your hometown that I named my private secre-
> tary Lamont.[24]

For the crowd gathered at the station, largely Democrats, the ticket of Bryan for president and Altgeld for governor was the finest that had ever been put before the public. It
was viewed by them as the answer to the depression and economic woes of the farming
and labor classes. Altgeld had demonstrated that a caring official could prevent strike
violence and settle labor disputes. He was a hero to those Lemonters that worked the
quarries, the two canals, and the railroads. He was also a hero to liberals such as Brand
Whitlock, who wrote later about that campaign that "politics in those days — and not
alone in those days either — were mean . . . it did fill me with disgust and made the whole
business utterly distasteful. Politics were almost wholly personal."[25]

However, Altgeld was not a hero to the opposition. He had over the course of the
campaign been portrayed as the devil incarnate, an anarchist, an evil force directing and
moving the presidential candidate, Bryan. The Republican candidate, William McKinley,
was so poor a match for Bryan's oratory that his manager, Mark Hanna, let him sit out a
large part of the campaign.[26] Hanna needed an issue and he found it in Altgeld. The governor of Illinois had interfered in labor disputes, such as the Lemont and Pullman Strikes,
had defied President Cleveland over the use of federal injunctions, and had pardoned the
remaining Haymarket conspirators.

Some Lemont Republicans were also upset by the actions of President Cleveland's
vice-president, Adlai E. Stevenson of Illinois. Stevenson served as first assistant postmaster in Cleveland's first term, and in that position removed almost all Republican
postmasters. It was said that "he beheaded GOP postmasters with the dispatch of the
French guillotine." One of his victims was Lemont's popular John Bodenschatz, who was
replaced in 1894 by James Noonan, a loyal Democrat.[27]

Pro-McKinley speakers were sent out to every section of the United States. These speakers belittled the silver issue and portrayed Altgeld as the real leader of the Democratic
Party. Because of Altgeld,[28] Illinois became the battleground of the campaign.

To counter this publicity, Bryan undertook to travel over 18,000 miles and to make
over 500 speeches. In spite of overwhelming opposition from the media and the power
brokers, Bryan drew large and enthusiastic crowds.

It was just such a crowd that greeted Bryan when his train reached Lemont. The *Chicago Tribune* reporter who accompanied Bryan recorded the Lemont speech as number
474 of Bryan's campaign. His speech was a magical joining of a number of speeches he had
used throughout the campaign:

> He, McKinley, says every dollar is worth 100 cents. I want to
> show you that free coinage of silver, instead of bringing a panic
> will stop the panic that people have been suffering for years.
> Now if anyone tells you the gold standard is good — you ask
> him why in all these years . . . No political party has declared
> it a good thing?

And to those who would exploit labor:

> I believe that all classes which rest upon the producers of
> wealth can only prosper when the producers of wealth are

prosperous; and, therefore, I am not unselfish when I desire laws as will enable the people to have more than enough to eat and drink and wear. I want them to have enough to be comfortable, because until they produce there is nothing to distribute, and if they simply produce without enjoying, the production of wealth will be so discouraged that it will finally cease.

The crowd listened and cheered. After the speech the train headed for Chicago. Perhaps Bryan was thinking of crowds like those in Lemont when he said later, "I have been taught to believe that all labor is honorable and that in this nation, the man who works for a living is a better citizen than the man who must live on what someone else earns."

Words and crowds, though, could not elect Bryan. In the end Hanna's forces won. The campaign lasted through election day. Lemont's working men, including those working for Western Stone, were told that if Bryan won, they need not return to work the next day. Some factories closed down posting signs that read, " This plant will re-open if McKinley is elected. It will remain closed if Bryan is elected."[29] In the end farmers and laborers voted their pocketbooks and not their hearts. Bryan and Altgeld lost. It was the first Republican victory ever recorded in the village of Lemont.

Brand Whitlock summed up the time and events, "There were here and there in the land dreamers of a sort, who had caught a new vision. The feeling of it, the emotion, was to find expression in Mr. Bryan's campaign in 1896."[30]

ENDNOTES

[1]The actual date was September 18, 1793. George Washington laid the stone in a Masonic ceremony.

[2]Emmett Dedmon, *Fabulous Chicago* (New York: Atheneum, 1983) p. 231.

[3]Roy McCarthy served from 1929 to 1936. He was only three at the time of the ceremony, yet he claimed to have remembered the day.

[4]A reference to the I & M Canal.

[5]Dedmon. *Fabulous Chicago,* p. 237

[6]Note that the trend in school design today is more like commercial buildings. What does the design of a school say about its symbol and role in a community?

[7]Nathan Ricker developed the architecture department at the University under the school of engineering. He was influenced by the newer American ideas of architecture, especially the designs of H.H. Richardson. His best known work is Altgeld Hall on the campus.

[8]Lemont certainly needed some positive publicity at this time.

[9]There has been a controversy over whether Old Central was built to house a secondary school. It would seem that was its original intent.

[10]Lloyd Wendt and Herman Kogan, *Lords of the Levee* (New York: Garden City Publishing, 1944), p. 133.

[11]*Ibid.*, p. 124.

[12]Mike McDonald was a gambling czar and Democratic political power broker who owned quarry land for a period of time. Sol Van Paang served in the state legislature and also was involved with gambling and politics. Both men were delegates to the State Democratic Convention that nominated John Altgeld for governor on the 1892 ticket.

[13]Sonia Kallick, "Continuous Battering Marked Championship Fight," *The Lemont Metropolitan*, July 21, 1977, p. 4.

[14]The gloves were skin tight with no padding, one step up from the usual bare-knuckle fight.

[15]*Chicago Tribune*, September 16-17, 1895. Also information from *Tribune* sports desk boxing editor, 1976.

[16]*Sears Consumer Guide, Fall, 1900* (Northfield: Digest Books) p. 394. It was made of French tanned leather, well padded on top and double stitched with silk. Order # 37812. A set of four gloves cost $4.75.

[17]*Chicago Tribune*, April 8, 1943.

[18]When Cleveland was elected in 1892, he was faced with paper dollars "circulating to an extant five times greater than the gold in the treasury." Each dollar was payable in gold. At the same time every silver dollar outstanding was exchangeable for one in gold. This caused a drain on the gold reserves and deflated the value of the dollar. See Mark Sullivan, *Our Times: 1900-1925.* (New York: Chas. Scribner & Sons, 1926) vol. 1, pp. 170-171.

[19]Louis Uchitelle, "Just a Little Inflation and Everybody's Happy," *The New York Times*, September 8, 1996, Section E. The author points out that this struggle has gone on since the 19th century. It simply takes different names through the years such as hard money vs. easy money, or tight monetary policy vs. easy policy.

[20]A bi-metal paper, or position, was one that favored the use of both gold and silver to back the dollar.

[21]Harry Barnard, *Eagle Forgotten* (Secacus NJ: Lyle Stuart, 1973), pp. 368-370.

[22]Louis W. Koenig, *Bryan: A Political Biography of William Jennings Bryan* (New York: G.P. Putnam's Sons, 1971), pp. 196-198.

[23]The irony here is that Bryan and the silver Democrats defeated Cleveland's forces at the Democratic Convention in 1896.

[24]His secretary was Don Lamont.

[25]Brand Whitlock, *Forty Years of It* (New York: Greenwood Press, 1968), pp. 94-95.

[26]Historically referred to as the "front porch campaign."

[27]Leonard Schlup, "Gilded Age Politician: Adali E. Stevenson of Illinois," *Illinois Historical Journal* (Springfield: Illinois State Historical Society, 1989) vol. lxxxii, no. 4, p. 221.

[28]Barnard, *Eagle Forgotten,* pp. 359-379. See also Koenig, *Bryan: A Political Biography,* p. 253.

[29]Barnard, *Eagle Forgotten,* p. 388.

[30]Whitlock, *Forty Years of It,* pp. 94-95.

CHAPTER TWENTY-THREE

LEMONT ENTERS
THE 20TH CENTURY

Economic and Social Changes: 1897-1900

By 1896, as Ship Canal construction moved on to the Lockport section, the population of Lemont dropped from 9,897 in 1895, to 6,574. The *Lemont Observer*, while not denying a large exodus of people, felt that the report was incorrect. The paper thought that the original count in 1895 was too high or the count for 1896 too low. In any case, the effect on the economy of the town was clear.[1] Lemont began to suffer the economic problems that had plagued the nation since 1893.

In January of 1897, the Norton Store at 103 Stephens Street declared bankruptcy. A fixture in Lemont, the store and grain elevator were part of the Norton Enterprises of Lockport, Lemont, and Chicago. Started in 1870 by S.W. Norton,[2] management was turned over to his son H.S. Norton[3] in 1877, who modernized the store, advertising in the *Lemont Phoenix* that "Norton's now deals in grains, flour, provisions, dry goods, crockery, and glassware. We have taken a departure from the OLD CREDIT SYSTEM and are selling for CASH at prices that offer unusual inducements to buyers from Lemont and surrounding country and to all who make Lemont a purchasing center."[4]

Norton's grew in size and services offered. Herbert S. Norton became a stockholder in many Lemont businesses, the bank, the savings and loan, Lemont Power and Light, and some quarry operations. This network was tied to the rest of the Norton family: S.W. Norton and D.C. Norton in Lemont, and J.L. Norton and L.D. Norton in Lockport. Together they held all or part of the following: Norton's Flour Mill, Lockport; Lockport Power and Light; Norton's Chicago Flour Mill; Lockport's Norton's Merchandise; Lockport's Norton's Machine Shop; a cooper shop; and a grain storage at Romeo and Lemont.

Their economic power was so great that whenever the family needed money for expansion or grain purchases, they sold notes to the public against their grain holdings. Not only did the Nortons sell these notes, but in Lemont, the store also served as a company store bank. Quarry workers would deposit their wages with the store on account and gain a cash discount on items purchased.[5] Since the store sold almost all goods needed by a family, the system helped carry quarry families over the lean months of winter, when the quarries were closed.

The crisis began when L.D. Norton, in Lockport, began to speculate in wheat in 1896, along with Joseph Leiter. He thought he could enter into a big corner on wheat, when Leiter reported European crop failures. A corner begins whenever a commodity sold for later delivery is so controlled by the purchaser that the seller cannot make delivery except by buying from the purchaser.[6] L.D. Norton sold over 200,000 dollars worth of notes to local people to raise cash to buy wheat. The scheme did not work when they found themselves up against the meat packer, Philip Armour. Armour held 30 percent of Chicago's wheat and was so tough a businessman that he ordered a fleet of grain ships to sail from Duluth through Lake Michigan's winter storms to cover the contracts.[7] In a move to avoid loss, J.L. Norton tried to dissolve the family partnership, but it was too late.

In Lemont, both Herbert S. Norton and his father struggled to find the capital to pay their outstanding debts, but there was no one with the money, or the desire to cover them. Confessions of judgement within the family included Mabel Norton, J.L. Norton, and Clare Norton. They also owed the Lemont State Bank 7,500 dollars. Their total assets were 20,000 dollars, while their liabilities amounted to 30,000 dollars. They owed money to townspeople, the bank, and to the Lemont Building Loan and Homestead Association, where Herbert served as a director and treasurer.[8] The store closed and was placed under the trusteeship of Frank Welch.[9] Welch had to advertise for sealed bids for the entire stock of the store. The idea of retailing it was abandoned, as cash was a scarce commodity in town.[10]

The family fortune was gone. Lockport's Dorothy Dow Fitzgerald, poet and author, painted a sad word picture of the fallen fortunes of the Nortons when she wrote of L.D. Norton's wife:

> Mrs. Norton
> Stiff with the memory
> of great wealth
> before the depression of the
> Nineties.[11]

The effect of Norton's collapse was disastrous on the whole community. It was rumored that two Lemonters attempted suicide after learning of the failure because of their losses. One was Thomas Huston, an outstanding civic leader and city treasurer, who was also the secretary of the Lemont Building Loan and Homestead Association. The other was Mrs. Ray, a widow who had lost most of her savings in the collapse.

Thomas Huston did die drinking carbolic acid in a hotel room in Chicago. His death prompted a review of the books of the loan association and all accounts were found in order. H.S.

Norton's store, photo circa 1890s. Grain storage building is on the right. (Photo courtesy of Lemont Historical Society)

Norton was upset by the implication that there could be a problem with the funds. He told the *Observer* that he felt the references to him in the Chicago papers in the matter of Mr. Huston's death did him an injustice, there being no liabilities between them.[12] Many suggested that Huston's death was not really related to Norton's failure, but to the mental and physical suffering that had tormented him since his service in the Civil War.[13] Mrs. Ray survived and the family reported that she had not attempted to take her life, but accidently shot herself while trying to hammer some tacks with the butt end of a pistol she thought was unloaded. Norton's reopened in 1899 and was incorporated as S.W. Norton and Company.

By the fall of 1897, Wold Brothers Soda Company also failed and was forced to reorganize, leaving its stockholders suffering losses. Many other Lemont businesses closed as population dwindled, including the large Joliet Clothing Store on Canal Street. As a result, the downtown presented a number of boarded up buildings, aside from the Smokey Row dives, that tempted vandalism and arson. Fires of known incendiary origin[14] occurred at the east end of Illinois Street, destroying two frame homes, in the stable of Western Stone at the northeast corner of State and the I & M Canal, and at Norton's warehouse.

Within two years, Lemont's other large general store, Tedens & Thormahlen declared bankruptcy. The death of John Tedens Sr. hastened the store's demise. It was assigned to Frank Welch and reorganized as Tedens & Dystrup, with John Tedens Jr. and Andrew Dystrup as the new partners. John Thormahlen Jr. took the leather and harness business and opened his own shop on Main Street.[15]

Some Lemonters, facing hard times, found unique methods of surviving. One scheme was to steal tools and scrap iron from the canal contractors, which were sold to middle men for cash, no questions asked. The tools were often redeemed by the contractors, as this was cheaper than buying new tools. Almost all attempts to catch the thieves failed. The junk and old metal buyer in Lemont, S. Nathan, would not reveal names, and the local police were not interested in what they considered petty theft. Scrap metal sold at high prices and this led to the theft of bolts and rails. A Myler derrick at the Ship Canal site was completely emptied of its bolts one night and, as a result, toppled over into the canal diggings. Even the work bell at Hastings quarry was taken and sold out of town.[16]

The paper editorialized on the loss of revenue with the completion of Lemont's portion of the Ship Canal, "Sleeping hills of disembowelled rock at 70 cents per cubic 'disembowelment' made fortunes for contractors. It would have been better for the con-

J. H. TEDENS & CO.,
DEALERS IN
DRY GOODS,
Groceries, Provisions, and Farmers' Produce;
AND ALSO MANUFACTURERS OF
BOOTS & SHOES
CLOTHING & HARNESS.

Advertisement for J.H. Tedens & Company from 1880s. (Illustration courtesy of Lemont Historical Society)

Picnic at Peterson's Park, later called, possibly inappropriately, Brown's Woods. (Photo courtesy of Lemont Historical Society)

tractors and for Lemont had the work proceeded more slowly."[17] Once busy Lemont took on a deserted look. It fell on the village board elected in the spring to attempt the task of revitalizing the community.

Politics remained a passionate pastime in town. When J. McCarthy announced he would not run for mayor, several candidates came forward, many still polarized by the McCarthy-Clancy struggle. The winners were Daniel Murphy, as mayor, and more moderate men for trustees, including J. Skarin, A.J. Helbig, Kasimieriz Bushkiewicz, John Powalisz, Michael New, and John Wagner.

Over 100 people attended the swearing-in ceremony in the Village Hall, many interested in obtaining work in the new village government. Their hopes were dashed when it was revealed that the village had only $4.82 in its treasury.[18] Mayor Murphy was accused of making some nasty remarks about the old administration, but he denied any intentions of casting slurs against them. He did, however, establish new rules for village board meetings. There would be no smoking during the sessions, and no member could come to the meetings intoxicated, or such offender would "be asked to vacate his seat."[19]

Those who won appointments were Michael Wagner and John Schultz, marshals; H. Losey and M. Welch, engineers; P.A. Nelson, treasurer; Wm. Murphy, water tax collector, timekeeper, and coal inspector; Tom Godson, teamster; and Dennis Noonan, janitor.

To stabilize the economy, the board dropped the bi-yearly license fee for saloons still in business, and to gain revenue they permitted the operation of a horse market by Charles Nathan twice a month on east Talcott Street. Most towns discouraged horse markets as they tended to bring in a rough crowd. These markets were often outlets for used, sick, older horses, and, at times, for stolen animals. There was even a fear that the market horses could carry diseases that would be transmitted to the horse population in town. The main source of the animals sold in Lemont probably came from the Ship Canal contractors. Many animals were purchased for slaughter and for rendering. It was a sad, sorry enterprise and with Reverend Clancy gone, the horse market could not be "Clancyified."

The village also set water rates to gain revenue. The fees were 50 dollars a year for livery stables and soda pop factories;[20] 10 dollars to five dollars for bathtubs; 25 dollars for undertakers; five dollars for barbershops; 10 to 20 dollars for laundries; three dollars for a private key to a hydrant; two dollars and fifty cents for a lawn hose; and three dollars for water closets.[21]

Another problem the board faced was how to establish wages for those few men that they could hire. The problem was solved by basing all pay on wages received by the quarry workers. There were also plans for revitalization of the town. Talty and O'Neil, of Smokey Row fame, added a private gym in their basement for the use of their customers. Meanwhile, the village upgraded and developed the triangle of land in front of the Alton Station to make a park.[22]

Amusement for Lemonters was offered at Teden's Opera House above Teden's store. A variety of entertainments could be had for a little as ten cents. Professional productions ranged from Mozart quartets and the Francis Owen Company's play *The Vendetta,* to Earl Doty's production of *An American Girl in Cuba.*[23] The stage also served for the many amateur productions and public ceremonies that were so much a part of community life.

There was also less cultural entertainment, such as the rat killing contests at Otzenburger's saloon. The champion rat-killer, a dog owned by Mr. Stein, killed 89 rats in 13 minutes, a testimony not only to the dog, but to the kind of people who viewed such events, and to the availability of rats in Lemont.

Other entertainment included church socials, picnics in Brown's Woods, nutting parties in the fall, sleigh rides in the winter, hunting and fishing in the valley, and dances in the Village Hall and Tedens Opera house. Summer days were given to the local baseball clubs. In April of 1897, the *Observer* noted that the season had started and commented that the Lemonts had organized and the nine were made up of the same men as last year, as was the team called the Rivals. There was also talk of a new club, the Marquettes, being organized. The paper editoralized, "Line them up boys, baseball is a fine game, an innocent game, a healthful sport if you keep it so. Let every game the coming summer be a game that Ladies may attend. If you have a member in your club who plays more with his mouth than his hands, drop him. Give us clean ball and lots of it."

Still it was politics that entertained most of Lemont. The village election was exciting, but nothing beat the school board election in April of 1897, for it was the first election where women were allowed to vote. The issues were emotional, and again the McCarthy-Clancy fallout clouded the election. C.A. Talty was president of the school board and had directed part of the construction of the old 1896 Central School Annex. He was opposed by Dr. J.J. Leahy. The main issue was the question of whether the grade school district should continue using tax monies to support post-eighth grade classes. The new school annex had been built with revenue from Smokey Row, with the idea of continuing secondary instruction. Evidence of this can be seen looking at the front of Old Central School.

Carved there are the words "Lemont High School 1896," but the word "High" is faint due to a futile attempt to remove it. Fifteen students completed the course in 1891,[24] and by 1896, there were 40 students enrolled in these classes. They paid two dollars a month tuition, but the burden of tuition costs fell on the grade school's taxpayers.

The first annual high school commencement was held on June 30, 1891. The graduates were Cornelia Robinson, Lizze Brown, Robert Ries, O. R. Derby, John Welch, Mamie Welch, Alfred Roebuck, Henry Welch, Willie Kettering,[25] Theresa Smelzer, Lena New, Anna Welch, Elmer Huston, Lara Spence,[26] and Lee Brown.[27]

No attempt had been made in the township to develop or fund a township high school taxing district. Most rural families of the township were content with the ungraded country school. Those who sought more education for their children usually boarded them in town in order for them to attend Old Central or St.

LEMONT HIGH SCHOOL

First Annual Commencement,

Lemont, Ill., June 30, 1891.

PROGRAMME.

MUSIC.—Quartette.....Misses Cornelia Robinson, Lizzie Brown.
Messrs. Robert Reis, O. R. Derby.
RECITATION.—"Mary Garvin." *Whittier*.............Mamie Welch.
ORATION.—"Immigration,".................Alfred Roebuck.
ORATION.—"Immigration,"....................Henry Welch.
MUSIC. Song.—"The Dago Banana Peddler.".. Willie Kettering.
ESSAY.—"The Heroic in History.".........Theresa Schmelzer.
RECITATION.—"The Order for a Picture." *Cary*.....Lena New.
ESSAY.—"Mistakes.".......................Anna Welch.
MUSIC. Song.—"Supposing."................Lizzie Brown.
ORATION.—"Labor.".....................Elmer Huston.
ORATION.—"The Public Schools of America."......John Welch.
ESSAY AND VALEDICTORY.—"Tongues.".......Lura Spence.
RESPONSE TO VALEDICTORY.................Lee Brown.
MUSIC. Song.—"Bonni Dundee.".............Lena New.
PRESENTATION OF DIPLOMAS.

Program for first commencement at Lemont High School. (Illustration courtesy of Lemont Historical Society)

James Academy. Some were sent to Chicago or other communities that offered secondary education.

Talty defended the plan for high school courses, mainly because he wanted to train local students to become teachers. Talty and his board strongly favored hiring local people to teach, and without classes available to Lemont grade school graduates, there would not be a supply of local people qualified to teach.[28]

Dr. Leahy, like many others at his time, opposed spending tax money for anything more than eight grades of education. His view of public education was part of a general tax opposition sweeping most public schools, including Chicago. Many felt that all that was needed for an educated work force was basic eighth grade instruction, and any class work beyond that was not the obligation of the taxpayer.

Part of this opposition was directed at the cost of educating children of new immigrants. Some members of Lemont's older families resented newcomers, especially the foreign born, since most were willing to take jobs at a pay lower than the prevailing wage. The paper editorialized on the situation, reporting that Talty and his board "believed in giving places to home talent. At the present time three teachers are Lemonters. If the men who advocate the abolition of high school will look facts in the face . . . they will see that the extra school is needed for our students to compete."[29]

The effect of the women's vote in that election is hard to determine, but the social effect was remarkable.[30] The *Lemont Observer* reviewed the event:

> The great day dawned at last . . . There was business from the start at 10:00 a.m. to 4:00 p.m. We never saw such a lively day in Lemont. How the women did vote. All day long they came in loads. The Saturday cooking was left to the care of itself,[31] and the babies did likewise. The "New Man" has not yet evolved to take the place of the "New Woman" when she is away voting or electioneering. Eighteen year olds wanted to vote but they couldn't. Nearly 1500 votes were registered in the two precincts.

When the votes were tallied, Talty was declared a winner by 380 votes. Leahy called for a recount, claiming vote fraud, so a court hearing was scheduled. Judge Carter, from Chicago, was summoned to hear the case. Talty was represented by the school board lawyer J. Coburn, while Leahy hired the influential Chicago firm of Kicham and Scanlon. It was a long hot summer of hearings in the Village Hall, hearings that were a series of petty arguments, accusations, name calling, and old gossip. Finally, Judge Carter, who the papers said slept through most of the sessions, declared Leahy as the official winner. On hearing the news, his supporters paraded through town with a small brass band. Dr. Leahy claimed his seat at the August school board meeting.[32]

The disputed cornerstone. (Photo courtesy of Lemont Historical Society)

Tensions on the board created problems for those seeking jobs or payment for work done. The old and new members, James Ash, Joseph Frelichowski, Theo. Losey, J.J. McGraw, John O'Brien, John Skarin, and Frank Welch[33] clashed so often that it became hard to do necessary business. The most foolish episode of this behavior fell on a stone cutter, Mr. Rogan. He carved the front Bedford Stone arches on the 1896 school annex and the cornerstone names. When he presented his bill, Dr. Leahy, as board president, refused to pay it unless his name was added to the cornerstone. The old members of the board would not support the addition of his name since he was not on the board when the annex was planned and built. Rogan, wise to the ways of Lemont politics, refused to do any other work until he was paid for his past work. He continued to present his bill every year for five years and was refused each time. He did not collect his 100 dollars until a new board was elected. Another person forced to wait for payment was the board lawyer, J. Coburn. Hired to defend Talty, when Talty lost, the board refused to pay him. He also finally collected his fee in 1906 for the long "hot summer of the recount."

The population decrease in town, coupled with the depressed economy, also affected the private schools. The *Observer*[34] noted that by late fall of 1897, many families were moving to South Chicago or Joliet, where there was promise of work. Tuition costs and lower enrollments forced St. Cyril's to close several of its classrooms and transfer some students to Central School. This move put an added burden on the village's public school system. Still, in spite of Leahy's opposition, the other board members overruled him and continued post-eighth grade course offerings. These older high school students were a vocal group. They even petitioned the board asking for a dismissal at 3:00 p.m. instead of 4:00 p.m. However, their petition was rejected by School Superintendent Haley as impractical under the "intense" course of instruction offered.[35]

In order for St. James Academy to continue operating, they added adult education classes to their curriculum. The Sisters introduced such courses as music lessons, including vocal, mandolin, guitar, and piano. They also offered instruction in all types of needlework and, more importantly, classes in bookkeeping, shorthand, and typewriting.

There were other events to distract Lemonters after the "boom times" of the mid 1890s. Among them were the fall church fairs given by Reverend Father Bollman of St. James of the Sag. One of the unique features of the Sag Church is its cemetery. The original eight acres were deeded to the church parish by James and Bridget Murphy and John and Catherine Sullivan, who had farms adjoining the church land. At the deeding ceremony, Bridget Murphy suggested adding a clause that stated that "any poor may bury his dead in the cemetery without cost."[36] Because of what was a verbal agreement, an acre was set aside for any non-member of the parish to bury his dead without cemetery or sexton fees. The deed was recorded on October 13, 1858. Father Bollman said that as far as he knew, this acre, called "the acre of God," was the only cemetery of its kind in the world. Here people of all stations in life would rest. There were even spots for the stranger, the unbaptized, and the suicide in the northwest corner of the plot.

St. James of the Sag Church. (Photo courtesy of Greg Kolack)

The free burial policy became known along the I & M Canal and in Chicago's Irish Catholic communities. The poor would come out on the Alton train line with their dead.[37] Often the mourners held movable wakes highlighted with drinking. This presented problems for Father Bollman and for Marshal Coen of the Sanitary District Police. Both recalled one wake in particular. The group arrived early in the morning from Bridgeport. The day was cold and the coffin heavy, so the bottle was freely passed to ease the ordeal. The party dragged the coffin up the steep hill looking for a gravesite. Upon hearing the commotion, Mike Stepps and Tim Caroll, the gravediggers, came forward to offer their services, but the mourners preferred to dig the grave themselves. Mike and Tim were not only sorry to lose the fee, but they also wanted to avoid the need to rebury the body later. Too often the dead were inadequately interred by amateurs, and clearly this group would either dig too shallow a grave or place the coffin on top of an older internment.

The ground was hard and the winds even harder, so more spirits were passed around. Someone sang, "Gra Machee a coolin baun."[38] Finally, as afternoon approached, the party realized that they had no place to stay until the evening train to Chicago. They decided to go to the parish house. Father Bollman was away, and only his housekeeper was there baking bread. The members of the wake broke into the house screaming, singing, and laughing. The housekeeper became so terrified that she ran upstairs and locked herself in an unheated room, where she nearly froze to death before her rescue later that evening by Marshal Coen.

Friends of the departed built a fire, helped themselves to the bread, passed the bottle and continued singing. When the Reverend Father came home, he stood in the doorway viewing the crowd.

"I wonder who his giblets is?" asked a tipsy member of the wake. "Say mister if you can find a place to sit, why not have a drink?"

"Thanks for your hospitality, but this is my house. I am pastor of the parish and would like you to get out of here."

But the wake refused to move. No amount of persuasion would work. Father Bollman was forced to call on Marshal Coen. It took the Marshal and 30 of his men to remove the crowd. They were escorted to the station to be sent back to Chicago and the flats of Bridgeport, singing all the way.

Once a month for the 21 years Father Bollman served at St. James, he would say a low mass for the unknown dead in his "Acre of God." He always remembered that rowdy wake as a symbol of so many of the poor, strong enough to be able to bury their dead and celebrate life at the same time.

In September of 1897, Father Bollman held his annual fair in the large hall at the bottom of the church hill to raise funds for the parish, an event that was to become one of Lemont's legends. Over the years the fair had been successful with the older parishioners, but the young people had shown little interest in it. To attract them, Father Bollman hired two Chicago Irish musicians, William Loney of 3326 Charlton Street, and John Kelly of 200 W. Taylor Street.

Loney and Kelly's harp and flute music brought out a large crowd, and dancing lasted until 1:00 a.m. Sunday night. Not wishing to travel when it was so late, the two musicans fixed up cots in the upper floor of the hall and settled in for the night. Kelly fell asleep rapidly, but Loney was restless. The night was cold and the moonlight coming through the window cast an eerie light on the unfamiliar surroundings.

Suddenly he heard the gallop of a team of horses and the rumble of wheels. He wondered what event could send someone out in such a hurry so late at night. Looney jumped out of the cot and ran to the window. The moonlight cast light on the tombstones in the church graveyard, the steeple, and on the gravel lane. The sound of galloping horses and crunching gravel continued louder, but no carriage or team was visible. The sound came to the front of the hall, passed with a rush, and faded down the road.

Looney, terrified, woke Kelly and told him what he had heard. As they were talking, the sound of galloping horses and the carriage returned growing louder and louder. Both men went to the window, but saw no carriage or horses. What they did see was the form of a woman in white standing in the road. She was young and tall, with black hair that hung down her shoulders "in tangled confusion." Her hands were raised above her head and she moved in a gliding motion. "Deep sadness was reflected from her sepulchral eyes that rolled about with the intensity of some soul-eating despair." The young men were about to call out to her when she glided over the road through a rail fence and wandered about the field.

Again they heard the sound of galloping horses, but this time they appeared. They were snow white and covered with fine netting. A light glowed from the forehead of each.

The carriage was dark and no driver could be seen. The young woman frolicked over the road as the carriage swept by. She raised her hands and then lowered them. A dark shadow gathered about her and she began sinking into the shadow until she, the carriage, and the horses disappeared. The two men stared not knowing what to do. Then the sound of the horses returned and the young woman reappeared; as the horses appeared the men heard her call, "Come on." She waved her hands and disappeared into the ground. Kelly and Loney did not wait to see more. They got into their cots and stayed awake until dawn. At dawn they rushed to the police station with the story.

Marshall Edward Coen of the Sanitary District Police, who lived in the Sag, took down their story and reported that "both men are willing to make an affidavit of the events." William Loney added that he would be willing to tell a priest that it was the truth and added, "I have never told a lie to a priest in my life." Marshall Coen added:

> I know nothing as to the truth of the story but this much I will say. Both Kelly and Loney are fine young men and I have no reason to disbelieve any statement they have made. They evidently saw something which has impressed them greatly. I do not believe there is anything of the practical joke in the affair. That would be dangerous in this locality. Everyone out here carries weapons since rough characters have been brought in for the building of the canal. It would be tempting death to try such a thing, for any person so foolish would is likely to receive a bullet. Both men are sober fellows. There was no liquor at the dance. I believe that these boys are telling the truth. I can make nothing else out of it.[39]

Old settlers of the area said that the ghosts were those of two young people who fell in love in the early 1880s. He was a young priest who served as an assistant to the mission priest at St. James and she was a housekeeper. They fought against their feelings for one another until they could bear it no longer. Against all social conventions of the day they decided to elope. Late at night he hitched up the team and wagon and told her to wait for him halfway down the hill so they would not be seen. She called, "Come on," as he approached with the wagon. As she boarded, the horses bolted, turning the wagon over and killing them both. They were buried together in an unmarked site in the St. James "Acre of God" and on moonlight nights are doomed to reenact their attempt to run away.

The event kept the town excited and, as reported by the paper, it encouraged several of the local kids to spend that fall running around at night wearing white paper coats to scare the village. It must have been a time of gothic imagination in town as the people on Talcott Street added to the mystery by reporting flying airships, airships that appeared only on their street.[40]

In the spring of 1898, Lemont, like the rest of the nation, was swept up in the emotion of the Spanish-American War and the Cuban struggle for independence. It was said that Lemont men who wanted adventure had two choices, to fight for Cuban independence or to go to Alaska to search for gold.[41] The paper ran "facts about Alaska" in their columns including such strange myths as "the mosquitos are numbered by the billions and are poisonous. Gold fillings in teeth contract from the cold and fall out, anyone intending to mine should have amalgam fillings." They also warned that men born in the southern latitudes can go insane from the long dark.

Edwin Walker Whiting's grave at Rosehill Cemetery. (Photo courtesy of Lemont Historical Society)

The Spanish-American War lasted only three months and 22 days. Over 200,000 men served, and of that number 379 were killed, 1,604 wounded, and 4,000 died of disease or spoiled food. Lemont records six men buried here as veterans who served in that conflict; they were Michael Heinz, Peter Heinz, Anthony Hesserich, Fredrick Reed, Peter Meyer, and Clayton Conly.[42]

Edwin Walker Whiting, grandson of Edwin Walker, was one of the Lemont men who died of yellow fever during the war. His stone at Rosehill cemetery reads: "Edwin Walker Whiting, died Santiago de Cuba, August 8, 1898," and above it the phrase, "Pro Patria. He gave his young life for his country."[43]

One Lemont man played a unique role in that war. His name was Ralph Paine and he was born in 1871, when Lemont was still part of the frontier West. His father, Reverend Samuel Delhaye Paine served as minister to the Lemont Methodist Church. However, pay and prestige were scant for frontier clergy, so when Ralph's father was offered a church in Florida, he accepted. Ralph had to leave the small town life for the East. He went to school at Yale and began writing sports coverage for the school paper and for the *Philadelphia Press*. Graduating in 1894 and eager to make a name for himself, he set off for New York, then the center of journalism. Competition between two newspapers, Pulitzer's *New York World* and Hearst's *New York Journal* had created a new style of news writing; reporters were encouraged to get scoops, play up events, and even make the news themselves — anything to sell papers.

Trouble in Spanish-held Cuba had been going on for ten years. Unhappy under Spanish rule, many Cubans had come to the United States to raise money and acquire arms for an army of independence. Their efforts had become a popular cause, championed by the press. To get a job, Ralph Paine came up with a scheme that he thought he could sell to William Randolph Hearst. He would arrange passage on a ship supplying illegal arms to the Cuban insurrectionists and report on the voyage.[44] Hearst bought the idea and added a twist to the scheme. His organization had raised money for a fancy presentation sword for the hero of the rebellion, General Gomez. Hearst asked Paine to deliver it and write the story. He did add the warning, "I will be perfectly frank with you. This would be devilish hard to explain to the Spanish army, if you happen to be caught."[45]

In Jacksonville, Paine arranged passage on the *Tres Amigos*, a ship with the reputation of being the "Flying Dutchman" of the illegal arms trade. There was a standing reward by the governor of Cuba for the capture or destruction of the ship. All went smoothly on the *Tres Amigos* until it anchored in a small Cuban bay to unload the weapons. Suddenly, a gunboat attacked and drove them into open waters. There the *Tres Amigos* returned fire and damaged the Spanish gunboat. Paine had his story of adventure at sea, and with approval from Captain "Dynamite" Johnny O'Brien, he transmitted it by wire to New

York. When they arrived in Key West, to his surprise the ship was impounded and Lemont-born Ralph Paine found himself one of the few Americans ever charged with piracy on the high seas. He went into hiding.

The government was forced to act because Hearst had made his story a *New York Journal* front page scoop:

> *Piracy Strikes Terror*
>
> Tres Amigo's filibusters in fear of their lives. If convicted of
> the crime they will be sentenced to death.[46]

Hearst found the story useful in his campaign to get the American government to intervene in Cuba. He ran an editorial lambasting President Cleveland for his inaction and decrying the fate of Paine and the crew:

> When he [Cleveland] undertakes to have American citizens
> hanged by the neck until dead because they beat off Spanish
> armed vessels . . . he exceeds even his limits of power.[47]

Ralph Paine, the pirate reporter, sailed with other ships while avoiding the law. He continued to carry the sword for Gomez, but never got it to him and finally turned it over to Cuban agents for delivery. The piracy charges were dropped for lack of witnesses and Paine returned to other reporting until the battleship *Maine* blew up in Havana harbor. With that act, America went to war with Spain. Paine served as a correspondent with such legends in the newspaper world as Ed McCready, Richard Harding Davis, and Stephen Crane. Crane made Paine the hero of one of his short stories about the war called "The Lone Charge of William B. Perkins: A True Story." Paine's early childhood in Lemont must have been a part of his personality, for Crane marked him as a western man in his story with these words:

> Perkins [Paine] had no information of war and no particular
> rapidity of mind for acquiring it but he had that rank and
> fibrous quality of courage that springs from the thick soil of
> Western America.[48]

Paine continued his career covering the Boxer Rebellion in China, serving as a correspondent in England, working as a muckraker in the newspaper crusade against the beef trust, and as an expert in naval affairs. He also wrote several children's books.[49]

With the war, the United States entered the new century as a world power. But in Lemont, the town was still struggling with change from an agriculture and quarry based economy to an industrial age economy. Much of the town's income had hinged on the stone quarries and as they slowly closed or downsized the only large industry to offer work was Illinois Pure Aluminum. The plant had 100 workers and was planning expansion. What advantage Lemont did have was its transportation corridors. Already, the I & M Canal was outdated, so hope rested on the new canal.

As the "Drainage Ditch," a name favored by locals but not by the Sanitary Board,[50] neared completion, the anticipated economic boom failed to appear. There were even those who predicted that the massive engineering project would be a failure. It was thought that the water flow would be as unsuccessful in moving Chicago sewage as was the I & M Canal. This new project depended on a strong flow from Lake Michigan to dilute the sewage, a plan opposed by many communities along the lake.[51]

As for the towns downstream along the Illinois and Mississippi Rivers, they became concerned about the effect of the sewage on their own water supplies and began to plan action against the Sanitary District. On January 2, 1900, a small needle dam between the Chicago River and the new canal section to Lockport was opened and the waters of the Chicago River began to fill the channel. The project was three months late, as the completion date had originally been set for October of 1899. This initial fill was done because the trustees of the Sanitary District were afraid that downstream cities, especially St. Louis, would attempt an injunction before the official opening day scheduled for January 20, so the board decided to act before any legal action could halt the project.

It took two weeks to fill the Chicago to Lockport section. On the night of January 16, two trustees and two commissioners took a special Santa Fe train to Lockport and inspected the controlling gates. Governor Tanner was called and he gave his permission to open the locks before St. Louis could file its injunction.[52]

At 11 a.m. on January 17, the small group watched as the gates were opened. Water from Lake Michigan and the Chicago River flowed through the gates and on to the Mississippi. Once begun, the flow could not be easily stopped. St. Louis's suit was dismissed in 1906.[53] Work on the Lockport to Joliet section was done from 1903 to 1907. In 1910, the U.S. War Department approved the construction of a secondary channel from Lake Calumet to the Sag. This was to add additional water without taking more from Lake Michigan. Called the Cal-Sag Channel, it was completed in 1922.

Since the official opening was less than spectacular, the politicians felt that more publicity would help their image. So in May, when Admiral Dewey, the hero of the War with Spain in the Pacific, scheduled a visit to Chicago, it was decided that he should have a tour of the new canal, the modern engineering wonder of the world.

Excitement ran through Lemont on that May morning. Children and adults sang the favorite ditty of the day:

> O! Dewey was the morning
> Upon the first of May,
> And Dewey was the Admiral
> Down in Manila Bay.
> And Dewey were those regent's eyes,
> Them orbs of royal blue
> And do we feel discouraged?
> I do not think we do.

Not great music, but a reflection of the popularity of Dewey in those early days of American power. School children practiced the song while adults decorated the stretches of spoil bank left by canal construction. The students were dressed in their best clothes. Miss Reagan, the first grade teacher, gave each child a small 45-star flag as they lined up for the march down Stephen Street to the Canal.[54]

Admiral Dewey had arrived in Chicago a few days before and had been honored at parades, dinners, and receptions. It had been two years since his great victory over Admiral Montojo's fleet in Manila Bay, a victory immortalized by the words, "You may fire when ready, Gridley." In those two years Dewey had developed political ambitions. He married into the family that owned *The Washington Post,* and there was talk of his possible candidacy for president on the Democratic ticket, a fact that upset both the Silver Democrats and the McKinley Republicans.

Chicago's Mayor Carter Harrison II[55] had difficulty getting a reception committee together because of the political undercurrent. He finally got help from a former Lemonter, Chicago alderman Martin B. Madden of the Republican Central committee. Madden agreed to organize the event because it would focus on his interest in canals, especially the idea of an isthmus canal across Central America. Madden was able to bring together a group to honor the Admiral.

The day started with Dewey and a party of over 200 taking a train to McCook. At McCook, the main party boarded the cutter "Hilda," while the rest of the dignitaries boarded other vessels.

The public outpouring was so warm that several major strikes were canceled for the day in order that the trip go smoothly. Even the construction workers, who had been in a bitter strike, came to work to build a platform used to board the cutter. The only evidence of their feelings was a hand-painted sign that read, "Made by union labor." It is not known if the Admiral saw it.

The party was served a large lunch with the best of food and drink for all. Isham Randolph recited the usual poem for the occasion:

> Glad welcome, gallant sailor,
> Oh, Navy's chief and pride
> Whose name thrills every sailor's heart
> Where ever our war ships ride.
>
> Ours is a man made river,
> Now flowing full and free,
> From the Great lakes of the Northlands,
> To the far off southern Sea.[56]

As the flotilla sailed toward Lemont, the wind picked up and clouds began to gather. The only break in the weather came when they entered the Des Plaines Valley. The *Chicago Daily News* reported that "the countryside had a green look and the sun came out and lit the hills of Lemont, Romeo, and Will County in honor of the occasion."[57]

At Lemont the sun was bright as the first sight of the Admiral's flag was seen in the distance. The crowds waved and cheered the hero of Manila Bay. Dewey and the officials stood on the deck and responded to Lemont's reception. As the fleet turned the bend in the Ship Canal toward Lockport, it began to rain. On board the cutter, the captain, an old barge man, was feeling good. He had eaten a fine lunch, drunk a good deal of spirits, and he was commanding a ship with the main Admiral of the American Navy as his passenger. The crowds and liquor gave him a sense of power. In this state, he overlooked the fact that the undercurrent was stronger than usual, because Chief Engineer Isham Randolph had ordered extra water for this special day and it was creating an undertow.

As the ship approached the controlling gates at Lockport, Dewey, in the center of an admiring group, stepped to the rail to give the works a glance. He then called to Mayor Harrison, "You had better suggest to our captain to give the controlling works a wider berth."

Harrison went to the captain with Dewey's suggestion and the old barge man replied, "I know my business and want no advice or interference." Harrison went back to the deck, but could not find the Admiral. Returning to the bridge, he found Dewey, alone, at the helm. Dewey, now in charge, said, "It's all right Mr. Mayor. I am getting her from the undertow at the dam, but when I took the helm we were in greater danger than I was anytime in Manila."

The captain was found in another room cursing and screaming, "This is mutiny on the high seas! Dewey is a blankety-blank mutineer. I've a mind to put him in irons, in solitary and fed on bread and water!" It took a while for the captain to sober up. [58]

Meanwhile the crowds at the dam, unaware of the little drama, cheered Dewey, not knowing that he had saved the party from a small naval disaster on the Ship Canal. On shore another mishap took place when a 12-pounder cannon, designed for a salute, discharged too early, mortally wounding Sergeant Richard Popp of Fowler's Battery.[59] All must have been grateful that the trip back to Chicago on the Santa Fe Railroad was an uneventful one.

ENDNOTES

[1]*Lemont Observer*, February 18, 1897.

[2]The whole family had a tendency to use only initials instead of first names.

[3]Lemont had another H.S. Norton, Horace Singer Norton, who was the son of Dewitt Clinton Norton. The two often get mixed up in the Lemont records. S.W.'s son was Herbert Norton. D.C. Norton, mayor and quarry owner, was S.W. Norton's cousin.

[4]Sonia Kallick, *Lemont Walking Tour Site 17* (Lemont: Lemont Historical Society, 1974).

[5]The arrangement was not entirely out of concern for the worker, but an outgrowth of the 1885 strike and the need for quarry owners to control the workers.

[6]*Federal Trade Commission Report On Grain Trade* (Washington D.C.: U.S. Printing Office, 1920-1926) vii, p. 241.

[7]This action by Armour is part of the colorful history of the Chicago Board of Trade. It is the basis for Frank Norris' novel, *The Pit*. See William Cronon, *Nature's Metropolis* (New York: W. W. Norton & Company, 1991) pp. 248-249. The Norton holdings were probably in trouble before 1896. Certainly the depression of 1893 affected their business. Horace Singer Norton, however, blamed the downfall on wheat speculation. See *The Lemonter*, December 15,1938.

[8]*Joliet News*, January 2, 1897.

[9]Welch was a local lawyer who began his study of law while working as Lemont's first librarian in the Union Library in 1888.

[10]*Lemont Observer*, February 6, 1897.

[11]This is part of an autobiographical poem called *Flowers of Time*. For an interesting story of the life of this woman, see Michael Conzen, ed., *Lockport Legacy* (Chicago: University of Chicago, 1990), p. 135.

[12]*Lemont Observer*, February 20, 1897.

[13]See Chapter 13 and Huston's service experience.

[14]The smell of kerosene was reported before the fire.

[15]*Lemont Observer*, January 14, 1899.

[16]*Ibid.*, January 23, 1897.

[17]*Ibid.*, December 12, 1896.

[18]Barbara Bushman, ed., *Lemont, Illinois: Its History In Commemoration Of The Centennial Of Its Incorporation* (Des Plaines: King/Mann Yearbook, 1973), p. 26.

[19]*Lemont Observer*, May 15, 1897.

[20]This fee probably pushed the struggling Wold Company into receivership.

[21]Just how many water closets there were in Lemont at this time is questionable since there was no village sewer system. Some "fancy" homes may have had toilets, but the outflow had to be into unregulated septic systems or into ditches or cesspools.

[22]Land was donated by N.J. Brown.

[23]*Lemont Observer*, March 20, 1897.

[24]This is the actual date of the founding of Lemont High School, 15 years before the date usually given, 1906.

[25]William Kettering went on to get more secondary school work in a Chicago high school.

[26]Lara was class valedictorian.

[27]Archives of the Lemont Area Historical Society.

[28]Two years beyond grade school would qualify teachers for most rural primary schools at the time. In Cook County, candidates for teaching had to take an exam and pay a dollar fee.

[29]*Lemont Observer*, April 10, 1897.

[30]The Illinois General Assembly granted women the right to vote in school board elections in 1891. Lemont women had to wait until 1897 to be allowed to exercise their right.

[31]This was the time when the traditional work week was laid out for women. Monday was wash day. Tuesday was ironing. Wednesday was for sewing and mending. Thursday was semi-rest, a day for fancy work such as embroidering and quilting. Friday was cleaning day. Saturday was cooking day, the day to make the week's breads and pies, and Sunday, the day of rest, was the time to cook the big family dinner

[32]*Lemont Observer*, August 20, 1897.

[33]He served as clerk and lawyer to the board.

[34]*Lemont Observer*, September 24, 1897.

[35]*Ibid.*, October 8, 1897.

[36]There is no written record of this clause in the Diocese or on the deed in Cook County. See *150 Years in the Kitchen: A History and Cookbook of St. James Of The Sag* (Sag Bridge: St. James Tabernacle Guild, 1983) pp. 91-93. Still this fact seemed to be known along the I & M Canal.

[37]This tradition continued for almost 60 years. *Ibid.*, p. 91.

[38]"Oh little jug, my own heart's love."

[39]*Lemont Observer*, September 30, 1897. See also *Chicago Tribune* for that date.

[40]*Ibid.*, April 17, 1897.

[41]Gold was discovered in Klondike Creek, Yukon Territory, on August 12, 1896. There were still those around who had gone to California in the 1849 rush.

[42]*The Lemonter*, May 29, 1930. There probably were others, but their service was not recorded by the local Veteran's Organizations.

[43]"For Country."

[44]The U.S. government under President Cleveland attempted to suppress the trade in an effort to avoid war with Spain.

[45]Ralph Paine, *Roads of Adventure* (Boston: Houghton Mifflin Company, 1922) pp. 61-64.

[46]*Ibid.*, p. 130.

[47]*Ibid.*, p. 160.

[48]Stephen Crane's book is *Wounds in the Rain*. The story about Ralph Paine first appeared in McClure's Magazine.

[49]See his autobiography, *Roads of Adventure*, 1922.

[50]The board preferred the better sounding Sanitary and Ship Canal, or the Sanitary Ship Channel.

[51]*Lemont Observer*, September 3, 1897. This did lead to a number of legal actions that restricted the amount of water Chicago could draw for the Ship Canal.

[52]The Sanitary Board had a friend in St. Louis who warned them, by phone, of the impending suit.

[53]Louis Cain, "The Creation of Chicago's Sanitary District And The Construction Of The Sanitary And Ship Canal," *Chicago History* (Chicago: Chicago Historical Society, Summer 1979), vol. VIII, no. 2, p. 110.

[54]Walter Tedens' recollections in *Where the Trails Cross* (South Holland: South Suburban Genealogical Society, 1971) vol. 1, no. 4, p. 113.

[55]Son of Carter Harrison Sr. who spoke at Lemont's Village Hall dedication in 1893.

[56]*Joliet Daily Republican*, May 2, 1900.

[57]*Chicago Daily News*, May 2, 1900.

[58]Carter Harrison, *Growing Up With Chicago* (Chicago: Ralph Fletcher Seymour, 1944) pp. 154-156.

[59]*Joliet Daily Republican*, May 2, 1900.

CHAPTER TWENTY-FOUR

LEMONT IN THE FIRST DECADE OF THE 20TH CENTURY

With the turn of the century, Lemont continued its economic and political worries. Its major industry, quarrying, was largely under the control of one strong monopoly — Western Stone — which faced stiff competition from Indiana quarries and a declining market for dimension stone. In an attempt to compete for what market remained, Western Stone continued to drop wages and discharge workers, a fact that hurt the local economy.

There had been a strong belief that the new Sanitary Ship Canal would bolster growth, but most of its traffic bypassed Lemont, while the old I & M Canal fell into general disuse. In 1900, the village board asked the Metropolitan Sanitary District for permission to place a pipe into the I & M Canal to take water from the canal in the case of a fire emergency. This was granted, so it was clear by the start of the century that the District did not feel any great pressure to maintain water level in the old canal.

The 1900 Lemont Village census showed that 47 percent of its employed were working in the town's three major industries. Of that group 30 percent worked for the quarries or stone-related industry. The two railroads employed ten percent and Illinois Pure Aluminum seven percent. Lemont had become diversified enough so that 53 percent listed other occupations; however, many of those were dependent on the payroll from the three major industries.[1] The other work force had seven percent registered as merchants; four percent as salesmen; two percent in the health fields; one percent in law-related enterprises; five percent in transportation;[2] nine percent in small manufacturing; 12 percent in food, drink, and hotel services; two percent in teaching; two percent farmer-laborers living in town; three percent clerical; and five percent general unskilled labor.[3]

It is interesting that of those employed full-time, 15 percent were women: ten were teachers, three stenographers,[4] one nurse, one midwife, one physician,[5] one farmer, one photographer, one postal clerk, four merchants, 17 at Illinois Pure Aluminum,[6] 14 paid housekeepers, 17 servants, ten washerwomen, and one janitor.[7] Women contributed a good deal to the local economy.

On August 2, 1900, the old pioneer N.J. Brown passed away. His death caused excited interest as the family became embroiled in a legal contest over his will, or to be more exact, over his two wills. It seems that N.J. Brown had signed a new will just before his death. The newspapers reported that the two wills, both made out at his request, were radically different. The will he signed on his death bed gave most of his estate to his nephew L.L. Brown. The other relatives who had been "well remembered" in the first will were left out in the second one. There were over 75 near and distant relatives of N.J. and over 50 percent of them were cut off with no bequest.[8] He left property estimated by the family of over 500,000 dollars,[9] but the will listed assets of only 125,000 dollars. Those who received special bequests were his brother, Daniel Brown, 5,000 dollars; Emma Jenks, a niece, 1000 dollars; Anson Brown, a nephew, 1,000 dollars; Herman Welk, Brown's lawyer, 1,000 dollars; The Methodist Church, 1,000 dollars; and 5,000 dollars for a "suitable tombstone shaft" to be placed over his grave in the Brown Cemetery.[10] Most shocking of all was his bequest of the Brown homestead to Grace Robinson, his housekeeper for many years.[11]

It was not long before the rumors about the circumstances of Brown's death began to circulate. Dr. Dougal's papers include a diary entry that reveals some of the local gossip:[12]

> Joliet, Illinois Aug, 3, 1900
>
> Yesterday, I went to Chicago to transact some business as director of McDonald's Brewery,[13] got through and went on the three p.m. train for Lemont. While asking for a ticket from any passenger on the train, John Peterson sold me one[14] and we got acquainted and talked together all the way to Lemont. He told me that he owned the Alton Park at Lemont and got his lease from N.J. Brown for forty years. I said Brown died yesterday and he said, "I was there when he died." I said, "There was some funny business about his will reported in the papers." He replied, "I was a witness to the will." I said, "Was he able to write?" He said "About as good as a dead man. Another man took his hand and made the writing." He spoke more about it but I do not remember the exact language he used.

Still interested in the story, Dougal has an entry on October 10, 1900, describing a conversation with Dr. Leahy, the Lemont physician:

> [Leahy] said he was also a witness [to the will] and expected to have trouble on the witness stand if called. He also said Brown signed his will 14 hours before he died and that his mind was bright.[15]

It took a year to settle the estate and the final will was held valid, but administration was turned over to Anson B. Jenks, a lawyer and a nephew. Herman Welk, the original lawyer, was awarded 6,400 dollars by the probate court. As for the housekeeper and the homestead, nothing is recorded. Apparently she was bought out. Even "Governor" Brown could not control the world after his death.

The slowdown in the quarry industry led village trustees to form an economic council designed to attract new industry. From this group came a contribution by the holding company of Cheese, Brown and Huston of an acre of land free to any industry that would locate in Lemont and employ 50 or more persons. The land they offered was part of a parcel they had acquired between the Des Plaines River diversion and the Santa Fe tracks. Cheese, Brown, and Huston[16] had invested in this land believing that the presence of the Sanitary Ship Canal would open new business along its route. This did not happen as the Metropolitan Sanitary District took control of most of the adjoining lands. The District even offered free docking space for 20 years to Western Stone, thus removing most of the traffic, tolls, and services from the I & M Canal in Lemont.

Owen Earnshaw of Lockport was the first to take advantage of the offer and he leased land with a plan to open a quarry in the spring of 1901. However when a proposal to operate a lithograph quarry in Custer, North Dakota, was announced, a number of his men went west to work. His foreman, George Earnshaw, left leaving Owen without skilled help. George Earnshaw took such experienced stone men as Theo. Adams, Jacob Schartz, Mike Hettinger, William New, and John New, Jr. with him.

Other economic enterprises faded from the scene. The fixtures of the Lemont Building Loan & Homestead Association were sold at auction as that troubled institution finally closed its doors.[17] Meanwhile, rumors about outside owner mismanagement of the Lemont State Bank reached a fever pitch, and on January 11, 1901, between 9:00 a.m. and 4:00 p.m., there was a run on the bank. Lemonters demanded payment on their savings, but all they received was 40 percent and a promise of full payment at a later date. By the 17th, the bank closed with no further payments, and all its equipment was offered for sale to the highest bidder by Floyd Jennison of the firm of Darrow and Thompson. The equipment was purchased by Dr. William Dougal, who put up a 200 dollar draft from the Corn National Bank on the account of the Illinois Pure Aluminum Company.[18]

The Walker and Dougal[19] families then formed the Lemont City Bank with George Walker as head cashier. Capitalized with 10,000 dollars, the bank opened in the Fischbach Building on Lemont and Canal Streets in February. It proudly advertised that it was "Insured Against Bank Robbers — Day and Night."[20] Walter Tedens and Sarah Smelzer served as the first clerks. The bank was so successful that they had to telegraph to Chicago for 1,000 dollars cash to meet payroll checks presented on the first day. In a letter to Dougal, George Walker commented, "I think this will be a good thing after we get going."[21]

SS. Cyril's and Methodius parade for visiting Bishop. View on Main Street east to Stephens. (Photo Courtesy of Lemont Historical Society)

Others believed in Lemont's future, and part of the failed bank building was rented by Julius Ott for a shoe store, while John Woods took over Patrick Hunt's building on Canal Street for a grocery. Other businesses that were successful were the clothing shops. The vest factory reported adding 12 sewing machines to meet orders. Of course, lack of work in the quarries forced many women into the needle trade to support their families, often on a part-time basis. This part-time "sweated trade" was harsh. Thomas Hood, in his *Song of the Shirt*, captured the feeling of this toil:

> With fingers weary and worn,
> With eyelids weary and red,
> A woman sat, in unwomanly rags,
> Plying her needle and thread.
>
> Oh, men with sister dear!
> Oh, men with mother and wives!
> It is not linen you are wearing out,
> But human creatures' lives!

Conditions in Lemont needle shops varied with the ownership. Some were kind employers while others were not. At least the shop work in Lemont was on a small scale and the workers were friends who held a special bond with each other most of the time, a bond that was sometimes disrupted by the those employers who feared unionization. When threatened, the bosses used piece work pressure and ethnic divisions to control workers.[22]

Another reason for the large number of clothing manufacturers in town was because of the number of abandoned buildings. Rents were low for the deserted Smokey Row dives, and all that was needed to start a business were skilled women and sewing machines.

Revitalization of Canal Street and Lemont was set back on February 22, 1901, when a fire started in the Hennebry Building. Supervisor James Hennebry, his brother Patrick, and their families had a narrow escape. It took the volunteer fire department four hours to put out the fire that had started in the front dry goods store belonging to Nick Pinter. From there it spread to the second floor residence and the third floor lodge hall. Before it was under control, it broke through to the Hennebry Meat Market. One unique aspect of the fire was the fact that the lodge hall housed a live mascot, a goat. The goat was rescued and spent the night capering up and down Canal Street, getting in the way of the firemen.[23] The Hennebrys voiced determination to rebuild, a fact that gave support to their faith in the town.

Politics at the start of the century remained heated. The McKinley-Bryan election of 1896 had resulted in a victory in town by a small margin for McKinley, the first Republican victory in Lemont since its beginning.[24] As a result, partisan politics crept into our local government. Although the community elections were supposed to be bi-partisan, supporters of the national parties tended to support one slate or the other. This was reflected in the spring election when two slates were presented to the voters, the Citizens Party and the Peoples Party.

A number of local issues divided the candidates. The village trustees, already 20,000 dollars in debt with outstanding water bonds, had considered selling the village waterworks to the private Lemont Power and Light Company,[25] a suggestion that not only upset the bond holders but many citizens as well. The situation with the village and the Lemont Power and Light Company continued for a number of years. In 1903, the Light Company was forced to sue the village to collect money owed. There was also the matter of John

Peterson's resort, of Alton Park. He had obtained his saloon license renewal on the condition that the picnic grounds close at 8:00 p.m. However, complaints about late closings and rowdy crowds were so numerous that a number of petitions were presented to the village board in an attempt to close his park. Only one sitting trustee supported the opposition to Peterson's Park, and that was A.D. Brown. Brown's motives may not have been entirely for the general welfare. After all, Peterson was spreading gossip about the circumstances of N.J. Brown's death and still held a 40-year lease on a prime piece of the Brown estate inheritance.

The candidates for the Citizens Party were, Peter Fishbach for president; Nels Anderson for clerk; and A.D. Brown, John Powalisz, M. New, and John McGraw for trustees. Patrick McCanna also ran on the ticket for Police Magistrate. The Peoples Party presented Martin Wagner for president; Thomas Talty for clerk; and John Riordan,

John Erickson trimming the electric arc lights at Canal and Stephens Streets, 1903. (Photo courtesy of Lemont Historical Society)

Emil Wend, John Gorski, and Swan Swenson for trustees. The Citizens Party won the election.

Not all of the Citizen's Party were affiliated with the Republican Party, but the more vocal ones were. They opened a campaign headquarters in part of the old bank building. During the fall presidential elections of 1900, they supported one of the largest Republican rallies ever witnessed in Cook County. It was held under a huge tent, and the crowds were brought to Lemont on the Santa Fe line for free. The train started from downtown and stopped at McCook, Willow Springs, and Byrneville. When they arrived, they were treated to "a grand chorus of sixteen ladies, a professional male glee club, and the Phinney U.S. Band," as well as speeches from Lemont's own Martin B. Madden, Congressman Lorimer, and Charles Deneen.[26] McKinley won the election and he carried Lemont, the second Republican victory in its history, the Bryan-McKinley election of 1896 being the first.

In spite of financial problems, the Lemont Village of 1900 was a stable community. There were 2,449 residents, and of that population almost 1,600 were born in the United States. Ties to Europe were still strong, however, as 83 percent of Lemonters had parents who were foreign born. Many homes were bilingual and our churches offered services in German, Swedish, and Polish. As a result, Lemont continued to support a number of small general stores because their owners could speak a second language. This was in contrast to the developing national trend of larger and chain stores.

The census reported Lemont's ethnic breakdown on the basis of parental origin as follows: 30 percent Polish, 28 percent German, 18 percent Scandinavian, 16 percent Irish, four percent English, and four percent listed as "other." Of those who could speak English, it

East Main Street, circa 1900. (Photo courtesy of Lemont Historical Society)

was recorded that 91 percent of the Scandinavians, 89 percent of the Germans, and 54 percent of the Poles had mastered the language.[27]

Real community stability is reflected in home ownership, and by 1900, 72 percent of village residents owned their own homes, a remarkable achievement. Of that number, the Poles led with 85 perent, due in large part to the subdivision of Jasna Gora[28] on Blue Hill, the planned development designed by Father Leopold Moczygemba around SS. Cyril's and Methodius Church. Germans in the village had a 76 percent home ownership, while about 50 percent of the Scandinavians and Irish owned their own homes.[29]

Another interesting reflection of the community after 1900 is in the number of saloon licenses issued. From a high of over 100 in 1896, the village issued 15 in 1902. They were held by Anthony Burkhart, Christian Boe, Emil Wend, Mrs. J. Otzenberger, Miss Anna Schmitt, George Losey, Edward Mitchell, S.P. Swanson, W.H. Slavin, M. Bethke, Jas. Wagner, Mrs. T. New, B. Jungles, J. Powalisz, J.G. Bodenschatz, and Peter Peterson. Burkhardt and New operated hotels and served meals, Slavin and Wagner had liquor stores, and Bodenschatz had a small bar, but also held the license as part of his pharmacy.

Economic and factional circumstances had changed in Lemont and the nation so that by the early 1900s, Labor Day[30] was looked at as a recreational holiday rather than a day to demonstrate for better working conditions — not that labor had gained what it had wanted, but by moving the day to the fall it became an event that celebrated the end of summer. Lemont has had such celebrations dating from 1903. The first were sponsored by the Merchants Association, and then they were taken over as money-raising projects by the Volunteer Fire Department. The 1903 event was a community picnic with horse trotting and bicycle races for entertainment. It was reported as a wild day:

Afternoon tea in Lemont. (Photo courtesy of Lemont Historical Society)

Runaways, collisions, and numerous accidents, none of which were fatal, marked the Labor Day demonstrations at the race course at the flats.[31] Almost every event had an unexpected happening. While F. O. Earnshaw was exercising his horse, a man from Chicago got caught between the shaft and the wheel of his trotting cart. The wheel fell off, Earnshaw was thrown and the horse ran away. The loose wheel struck Peter Wagner of Lockport injuring him slightly. While warming up for the free-for-all race, Art Clarke of Naperville ran into Sam Squire's cart. Clarke was thrown sustaining a broken wrist. No sooner had everything calmed down when Jacob Klein's horse ran away, twice. The second time his son was driving it and the stubborn animal decided to climb a telephone pole. The pole was broken and the runaway horse continued on to smash Frank Chilver's buggy and damage John New's cart. The bicycle races fared little better. Some of the same men who had mishaps on their horses found the bicycles as hard to handle. Broken wheels were sustained by Jacob Klein, Fred Earnshaw, John New, John Dom, and Art Clarke. The first race for a five dollar prize went in four heats; first won by George Davey, second by Jacob Klein, third and fourth by George Davey. It was an eventful day for both participants and observers.[32]

Even as the village financial base was sustained by some quarrying,[33] small manufacturing, and transportation, the township continued to supply agricultural products, but the traditional general farm was slowly being replaced by specialized farming such as dairy and meat production. During this period Lemont shipped 300 to 500 cans of raw milk to Chicago dairies each day,[34] while butter and cheese production fell as the local companies could not compete with larger manufacturing plants such as J.H. Wanzer and Borden & Company. Lemont's small dairy farmers were caught in a situation that made it hard to offer a final product at a competitive price. However, there were six local dairies supplying milk to our area — they were Lemont Sanitary Dairy, Lemont Jersey Farm Dairy, Bomberg's Dairy, Burr Oak Farm, and The Milk House.

For larger dairy volumes, it was easier for most Lemont producers to ship raw milk to Chicago for processing because the state had begun to demand a safer milk supply. The equipment needed to pasteurize and process milk under controlled conditions added more cost to production. By 1906, John Skrzypczynski found that these overhead costs made it possible for him to profit without using local sources. He sent processed milk collected from Chicago dairy collection plants to Lemont, under the name of the Lemont Dairy.[35]

Farms remained the main source of food for the farm family itself. Vegetables, milk, and meat were plentiful, and any extras could be sold at the local markets. It was the need for a cash crop to buy supplies and modern machinery that increased pressure toward specialization. As pointed out before, early in Lemont's agriculture history wheat was the main crop, but production dropped as the new Western lands were able to supply wheat at a lower price. During the late 1800s, Lemont's main grains were corn and oats, mostly used to feed livestock. Many area farmers, because of the proximity of the Union Stockyards, began finishing cattle and hogs; that is, they fattened the animals for slaughter. Local cattle breeding dropped as Texas range cattle arrived in the Midwest at a much lower price than home-bred livestock. Western cattle sold at a cheaper price because they had been fed on the open range and brought to the rail heads on cattle drives, thus cutting the cost of transportation.[36] Lemont farmers could then purchase these animals and use their own grain and pasturage to fatten the animals for a higher profit at the stockyards. Clean pastures and clean silage[37] became so important in this process that townships appointed Canadian thistle inspectors who had the power to fine anyone with thistles on their property.[38]

The Alton Railroad on Main Street developed huge holding pens for livestock located west of the station, so it was not unusual for townspeople to see herds of cattle and even hogs driven down the streets. These "Lemont cattle drives" often led to unexpected adventures, such as small stampedes that sent shoppers scurrying for cover. On one such drive, led by Frank Chilvers of Downers Township, a cow jumped into the new Ship Canal and it took considerable effort to rescue the animal.[39]

As the village grew there was pressure on the surrounding farmland for new home sites, thus driving up the price per acre. In fact, even without a profit from crops, the early landholders increased their potential wealth in the value of their land.[40] This led many farmers to sell parcels to those who desired smaller "farmettes," ranging from five to 20 acres. By doing so, they made their own farms too small to compete with the mechanized farming to come. This desire for land for expansion is happening in the township even today. When land prices become too high, the farmer is faced with higher taxes and a higher cost of farming and must move on. Those who wish to remain in farming have to move to less developed areas. The transportation systems that make our township desirable for shipping agricultural products also work to destroy farming, for easy transportation has opened up the suburban areas to residential and manufacturing growth.

Still, in the early 1900s, Lemont was a rural village. Not only was there farming, but there was a good deal of hunting and fishing. Quail was especially plentiful and the spring of 1901 drew many out to take part in the bounty. There was one small mishap that season when Barney Jungles was shot in a "very delicate place" by his hunting partners, M.S. New and A. Erickson, when they became overly-excited at flushing up a large bevy of quail. Interestingly, the state had a fish commission as early as 1888 that had introduced carp into the Illinois River system for commercial purposes. This was done because almost all other coarse fish were extinct.[41] They must have also had some stocking programs in the Des Plaines system because Lemont reported a three-day spring catch in 1901 of over 2,000 pounds of black bass, pickerel, and carp.

As the new century began, another mode of transportation developed that was to again change the way people lived and moved. This, of course, was the automobile. The Stanley Brothers Company built steam cars for those willing to pay the cost. Steam "horseless carriages" were sold as early as the 1890s, but were never considered more than a novelty. People had a fear of steam in spite of the fact that it was a major source of power in the late 1800s. The steam car had considerable power. In 1906, a Stanley Steamer set the world speed record at 127.66 mph, but few raised in the horse era had a desire to go that fast.

Credit for the commercial development of the gasoline powered internal combustion engine for transportation goes to European inventors Carl Benz and Otto Daimler. Both men had built and run gasoline engines by 1885. In this country, Frank Duryea and his brother Charles built their first auto in 1892-93. The two had a bicycle shop in Springfield, Massachusetts, where they tinkered with the idea of a self-propelled machine.[42] For years they fought over which one was responsible for the American prototype auto. It appears that Charles had the idea and Frank built the car. By 1896, they had sold 13 copies of their one-cylinder car. This is considered the beginning of the United States auto industry, now over 100 years old. Frank and Charles went their separate ways for a while, and in 1899, Charles was building an auto called the Duryea Trap in Peoria, Illinois.

The Dureya won the first auto race in Chicagoland in a contest sponsored by the *Chicago Times Herald* in 1895. A machine driven by Frank Dureya went from Jackson Park to Evanston and back in nine hours.

By 1898, there were more than 50 small companies in the United States hand building cars under all kinds of trademarks. Most of these were buggies or wagons with a one-cylinder gasoline engine geared to a rear axle by a bicycle chain.[43] A few were electric-powered. The public had a hard time trying to find names for these contraptions, calling them the machine, diamote, electrobat,[44] paramount, autokinetic, autobaine, locomotive car, bolvete, motorig, oleo locomotive, mocole, autometon, motorfly, automotive, and electric. Yet, few considered that these unreliable machines would replace the horse, in spite of the fact that in 1901 Oldsmobile sold 425 cars and, three years later, had sold 5,000 units. Ford entered the business in 1903; General Motors was formed in 1908. Sears even sold a car from 1906 to 1911, at a cost of 485 dollars for the closed coupe model.

In the beginning, cars "were viewed as playthings of the rich."[45] In 1905, President Theodore Roosevelt said he had only two auto rides during his term in office and reported he would take no more, while Woodrow Wilson warned the students at Princeton[46] that riding in an auto was dangerous because, "nothing has spread socialistic feelings in this country more than this picture [the auto] of the arrogance of wealth."[47]

It was during this time of fascination with the auto that Lemont became the scene of one of the first "one way auto rides" in history. Around 6:30 a.m. on Saturday, November 19, 1904, Peter Frehaus, a farmer living on Archer Road about two miles south of the Sag, went to his barn to tend to his morning chores. One of his cows became disturbed and kicked over the milk pail and ran away. Irritated, Frehaus chased the animal around the yard. As he approached the fence, he saw an automobile, a very rare sight, at rest facing north toward the Sag.[48] Curious, he went over to examine the machine. There he discovered the body of a young man slumped over the steering wheel, with a bullet wound in the back of his head.

Police were summoned from Lemont and Joliet in order to preserve any clues left at the scene. Since the body was discovered in the township, Town Constable Frank Frelichowski took charge of the investigation. The body was taken to O'Brien's Undertaking Parlor at 312 Canal Street, and the Will County coroner was notified.

Examining the car, the police determined that it was a Toledo make with the Chicago license number of 278. From the tracks on the dirt road it was evident that the car had been turned before the killing. It had been going south and then turned north for about a half mile. The engine was running at the time of the murder, because the controlling levers were in a running position and set for four miles an hour.[49] Power to the engine was stopped when the dying man's foot slipped off the safety control. It appeared that the killer (or killers) had pushed the car to the side of the road, for the wheels were blocked with clods of mud to keep the car still while the engine ran down. The side lamps had been extinguished and were covered with bloody finger marks. There was a pool of water under the car from an opened water tank. The police noted, for reporters, that this was a trick known to the chauffeuring profession as a way of disabling a car without damaging it.

Other evidence included bloody stains on the steering gear, and, most puzzling, blood stains under the rear seat cushion, along the hood, and under the rear wheel. It was suggested that someone other than the victim had been dragged out of the seat on that side. The license was traced to the Canary Company in Chicago and the owner came out and identified the driver as John Bate. Bate worked for the livery service and was on duty the night of November 18, when a call came in from the affluent Auditorium Hotel on Michigan Avenue. A "Mr. Dove" had requested that a car be sent around to the hotel. He had inquired about the fee, five dollars per hour, first objected to the price but later agreed to the terms.[50] Mr. Dove said there would be two in the party. The other driver on duty that night, Edwin Archer, refused the fare even though it was his turn, so Bate elected to go.

The hotel clerk reported that Bate picked up his single fare at 9:25 p.m. It was also revealed that no Mr. Dove was registered at the hotel. He had come off the street to order the car. Dove's description was as follows: about 27 years old, weight about 130 pounds, height about five feet, six inches. He was wearing a light topcoat, checkered suit, red necktie, had on a large diamond ring, and was carrying a tan-colored suitcase.[51]

The Chicago newspapers, eager to increase circulation, played the gory details on the front pages. The *Chicago Daily News* sent special editions to Lemont on the Santa Fe. These were hawked up and down Lemont streets by tough Chicago news boys. The copies sold quickly as Lemonters were eager to get news of the crime. It was believed that the murderer was hiding out in the village or township, so a manhunt was organized to find him.[52]

Led by Constable Frelich-owski and Village Police Chief Klukowski, a posse of towns-people, reporters, and detectives organized to search the valley from Lemont to Lockport. Farm-ers driving produce from Romeo to Lemont reported seeing a campfire in a ravine near the I & M Canal. This led the citi-zens to believe that "Mr. Dove" was hiding in the Des Plaines Valley. Many hoped to catch him for the glory and the reward. The newly formed Chicago Auto Club, enraged that such a fate should befall a driver, was offer-ing a reward for Bate's slayer. The search was a spectacle, as the posse did not opt for horses but instead used an old steam engine and the abandoned tracks left from the construction of the Sanitary Ship Canal. With this small engine they moved up and down the valley searching for the killer. It was hardly a noiseless search to find a "mad killer," but it was a great adven-ture. After two days of chugging up and down the valley, the posse gave up the hunt.

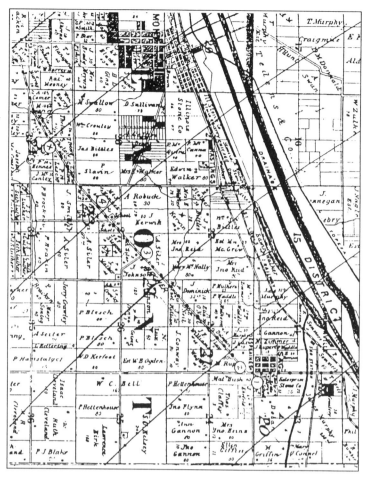

1904 Route of Lemont's "one-way ride." [1] Kirks Corner in Sag Bridge. Dove stopped there to ask for Hogan. [2] Mrs. Ruppers sees headlights. [3] Seiler place, where one occupant tried to enter. [4] Hennes Place. [X] Friehous Farm, where auto and Bates body were found. [5] 131st Street.

The publicity increased local fear, and anyone with a red tie, light suit or overcoat, or suitcase was suspect. There was a good deal of local crime and Lemonters were paranoid. R. Tessem, manager of the S.W. Norton Store,[53] reported to police that he had seen a strange man in Lemont a week before. The man was wearing a light checkered suit and topcoat. He had passed the store a number of times and Tessem became suspicious be-cause of recent safe bombings in town. Tessem said that he followed the man to a saloon where the stranger ordered a beer, paid for it and left without drinking it — certainly strange behavior. This same man was seen again the next day with two "shifty" characters.

Witnesses were slow to come forward with information until they felt that the killer had left the area. Investigators found it took time to put together the facts of the fateful one-way ride. Charles Keuper, owner of a saloon at 58th Street and Archer, told police that Bate and a man fitting the description of "Mr. Dove" came to his place Friday evening and bought a number of drinks. They spent about 15 minutes drinking and talking. No one was with them.

Later, the car was seen by a bartender at Bank's and Keller's Saloon in Willow Springs. The auto, naturally, attracted his attention as it passed his window around 11:00 p.m. Friday night. The bartender stated that there was a large modern electric sign nearby and he had a good view of the auto and its passengers. When he saw the auto it had two men plus the driver and contained a large package. His story was backed by Marshall Herzog of Willow Springs who had also seen the car. If what they saw was correct, Bate and "Dove" had picked up another passenger somewhere between 58th and Archer and Willow Springs. The third sighting of the auto came from near Kirk's Roadhouse in the Sag. Mrs. Rose Fous saw the car, this time with only two occupants. At Kirk's, a man with "Dove's" description asked for Ed Hogan. Hogan was known to the owner, but was not in the tavern at the time.

Mrs. Ruppert, who lived in the area, told police that she was awakened about midnight by the sound of an auto coming into the Sag from Archer Avenue. The headlights flashed in her window as the car came down the hill a quarter of a mile from her home. She reported, "The shouting was like that of a madman or a drunkard. Suddenly there were two shots. The shouting continued and the machine did not slow up its speed but continued across the valley and up the hill."[54]

Two miles south on Archer, Peter Seiler reported that on Friday night he heard loud raps on his front door a short time after midnight. At first he did not answer, fearing it might be a burglar. After a period of time he asked who was there. The reply came in hushed tones, "Let me in. Let me in quick." Seiler asked the stranger's name but there was no reply only a repeated, "Let me in." Since the person did not give his name, Seiler did not open his door and the caller left.[55]

Half a mile down the road, Mr. Connors reported that he was awakened by the sound of an automobile in front of his place. He could not tell how many passengers were in the car but they stayed outside of his house for a while until one got out and knocked on his door. Conners, too, was afraid and did not answer. So the men returned to their auto. Later that night Peter Frehaus thought he heard angry voices followed by a shot, but did not think about it until he made the grim discovery by his house in the morning.

One other witness, a young farmer, John Hennes, claimed to have seen the car. He told the papers that he was awakened at 11:00 p.m. by the sound of an automobile. "I did not pay attention at first, but just as the machine neared our place . . . I heard quarreling. I rose from my bed, drew the curtain . . . and could see the outline of the auto perhaps 100 feet away. The car seemed to be swaying from side to side." He went on to describe seeing one of the occupants fire straight ahead twice, but did not think anyone was hurt until he heard of the murder. The police accompanied him to the spot where he said the shooting occurred. It was overhung with trees blocking any view. His time sequence was also different from the other witnesses. Under police pressure, he admitted that he had seen nothing but had been influenced by the newspaper coverage and publicity and desired some attention.[56]

All trace of the killer seemed gone until Fritz Boehme, a saloon keeper in Romeo, reported that someone of "Dove's" description had been seen there. Upon further investigation, it was learned that the stranger went from Boehme's place to the Santa Fe Station in Romeo. The man asked the telegraph operator, Peter Startz, where he could wash his hands and was shown the horse trough. He asked to bed down in the station until there was a train to Joliet or Streator. He did not care where he went as long as he could get out of Romeo. Since there were no local trains that early in the morning, he left. He was next seen at the Chicago, Joliet, and Elgin electric station in Romeo where he boarded the Joliet car at 7:30 a.m. Saturday. The conductor noted his light overcoat, suitcase, and red tie.

In Joliet, on Saturday, a man fitting the description appeared at the Hauser boarding house one block from the station. He seemed tired, nervous, and ill, so Mrs. Hauser rented him a room. He remained in his room all day except for a trip to Brown's Drug store at Joliet and Jefferson. There he purchased 16 ounces of benzine and nerve tonic. He stayed in his room for the rest of the weekend and left at night on Sunday. He was last seen walking toward the Sanitary Ship Canal. The next day, boarding house guests reading about the sensational murder in Lemont began to suspect that their mysterious visitor might be the killer. They notified the police but it was too late — "Dove" had vanished.

Fueled by the Chicago papers, the police began to develop a list of suspects. That list was a complicated cross-section of society in 1904 and the world of the professional automobile chauffeur.

Edwin Archer, the other driver on duty that night, was one of the first to come forward with a possible motive for the murder. He confessed that he had refused the commission that night out of fear for his safety. Archer believed Bate was shot in a case of mistaken identity. He thought the killer was after him, because he had testified in a case of conspiracy in criminal court. His testimony had led to the indictment of a criminal court clerk and a burglar, but both were acquitted and Archer had been in fear for his life since their release. The police discounted this idea as it appeared that Bate and his killer knew each other as they shared drinks at Keuper's Saloon.

Dan Canary, the garage owner, told reporters that he believed that Bate was murdered in a dispute over the fare, as there was no money found on his body. Canary said that almost all livery drivers had experienced difficulties collecting fares from some passengers. Canary felt that either Bate collected his money in advance or was talked into taking the long trip beyond Summit. If he collected in advance, he was robbed by the murderer, or he might have been persuaded to go from place to place until he realized that his passenger did not know "what he was about" and turned to head for the city. This could have angered the drunk or crazy passenger into shooting Bate. Canary said that he was sure that Bate would not have gone beyond Summit without telephoning for instructions unless he felt the trip was nearing its end.

The police, following this information, began to look for people who rented autos for night use, and also followed up on the fact that "Dove" had asked for Ed Hogan at Kirk's roadhouse. It was revealed that Hogan frequently rented cars while working as a "con man" in the southwest suburban countryside. Hogan had an alibi for the night of the murder, since he was in New York at the time. However, his occasional partner in confidence games, Joseph Weil, was in the city. Weil was already under indictment on two counts — one for securing, by fraud, 1,000 dollars from a Grayslake farmer, and the other for not paying a fare of 62 dollars and 50 cents to the Green Motor company for an auto rental in July.

Newspapers soon began developing a case against Weil. On hearing that the police were looking for him, Weil came forward with his lawyer. Weil had already developed a reputation as one of the greatest of Chicago's con men. Known as "Yellow Kid Weil," his exploits were already legendary.[57] His stings were based on the greed of the sucker and often the victim refused to admit he had been taken. The publicity brought forth another garage owner who claimed that he had been cheated out of a fare by Weil. The owner, Mr.

Coey, was especially angry with Weil because of a sting played on him a year before by Weil and Ed Hogan. It seems that Coey liked the sporting crowd and prided himself on knowing the rich horsemen that he drove around. He took special pleasure in bragging to everyone he met about his friendship with Charles Ellison, an important owner and breeder. One day Coey got a personal call from Ellison who informed him that he had inside knowledge of a sure thing on a horse race in Worth. If he wanted to make some fast money he was to bring cash to the Palmer House and meet Ellison.

When Coey got to the Palmer House, Ellison was not there, but Weil and Hogan met him and said Ellison had already gone to the track. Hogan would take care of everything. Coey gave Hogan 200 dollars. At that point Hogan and Weil urged him to put up more money as the race was fixed, and so Coey got 600 dollars more and gave it to the two. The horse won, so Coey called Ellison the next day asking for his money. Charles Ellison did not know what he was talking about. He had never called, nor sent an agent. Furthermore, he was highly insulted by the suggestion that he would have anything to do with fixing a race and terminated his association with Coey's garage. Coey called the police who picked up Hogan and Weil, but the money was gone and the case dismissed for lack of witnesses. Coey was still so angry that he said that he believed Weil would do anything for money — even murder.

Weil loved publicity and after being listed as a suspect he demanded that the police, the reporters, and his lawyer go to the Auditorium Hotel to confront those who saw "Mr. Dove." Weil forced his own personally controlled and conducted line up. Of course, under such circumstances, both the doorman and the telephone operator swore he was not the "Mr. Dove" they had seen that night. Weil even had a strange endorsement from his sister-in-law who told the police that murder was not in Joe's line at all.[58]

The leads became more difficult as the weeks passed. Many believed that the simplest reconstruction was the best. Bates left "Dove" in Lemont and was returning to Chicago when he was murdered. That suggested that the killer could even be a Lemont resident. Some hinted that the auto frightened a local pedestrian or man on horseback, who drew a revolver and began shooting, accidentally wounding Bate, and then, perhaps, robbed him. This idea was suggested by the Chicago papers, which noted that many Lemonters and Sag residents carried side arms. The coroner of Will County added that "residents of that locality are quick enough to shoot."[59]

It took a year for the next real suspect to be developed by detective work. On August 17, 1905, Chicago's Harrison Street detectives announced to eager reporters that they believed they had found a major clue in the Lemont auto mystery.[60] It seems that early in the investigation they got a tip from a Joliet express driver reporting a shipment of two suitcases to Kansas City a week after the Bate slaying. One was old and fit the description of Dove's case, and the other was new. They were shipped by a Bennett Marsh. The authorities in Kansas City were contacted and asked to report anyone attempting to claim them. Months passed and they were not claimed, so the detectives asked that they be forwarded to Chicago. Upon arrival they were opened and found to contain a light overcoat, new clothes, a set of tools used by professional chauffeurs, several letters, an envelope addressed to Marsh Cycles, Brockton, Massachusetts, and an auto license issued to George Lawrence. One letter started, but not finished, told of plans to go to St. Louis in the fall. The other letter addressed to Bennet Marsh was postmarked Boston and signed by "Flo," but the author of the letter wrote the name George in the salutation. She must have been aware of his use of an alias.

On March 27, 1905, Bennett Marsh appeared at the express office and was told that his cases had been returned to Chicago. If he would return in three hours, arrangements would be made to ship them to Kansas City. The police were notified, but Marsh never returned. The detectives reported that their investigation had revealed that Bennett Marsh (a.k.a. George Lawrence) had worked for several months at the Canary company along with Bate. He then got a position as a private chauffeur for Jay Morton, the millionaire banker and heir to the salt fortune. Marsh was loud and boastful, so it was his habit to come back to the garage to tell the other drivers what an important job he had.

Marsh's personal tale of woe began as he was driving a society woman, Madison Kennedy, home from a quiet evening with Mr. Morton. Mrs. Kennedy lived at the fashionable Metropole Hotel at 2300 South Michigan Avenue. When the auto crossed Garfield Boulevard near Calumet Avenue, Marsh struck a 57 year old man. The man was badly hurt and rushed off to the hospital in critical condition. The police, sick of the number of injuries caused by reckless driving of this new invention, decided to make an example out of Marsh and he was arrested for assault. The hearing set for November 12, 1904, but was extended to await the condition of the patient. Sick and nervous, Marsh went down to the Canary garage to gain comfort from his old fellow drivers. They saw a chance to get back at a chronic braggart and began to work him over. They convinced Marsh that they had heard that the victim was on the verge of death and he would be charged with manslaughter and sent to jail. Adding to Marsh's nervous state was the fact that he had been injured in the accident and was having some mild hemorrhages from an old lung infection.

Marsh came to the garage on the morning of the murder and told one of the owners that a rich man had given him money and a ticket to San Francisco and he planned to "dig out" before the next court date. If there was a ticket issued to Bennett Marsh for San Francisco, police found it was never used.

Marsh did not appear for his court date on November 22, four days after Bate was shot and the same day someone by the name of Bennett Marsh shipped the two suitcases to Kansas City.[61] It was from these facts that the detectives developed their circumstantial case. Before any warrants or grand jury proceedings, the police gave the newspapers an imagined scenario: that Marsh, fearful of the outcome of the trial, decided to get out of Chicago. He called the garage knowing that any of the drivers would take him as a fare. When Bate drove up to the Auditorium Hotel he recognized who "Dove" was and felt sorry for him and took him for some drinks to calm him down. The detectives decided that Marsh then became drunk and agitated. The longer they drove, the worse he became and when Bate decided to turn back to Chicago, Marsh shot him.

The police explanation of the slaying did not reveal why some witnesses saw three people in the car. It also did not explain the blood stains on the rear seat, along the hood, and the rear wheel. However, since the other facts made a plausible case the conflicting clues were ignored. The newspapers were satisfied and sent out extra editions. All that was needed was an eyewitness to establish that Marsh was in the Lemont area on the night of the murder. That eyewitness was Peter Startz, who saw him at the Romeo Santa Fe Station on that night.

Mr. Startz and a detective went to see Marsh, who was located in Brockton. Armed with warrants they confronted Marsh. He was on his sickbed dying of tuberculosis and the visit aggravated his condition. Startz viewed the accused carefully and stated that he was not the man he saw that night. The last substantial lead was gone. Marsh died without any confession of guilt. As in so many cases, the killer was never found, but, unlike many unsolved murders, there persisted local stories that all of the truth of that night had not been revealed. Rumors that some Lemonters had been involved or had some information were so strong that as late as April, 1929, the *Chicago Daily News* offered a 500 dollar reward for any information leading to a solution of the Lemont auto murder. The *Lemont Optimist News* responded with a comment, "The guilty party was never brought to justice though local people freely mention the name of one they suspect of the crime. This party was living near the scene at the time of the killing. Here is your chance to make money enough to buy your own car, or what ever you please."[62] No one revealed a name. The money remained unclaimed.

The first reference to local police or citizen action against an automobile was in September of 1905. Paul Bergholz appeared before Justice of the Peace Weimer where he swore out a warrant against an "automobilist who ran into him in Sag Bridge." His wagon was destroyed and his horse had run away. No offender's name is listed but it showed that a few in the area were already driving around in some form of automobile.[63] The first local newspaper ad for a car appeared in January of 1907. The Joliet Auto Company at 100 Cass Street offered for its Lemont and Lockport readers the Buick Auto which had 22 horsepower, a top, horn, and headlamps for 1,350 dollars. The company also acted as agent for the Cadillac, Knox, and Winton makes.[64] By 1910, Tedens and Dystrup on Stephens Street was selling the Velie auto, a car backed by Deere and Company of Moline.

With the automobile[65] came the need for better roads and bridges. The first cars were not capable of the power of a horse to pull a wagon out of the spring mud and the suspension systems were primitive. A joke that made the rounds had to do with Henry Ford's mass production system and the ride that the early Fords offered:

> Guide on a tour of the Ford plant: Do you know what would happen if that man on the right side ever missed a day of work?
>
> Onlooker: No, what would happen?
>
> Guide: 2,261 Fords would go out of the factory without springs.
>
> Onlooker: Say mister, that fellow's been sick a lot, ain't he!

Roads had been a secondary concern as long as the route to the rail station was acceptable. Only when the auto offered a cheaper means of travel that did not require a barn, stable, food, and fresh water did the idea of a network of good roads and bridges become important. By 1905, it was clear that the wooden bridge over the Des Plaines River was no longer safe. It stood in marked contrast to the new steel bridge over the Sanitary Ship Canal. Township commissioner, John O'Brien, proposed a new bridge and had plans drawn for a steel structure and displayed them in his store window on Canal Street prior to a bond referendum for the township,[66] but the citizens of the township did not feel that they should bear the burden of the full cost of the bridge. They were bitter because the construction of the Ship Canal, that had been a short boon to the village, had destroyed so much of the natural beauty of the valley and had not returned any great economic growth. Before the Ship Canal construction the river could be crossed most of the year at almost any site. The Des Plaines was a shallow waterway that wandered over much of the valley and a bridge was usually not necessary. Changes brought about by the

Ship Canal included the channelization of the Des Plaines which raised the water level to a point where a bridge was needed. Angry voters turned the proposal down in April.

The problem did not go away, and in June of 1906, James Ash, the new road commissioner, called a citizens meeting to discuss the bridge. J.W. McCarthy, always a "good-roads man" gave an impassioned plea for the construction of a new bridge. He felt that economic growth of the town would be hindered if it was

The masonry bridge. (Photo courtesy of Lemont Historical Society)

not built.[67] He finished his presentation telling the crowd that if they failed to improve the bridge the township and village would be responsible if any injuries occurred. The argument hinged on steel versus other materials. McCarthy and alderman Spence[68] favored a steel structure; they reported that stone would cost twice the price and would have to be built in an arch shape that would raise the span six to eight feet. Spence also stated that it would take six to eight months to complete a stone or concrete structure, while a steel one would take only thirty days. Hearing an old stone man argue the merits of steel gave many in the room an uneasy feeling about any future for Lemont's once great stone industry.

Two spoke in favor of a masonry bridge, Francis Keough and L.L. Brown. Keough had conferred with the Cook County Commissioners and found that they favored an arched span for recreational traffic. Brown reported that the county would pay for half if the design met with their approval. The county favored a traditional masonry span and such a design was submitted by Joseph Heineman of Chicago. This time the bond issue was approved by a vote of 115 to 15. Most of the bonds were purchased by the Lemont City Bank.

The bridge, now gone, was styled after early Roman bridges. It had a Victorian flavor with four seated lions guarding each corner, holding lights. It clearly represented a past, Romantic tradition, perhaps a bit out of place in our valley which was entering the industrial age, for by 1910, the needs of the internal combustion engine for industry and transportation had already set in motion plans to build the first refinery in the Des Plaines Valley in Lockport,[69]

The Aluminum Products Company. (Photo courtesy of the Lemont Historical Society)

a forerunner to the petrochemical industry in the valley today. The old romantic bridge was torn down when the new high rise span was completed. All that is left are parts of the lion decorations now at the Lemont Historical Society.

By the end of the first decade of the 20th Century, just over 60 years from the completion of the I & M Canal, Lemont was a town of 3,500 people. Agriculture continued to be part of the economic base, as did crushed stone. However, the presence of skilled and unskilled laborers offered a labor pool that encouraged the development of industries of various types. There were two aluminum plants, Illinois Pure Aluminum on Talcott Street (founded 16 years before) and the Aluminum Products Company on west Main Street.[70] There was also The Chicago Structural Tile Company, Lemont Manufacturing Company, Nagel Cement Block Company, Lemont Limestone Company, Illinois Stone, Lincoln Park Nursery,[71] The Flux Company, five vest manufacturing firms, branch warehouses of two brewery firms, a cigar manufacturer, two lumber yards, and several contractors.

The community advertised that it could offer cheap hydroelectric power from the Ship Canal through a power plant owned by the Public Service Company of Illinois. Based on what was to be an "ever increasing flow of water," the community fathers offered rates much lower than those produced by steam.[72] Lemont had three sources of electric power including the privately owned Lemont Power and Light Company. Other inducements to manufacturers included cheap, soft coal from Will and LaSalle Counties, low freight rates for water transportation, two train trunk lines, and the electric railway.

Lemont could boast such amenities as a bonded debt of 1,000 dollars, a city water works capacity of 200,000 gallons daily, a volunteer fire department of 43 members, a good police department, five schools, eight churches, one bank, three hotels, four department stores, 26

Illinois and Michigan Canal, Lemont, 1997. (Photo by the author)

passenger trains daily, 21 fraternal societies, cheap gas service, three doctors, a dentist, and a drug store. It was a community that offered a wide range of services for the growing area.

Yet it still had the feel of a frontier town, for as late as 1910, the township had to vote extra funds for Frank Frelichowski for his work in arresting two men charged with horse stealing and robbing the mails at Sag Bridge. That fall, George New also received money for the arrest of another horse thief.

The biggest symbol of change in Lemont came so quietly that few recognized its significance. In 1910, the Illinois and Michigan Canal was closed to all traffic from Chicago to Lockport. The canal that had built Lemont was finished. Its only role for the next years was to serve as a sewer for storm water. The Lemont Commercial Association was concerned about the closure and sent a resolution to the Metropolitan Sanitary District Board of Trustees requesting that they supply enough water flow through the abandoned canal to prevent disease from stagnant water. The canal that had seen so much of Lemont's history was now looked on as the "main and principal sewer for the village carrying away both the sewage and the surplus drainage."[73] So it remained abandoned and neglected for most of the 20th Century until the development of the Illinois and Michigan Canal National Heritage Corridor in 1984.

Today, finally, the old canal is recognized as the spine of a unique economic and recreational area that serves to tell the story of the growth of Northern Illinois, of our canal town, and of the people who made its history.

ENDNOTES

[1] Robert J. Williams, "A Social Profile of the Community in 1900," *Looking For Lemont*, Michael Conzen and Carl Zimring, ed. (Chicago: University of Chicago Press, 1995), p. 215. See also the *U.S. Census for Lemont 1900*.

[2] Transportation other than the railroads. This would include teamsters, canal boaters, and boat engineers.

[3] Williams, "A Social Profile," pp. 218-219.

[4] A new field for women that became available with the introduction of the typewriter and high school training in shorthand and bookkeeping.

[5] Ella Camp, M.D. served the community from 1892 until 1901. In 1901 she left for Iowa to tend to a family member who was ill.

[6] One was a foreman.

[7] Williams, "A Social Profile," p. 220.

[8] N.J. Brown never married.

[9] Including property on Lake Shore Drive.

[10] Such a monument was never established. A visit to the Brown Cemetery on the Methodist Church property reveals only a small headstone for the old pioneer.

[11]*Joliet Daily Republican*, August 9, 1900.

[12]Wm. Dougal, M.D., was the son-in-law of Edwin Walker, the quarry owner and contractor.

[13]Wm. Dougal had extensive business interests aside from the practice of medicine.

[14]Dr. Dougal apparently bought a discounted weekly or monthly pass ticket, thus saving money on the fare.

[15]"Walker-Dougal Papers," Lemont Historical Society.

[16]A.D. Brown, E.L. Huston and Ed Cheese.

[17]This was the loan association associated with the Norton family.

[18]"Walker-Dougal papers," Lemont area Historical Society Archives.

[19]His name is spelled on documents two different ways, both with one *l* and two *l*'s.

[20]*Lemont Phoenix-Advertiser and Observer*, February 9, 1905. Note that the local newspaper was victim of the merger mania of this period, not unlike the town newspaper situation today.

[21]This is now The Lemont National Bank and Trust. See "Walker-Dougal papers," Lemont Historical Society.

[22]Piece work standards could be set by the work produced by the most gifted seamstress. This made it almost impossible for the others to meet the standards. As for the ethnic divisions, any foreman from one group, Polish, German, or Irish, could clearly favor some workers over others. This would lead to disruptions.

[23]*Lemont Observer*, February 23, 1901.

[24]Records for the early elections in Lemont are not available. If the *Joliet Daily Republican* newspaper is correct, then Lemont did not give Lincoln a majority in either his first or second election. It is possible that our strongly Democratic community did not vote for Lincoln. He probably did not have majority community support until the last year of the Civil War.

[25]From 1900 to late 1903, the Lemont Power and Light Company, the private power company, had trouble collecting from the village. By 1903, they were forced to sue the village to collect for electricity supplied for street lighting.

[26]*Joliet Daily Republican*, October 6, 1900.

[27]The Polish community was one of the last to come to Lemont before 1900. That is why so few spoke English

[28]Its real meaning is "Bright Mountain."

[29]Williams, "A Social Profile," p. 217.

[30]The official Labor Day in the United States was changed to the fall to avoid any association with May Day labor demonstrations of the past and with radical movements. This in spite of the fact that the worldwide May 1st celebration began in Chicago.

[31]The area along River Road by the Santa Fe trackage.

[32]*Lemont Observer & Optimist News*, September, 1903. See also Sonia Kallick, "Earliest Keepataw Days Explained," *The Lemont Metropolitan*, September 2, 1993, p. 12.

[33]By the 1900s, most of the stone was for gravel and rip-rap.

[34]Barbara Bushman, ed., *Lemont, Illinois: Its History In Commemoration of the Centennial of Its Incorporation* (Des Plaines: King/Mann, 1973), p. 30.

[35]Frank Bradbury, *History of Lemont Bottles* (Lemont, 1979), pp. 6-7. Lemont Historical Society Collection.

[36]The importation of Western cattle presented a problem — the introduction of cattle diseases from the plains that entered into the local population. This led to attempts to control cattle and livestock through the Illinois State Agriculture Department. See John Keiser, *Building For the Centuries: Illinois, 1865 to 1898* (Urbana: University of Illinois, 1977), pp. 116-148.

[37]Chopped fodder stored for animal feed.

[38]The idea may have had merit but it is clear today, looking at the open lands in the township, that the thistle far outlasted the thistle inspectors.

[39]*Lemont Observer*, March 23, 1901.

[40]Keiser, *Building For the Centuries*, p. 148.

[41]*Ibid.*, p. 133.

[42]The bicycle was also a modern means of transportation. It became part of a craze that swept the country dating from its successful introduction in the late 1880s. It is interesting to note that two small bicycle repair shops made major contributions to the transportation industry of the 20th Century, that of the Duryea Brothers and, of course, the Wright Brothers.

[43]Samuel Morison, *The Oxford History of the American People* (New York: Penguin Books, 1972), vol. 3, p. 223.

[44]Some cars were designed as electric runabouts, but they suffered energy problems. New and redesigned electric cars may yet become the auto of the future.

[45]Morison, *The Oxford History of the American People*, vol. 3, p. 223.

[46]He served a president of Princeton from 1902 to 1910.

[47]Morison, *The Oxford History of the American People*, vol. 3, p. 223.

[48]In 1904 only 70,000 cars were registered in the United States.

[49]The regulation speed for hill climbing for the car. It had been set to climb the grade from the Sag to the higher part of Archer Road.

[50]The average wage then was $1.75 a day.

[51]*Chicago Daily News*, November 19, 1904.

[52] *Ibid.*, November 22, 1904.

[53]Now reorganized and under Tessem's control.

[54]*Chicago Daily News*, November 22, 1904.

[55]*Ibid.* This story reveals a real fear of crime in Lemont during the early 1900s, especially in the rural sections of the township. We like to think of the "good old days" as safe from violence and crime. This was not true.

[56]*Ibid.*

[57]The name came from a popular comic strip of the day. The "Yellow Kid" was a sharp, fast talking character.

[58]Weil served little time for his swindles. The movie *The Sting* is based on one of his schemes. He made fortunes and lost them, and died penniless and a public ward in 1976. If he knew anything about the Bate murder, or was the third man in the car, he never told.

His body is at rest in a pauper's grave in Willow Springs, near the road that he or a friend may have taken that night in 1904.

[59]*Chicago Daily News*, November 22, 1904.

[60]*Ibid.*, August 17,1905.

[61]The case was dropped as the victim was improving. Mrs. Kennedy, the passenger, came to an out-of-court settlement with the victim. Strange that the passenger should pay for the injuries; however, the lawyer was delighted with the settlement and spoke of Mrs. Kennedy's generosity.

[62]*Lemont Optimist News,* April 29, 1929

[63]*Lemont Phoenix-Advertiser and Observer*, September 7, 1905.

[64]*Ibid.*, January 10, 1907.

[65]The bicycle craze of the last half of the 19th Century was also a factor in the demand for good roads. Historians often neglect the importance of the bicycle as a mode of transportation.

[66]*Lemont Phoenix-Advertiser and Observer*, February 9, 1905.

[67]The fact that McCarthy had a new subdivision development east of town probably had something to do with his ardor for the cause.

[68]Alderman Spence was a quarry supervisor.

[69]The Texaco plant began in 1911.

[70]This plant was a division of Reynolds Aluminum based in LaGrange, Illinois.

[71]This nursery was part of the Chicago park system. Plants were grown here for use in the parks. The remains of this complex remain in the Waterfall Glen Forest Preserve. Hikers in those woods who stumble on the ruins labeled LPN often wonder about their source.

[72]Political and territorial fighting over Chicago's right to draw unlimited water out of the Great Lakes eventually doomed widespread use of the hydroelectric plant at Lockport.

[73]Lemont Town Council notes, July 27, 1910.

U. S. HISTORY

1900: *McKinley Elected President — Gold is Unit of Money Standard in U.S. — Doctor's Study Yellow Fever in Cuba — Western Baseball League Named the American League.*

1901: *Cuba Made a U.S. Protectorate — McKinley Assassinated — Teddy Roosevelt Becomes President — Treaty for the Panama Canal — First Radio Messages.*

1902: *U.S. Establishes Civil Government in the Philippines.*

1903: *Iroquois Fire in Chicago, 600 Die — Alaskan Frontier Settled — First Teddy Bears — First Coast-to-Coast Crossing by Car, 65 Days — Ford Motor Car Company Formed.*

1904: *Teddy Roosevelt Wins Presidential Election — Work Begins on the Panama Canal — Steerage Rates to U.S. for Immigrants is $10.*

1905: *International Workers of the World Formed — First Neon Signs.*

1906: *President Roosevelt Visits the Canal Zone — San Francisco Earthquake Kills 700+ — White Sox Beat Cubs in Chicago's Only Intercity World Series — Hearst Begins Restoration of New Salem Near Springfield.*

1907: *Roosevelt Bars Japanese from Immigrating to America — Oklahoma 46th State — Bank Panic and Economic Depression — First Daily Comic, Mutt and Jeff.*

1908: *Cubs Win World Series — William Taft President — Wilbur Wright Flies 30 Minutes.*

1909: *Burnham Plan for Chicago — Robert Peary Claims to Have Reached the North Pole.*

LEMONT HISTORY

1900: *Sanitary Ship Canal Finished — Admiral Dewey Visits Lemont and Lockport — Lemont State Bank Fails.*

1901: *Chicago & Joliet Electric Opens, September 25 — Lemont City Bank Opens (Now Lemont National) — Harriet Singer Public Library is Open.*

1902: *The Electric Trolley Crashes at Walker and Main — Ex-Governor Altgeld Dies in Joliet While Speaking Out against the Boer War.*

1903: *Smallpox in Lemont, Town Isolated Because Village Will Not Act.*

1904: *Horse Racing on the Flats by the A.T. & Santa Fe a Weekly Event.*

1905: *Building East of Hennebry Building on Canal Erected Called the Leahy Building — Anderson & Alberg are in the Friedley Building — Peterson's Park, the Gambling Resort, Becomes Alton Park — Bridge over the Des Plaines River Diversion is Built — Peter Kiolbassa, Well-Known Polish Organizer and Politician, Dies — the Dove Auto Murder Mystery Begins.*

1906: *Police Chief Peter Kane on Trial for Shooting Leader of the "Hot Air Gang," Found Not Guilty.*

1907: *Edwin Walker Dies — Archbishop Quigley Comes to Lemont April, 13 — Swedish Mission Church Dismantled — T.E. Sullivan Mayor — New Trustees are John Erickson, Axel Anderson, and Tom Ludwig — Shering Brewery Distribution Built on State Street Next to Santa Fe.*

1908: *Vasa Order of Odin #132 Formed.*

1909: *Lemont Commercial Association Formed — Billiard and Pool Tables in Town Subject to License — Plan for Lincoln Park Nursery Set for Area Across the Valley.*

1910: *I & M Canal Abandoned for Navigation from Joliet to Chicago, in Use for 60 Years — The Commercial Association Sends a Request to the Trustees to Establish Enough Flow through the Canal to Move Drainage and Sewage.*

EPILOGUE

I began this book by stating that history is written in the landscape, that our political, economic, social, and cultural record is a product of our surroundings. Lemont's unique story is due, in large part, to its geography and geology. We are here because of the Des Plaines River and the Illinois River Valley, a corridor traveled by Native Americans, explorers, and the settlers who followed.

The topography of the valley made it a natural course for the construction of the I & M Canal, the railroads, and the Sanitary and Ship Canal. With these transportation corridors came settlers, quarry workers, and immigrants from all over Europe. These pioneers added to the unique ethnic flavor that is still part of Lemont's social and cultural heritage.

What Lemont is today is reflected in its past, for any community carries with it the roots of its past just as a family does. In spite of modern changes, we are still at heart a classic canal and labor town. This volume covers mainly the 19th Century through the period of 1910 and the closing of the I & M Canal, the time of Lemont's birth and adolescence, and was written to try tell who we were then. There is still much more to be written, beginning with the 20th Century, to tell who we are today.

APPENDIX

A DOWNTOWN WALKING TOUR OF LEMONT SITES

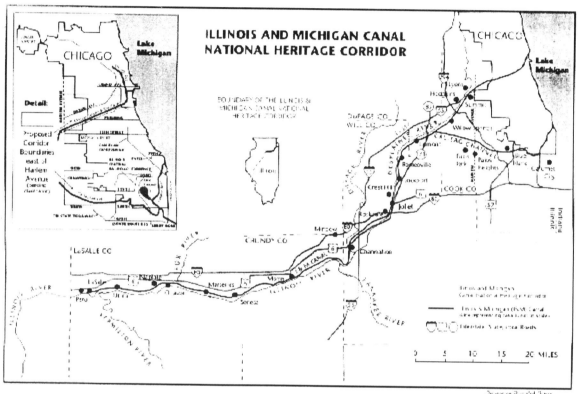

The Illinois and Michigan Canal National Heritage Corridor. (Illustration courtesy of the I & M Heritage Commission)

The following is a short walking tour of sites mentioned in the book. It is easier to relate to history when you visualize where events occurred, so included here is a short review outline about the locations. Some newer, post-1910 places are listed for general information. Sites that are part of the time period from 1673-1910 are marked with an asterisk. For more information on any of these locations visit the Lemont Area Historical Society.

1.*OLD STONE CHURCH — LEMONT AREA HISTORICAL SOCIETY
306 LEMONT STREET.

Begin your tour at the Historical Society Museum and Library for an overview of Lemont history. The building was placed on the National Register of Historic Places on May 5,

1986. It was built in 1861 of stone tailings, broken pieces of quarry stone. Members of the congregation hauled the stone from Brown's Quarry, west of Lockport Street on stone boats (flat sleds with log runners pulled by horses). The walls are self-supporting and measure 22 inches thick. It is the oldest church structure in town and rests on land donated by Benjamin Brown. Its style is reminiscent of the New England churches of its founding members who included the prominent pioneer families of Brown, Wells, Singer, Talcott, Martin, Clifford, and Luther. The building was a Methodist-Episcopal Church in its early years. Later it became a Methodist Church. It served until 1970, when a new church was built at the west end of Division Street. In 1861, just after the building was completed, it was a recruiting station for the Civil War. From this building Lemont's Reverend Clancy led his crusade against Smokey Row in the 1890s. The author, adventurer, and newspaper reporter, Ralph Paine, spent his early years here while his father ministered to the congregation. The stained glass windows were installed in the 1890s and the present pews in 1900. The metal ceiling was manufactured by the Friedley & Voshardt Company of Chicago. Relatives of that company were members of the congregation. (See Chapters 13, 16, 21, and 22)

(Look across the street from the Historical Society.)

2.*SAINT MATTHEW'S EVANGELICAL LUTHERAN CHURCH
SOUTHEAST CORNER OF LEMONT AND ILLINOIS STREETS

By 1869, there were enough German Lutherans in the Lemont area to establish a preaching station, and by 1874, the parish was formally organized above the Tedens & Thormahlen Store at 102-106 Stephen Street. John Tedens was elected chairman of the group and John Thormahlen, Peter Bose, Andreas Hiss, and Joachim Ahrens were elected trustees. They selected the name *Evangelical Lutheran Mataeus Congregation*. The church was built in 1888 in a Gothic-Roman Revival style of Lemont native stone. The walls are almost three feet thick. The windows are Gothic in style while the design around the steeple is Neo-Roman. The original steeple was a tall, tapered, traditional structure, but was destroyed in a fire on January 18, 1918. The steeple, roof and interior were ruined, but the stone walls stood, so the church was rebuilt without any exterior changes except for the tall steeple, which was omitted. The congregation kept the original simple design including the opalescent glass windows fashioned to give a play of light similar to an opal. The new addition in the rear of the church is on the site where Horace Singer's private school was moved after it closed. Over the years the school has served as a parochial Lutheran school, a Sunday school, and as the first meeting place of the congregation. It was demolished in 1972.

(Turn north [left] and stop at the southwest corner of Lemont and Illinois Streets.)

3.*OTZENBURGER'S HALL
NORTHWEST CORNER OF LEMONT AND ILLINOIS STREETS

The present red brick building was remodeled in the 1920s. The central portion was redone in 1894. Before that it was the site of another building that served as a social and athletic hall. The German Benevolent Society and the Turnverine Vorwaerts met here. At this site, Albert Parsons, the laborer organizer, spoke during the Lemont Strike of 1885, calling on the Lemont workers to organize, but they did not out of fear of losing their jobs.

At the north end of this building there was a succession of taverns. During the canal days it was a popular spot for canal men, who were a tough lot. One of their favorite sports was to stage rat-killing fights. The champion dog belonged to Mr. Stein; it killed 89 rats in 13 minutes. The customers supplied the rats as they were freely available under the town's wooden sidewalks and along the canal. It was at this corner that the "Hot Air Gang" met until the fatal shooting of its leader. Finally, the widow of Mr. Otzenburger married Peter Kiolbassa, an important Polish-American politician of early Chicago. (See Chapter 15)

(Walk down the south side of Illinois Street. Note the typical early frame homes on this block and the limestone foundations that predate concrete basements. These homes are over 100 years old. The frame house on the southwest corner was the home of Lemuel Brown, the man who named Lemont. Continue west to the next stone building.)

4.*SAINT JAMES ACADEMY

SOUTH SIDE OF ILLINOIS

Completed in 1883, this Italian-style building served as a private secondary school when there were no other secondary schools in the area. It was one of the most imposing buildings in the Catholic Diocese for many years. Built and conducted by Reverend James Hogan, it served students from the first to the twelfth grade. Many non-Catholics attended, some boarding away from their remote rural homes. The public school system did not offer post-eighth grade classes until 1887, and did not offer a full four- year program until the early 1900s. An honored pupil of St. James was Francis Keough. Upon graduation from the academy, he went to Notre Dame where he played football on one of the first "Fighting Irish" teams. Later he completed law school and returned to Lemont to serve as a civic leader and mayor of the town for 18 years, beginning in 1909.

St. James Academy on the left and St. Patrick's on the right. (Photo courtesy of Lemont Historical Society)

The building has simple lines and an interesting roof line with Italianate brackets. Note the elevated entrance that leads to the second level; this is typical of buildings of this style and period. Also, note the memorial stone on the front of the staircase, an excellent example of granite etching. The back portion of the building contains the remains of the first stone residence built in Lemont by Joel Wells. He came to Lemont in 1845 and served as the first mayor in 1873. (See Chapter 23)

(Continue west on Illinois Street.)

5.*SAINT PATRICK'S CHURCH
200 ILLINOIS STREET

During the construction of the I & M Canal, Lemont's catholics were served by two priests. One was the French Father Hypolite DuPontavice and the other was Father Plunkett. Both were mission priests who went from church to church. Over the years there have been two other sites for this church before the present one was built in 1895. The first one was at Main and State, near an area called Corktown, and the second one at the top of the hill on McCarthy Road (east of the present grade school). The second one was called St. Mary's for a while. This building was designed by Martin A. Carr under the pastorship of Rev. Michael O'Sullivan. The design of this church is different from the others in town. Note the half walls projecting out on the side, typical of the style of Irish country churches. The design comes from Roman buildings remembered by the early missionaries who brought the faith to Ireland. Romanesque and Norman churches such as St. Patrick's concentrated on interior design, keeping the exterior simple. The tower and steeple of St. Patrick's is Romanesque as are the arches which are more rounded than pointed. Also interesting are the three front windows that act as a triptych. The stain glass windows in this building are exceptionally interesting. N.J. Brown donated a bell to the new church which was inscribed from "N.J. Brown, The 'Father of Lemont.'" (See Chapters 7, 8, and 9)

(Continue to the junction of State Street.)

6.*THE DERBY HOUSE
SOUTHEAST CORNER OF STATE AND ILLINOIS STREETS

This house was built around 1873, by the lumber dealer Sylvester Derby, a member of one of the pioneer families, who made his fortune dealing in the lumber trade on the I & M Canal. The style is a straight-forward Midwestern farmhouse design in an "L" shaped plan with a cross gabled roof. It was considered a fancy home in its day. The concept of showing wealth or status through the exterior of the home had not come into fashion yet. However, inside there were chandeliers in both the living and dining rooms, plus a front and back parlor and a one-story full width porch. The main kitchen, breakfast and work areas were located in the basement away from the main rooms, in the English style. The parish purchased the home in 1938 for use as a rectory and has since remodeled the front facade.

(Cross Illinois Street and proceed north on the High Rise Bridge.)

7.THE HIGH RISE BRIDGE
STATE STREET

The High Rise Bridge begins by spanning Main Street. If you look east, you can view buildings in styles that range from the 1860s to the 1970s. In the distance you can see the Village Hall at Main and Fremont Streets and the Budnick Building at Main and Stephen. It is from this bridge that one can view the importance of transportation corridors to the growth and development of Lemont and the Des Plaines Valley. From here to the river, you cross one valley trail and road — Main Street, the old electric route, the old Alton Line, the I & M Canal, the Santa Fe tracks, the Sanitary Ship Canal, and the Des Plaines

River. On *Main Street, the Chicago and Joliet Electric Trolley ran from 1901 to 1933. It offered transportation to Joliet and Chicago and served as a simple and cheap means of transportation for the community. (See Chapter 18)

(Turn and look back to town.)

From here you can see the steeples and towers of Lemont. Looking from left to right: on your far left is SS. Cyril's and Methodius Church, then Old Central School, Saint Matthew's Church, The Old Stone Museum and Historical Society, Bethany Church, Saint James Academy, Saint Patrick's Church, and Saint Alphonsus' Church. Higher on the bridge look west and you can see the modern roof line of the New Methodist Church. Turn back north and see the towers of the Hindu Temple of Greater Chicago.

(Continue north on the bridge.)

The second street spanned by the bridge, after the I.G.C. tracks (once the Chicago and Alton) is *Canal Street. The buildings on the second block of this street have the look of the 1880s and 1890s when the Illinois and Michigan Canal and the railroads were the main means of commercial transportation. Canal Street is narrow because it was designed for horse and buggy traffic, not automobiles. Canal Street, along with North Stephen and River Road, were the main parts of "Smokey Row," Lemont's notorious sin strip of the 1890s. Canal Street takes an odd angle because when the downtown was first subdivided into lots and blocks as the town of Keepotaw in 1836, the plat was laid out true north and south. Later subdivisions were platted in relationship to the canal and railroad. (See Chapters 6,7,8,9,21 and 22)

(Stop at a place above the I & M Canal.)

The *Illinois and Michigan Canal below is over 150 years old. Lemont has one of the finest portions left of this waterway. Begun in 1836, it was opened for navigation in 1848. The canal linked Lake Michigan with the Illinois River. Trips from Chicago to LaSalle took a long time, traveling at two to four miles an hour, but it was better than land travel which meant mud or dust and washboard roads. The main part of the canal fronting Lemont was completed from 1837 to 1840, and it did three things for the town. First, it brought people here to dig the canal and to contract the digging. Most of the laborers were Irish, French-Canadian, and German. It also opened the land for sale to farmers, and it led to the discovery of our dolomite quarry stone. That stone became the major industry of Lemont for over 80 years. The canal was closed in 1910 when the Sanitary Ship Canal became fully operational. National Park Drive on the north side of the canal was part of the towpath. The Drive was enlarged by the Civilian Conservation Corps in the 1930s. The area was to become a national park. It took 50 years for that to happen with the passage by Congress on August 24, 1984, of the Illinois and Michigan Canal National Heritage Corridor designation. Today the General Fry Landing Park offers a unique bike and hiking path along the canal. There is also a fine Friendship Garden along the pathway. Looking down on the waterway that shaped Northern Illinois it is hard to imagine the traffic it carried from 1848 to 1910. Some land uses along its banks have not changed. The 1886 maps show a lumber and gravel yard where there is still one located today. (See Chapters 5,6,7,8,9, and 10)

(Continue north on the bridge.)

Now look at the *Des Plaines Valley. From this point you can see the result of the geographical forces that shaped Chicagoland and Lemont. The valley is about one mile wide and is 70 to 100 feet deep. Look at the bluffs and try to imagine the amount of water it took to form the valley. Millions of years ago during the Silurian Period of the Paleozoic Era, all this land was at the bottom of a tropical sea. Sediment deposited over time and under pressure formed Lemont's bedrock limestone. This layer of stone runs from 200 to 450 feet deep in the area. After millions of years, the glaciers from this age left clay and rock covering most of the limestone. As the glaciers advanced and retreated they deposited rings, ridges, debris, and sand. Here on the bridge you can look east to Mount Forest Island (a glacial ridge) on which Saint James of the Sag Church stands. Look west to the sand and till deposits along New Avenue near the oil refineries.

It was the last ice sheet, however, that created most of the surface formation that makes Lemont unique. As the last glaciers melted the water collected in a huge basin. The water build-up found outlets in two places. One was the Des Plaines River, later the route of the I & M Canal; the other was the streambed along the route of the present Cal-Sag Canal. Both of the waters met here in our valley at Mt. Forest Island and rushed south and west to the Illinois and Mississippi Rivers. The water washed out much of the earlier clay deposit and exposed our limestone bedrock on the valley floor and bluffs. (See Chapters 1,and 10)

(Move north to the highest point on the bridge.)

Look at the *Santa Fe Railroad tracks and rail bridge* over the Ship Canal. Built in the 1880s, the tracks were elevated at the time of the Sanitary Ship Canal construction. The tracks follow the original course of the Des Plaines River, which explains the name of River Road on the street below. The Sanitary District engineers decided to divert the river north of the ship canal and the Santa Fe Railroad used the fill to elevate their trackage and to cross into town. The construction brought another railroad into Lemont, but the beauty of having the river as part of the downtown view was lost. The sharp angle of the track, known as Tedens' Curve, caused a number of accidents and derailments over the years. The worst one was in the early 1900s when two men were killed. (See Chapter 18)

Now view the *Sanitary and Ship Canal.* Constructed from 1892 to 1900 as part of the Sanitary System of Chicago, it was designed to carry flood and sewage water away from Lake Michigan, the source of Chicago's drinking water. The construction of this canal decreased the number of deaths from waterborne diseases. The canal was also designed for shipping, since it was much larger and deeper than the old I & M Canal. Methods of construction devised for this project were later used to build the Panama Canal. Like the I & M Canal before, this project brought many new immigrants to Lemont, mainly Scandinavian, Polish, and Italian. (See Chapters 19, 20, 21, and 22)

(Still north on the bridge until you reach the Des Plaines River.)

It was from the *Des Plaines River* that Marquette and Joliet first saw the future Lemont in 1673, but Native Americans had traveled the river long before that. The river here runs straight and does not meander like a normal waterway. Note how little watercourse vegetation is growing along the banks. This is for two reasons: first, this part of the river is less than 100 years old because it is a channel created for the river during the Ship Canal construction; and, secondly, the top soil is very shallow, laying on huge beds of limestone. Before the river diversion there were three islands in the river as it passed through Lemont Township: Shermans, Walkers, and Sag Island. (See Chapters 3 and 19)

(Return south to the steps at Illinois Street. Note the view of the town from here, how the houses and building climb up the hills to the highest points, on Blue Hill with St. Cyril's, and on Singer Hill with St. Alphonsus. Take the steps down to Main Street.)

8. MAIN STREET AND NEW AVENUE

This is the site of the old *Chicago and Alton Railroad*. The track was laid in the early 1850s and the station dates from 1853. It is one of the oldest stone buildings in Lemont and, along with Lockport's station, one of the oldest continuously used local rail stations in the Chicago area. It became the center of all traffic and commerce as use of the I & M Canal declined. In 1865, the townspeople gathered here in silent tribute to Abraham Lincoln as his funeral train passed slowly through town on its way to Springfield. During the quarry strike of 1885, the station was the center of violent activity. In 1893, during another bloody strike, Governor Altgeld spoke to Lemonters from this station, assuring them that the militia was under control and would not repeat the shooting incident of 1885. From this station men went to the Civil War, Spanish American War and World War I. William Jennings Bryan also spoke here, as did President Cleveland. (See Chapters 12, 15, and 20)

(Look south of the station and west along Main Street.)

9. *THE LEGION PARK AREA

MAIN STREET, NEW AVENUE AND LOCKPORT STREET

This triangle park was dedicated to all Lemont's war dead by the American Legion. It was first developed by the village in the 1890s as a gift from the Brown family. At its eastern corner is the site of the first St. Patrick's Church. It also is the site of the first village public school. The park was part of a violent strike in 1885. On May 4, the Illinois Militia under Colonel Bennett was sent to force striking quarry men back to work. At this place the townspeople and the militia met. The crowd was fired upon and three people were killed. The event was a rallying point for the early labor movement. Albert Parsons gave it the name "Lemont Massacre." The affair was investigated by state authorities and a report of the 1885 strike helped Governor Altgeld decide to come here during the 1893 strike. (See Chapters 11, 15, 16, and 20)

(Cross to the north side of Main Street and go east.)

10. *MAIN STREET

Note the building styles as you walk along the street. One hundred years ago, across from the parking lot on the south side, stood the Marble City House. On the north side of the street was the first community well. Much of this area was changed when the High Rise Bridge was built in the late 1970s. Philip Schmitt, a tombstone carver, ran the Lemont Marble Works along this street in the 1880s. His distinctively styled carved limestone footings for monuments can be seen at Saint James of the Sag and elsewhere. It was a good location since Joseph Gerharz operated a furniture store and funeral parlor across the street at 226 Main Street.

As you walk east, note the restored buildings along the route, the 1906 Werdeling Building and 219 Main Street.

(Continue east on Main Street.)

11. WORLD WAR II MEMORIAL
NORTHEAST CORNER OF LEMONT AND MAIN STREETS

In 1942, when so many Lemont men were away in service, J. Driscoll and C. Nicholas wanted to do something for the war effort. They developed an organization that sent 50 to 300 packages of wanted items each month to Lemont servicemen. The group also decided to create a permanent memorial to all those who had served. The land was donated by Joe Rose and the stone came from Wunderlich Company. It cost 5,000 dollars. Names were collected by Mrs. Nissen and Pat Doolin. All 600 men who served from Lemont are listed. The 22 who did not come back from the war are marked with a star.

(Walk to the intersection of Lemont and Canal Streets and go east on the north side of Canal Street.)

12. *LEMONT BUILDING AND LOAN
308 CANAL STREET

This was the site of a clothing store from the late 1880s to the early 1900s. Upstairs the Lemont Building Loan and Homestead Savings was founded. It lasted from 1885 to 1899 when it collapsed with the Norton failure. The colonial revival facade was added in the early 1900s. It was also the site of The First National Bank of Lemont, a bank with a checkered history, no longer operating. On April 10, 1929, it was the scene of a daylight holdup. The gangsters, unhappy with the small amount of money in the vault, locked the workers and the customers in the basement, who tried for a long time to get attention by yelling through the basement grate. Finally, someone heard them screaming, "We have been robbed and we are locked in the basement." The individual passing had little faith in banks and bankers operating out of that building. He replied, "Well, that's a good place for all of you," and walked away, leaving them to find their own way out.

13. *HENNEBRY BUILDING
312 CANAL STREET

The building was the site of James Hennebry's Meat Market, founded in 1885 after it was purchased from J.H. Laughlin. Later his brother Patrick took over the business and expanded the building to include a clothing store in the early 1900s. It was here that the mascot goat of the upstairs lodge hall was rescued from a fire in 1901. The building was later occupied by O'Brien and Boe Undertakers. Here Lemont's Air Ace, Rudy Kling, built his plane named "Jupiter: Pride of Lemont." Local children would come by to watch the progress on his cream and red Folkert SK3. With this plane, Rudy won the Cleveland Air Races of 1937. He became a national hero that "put Lemont on the map." He died in a airplane crash three months later and is buried in Saint Matthews Cemetery.

14. *FRIEDLEY BUILDING
311 CANAL STREET

This is one of the more interesting buildings on Canal Street because of its decorations. Built in the 1870s, it reflects the Romantic trend in taste that developed after the Civil War, as a reaction to the simple Greek and Roman Revival style that was popular in the first half of the 1880s. If you compare this building to the style of the Old Stone

Church, the back half of Old Central School, or the train station, you can see the difference in taste. The cornice is made of a composition material. At one time the roof line had two large cherubs attached to the center peak. The building was constructed on a true north-south line, marking it as one of the older buildings in town, since such buildings are all set on an angle. It was occupied for many years by the T.F. Friedley Hardware Company which sold farm machinery, roofing, and metalwork. Friedley-Voshardt embossed ceilings were sold from here.

(Continue to the corner of Stephen and Canal Streets.)

15. *BODENSHATZ BUILDING
118 STEPHEN STREET

One of our early post offices was located at the back end of this building. It was here that the Deputy Sheriff of Cook County read the Riot Act to Lemonters during the 1885 strike, and it was here that they learned that the Illinois militia was going to occupy the town. In the days before suffrage, Miss Amelia Bodenschatz served as an assistant postmistress. She took over all the duties for her father, Gustav, who operated the drugstore. Miss Bodenschatz served during Grant's administration until 1882, when she married. Before the days of medical clinics, doctors and dentists often located above a drug store, as they did here and at Budnick's.

(Look back from the corner to Mural Park and to the Mural.)

16. THE BICENTENNIAL MURAL

This mural was a project of the Lemont Bicentennial Commission and the Lemont Historical Society. Dedicated in 1975, it was painted by Caryl Yasko, a member of the Chicago Public Art Group. The mural shows quarry workers at work along with their families building Lemont. Yasko chose the theme after interviews with Lemonters. The water represents the river, the canals, and rebirth; the steeples are for the "Village of Faith"; and the round reactor for Argonne and the future. Note the use of triangles in its composition. The large female is symbolic of the support women offer in building a community. The men in the mural are working together for the common good, along with children. During the quarry days, children often left school at age 10 to work 12 to 14 hours a day. This mural has been reproduced in artbooks in the United States, England, and Germany. The park is a new addition completed in 1996.

(Turn north and go along the west side of Stephen Street.)

17. *TEDENS AND THORMAHLEN'S GENERAL STORE
102-106 STEPHEN STREET

This was an old general store. One has been on this site since 1861, when John Tedens and John Thormahlen founded the first store. The present stone building was erected in 1896. The store served not only Lemont, but sold goods up and down the I & M Canal. It was the only store from Chicago to LaSalle that held property rights directly on the canal. To make loading and unloading of barges easier, the owners built a tunnel from the canal level to their adjoining building. The present building, made of local stone, has a smooth cut face, a style not frequently seen in Lemont. This stone was cut and polished at the quarry with steam power equipment and brought to the site. The building is a vernacular style, a stone copy of the typical frame commercial buildings of the 1890s. Tedens Opera House upstairs offered vaudeville and minstrel shows. Here both the public and parochial schools held graduation ceremonies and school plays for many years. The Opera House later became a movie house. Downstairs is a vault that was for rent for townspeople to store valuables. The vault is so strong that it held off three attempts to rob it over the years. The front of the building has cast iron supports, popular in the 1880s. Such styles were selected out of catalogs and brought to the site. Note that for some reason these iron supports do not match. The building was used for a movie staring Dolly Parton.

(Continue north on the west side of Stephen Street.)

18.*THE ILLINOIS AND MICHIGAN CANAL

This is a good opportunity to see the canal up close. Note the stone work and try to visualize how long and narrow the barges had to be in order to pass each other. The water level was never more than six feet deep and often only two to three feet deep. In the 1850s, the Canal Towing Company, which provided horses and mules, operated on a site along the canal about three blocks east. However, horse and mule power was soon replaced by steam. There were four docking points along the canal in Lemont Township, most for the transport of stone. It is amazing that this small hand-dug ditch could have such a profound effect on the history of our area. Take some time to see the General Fry Park and walk the trails. The park was named after one of the commissioners of the I & M Canal. Northeast of the canal, Singer and Talcott had their main cutting and trimming plant. Here too, our first Smokey Row began. (See Chapters 5, 6, 7, 8, 9, and 10.)

(Cross the McCarthy Bridge and look east and west to view the canal.)

19. THE LEMONT POST OFFICE

Built in the 1930s as a Works Project Administration (WPA) project, the post office is in a typical functional "Art Deco" style. Note the simple lines and the Art Deco lettering. Go inside and view the mural. This scene on the I & M Canal was done by Charles Turzak as part of the Federal Arts Project. The style is typical of the 30s murals, but notice how he treated the wooden barge and the water — more like an impressionist painter. Here he emphasizes the family unit and uses a pole to unify his composition. These very same ideas were used by Caryl Yasko in the Bicentennial Mural, although she had not seen his work. Turzak completed the painting in 1938. Some other examples of his work were at the main post office in Chicago (now gone) and the University of Chicago. He died in 1986.

(Cross at the post office to the east side of Stephen Street.)

20.*NORTH STEPHEN STREET

Although the Ship Canal sin strip had places all over downtown, the worst dives were concentrated in this section. A number of the homes you see here once were part of Smokey Row. The underpass for the Santa Fe Railroad was completed in the 1890s and helped to move traffic when the entrance to town was along this route across two bridges. The bridges were over the Des Plaines River and the Ship Canal. Most of the Smokey

Row's worst dives closed by 1898; those few that remained into the 1900s were located in this area and between the underpass and the Ship Canal.

21. *THE WATERWORKS BUILDING

This Lemont Stone building was constructed to house pumping equipment and the village well. Later it also was part of the headquarters of the Lemont Power and Light Company. It is now a commercial building. This is another fine example of a Lemont Stone building. Simple in style with ashlar dressed stone, it has a more classical feeling than the Village Hall or Old Central School. One of the reasons for that impression is the use of smaller stone blocks across the top in a repeated pattern. (See Chapter 17)

(Continue south on Stephen Street crossing the I & M Canal.)

22. *THE NORTON BUILDING
101 STEPHEN STREET

This building of smooth faced Lemont Stone was constructed in 1870 to house the growing department store of S.W. Norton. Note the round arch windows and the symmetry of the design. There was a grain elevator where the parking lot now stands. It was part of the Norton family holdings that stretched from Lockport to Chicago. It was demolished in the 1950s. S.W. Norton managed the store until 1877, when he turned it over to his son Herbert Norton. Grain speculation by L.D. Norton in Joliet led to the store's bankruptcy here in 1896. Because Norton's was a company store and because many in town held grain receipts from Norton's, the bankruptcy caused a number of Lemonters to lose their lifes' savings. (See Chapters 21, 22, 23 and 24)

(Continue south to the northeast corner of Stephen and Talcott.)

23. *THE FRUHAUF BUILDING
107 STEPHEN STREET

This ashlar faced Lemont Stone building was constructed in 1871. The name of the owner is in pressed metal relief on the arch frieze. The building, like most well-constructed commercial buildings, has had a number of businesses. It was a saloon on the 1886, 1894, and 1910 maps. It once served as the Lodge Hall for the Knights of Pythais. This fraternal lodge met upstairs and called the room Castle Hall. Here the members could gather for an evening away from wife and family and talk sports and politics without the stigma of spending time in the saloon. Over the years the upstairs has served as a vest making sweatshop, a dance hall, and a bookie joint.

The building has a deep cellar, and this fact served some elements of the community during the dry days of prohibition. A large still operated here, but was raided only once. After a great deal of planning and preparation, the Cook County Sheriff and his men raided, only to find nothing. The still had been taken down for cleaning and the operators were nowhere to be found. (See Chapter 17.)

(Continue south along Stephen Street.)

24.*111 STEPHEN STREET

This fine example of a commercial Lemont Stone building was constructed around 1865 by Anthony Duter as a saloon, and served in that capacity until the first decade of the 1900s. Note the typical bracket cornice and flat roof. Aside from a saloon, it has been a hardware store, the town post office, and the home of the Lemont National Bank (originally Walker's Lemont City Bank) before it moved to Main Street. The building was also the home of Lemont's Vasa, a Swedish health and benefit society. It was known as Odin Hall, after the Scandinavian God of war and poetry. This was the block involved in Lemont's Great Fire of 1888. The building was used in Steve McQueen's last movie, *The Hunter*. (See Chapters 14, and 17)

(Continue south across the tracks.)

25.BUDNIK'S

400 MAIN STREET

Built in 1926 on the site of the old Murphy Building, this is an excellent example of the brick and terra cotta style of the 1920s. Budnick's still has the character of an old time pharmacy.

(Go east on Main Street to the Village Hall.)

26.*THE VILLAGE HALL

416-418 MAIN STREET

Constructed by C. A. Talty of Lemont at a cost of 13,000 dollars, the hall was dedicated on September 17, 1893, by Carter Harrison, the mayor of Chicago. The architect was H. Boehme of Joliet. Originally there was a wood frame bell tower between the gables. The upstairs was a community hall and also served as court rooms. The building has been remodeled over the years. In 1938, as a WPA project, the basement was dug out for club rooms and public library space was added. At one time the mayor, the police, and fire department shared the building. The building is Romanesque in style, but it is not as detailed as Old Central School. The 1938 architects were Stormsland and DeYoung. Recent extensive remodeling and preservation was done by David Krope. (See Chapters 17, 19, 20, and 21)

(Look east across the tracks toward Holmes Street.)

27*SITE OF THE ILLINOIS PURE ALUMINUM BUILDING

HOLMES AND TALCOTT STREETS

The building is gone in spite of efforts to save it, but the site is important, for here the Illinois Pure Aluminum Company started in 1892. It was the oldest manufacturer of drawn aluminum cookware in the United States until it closed in the 1970s. Items made here were displayed at the Colombian Exposition of 1893. The products were marketed under the name Walker Ware for the name of its owners. Edwin Walker came to Chicago in 1856 and became a building contractor. In order to have stone, he purchased quarry land in Lemont and contracted stone for the Chicago Water Tower and many other landmark buildings. He bought the aluminum plant when the original owners defaulted. The company remained an important part of Lemont's economy for over 80 years. (See Chapter 16)

(Return to Main and Stephen Streets and climb the hill to the Old Central School.)

28.*OLD CENTRAL SCHOOL APARTMENTS
McCARTHY ROAD AT THE TOP OF THE HILL

This building was listed on the National Register of Historic Places in 1979 as the oldest grammar school in continuous use in the state. The building has since been re-adapted for apartments. The south half was built in 1869 and the north half in 1896. John Barnes of Joliet was the architect of the 1896 section, which was similar to Lockport's Central Square. The building is made of the same dolomite stone that made Lemont. Note the building differences between the back and front half. The back is neoclassical, while the front is Romanesque. Stone for the back was cut and fit on site, requiring excellent stonemasons. Stone for the front was a product of steam-powered machinery; that is why the blocks are so even on the front. The stone industry had changed from mostly hand cutting to machine power in the 20 years between the building of the two parts. When the clocks in the tower were in place, they served as time keeper for the whole town. (See Chapters 16 and 17)

(Go to the back of Old Central and down the steps to the Bowl.)

29. THE BOWL

The Bowl is a natural formation, a small "sag" or depression caused by a block of melting glacial ice. It existed as a ravine, cutting across the village, that ran from above Logan Street to the Des Plaines River. The glacial till material, here and along parts of west New Avenue is a unique deposit that seems to date from some other geological event than the last Ice Age melt. The ravine had a gully that bisected Cass Street and cut through town. When the I & M canal was built, the engineers added the runoff to the I & M Canal. In the 1930s, the WPA created a better drainage system that still flows into the canal. They also built the retaining and drainage walls and the "castle," actually a bandstand. In the 1920s, the area of the Bowl was cleared and a 50 by 70 foot pool was built that was four and one half feet deep at the center. The wading pool was used until September of 1929, when a six year-old drowned in a tragic accident. The following years, with decreasing attendance and a higher cost of maintenance, the pool was closed and filled in. During the WPA work, two Native American skeletons, a calumet, and numerous Indian artifacts were found. The Bowl must have been an encampment site for the early Native Americans.

(To the east is SS. Cyril's and Methodius Church.)

30.*SS. CYRIL'S AND METHODIUS CHURCH
CORNER OF SOBIESKI AND CZACKI STREETS

In 1882, Father Leopold Moczygemba, who had been serving as pastor at Saint Alphonsus Church, was asked by Archbishop Feehan to form a new parish in Lemont to accommodate the growing Polish population. He bought 20 acres and named it "Jasna Gora," and dedicated it to Our Lady of Czestochowa. The title to the top of the hill, the highest point in Lemont, was set aside for the church and the rest of the land was subdivided into 50 by 135 foot lots, which sold for 50 to 100 dollars each. This manner of financing not only helped build a church, but allowed the Polish community in Lemont to own homes. With this money and other contributions, a frame church and school were built by 1884. The original church burned down in 1928, and the present structure was finished in 1930. It was designed by the firm of Brielmaier and Sons of Milwaukee. The building is simple gothic. Note the two round rose windows in front and the triple arches that form the entry way. The arch pattern is repeated in the windows and in the design on the tower and roof line. This section of Lemont is unique with such street names as Sobieski and Ledochowski, names chosen by Moczygemba to honor Polish heroes. (See Chapters 20, 23, and 24)

(Return up from the Bowl and go down Cass Street. Stop at the corner of Lemont Street and walk up to Bethany Church.)

Members of the Bethany Lutheran Church building the 1895 church. (Illustration by Don Zinngrabe)

31.*BETHANY CHURCH
LEMONT AND LINCOLN STREETS

The Scandinavians came to Lemont beginning in the 1860s, and by the 1870s, they were gathering in homes for social events and prayer services. There were Norwegians, Swedes, and Danes represented, but the largest group was Swedish. For a period of time, a Swedish Covent Church operated, but most wanted a Lutheran church. In 1872, the group adopted the Augustana Synod Constitution and formed Lemont's *Svenska Evangeliska Lutherska Bethania Forsamlingern.* They built a frame church which was used until 1894, when N. J. Brown offered the congregation a gift of an adjoining lot if the congregation would build a church of brick or stone costing not less than 3,000 dollars and have it finished within two years. It was finished in 1895. The stone workmanship is an excellent testimony to the craftsmanship of the congregation. The north side has some Romanesque features including the stone design along the top. The windows are a fine example of the Gothic revival arch. The windows are placed in a carefully ordered pattern, designed by men and women who believed in an ordered universe. The bell here is a gift of N.J. Brown, who loved bell music. It is unique in that it is a handcast bell with a D flat tone.

(Go up Lemont Street to Saint Alphonsus Church.)

32.*SAINT ALPHONSUS CHURCH
STATE AND CUSTER STREETS

The second largest immigrant group to arrive after the Irish were the Germans. They began coming in large numbers after 1850. Those Germans who were Catholic worshiped at Saint Patrick's at State and Main Streets and then at St. Mary's at the top of Stephen Street, but were not content until they could have their own church. They contacted the Redemptorist Fathers in Chicago and had their first service in 1867. By 1868, they had built a frame church on the site and had organized a school for their children. The present church was planned in 1919, but it took until 1921 to finish. It was designed by Charles

Wallace of Joliet. The brick work was done by Fred Fries of Lemont, the carpentry by A.J. Helbig & Sons, and the foundation by August Nagel. Note the stone cross on the northwest corner. Dolomite is hard to work into sculptural forms, so the workmanship of some forgotten mason is all the more remarkable. The base measures 60 inches by 60 inches and is rough-worked to resemble a stone outcropping. The inscription translates: "He who perseveres to the end will be saved 1874-1876-1882." It was erected to memorialize the successful missions of those years.

(The tour ends here, but this is only a small overview of the historic sites and buildings in town. To learn more, return to the Lemont Historical Society in the Old Stone Church.)

BIBLIOGRAPHY

PUBLISHED SOURCES

The Alarm, 1885. At the Chicago Historical Society.

Algren, Nelson, *Chicago: City on the Make* (New York: McGraw-Hill, 1951/1983).

Andreas, A. T., *A History of Cook County: 1885* (Evansville: Unigraphics, 1976).

Andrist, Ralph, ed., *The American Heritage History of the Confident Years* (New York: American Heritage Publishing, 1973)

Asbury, Herbert, *Gem of the Prairie* (New York: Knopf, 1940).

Ashbaugh, Carolyn, *Lucy Parsons: American Revolutionary* (Chicago: Charles Kerr Publishing Company, 1976).

Barnard, Harry, *Eagle Forgotten* (Newark: Lyle Stuart, 1973).

Bearss, Edwin, ed., *The 55th Illinois: 1861-1865* (Huntington, WV: Blue Acorn Press, 1993).

Beatty, William, "When Cholera Scourged Chicago," *Chicago History* (Chicago: Chicago Historical Society, Spring 1982).

Beecher, W. J., "The Lost Prairie," *Chicago History* (Chicago: Chicago Historical Society, Spring-Summer 1973).

Berkhofer, Robert, Jr., *The White Man's Indian* (New York: Vintage Books, 1979).

Bourne, James, "Occupaton and Ethnicity in Lemont: 1870-1880," *Looking For Lemont*, Michael Conzen and Carl Zimring, ed. (Chicago: University of Chicago, 1994).

Branaham, Charles, "Black Chicago: Accommodation Politics," *The Ethnic Frontier*, Melvin Holli, ed. (Grand Rapids: Eerdmans Publishing, 1977); "Black Chicago," *Ethnic Chicago*, Melvin Holli and Peter d'A. Jones, ed.(Grand Rapids: Eerdmans Publishing, 1984).

Brent, E. W., *Martin B. Madden*, (Chicago: 1901). At the Chicago Historical Society.

Brown, Virginia, ed., *Grundy County Landmarks* (Morris, IL: Grundy County Historical Society, 1981).

Bushman, Barbara, ed., *Lemont Centennial Book* (Des Plaines: King/Mann Yearbook, 1973).

Cain, Louis, "The Creation of Chicago's Sanitary District and the Construction of the Sanitary Ship Canal," *Chicago History* (Chicago: Chicago Historical Society, Summer 1979).

Carpenter, Allan, *Illinois: Land of Lincoln* (Chicago: Regenstein, 1968).

*Chicago Daily News**

Chicago Inter-Ocean

Chicago Tribune

Clifton, James, "Chicago Was Theirs," *Chicago History* (Chicago: Chicago Historical Society, Spring 1970).

Condit, Carl, *The Chicago School of Architecture* (Chicago: University of Chicago, 1973).

**Newspaper dates can be found in the endnotes*

Conrad, Howard, "Western Real Estate Speculation: Fifty Years Ago: Chicago's Famous Auction House, Nathaniel J. Brown," *The National Magazine* (Chicago: 1887).

Cook County Inquest Report: Lemont, May 5, 1885 (Springfield IL: Illinois State Archives).

Cronon, William, *Nature's Metropolis: Chicago and the Great West* (New York: W.W. Norton & Co., 1991).

Davenport, F., "The Sanitation Revolution in Chicago," *Journal of the Illinois Historical Society* (Springfield IL: Illinois State Historical Society, 1973).

Dedmon, Emmett, *Chicago: A Great City's History and People* (New York: Atheneam, 1981).

Densmore, Frances, *How Indians Use Wild Plants for Food, Medicine, and Crafts* (New York: Dover Books, 1974).

Dziewnik Chicagoski

Eastman, Zeb, *Chicago Magazine: 1857* (Chicago; Chicago Historical Bookworks, 1978).

Eaton, Conon, *Rock Island* (Sturgeon Bay, WI: Bay Print, 1979).

Edmonds, David, *The Potawatomies: Keepers of the Fire* (Norman, OK: University of Oklahoma Press, 1987).

Eisenbeis, Roland, "Bows and Arrows: Part Two," *Nature Bulletin* (Chicago: Cook County Forest Preserve, Feb., 1976).

Farr, Finis, *Chicago* (New Rochelle: Arlington House, 1973).

Federal Trade Commission Report on Grain (Washington DC: U.S. Printing Office, 1920-1926).

Ford, Thomas, *A History of Illinois: 1818-1841* (Springfield, IL: Illinois State Historical Society, 1995).

Fryxell, F. M., *The Physiography of the Region of Chicago* (Chicago: University of Chicago, 1927).

Funchion, Michael, "Irish Chicago," *Ethnic Chicago*, Melvin

Holli, ed. (Grand Rapids: Eerdmans Publishing, 1977).

Ginger, Ray, *Altgeld's America* (New York: New Viewpoints, 1973).

Gorner, Peter, "Back on the Map," *Chicago Tribune*, Tempo Section, Jan. 22, 1987.

Grant, Ulysses, "Vicksburg Campaign," *Battles and Leaders of the Civil War* (New York: Century Company, 1888).

Griffin, Richard, "Big Jim O'Leary," *Chicago History* (Chicago: Chicago Historical Society, Spring 1977).

Hansen, Harry, *Rivers of America: The Chicago* (New York: Rinehart & Co., 1942).

Harrison, Carter, *Growing Up With Chicago* (Chicago: Ralph Fletcher Seymour, 1944).

Hicken, Victor, *Illinois in the Civil War* (Urbana: University of Illinois, 1991).

Historic American Buildings Survey: Lemont (Washington DC: National Park Service, 1987).

History and Cookbook of St. James at the Sag (Sag Bridge: 1983).

Howard, Robert, *Illinois: A History of the Prairie State* (Grand Rapids: Eerdmans Publishing, 1972).

Hunt, Ben, *The Complete How To Do Book of Indians* (New York: Collier, 1973).

Illinois Labor Report For 1882 (Springfield: State of Illinois 1883).

Indians Of Chicago (Chicago: Field Museum of Natural History, 1970).

Jackson, Donald, *Blackhawk* (Urbana: Illinois Books, 1969).

Johnson, David, *Chicago Universalism* (Brookline, MA: Philomath Press, 1991).

Joliet Daily Republican

Joliet News

Joliet Signal

Joliet True Democrat

Karamanski, Theodore, *Brown Property Historical Evaluation: Lemont, Illinois* (Chicago: Loyola University, 1986).

Kaye, George, "Growth and Development of the Townsite," *Looking For Lemont*, Michael Conzen and Carl Zimring, ed. (Chicago: University of Chicago, 1994).

Keister, John, *Building For the Centuries: Illinois 1865-1898* (Urbana: University of Illinois Press, 1977).

Kinzie, Juliette, *Wau-Bun* (Portage, WI: The National Society of Colonial Dames in the State of Wisconsin, 1989).

Klowden, Kevin, "Maunfacturing in Lemont: The Fortuitious Rise of Industry in the Local Economy," *Looking For Lemont*, Michael Conzen and Carl Zimring, ed. (Chicago: University of Chicago Press, 1994).

Koeing, Louis, *Bryan: A Political Biography of William Jennings Bryan* (New York: G.P.Putman's Sons, 1971).

La Farge, Oliver, *Pictorial History of the American Indian* (New York: Bonanza, 1974).

Lamar, J. E., *Handbook on Limestone and Dolomite for Illinois Quarry Operators* (Springfield: State Geological Society, 1967).

Lamb, John, *A Corridor in Time* (Romeoville, IL: Lewis University, 1987).

Lane, James, *City of the Century* (Bloomington: Indiana University, 1978).

The Lemonter

The Lemont Metropolitan

Lemont Ledger

Lemont Ledger & Weekly Observer

Lemont News

Lemont Observer

Lemont Observer & Optimist News

Lemont Optimist News

Lemont Phoenix-Advertiser & Observer

Lemont Press

Longstreet, Stephen, *Chicago* (New York: David McKay & Company, 1973).

Lovoll, Odd S., *A Century of Urban Life: The Norwegians in Chicago Before 1930* (Champaign: University of Illinois and the Norweigan American Historical Association, 1988).

Mandell, Gerald, et. al., *Principals and Practices of Infectious Disease* (New York: Wiley & Sons, 1979); *Principals and Practices of Infectious Disease,* 3rd ed. (New York: Churchill Livingstone, 1990).

McNerney, Michael and Virgii Noble, *An Inventory of Known Archaelogical Resources in the I & M Canal Heritage Corridor* (Carbondale: American Resources Group, 1987).

Michael, Vincent and Deborah Slayton, *Joliet-Lemont Limestone* (Chicago: Landmarks Preservation Society, 1988).

Morison, Samuel, *The Oxford History of the American People,* vol. 3, (New York: New American Library, 1972).

Nevins, Allan and Henry Commager, *A Pocket History of the U.S.* (New York: Washington Square Press, 1956).

Ott, Elmer, "The I & M Waterway," *Lions Magazine,* Jan. 1966.

Paine, Ralph, *Roads of Adventure* (Boston: Houghton Mifflin Co., 1922).

Pasadena Star

Pease, A., *The Story of Illinois* (Chicago: University of Chicago Press, 1975).

Peterson, Jacqueline, "Wild Chicago," *The Ethnic Frontier*, Melvin Holli, ed. (Grand Rapids: Eerdmans, 1977); "The Founding Fathers," *Ethnic Chicago*, Melvin Holli, ed. (Grand Rapids: Eerdmans, 1987); "The Absorption of French-Indian Chicago 1816-1837" *Ethnic Chicago*, 4th ed., Melvin Holli, ed. (Grand Rapids: Eerdmans, 1995).

Pierce, Bessie, *A History of Chicago* (New York: Knoff, 1940).

Pineda, Manuel, *Pasadena Area History* (Pasadena: 1972). In the Pasadena Central library.

Pinkerton, Allan, "Communism and the Riot in Chicago," *The Prairie State: Civil War to the Present*, Robert Sutton, ed. (Grand Rapids: Eerdmans Publishing, 1976).

Preshlock, Dennis, "Peopling the Lemont Area to 1860," *Looking For Lemont*, Michael Conzen and Carl Zimring, ed. (Chicago: University of Chicago, 1994).

Putnam, James, *The Illinois & Michigan Canal: A Study in Economic History* (Chicago: University of Chicago Press, 1918).

Richardson, Katherine, "An Analysis of land Parcel and Landscape Change in LaSalle County," *Settling The Upper Illinois Valley*, Michael Conzen and Melissa Morales, ed. (Chicago: University of Chicago, 1989).

Ritzenthaler, Robert and Pat Ritzenthaler, *The Woodland Indians of Western Great Lakes* (Garden City, NY: Natural History Press, 1970).

Roediger, Dave, *Haymarket Scrapbook* (Chicago: Kerr Publishing, 1986).

Rosenburg, Charles, *The Cholera Years* (Chicago: University of Chicago, 1962).

Sandborn Fire Maps

Schauer, John, *Joliett and Marquette Expeditions 1673-1675* (Joliet: College of St. Francis, 1973).

Schlup, Leonard, "Gilded Age Politician: Adali E. Stevenson of Illinois," *Illinois Historical Journal* Springfield: Illinois State Historical Society, 1989).

Sears Roebuck and Company, Fall 1900 (Northfield: Illinois Digest Books, 1970).

Selman, Robin, "A History of the Lemont Quarry Industry," *Looking For Lemont*, Michael Conzen and Carl Zimring, ed. (Chicago: University of Chicago, 1994).

Spear, Allan, *Black Chicago* (Chicago: University of Chicago, 1974).

Spitznagel, Louis, *Canal or Railroad* (Lockport, IL: Illinois Canal Society, 1984).

Stead, William, *If Christ Came to Chicago* (Evansville: Unigraphics, 1978).

Strong, Robert, *A Yankee Private's Civil War*, Ashley Halsey, ed. (Chicago: Henry Regnery Company, 1961).

Sullivan, Mark, *Our Times: 1900-1925* (New York: Chas Scribner & Sons, 1926).

Sutton, Robert, *The Prairie State: Colonial years to 1860* (Grand Rapids: Eerdman's, 1970).

The Heartland (Lake Forest, IL: Deerpath Publishing, 1982).

Thornton, Nancy, ed., "Quarry Work Recalled in the Doolin Family," *Cornerstone Newsletter* (Lemont: Lemont Historical Society, Aug.-Sept., 1988).

Uchitelle, Louis, "Just a Little Inflation and Everybody's Happy," *New York Times*, September 8, 1966.

Ward, Carrington, "Staying on the Farm: Persistence, Growth and Turnover in Lemont and Palos Townships 1870-1880," *Looking For Lemont*, Michael Conzen and Carl Zimring, ed. (Chicago: University of Chicago, 1994).

Wendt, Lloyd and Herman Kogan, *Lords of the Levee* (New York: Garden City Publishing, 1944).

Werling, Rev. Norman, *The First Catholic Church in Joliet*, Surname Index by Nancy Thornton (Baltimore: Gateway Press, 1987).

Wharton, James, *Scenic Mt. Lowe Echo Mountain* (Pasadena: 1898).

Whiteford, Andrew and Herbert Zim, ed., *North American Indian Arts* (New York: Golden Press, 1973).

Whitlock, Brand, *Forty Years of It* (New York: Appleton, 1914).

Whitney, Ellen, "Indian History and the Indians of Illinois," *Journal of The Illinois State Historical Society* (Springfield: Illinois State Historical Society, May, 1976).

Wiley, Bell Irvin, *The Life of Billy Yank* (Baton Rouge: Louisania State University Press, 1992).

Williams, Ben, ed., *The Chicago and Interurban Trolley Guide* (Chicago: Norton and Company, 1908).

Williams, Robert, "A Social Profile of the Community in 1900," *Looking For Lemont*, Michael Conzen and Carl Zimring, ed. (Chicago: University of Chicago, 1994).

Witt, Donald, "The Electric Trolley," *Where The Trails Cross* (South Holland: South Suburban Geneological Society, Spring, 1977).

Woodruff, George H., *A History of Will County* (Evansville: Unigraphics, 1973).

World Almanac Book of Facts (Mawah, NJ: Funk & Wagnalls, 1996).

UNPUBLISHED SOURCES

Bossert, E.O., *The I & M Canal*, Joan Bossert Morsicato, ed., 1993.

Bradbury, Frank, *History of Lemont Bottles*, Lemont Historical Society Archives.

Brown Family Papers, Lemont Historical Society Archives.

Cornerstone, Newsletter of the Lemont Historical Society.

Doolin Family Papers, Lemont Historical Society collection.

Kallick, Sonia, *Lemont Walking Tour*, 1973, 1976, 1985, 1992, *Lemont History and Ancedotes*, 1975; assorted articles dealing with Lemont in the Historical Society's collection.

Lemont Village Council Notes and Minutes, Lemont Area Historical Society Archives.

Nels Norden Papers, Lemont area Historical Society.

Walker-Dougal Papers, Lemont Area Historical Society.